Columbia University

Contributions to Education

Teachers College Series

No. 82

AMS PRESS

NEW YORK

A SURVEY OF A PUBLIC SCHOOL SYSTEM

BY

HENRY LESTER SMITH, Ph.D.

TEACHERS COLLEGE, COLUMBIA UNIVERSITY
CONTRIBUTIONS TO EDUCATION, NO. 82

219477

PUBLISHED BY
Teachers College, Columbia University
NEW YORK CITY
1917

Library of Congress Cataloging in Publication Data

Smith, Henry Lester, 1876-
    A survey of a public school system.

    Reprint of the 1917 ed., issued in series: Teachers
College, Columbia University. Contributions to
education, no. 82.
    Originally presented as the author's thesis,
Columbia.
    1. Bloomington, Ind.--Public schools. I. Title.
II. Series: Columbia University. Teachers College.
Contributions to education, no. 82.
LA285.B6S6 1972   371'.01'09772255   75-177774
ISBN 0-404-55082-7

Reprinted by Special Arrangement with Teachers
College Press, New York, New York

From the edition of 1917 , New York
First AMS edition published in 1972
Manufactured in the United States

AMS PRESS, INC.
NEW YORK, N. Y.   10003

CONTENTS

LIST OF TABLES

CHAPTER I

THE COMMUNITY AND THE PLAN OF ITS PUBLIC SCHOOL SURVEY

CHAPTER II

NORMAL PROGRESS, RETARDATION, AND ACCELERATION

CHAPTER III

CENSUS, ENROLLMENT, PROMOTIONS, FAILURES, WITHDRAWALS, REPETITIONS

List of Tables

CHAPTER IV

FINANCES

CHAPTER VII

TEACHERS

CHAPTER VIII

SUPERVISION OF INSTRUCTION

CHAPTER IX
School Buildings

A SURVEY OF A PUBLIC SCHOOL SYSTEM

CHAPTER I

THE COMMUNITY AND THE PLAN OF ITS PUBLIC SCHOOL SURVEY

1. PLAN OF THE SURVEY

There are various possible motives that might operate in the inauguration of a school survey. It is conceivable that a survey might be launched by individuals, or by organizations outside the schools themselves. In such cases the incentive might be retaliation on the part of enemies, opportunity to advertise the community, or a sincere desire to discover conditions as a basis for helpful and constructive assistance to the school authorities. A survey started by the school authorities themselves might have back of it the desire to discredit a previous administration, to defend themselves against present attacks, to advertise their own efficiency, or to learn in order to make improvement possible. The latter motive, whether the survey is prompted by those without the system or by those within the system, is the only wholesome and promising motive to have back of such a movement.

With a survey determined upon, the next question concerns the forces that are to make it. It may be made by outside experts and this method has in its favor the arguments that such experts are prepared to do their work quickly and that they are likely to be unprejudiced. On the other hand, they are subject to the danger of not understanding thoroughly the local conditions and consequently of misinterpreting the data. Moreover, their work usually stops with a setting forth of conditions found and recommendations made. They do not usually have a hand in the inauguration of the remedies suggested for existing evils.

The survey might be made by the local school authorities, including school board, superintendent, principals, and teachers. Such a survey has the advantage of being made by those who are familiar with conditions. Furthermore, it stimulates interest and creates an attitude that goes a long way toward insuring the application of successful remedies to defects found. It is the opinion of some school men that very little help can be expected from principals and teachers in such surveys. My own experience justifies me in predicting that a survey undertaken by the teaching corps as a whole will soon reveal to the superintendent that some of the accomplishments of principals, buildings as a whole, or individual teachers will surpass even his own dream of what could be accomplished. Of course some of the work thus done will certainly be carelessly done by a few indifferen or negligent individuals, but the checking up of such work has a wholesome effect on them and frequently converts them to a more helpful attitude toward school problems. There is the danger, of course, that teachers may be overloaded and such a danger needs to be kept in mind, for the most faithful teachers will overwork rather than complain. In order to avoid the overstrain, much of the mechanical part of the work should be turned over to a competent clerk. Because of the amount of work connected with it, a survey made by local school officials must stretch over a much longer period of time than a survey by outside experts. Hence where time is an important factor the local plan would have its serious drawbacks.

Where such a thing is possible, the survey should be made by a combination of factors, the local people doing the bulk of the work under the guidance of the expert or experts from the outside. Under such a combination the advantages of two types of knowledge and interest are centered on the problem.

As to types, surveys may be classified under two heads, sporadic and partial on the one hand, and continuous and complete on the other. The first type is apt to result when full dependence is put in the outside expert. Both funds and time are usually limited under such a plan. Where the whole teaching corps is inspired through the habit of shouldering the responsibility for discovering and remedying defects, the conditions are ripe for a continuous, intelligent, and complete survey, especially where the guiding and organizing hand of the outside expert supplements local activity.

Organization for a school survey depends of course upon the type of survey undertaken, the funds available, the motives back of the work, the co-operative spirit of the community and of the teaching corps. Assuming that all of the above conditions are ideal, that the schools and the community are a unit in desiring thorough and accurate information that may serve as a basis for improving the educational system, it would seem that the best organization for the work would be an organization that would combine the services of educational experts from the outside, of representative organizations or interests in the community, and of school board, superintendent, principals, and teachers of the schools. Much of the tabulation of data can properly be left to an office force created especially for that kind of work. Such an office force will be considered indispensable when the necessity for continuous, intelligent surveying is fully realized.

The survey of the Bloomington public school system was undertaken with the twofold view of determining and remedying conditions. The survey covered a period of six years though the bulk of the work was done during the years 1912–13 and 1913–14. The work of the year 1913–14 was supervised and directed by Dr. G. D. Strayer, of Columbia University, who made a special trip to Bloomington and remained on the field three days organizing the work, after which he continued his suggestions and oversight of the work through correspondence. Some special problems were worked out independently by the superintendent, the principals, and certain individual teachers somewhat familiar with statistical methods. Much of the work was done in a co-operative way as is always necessary to the best results. As a result of this co-operation practically every teacher in the school system has contributed to the results. It was possible, also, to arrange to have some of the tests given or graded by outside experts. Dr. C. W. Stone once gave his own tests in sixth-grade arithmetic. Two other times he had Dr. E. E. Jones, of Indiana University, give the tests. Each of the three times the tests were given Dr. Stone supervised the grading of the papers. The Courtis Composition, Reading, Spelling, and Writing Tests were all graded under the direction of Mr. S. A. Courtis and by his own corps of graders. Professor H. G. Childs and his class in school administration gave the Drawing Test and graded the papers. Material assistance, too, was given in the survey by graduate students in the university, eight of whom worked out theses for the Master's degree on practical problems connected with the Bloomington schools. The majority of these studies were worked out under the direction of the author and with all of them he was familiar during the progress of the work. From the following five of these eight studies extracts have been taken and embodied in this thesis: "Progress through the Grades," by A. C. Burgin; · "An Investigation into the Causes of

Children Leaving School before Graduation and their Employment after Leaving," by Belvia Cuzzort; "The Retention in Rank of Eighty-Six Pupils in the Bloomington Graded and High Schools," by Charley Bruner; "A Comparative Study of the Standing of Township and City Graduates," by Clifford Woody; "A Social Survey of Bloomington, Indiana," by Marcellus I. Gragh.

2. SOURCE OF THE EARLY POPULATION OF BLOOMINGTON

Bloomington, the county seat of Monroe County, Indiana, situated as it is in the southern part of the state, has been influenced during its history more by southern ideas than by those of New England. In 1800 there were approximately two hundred white inhabitants in the state and these were composed almost wholly of French in and about the forts, and trappers originally from Kentucky and Virginia. People from Kentucky, Tennessee, and the southern states along the Atlantic coast steadily streamed into southern Indiana while the northern part of the state was noticeably tinged with New England stock. After the early thirties an occasional New Englander found his way to Bloomington. From 1820 to 1860, during that wonderful westward movement of population, many Scotch-Irish from South Carolina left their small farms and migrated up the east side of the Blue Ridge through the Cumberland Gap and Kentucky into the vicinity of Bloomington. Others of the same stock entered this community from Western Pennsylvania and Eastern Ohio. This stock came in large enough numbers to stamp itself permanently upon the community. Bloomington township in which a portion of the city of Bloomington is located was settled certainly by 1816 and possibly earlier than that. As early as 1817 buildings were erected on the present town site. On April 10, 1818, the county commissioners ordered the county seat laid off and named Bloomington. By 1830 the population of the town was approximately 700 and by 1847 it had reached 1200.

For a long time after the settlement of the state, Indiana was noted for her illiteracy. In 1840 out of a population of 268,040 over twenty years of age 38,100 were unable to read or write. Monroe County contributed her share to this illiteracy. Her attitude toward education is pretty well exhibited in the following vote taken in 1849 on the question of free public schools for the state:

	FOR FREE SCHOOLS	AGAINST FREE SCHOOLS
Bean Blossom Township	59	112
Benton Township	44	41
Bloomington Township	128	307
Clear Creek Township	76	85
Indian Creek Township	40	101
Marion Township	16	35
Richland Township	59	128
Perry Township	127	20
Salt Creek Township	39	60
Van Buren Township	43	113
Washington Township	36	38
	667	1040

From the very beginning, though, there was an element in the vicinity of Bloomington heartily in favor of education. This element, composed largely of South Carolina emigrants many of whom belonged to the Associate Reform, Seceder, and Covenanter religious denominations, was largely represented in Perry Township, in which a portion of the city of Bloomington is located, which voted in favor of free public schools by a vote of 127 to 20. Bloomington Township, in which another portion of the city is located, voted against free public schools by a vote of 307 to 128. The vote of the city itself is not given. The population in Bloomington Township at that time was largely from Kentucky and Virginia.

Educational interest on the part of some of the early inhabitants of the village of Bloomington is evidenced by the fact that school was taught in the log courthouse in the winter of 1818-19. The following year a schoolhouse was built. In 1863 graded schools which had been favorably voted on were introduced and the public school fund for this purpose was liberally increased several hundred dollars by private subscriptions. From 1835 to 1852, the date of the new school law, the county of Monroe provided in its county seminary opportunities for higher education in the community. At no time in its history has Bloomington been without adequate educational facilities either in her private or her public schools. On more than one occasion the state university situated in Bloomington was helped financially either by public or private contributions. These efforts prove conclusively that there has always been a strong element for educational advantages in the community though for many years alongside of this element there was another, almost continuously from the beginning of the city's history, that was indifferent and even hostile to education, particularly free public education. Since the 60's and 70's, however, there has been a healthy school spirit which has gradually grown to the present where it shows steady enough to bear willingly even at the hands of an administration elected on the platform of economy a local taxation for school purposes practically up to the legal limit and at a point reached by very few communities in the state. Even in 1873 the taxes for school purposes bore a favorable relation to the total taxation as is shown by the following statement of taxes:

Taxes for corporation purposes..................	20 cents on each $100.00.
Taxes for road purposes........................	5 cents on each $100.00.
For general poll tax...........................	25 cents.
Dogs...	$1.00 each.
For school building...........................	50 cents on each $100.00.
For school building...........................	$1.00 on each poll.

The total tax was 75 cents on each $100.00 of valuation and a poll tax of $1.25.

3. General View of Present Educational Facilities in Bloomington

In addition to the regular eight grades in the common school and four years in the high school, Bloomington has in its midst the state university. This institution provides educational ideals that stimulate both the public school teaching corps and the patrons of the schools to put forth extra effort to have efficient public schools. The university not only contributes toward furnishing the ideals but it also assists in working out those ideals. This stimulus has been contributed through the free use, to teachers, of the university library. There has been at work, too, for many years a spirit of co-operation between the department of education in the university and the public schools of the city which has resulted in mutual benefit. Such a relation could not fail to leave its stamp upon the efficiency of the public schools. Indiana University was established in 1820 and grew in a period of twenty years, 1892 to 1912, from an attendance of 497 to an attendance of 2522. This steady growth is an index of the faith of the people of Indiana in their state university and with the spread of this faith a larger and larger number of representative young men and women of the state sojourn in Bloomington during their college course. As a result of the advanced educational advantages many families of refinement have been attracted to the city and many of the younger children of these families are attending the public schools of the city. The present population within the city limits is almost wholly of native-born Americans.

4. A BRIEF DESCRIPTIVE VIEW OF BLOOMINGTON AND
ITS PEOPLE, 1912–13

Bloomington is a city with a population of something more than
10,000 in addition to the resident students of Indiana University.
The city is situated on almost the highest lands of the state at the
junction of the Illinois Central and the Monon railroads. It has
doubled in population within eight years. Bloomington is in the very
center of the Oolitic limestone belt of the United States, a small
belt of land some one hundred and fifty miles in length and from two
to fourteen miles in width. Since 1850 stone quarries have been
operated to a greater or less degree in and about Bloomington. At
present in Bloomington and Monroe County there are in operation
seventeen stone quarries, twenty-two stone mills, and fifteen complete cut stone 'plants, representing an approximate value of
$2,000,000.

Bloomington is situated in an agricultural district where general
farming is carried on. The surface of the country is undulating.
The top soil is a dark chocolate clay loam with a dark red clay sub-
soil underlaid with Oolitic limestone which lies from five to twenty-
five feet below the surface. Each year more than two million dollars'
worth of manufactured products are sent out of Bloomington through
her factories, including one furniture factory with more than eight
hundred names on the pay roll and an annual output of over
$1,000,000 dollars, one veneer plant, one basket factory, one harness
factory, two flouring mills, two machine shops, one book bindery,
one glove and mitten factory, one ice cream factory, one ice plant,
one glass factory, four saw mills, one creosoting plant, three planing
mills, one foundry, one storage battery works, five printing offices,
one gas plant, two power laundries, one creamery, one washing
machine factory, one broom factory.

There were employed in Bloomington at the time the occupational
survey was made, 1912–13, 4440 individuals, 85.8 per cent men
and 14.2 per cent women. Approximately 45 per cent of all the
inhabitants of the city were helping to support themselves or their
families.

Table I gives the principal occupations of the women with the
number employed in each occupation.

TABLE I

Domestics...................	111	Basket makers.............. ...	27
Teachers...................	98	Cooks	25
Clerks.....................	71	Telephone operators............	25
Machine operators...........	57	Stenographers.................	22
Bookkeepers................	29		

Table II gives the principal occupations of the men with the number employed in each occupation.

TABLE II

Unskilled laborers....	419	Foremen......................	55
Clerks......................	165	Farmers......................	49
Drivers.....................	159	Managers.....................	49
Merchants..................	133	Barbers......................	47
Teachers...................	130	Planermen....................	47
Carpenters.................	125	Painters.....................	45
Cabinet makers..............	94	Contractors...................	44
Firemen....................	72	Finishers.....................	44
Engineers..................	64	Packers (furniture).............	36
Stone masons and cutters......	57	Veneerers....................	33

TABLE III

OCCUPATIONS BY BUILDINGS OF PARENTS OF CHILDREN IN THE GRADES, 1913–14, IN ALL CASES IN WHICH THE OCCUPATION COULD BE ASCERTAINED

Each parent counted as many times as there were children in the family attending school. Only fathers counted where fathers were living.

OCCUPATION OF PARENT	CENTRAL BUILDING NUMBER OF PUPILS	MCCALLA BUILDING NUMBER OF PUPILS	FAIRVIEW BUILDING NUMBER OF PUPILS	COLORED BUILDING NUMBER OF PUPILS	TOTAL NUMBER OF PUPILS	PERCENTAGE OF PARENTS IN EACH OCCUPATION
Architect............	1				1	.1
Barber [1]............	9	8	4	6	27	1.7
Blacksmith...........	10	2	16		28	1.7
Boarding-house keeper.	7		1		8	.5
Bookkeeper..........	2	9	2		13	.8
Brick mason..........	1	2			3	.2
Cabman.............	2	4			6	.4
Cabinet maker........	6	8	6		20	1.2
Carpenter............	34	13	11		58	3.6
Carver..............		5			5	.3
Clerk...............	16	14	18		48	3.0
Commercial agent.....		1			1	.1
Contractor...........	12	7	4		23	1.4
Cook...............	3	1	3	9	16	.1
Dentist..............	2				2	.1
Draftsman...........	1	5			6	.4
Drayman............	3		4		7	.4
Dressmaker..........	1			2	3	.2
Dye worker and cleaner	1	4			5	.3
Editor..............	2				2	.1
Electrician...........	3	4	2		9	.6
Engineer.............	26	10	6		42	2.6
Engraver............			1		1	.1
Expressman.........		2			2	.1

[1] Read as follows: There were 9 children in the Central building, 8 in McCalla, 4 in Fairview, 6 in the Colored building, or 27 in all buildings whose fathers were barbers. 1.7 per cent of the fathers of all children in the grades were barbers.

TABLE III (*Continued*)

OCCUPATION OF PARENT	CENTRAL BUILDING NUMBER OF PUPILS	MCCALLA BUILDING NUMBER OF PUPILS	FAIRVIEW BUILDING NUMBER OF PUPILS	COLORED BUILDING NUMBER OF PUPILS	TOTAL NUMBER OF PUPILS	PERCENTAGE OF PARENTS IN EACH OCCUPATION
Farmer	29	20	9		58	3.6
Fireman	10	4	6		20	1.2
Florist	2				2	.1
Foreman	8	8	3		19	1.2
Gardener		1	1		2	.1
Glass worker			3		3	.2
House cleaner		1		2	3	.2
Housekeeper	19	13	9	2	43	2.6
House mover		3			3	.2
Industrial proprietor	2				2	.1
Inspector	4	3			7	.4
Insurance	4	2	1		7	.4
Janitor	12	9	3		24	1.5
Laborer	121	113	95	53	382	23.5
Laundry	2	1			3	.2
Launderer		4			4	.3
Lawyer	4	4			8	.5
Liveryman	4	1			5	.3
Librarian		1			1	.1
Lumber dealer	4		1		5	.3
Machinist	13	10	12		35	2.2
Manager	2	2			4	.3
Manufacturer	15	7	2		24	1.5
Mechanic	4		3	2	9	.6
Merchant	42	29	22		93	5.7
Miller	3		1		4	.3
Minister	7	3			10	.6
Nickel polisher			1		1	.1
Nurse		1			1	.1
Optician	1				1	.1
Painter	12	7	10		29	1.8
Physician	4	6			10	.6
Planerman	12		10		22	1.4
Plasterer	3	6	2	1	12	.7
Poolroom proprietor	2				2	.1
Pastor				4	4	.3
Printer	1	1			2	.1
Professor in University	13	30			43	2.6
Public official	17	4	9		30	1.8
Quarryman	32	2	31	1	66	4.1
Railroader	59	13	15		87	5.4
Real estate	2	4			6	.4
Registrar of University	1				1	.1
Rooming house		1			1	.1
Saloon keeper		1			1	.1
Saw filer	1				1	.1
Sawyer	2	3	5		10	.6
Showman		1			1	.1
Stenographer		1			1	.1
Stock buyer		1		2	3	.2
Stone cutter	18				18	1.1
Stone mason	19	19	6		44	2.7
Student	5	8			13	.8
Superintendent	14	2	6		22	1.4

TABLE III (*Continued*)

OCCUPATION OF PARENTS	CENTRAL BUILDING NUMBER OF PUPILS	McCALLA BUILDING NUMBER OF PUPILS	FAIRVIEW BUILDING NUMBER OF PUPILS	COLORED BUILDING NUMBER OF PUPILS	TOTAL NUMBER OF PUPILS	PERCENTAGE OF PARENTS IN EACH OCCUPTAION
Tailor..............		2			2	.1
Teacher.............	9	8		2	19	1.2
Timber buyer........		1			1	.1
Tinner..............	5				5	.3
Transfer............	10				10	.6
Traveling salesman....	3	7	1		11	.7
Truant officer.......		1			1	.1
Undertaker..........	1	2			3	.2
Waiter..............	2				2	.1
Washerwoman	5	5	1	6	17	1.0
Watchman...........	4	1	1		6	.4
TOTAL...........	710	476	350	90	1625	100.0

SUMMARY OF TABLE III

1. 9.5 per cent of all the wage-earning parents of pupils in the first eight grades are in what might be termed the professions.
2. 17.7 per cent of such parents are in business for themselves.
3. 35.7 per cent of them are skilled laborers.
4. 37 per cent of them are unskilled laborers.

5. SOCIAL CONDITIONS IN BLOOMINGTON

The following conclusions are based upon a limited amount of data gathered during the year 1913–14 by the teachers in the upper grades and high school and compiled under the direction of the superintendent of schools by Mr. Marcellus Gragh, a graduate student in Indiana University. Data were gathered from 535 families out of a total of 2592 families in the city. The 535 families were distributed as follows, 38.8 per cent in the northeast section of the city, 22.6 per cent in the northwest section, 15.6 per cent in the southwest section, and 23 per cent in the southeast section. After careful consultation with a map of the city interpreted by a leading real estate agent, families on the following streets were chosen as being typical of the families in the respective sections.

The names of the streets are given — each street accompanied by the per cent that the reported families living on it is of the whole number of families living on it.

PER CENT

North Grant Street, northeast section............................... 21.6
West Seventh Street, northwest section............................ 30.7
West Third Street, southwest section............................. 20.0
South Washington Street, southeast section...................... 27.8

For each item of information a distribution is made for the whole city according to the same ratio that the 535 families distributed themselves. Not all of the 535 families reported on each item.

A distribution of the total number of white families in residence periods, by the same ratios as the 483 white families reporting, reveals the following facts:

PER CENT

Families having a residence in Bloomington of from one week to one year, inclusive. . . . . 486 or 20
Families having a residence of from 1 year to 3 years, inclusive. . . . . . . 282 or 11½
Families having a residence of from 3 years to 5 years, inclusive. . . . . . 210 or 8½
Families having a residence of from 5 years to 10 years, inclusive. . . . . 457 or 18¼
Families having a residence of from 10 to 20 years, inclusive. . . . . 526 or 21
Families having a residence of 20 years or more. . . . . 513 or 20½
Families having a residence of 50 years or more. . . . . 62 or 2½
Families having a residence of 99 years. . . . . 5 or ⅕

On distributing in the same way the total number of colored families, the following facts are found:

PER CENT

Families having a residence of from 1 week to 1 year, inclusive. . . . . . . 6 or 5
Families having a residence from 1 year to 3 years, inclusive. . . . . 12 or 10
Families having a residence from 3 years to 5 years, inclusive. . . . . 18 or 15
Families having a residence from 5 years to 10 years, inclusive. . . . . . . 23 or 20
Families having a residence from 10 years to 20 years, inclusive. . . . . . 36 or 30
Families having a residence of 20 years or more . . . . 23 or 20
Families having a residence of 50 years . . . . 6 or 5
The last item is included in the residential period of 20 years or more, above.

The scholarship of heads of families, 780 white parents and 27 colored parents reporting, is shown as follows:

YEARS

Average number of years' schooling of husbands (white). 9
Average number of years' schooling of wives (white). 8.5
Average number of years' schooling for both. 8.75
Coefficient of correlation (Pearson's formula) between number of years' schooling of husbands (white) and number of years' schooling of wives. . 68
Average number of years' schooling of husbands (colored). 5
Average number of years' schooling of wives (colored). 5.9
Average number of years schooling of both. 5.6
Coefficient of correlation between number of years' schooling of husbands (colored) and wives. 63

Using the per cents by which white parents who made reports distribute themselves according to the amount of schooling, it is estimated that about 124 parents in Bloomington never went to school; about 1405 parents quit before reaching the eighth grade; about 1617 parents quit school in eighth grade or at the end of it; about 1010 parents have had some high school training; 792 parents have had some college work; and 445 parents are college graduates and post-graduates.

Of the colored population, it is estimated that about 44 parents never went to school; about 44 parents quit school in the eighth grade or at the end of it; about 95 parents quit school below the eighth grade; and about 53 parents have had some high school work.

The church and fraternal order membership of heads of families
as reported in answers to questionnaire is shown as follows:

White families   PER CENT
Church membership of all fathers reporting................... 74.6
Non-church membership of all fathers........................ 25.4
Club and fraternal membership of fathers.................... 55.7
Church membership of all mothers........................... 85.5
Non-church membership of all mothers....................... 14.5
Club and fraternal membership of all mothers................ 25
Sabbath school attendance of fathers and mothers based on their church
   membership... 14
Children in the public schools who attend sabbath school taken with
   those who do not attend sabbath school................ 80
Children in the public schools who do not attend sabbath school taken
   with those who do attend sabbath school............... 20

Total estimated membership of white fathers in all churches in Bloomington.. 1783
Total estimated membership of white mothers in all churches in Bloomington.. 2200
Total estimated membership of white fathers and mothers in all churches
   in Bloomington.. 3983

Colored families   PER CENT
Church membership of all colored fathers reporting.......... 55
Non-church membership of all fathers........................ 45
Fathers having club and fraternal order membership......... 10
Church membership of all mothers........................... 100
No non-church membership nor no membership in club or fraternal orders
indicated for colored mothers.
Per cent of sabbath school attendance of fathers and mothers based on
   their church membership............................... 9½

Total estimated membership of colored fathers in all churches in Bloomington.. 66
Total estimated membership of colored mothers in all churches in Bloomington.. 118
Total estimated membership of colored fathers and mothers of all churches
   in Bloomington.. 184

6. A Summary of Facts Regarding Home Conditions

Below is given a summary of facts from the tabulation of the
survey mentioned above. These facts are to some extent, at least,
an index to home conditions.

Houses:
   Out of 458 cases reported:
   Number of houses owned by occupants...................... 224
   Number of houses rented................................. 234
   Number of houses owned by the occupants and mortgaged...... 84
House conditions:
   Out of 464 reports on house conditions:
   Good house conditions................................... 282
   Fair house conditions................................... 138
   Bad house conditions.................................... 44
   Number of cases where one family lived in a house.......... 373
   Number of cases where two or more families live in the same
     house... 100
   (Last two items out of a total of 473 houses.)

Community and Plan of its Public School Survey 13

Furniture:
In 442 reports on furniture conditions:
Number of cases of good furniture conditions.................. 281
Number of cases of fair furniture conditions.................. 116
Number of cases of bad furniture conditions.................. 45
Number of cases having an ample supply of furniture.......... 373
Number of cases that did not have an ample supply of furniture.. 49
Yards:
Out of 453 reports on yard conditions:
Number of cases of good yard conditions..................... 194
Number of cases of fair yard conditions..................... 214
Number of cases of bad yard conditions 45
Adjoining property:
Conditions of streets and alleys adjoining property, 421 families in the report:
Number of cases of good condition........................... 297
Number of cases of fair condition............................ 93
Number of cases of bad condition............................ 31
Miscellaneous facts:
Number of families having bathing facilities.................. 164
Number of families not having bathing facilities.............. 61
Per cent of families reporting on this item who have bathing facilities.. 72.8
Number of families having cellars............................ 334
Number of families reporting sewer connection............... 222
Number of families reporting plumbing connections........... 209
Number of cesspools reported............................... 52
Water supply:
Number of families using wells........................... 63 or 9 %
Number of families using city service...................... 276 or 37½%
Number of families using cisterns......................... 391 or 53½%
Some families have more than one means of water supply.
Number of families reporting inside toilets.................. 196
Number of families reporting outside toilets................. 307
Per cent of families reporting who have inside toilets.......... 39%
Per cent of families reporting who have outside toilets......... 61%
A few families have both inside and outside toilets.
Heating:
319 families reported:
Number of families using stoves.......................... 201 or 63 %
Number of families using hot air furnaces.................. 65 or 20½%
Number of families using hot water....................... 42 or 13 %
Number of families using steam heat...................... 11 or 3½%
Lighting:
524 families reported:
Number of families using electric light..................... 223 or 42½%
Number of families using gas light........................ 115 or 22 %
Number of families using oil lamps .... 186 or 35½%
Some of the families have more than one means of lighting and heating.
Cooking:
470 families included in report:
Number of families doing cooking at home.................. 467 or 99¼%
Number of families not cooking at home................... 1 or ¼%

The above facts for colored families reported are as follows:
House conditions:
Number of houses owned by occupants...................... 8
Number of houses rented by occupants...................... 11
Number of houses owned by occupants and mortgaged......... 6
Number of families reported as having good house conditions.. 2
Number of families reported as having fair house conditions..... 11
Number of families reported as having bad house conditions ... 19

Furniture conditions:
    Number of families having good furniture conditions......... 2
    Number of families having fair furniture conditions.......... 6
    Number of families having bad furniture conditions.......... 13
    The above three items included in 21 families reported.
    Number of families having an ample supply of furniture....... 10
    Number of families not having an ample supply of furniture ... 10
    Twenty families included in the report on the two items last mentioned.

Yard conditions:
    Twenty families reported:
    Number of families having good yard conditions.............. 4 or 20 %
    Number of families having fair yard conditions.............. 12 or 60 %
    Number of families having bad yard conditions.............. 4 or 20 %

Adjoining property:
    Conditions of streets and alleys adjoining the property.
    Eighteen families reported:
    Number of families having good street and alley conditions.... 4 or 22 %
    Number of families having fair street and alley conditions..... 7 or 39 %
    Number of families having bad street and alley conditions..... 7 or 39 %

Miscellaneous facts:
    There is no report on bathing facilities among the colored families.
    Number of families having cellars.......................... 6
    Number of families having sewer connection................ 1
    Number of families having plumbing connections............ 1
    There were no cesspools reported.

Water supply:
    Twenty-two families reported: .
    Number of families having wells........................... 7 or 32 %
    Number of families having cisterns........................ 12 or $54\frac{1}{2}$%
    Number of families using city service...................... 3 or $13\frac{1}{2}$%
    No inside toilets reported.
    All families using outside toilets.

Heating:
    Seventeen families reported:
    All these families use stoves.............................. 17 cases.
    No other means of heating was reported.

Lighting:
    Twenty-two families reported:
    Number of families using electric light..................... 1 or $4\frac{6}{11}$%
    Number of families using oil lamps........................ 22 or 100%
    None use gas light; one family uses both electric light and oil lamps.

Cooking:
    Nineteen families reported:
    All the colored families do the cooking at home............. 19 cases.

SUMMARY OF CHAPTER I

1. The survey of the Bloomington schools was undertaken with a view to determining and remedying conditions.

2. To the end that these conditions might best be discovered and remedied the plan of survey decided upon was that of co-operation between outside experts and local authorities.

3. Bloomington, in its early history, contributed her share toward the illiteracy for which the state of Indiana was noted.

4. The inhabitants of Monroe County, of which Bloomington is the county seat, even voted in 1849 against free public schools by a vote of 1040 to 667.

5. From the beginning, however, a noticeable element in the population of Bloomington supported general education.

6. At the present time the city of Bloomington gladly supports public education by a tax considerably higher than that levied by the majority of other Indiana towns for educational purposes.

7. Approximately 45 per cent of all the inhabitants of Bloomington help to support themselves or their families, 85.8 per cent of this number being men and 14.2 per cent women.

8. Of all wage-earning parents of children in school, 9.5 per cent are in professions, 17.7 per cent in business for themselves, 35.7 per cent in skilled occupations, and 37 per cent in unskilled occupations.

9. The median number of years' schooling of white parents in Bloomington is: fathers, 9 years; mothers, 8.5 years. Of colored parents the median is: fathers, 5 years; mothers, 5.9 years.

10. It is estimated that about 124 white parents in Bloomington never went to school; about 1405 quit school before reaching the eighth grade; about 1617 quit in the eighth grade or at the end of it; about 1010 have had some high-school training; and about 792 have had some college work; while 445 are college graduates and post-graduates. Of the colored population about 44 never went to school; about 44 quit in the eighth grade or at the close of it; 95 quit below the eighth grade; and 53 have had some high-school work.

11. The per cent of white parents that are church members is: fathers, 74.6; mothers, 85.5. Of colored parents the per cent is: fathers, 55; mothers, 100.

12. Of the white families only 14 per cent of the parents who are church members attend sabbath school while 80 per cent of all white children in the public schools attend sabbath school. Of the colored families only 9½ per cent of the parents who are church members attend sabbath school, whereas 80 per cent of all the colored children in school attend sabbath school.

13. Of the white families a little over 50 per cent live in rented property. Of the colored families about 58 per cent live in rented property.

CHAPTER II

NORMAL PROGRESS, RETARDATION, AND ACCELERATION

In recent studies on retardation and acceleration various bases for determining normal progress have been used. The age-grade basis and the years in school and progress made basis are the two fundamental ones upon which to figure normal progress. Both of these methods have been used in the Bloomington studies. In the practices of those who use the age-grade tables alone there is lack of uniformity. Some count from six to seven years of age as the normal age for the first grade, seven to eight for the second, etc. Others allow a range of from six to eight for the first grade, seven to nine for the second, etc. In this study the median entering age of children in the 1B grade, the first half year of school, was determined. It proved to be approximately six and one-half years. With this age as the normal entering age normal progress was determined as follows: Six and one-half to seven years, 1B grade; seven to seven and one-half years, 1A grade; seven and one-half to eight years, 2B grade, etc. Unless a child made a half year of progress in school for every half year attended, assuming that each child entered school at the median age of entering, i.e., six and one-half years, he was counted retarded.

In the Bloomington survey normal progress, retardation, and acceleration are in most cases figured on the basis of six and one-half as the entering age and one-half year of progress in school for each additional half year of age. For the sake, however, of comparison with other systems that have worked out retardation and acceleration on the basis of allowing a range of approximately two years for each of the eight grades in school, i.e., six to eight for the first grade, seven to nine for the second, etc., and for the sake of comparing the Bloomington system of schools on this basis with itself at various times Tables V, VI, and VII are given.

The following table proves conclusively that the median or average age of beginning 1B pupils in the Bloomington schools is fairly close to six and one-half years:

TABLE IV — SUMMARY SHOWING AVERAGE AND MEDIAN AGES OF BEGINNING WHITE PUPILS BY SEX AND BUILDINGS FOR THE FIRST AND SECOND SEMESTER, SCHOOL YEAR, 1912–13

First Semester, Ages Taken September 9, 1912

BUILDING	GRADE	NUMBER OF BOYS	NUMBER OF GIRLS	TOTAL NUMBER OF BOYS AND GIRLS	AVERAGE AGE OF BOYS Yr. Mo. Da.	AVERAGE AGE OF GIRLS Yr. Mo. Da.	AVERAGE AGE OF BOYS AND GIRLS Yr. Mo. Da.	MEDIAN AGE OF BOYS Yr. Mo. Da.	MEDIAN AGE OF GIRLS Yr. Mo. Da.	MEDIAN AGE OF BOTH BOYS AND GIRLS Yr. Mo. Da.
Central	1B	16	17	33	6 4 12.1	6 5 25.1	6 5 4.2	6 3 15.5	6 2 9	6 3 2
McCalla	1B	34	32	66	6 10 14.5	6 9 19.9	6 9 19.9	6 6 15.2	6 5 13	6 6 20
Fairview	1B	18	19	37	6 7 25.6	6 6 8.8	6 7 1.6	6 6 9	6 5 20	6 5 25
Total	1B	68	68	136	6 8 10.7	6 7 10.6	6 7 25.7	6 6 0	6 5 9	6 5 13

Second Semester, Ages Taken January 27, 1913

BUILDING	GRADE	TOTAL NUMBER OF BOYS AND GIRLS	AVERAGE AGE OF BOYS AND GIRLS Yr. Mo. Da.	MEDIAN AGE OF BOTH BOYS AND GIRLS Yr. Mo. Da.
Central	1B	16	6 1 14.7	6 1 12
McCalla	1B	15	6 2 29	6 0 20
Fairview	1B	20	6 9 13.4	6 6 29.5
Total	1B	51	6 5 1.3	6 3 15

SUMMARY SHOWING AVERAGE AND MEDIAN AGES OF BEGINNING PUPILS BY SEX AND BUILDINGS FOR THE FIRST AND SECOND SEMESTERS, SCHOOL YEAR 1913–14

First Semester, Ages Taken September 1, 1913

BUILDING	GRADE	NUMBER OF BOYS	NUMBER OF GIRLS	TOTAL NUMBER OF BOYS AND GIRLS	AVERAGE AGE OF BOYS Yr. Mo. Da.	AVERAGE AGE OF GIRLS Yr. Mo. Da.	AVERAGE AGE OF BOYS AND GIRLS Yr. Mo. Da.	MEDIAN AGE OF BOYS Yr. Mo. Da.	MEDIAN AGE OF GIRLS Yr. Mo. Da.	MEDIAN AGE OF BOTH BOYS AND GIRLS Yr. Mo. Da.
Central	1B	31	30	61	6 8 12.2	6 8 25.3	6 8 21.7	6 6 22	6 6 2	6 6 22
McCalla	1B	26	34	60	6 9 9.9	6 6 5	6 7 16.2	6 9 28	6 6 17	6 6 24.5
Fairview	1B	20	21	41	6 7 14.3	6 5 1	6 6 6.7	6 5 10	6 5 1	6 5 3
Total	1B	77	85	162	6 8 16.7	6 6 25	6 7 19.6	6 6 28	6 5 28	6 7 7.5

Second Semester, Ages Taken February 1, 1914

BUILDING	GRADE	TOTAL NUMBER OF BOYS AND GIRLS	AVERAGE AGE OF BOYS AND GIRLS Yr. Mo. Da.	MEDIAN AGE OF BOTH BOYS AND GIRLS Yr. Mo. Da.
Central	1B	23	6 4 15.5	6 2 18
McCalla	1B	14	6 2 21.4	6 1 16.5
Fairview	1B	12	6 3 23.1	6 2 16
Total	1B	49	6 3 24.5	6 2 9

Table V gives the figures for retardation, acceleration, and normal progress of thirty American cities.   These figures with the exception of those from Bloomington are copied from page 191 of the Survey of the School System of Salt Lake City, Utah, which table, with the exception of figures for Salt Lake City and Butte, Montana, were

TABLE V

RETARDATION, ACCELERATION, AND NORMAL PROGRESS IN 30 AMERICAN CITIES

		PER CENT	
	RETARDED	NORMAL	ACCELERATED
Quincy, Mass.	19	31	50
Bloomington, Ind. (ages May 29, 1914)	22.4	66	11.6
Racine, Wis.	28	42	30
Amsterdam, N. Y.	28	23	49
Syracuse, N. Y.	29	29	42
Indianapolis, Ind.	29	37	34
Bloomington, Indiana { Oct. 4, 1913 / ages Sept. 1 }	29.5	62.9	7.6
Danbury, Conn.	31	31	38
Milwaukee, Wis.	31	41	28
Rockford, Ill.	32	40	28
Canton, Ohio.	34	38	28
Elmira, N. Y.	34	28	38
New Rochelle, N. Y.	34	30	36
Muskegon, Mich.	35	40	25
Niagara Falls, N. Y.	36	33	31
Topeka, Kansas.	36	38	26
Bloomington, Indiana { 1900–1912 / ages Sept. 1 }	37	52.2	10.8
Danville, Ill.	38	34	28
Trenton, N. J.	38	31	31
Reading, Pa.	40	35	25
Plainfield, N. J.	40	30	30
Perth Amboy, N. J.	41	32	27
Bayonne, N. J.	42	31	27
Hazelton, Pa.	42	36	22
Salt Lake City, Utah.	43	40	16
East St. Louis, Ill.	44	34	22
Elizabeth, N. J.	46	31	23
Kenosha, Wis.	48	36	16
Montclair, N. J.	48	34	18
New Orleans, La. (white)	49	31	20
Butte, Mont.	51	41	7
Passaic, N. J.	51	32	17

copied from Ayres' "Identification of the Misfit Child," Russell Sage Foundation, Bulletin No. 108.   In Table V pupils between six and one-half and eight years of age during last month of the school year are considered normal for the first grade as far as the Salt Lake City figures are concerned.   The ages for some of the cities in the table were doubtless computed from dates earlier in the school year. Dates for computing ages in Bloomington are indicated.   In the report for May 29, 1914, ages were computed as of May 29th, the last day of school, and pupils were counted as of the grades they were in before promotion on the last day. In Table V ages six to eight are considered normal for the first grade, seven to nine for the second, etc.

TABLE VI

NUMBER AND PER CENT OF NORMAL, RETARDED, AND ACCELERATED CHILDREN

All elementary school pupils entering Bloomington schools with classes beginning September 1900, January 1901, September 1901, January 1902, September 1902, January 1903, September 1903, and January 1904, and graduating June 1908, January 1909, June 1909, January 1910, June 1910, January 1911, June 1911, January 1912. All pupils entering these classes are included regardless of the year of entering or semester pupil was in. Each child counted each semester he was in. Ages as of date of opening of school in the fall. Normal age for first grade, six to eight years. Table computed from figures included in A. C. Burgin's study.

GRADE	I	II	III	IV	V	VI	VII	VIII
Boys	417	430	498	522	443	326	348	273
Girls	377	400	504	582	524	437	409	265
Total	794	830	1002	1104	967	763	757	538
Normal								
Boys	256	197	240	245	207	128	175	139
Girls	241	210	289	310	282	230	232	149
Total	497	407	529	555	489	358	407	288
Accelerated								
Boys	50	31	38	39	50	40	41	31
Girls	51	40	57	57	58	55	47	42
Total	101	71	95	96	108	95	88	73
Retarded								
Boys	111	202	220	238	186	158	132	103
Girls	85	150	158	215	184	152	130	74
Total	196	352	378	453	370	310	262	177
Per cent Normal								
Boys	61.4	45.8	48.1	46.9	46.7	39.2	50.8	50.9
Girls	63.9	52.5	57.3	53.3	53.8	52.6	56.7	56.2
Total	62.6	49.0	52.7	50.2	50.5	46.9	53.6	53.5
Per cent Accelerated								
Boys	12.0	7.2	7.8	7.5	11.3	12.3	11.5	11.4
Girls	13.5	10.0	11.3	9.8	11.1	12.6	11.5	15.8
Total	12.6	8.6	9.5	8.7	11.1	12.4	11.5	13.5
Per cent Retarded								
Boys	26.6	47.0	44.1	45.6	41.9	48.4	37.8	37.7
Girls	22.5	37.5	31.3	36.9	35.1	34.8	31.8	27.9
Total	24.7	42.4	37.7	41.0	38.3	40.6	34.8	32.9

TABLE VII

NUMBER AND PER CENT OF ALL WHITE PUPILS IN BLOOMINGTON SCHOOLS, OCTOBER 4, 1913, NORMAL, ACCELERATED, RETARDED

Ages as of September 1, 1913. Normal Age for First Grade, Six to Eight Years; for Second Grade, Seven to Nine Years, etc.

GRADE	I	II	III	IV	V	VI	VII	VIII
Boys	132	122	127	141	112	72	72	48
Girls	138	103	102	114	103	103	87	55
Total	270	225	229	255	215	175	159	103

Normal	I	II	III	IV	V	VI	VII	VIII
Boys	114	86	79	80	58	37	47	28
Girls	117	81	61	31	56	62	64	34
Total	231	167	140	111	114	99	111	62
Accelerated								
Boys	3	10	13	8	5	5	7	5
Girls	8	5	7	12	11	12	10	5
Total	11	15	20	20	16	17	17	10
Retarded								
Boys	15	26	35	53	49	30	18	15
Girls	13	17	34	71	36	29	13	16
Total	28	43	69	124	85	59	31	31
Per cent Normal								
Boys	86.3	70.6	62.2	56.8	51.7	51.4	65.2	58.3
Girls	84.8	78.5	59.8	27.2	54.3	60.2	73.5	61.8
Total	85.5	74.2	61.1	43.5	53.0	56.5	69.7	60.2
Per cent Accelerated								
Boys	2.2	8.2	10.2	5.6	4.4	6.9	9.7	10.3
Girls	5.8	4.9	6.8	10.6	10.6	11.6	11.5	9.1
Total	4.1	6.6	8.7	7.8	7.4	9.7	10.6	9.7
Per cent Retarded								
Boys	11.3	21.2	27.6	37.6	43.7	41.5	25.0	31.2
Girls	9.3	16.4	33.3	62.2	35.0	28.1	14.9	29.1
Total	10.3	19.1	30.1	48.6	39.4	33.8	19.5	30.0

A comparison of Tables VI and VII shows that for the Bloomington schools a much larger percentage of the children had made normal progress the fall semester of 1913–14 than for the earlier period. Only in the fourth grade is there an exception.

On the whole, there was less retardation in 1913 than in the earlier period, exceptions occurring in Grades IV and V. In the case of acceleration the advantage seems to be with the earlier period. This advantage is not as great as it appears, however, because children were allowed to enter at a younger age during the earlier period than later. Over 7 per cent of the children in the earlier period entered the schools before the age of six. The advantage seems more in favor of the earlier period than it really is for the reason, also, that the earlier study combines all pupils in both semesters of a year while the later study applies to the opening of school after a three months' vacation, which counts against acceleration. A similar study at the beginning of the second semester of 1913–14 would have shown a larger per cent of acceleration. The conclusion can safely be drawn that noticeable progress has been made in eliminating retardation in the schools in recent years compared with the period of entering from 1900 to 1904 and of graduating from 1908 to 1912.

Table V shows that in comparison with other cities Bloomington does not make a bad record so far as retardation and normal progress are concerned. The percentage of acceleration, however, is low in Bloomington. The table also shows that Bloomington has been making progress in eliminating retardation and in increasing the per cent of normal progress. As for acceleration, however, no progress can be claimed.

In succeeding age-grade tables Bloomington is .compared with itself from year to year. For these comparisons six and one-half years of age is considered the normal entering age and normal progress is interpreted as meaning one term of progress for each term in school.

TABLE VIII

SHOWING BY SEX, GRADE, AND BUILDINGS PERCENTAGES OF RETARDATION BASED ON AGE–GRADE TABLES FOR OCTOBER 4, 1913

Ages as of September 1. Normal age for entering, 1B grade, six and one-half years, Normal progress, one-half year for each half year of school.

	BOYS			GIRLS		
GRADE	CENTRAL	McCALLA	FAIRVIEW	CENTRAL	McCALLA	FAIRVIEW
1B	26	31.1	48.3	30.6	23.5	16
1A	38.5	38.8	20	12.5	43.8	42.2
2B	57.1	44.1	55.5	20	51.5	60.
2A	33.3	27.8	42.8	0	15.4	42.9
3B	35	57.5	47.8	50	38.1	60
3A	41.7	44.4	66.6	50	35.2	50
4B	57.9	58.1	63.6	40	44.4	50
4A	63.2	61.9	61.1	53.9	47.6	56.2
5B	52.4	62.9	47	75	25	64.7
5A	62.5	64.3	70.6	66.7	25	68.4
6B	77.8	45	60	64.3	15	61.1
6A	68.2	27.2		51.3	33.3	
7B	47.5			49		
7A	50			31.6		
8B	42.2			50		
8A	66.7			36.8		

SUMMARY OF TABLE VIII

1. In the Central building the per cent of retardation among the boys is greater than that among the girls except in grades 1B, 3B, 3A, 5B, 5A, 7B, 8B.

2. In the McCalla building the per cent of retardation among the boys is greater than that among the girls except in grades 1A, 2B, 6A.

3. In the Fairview building the per cent of retardation among the boys is greater than that among the girls except in grades 1A, 2B, 2A, 3B, 5B, 6B.

4. Among the boys in grades 1B to 6B inclusive Fairview has the greatest per cent of retardation in 5 grades, McCalla in 3, and Central in 3. Among the girls, Fairview has the greatest per cent of retardation in 6 grades, Central in 3, and McCalla in 1. In another grade Central and Fairview are tied for the largest per cent of retardation.

5. Among the boys Central has the least percentages of retardation in 5 grades, Fairview in 3, and McCalla in 3. Among the girls McCalla has the least per cent of retardation in 6 grades, Central in 4 grades, and Fairview in 1.

6. On the basis of the per cent of retardation beginning with the greatest per cent of retardation the various grades for the school system as a whole rank as follows: 5A, 4A, 6B, 4B, 5B, 8A, 6A, 7B, 3B, 3A, 8B, 7A, 2B, 1A, 2A, 1B.

TABLE IX

SHOWING BY SEX, GRADE, AND BUILDINGS PERCENTAGES OF ACCELERATION ON
AGE–GRADE TABLES FOR OCTOBER 4, 1913

Ages as of September 1. Normal age for entering 1B grade, six and one-half years. Normal progress, half year for each half year in school.

GRADE	BOYS			GIRLS		
	CENTRAL	McCALLA	FAIRVIEW	CENTRAL	McCALLA	FAIRVIEW
1B.................	51.6	34.4	38.7	44.4	44.1	52
1A.................	46.1	38.8	50	75	31.2	21
2B.................	38.1	38.2	27.8	60	24.2	26.6
2A.................	50	44.4	14.2	69.2	46.1	7.1
3B.................	40	30.3	34.8	33.3	47.6	25
3A.................	41.7	40.7	8.3	33.3	47.1	35.7
4B.................	15.8	25.8	27.3	40	33.3	18.1
4A.................	31.6	33.3	22.2	30.8	23.8	25
5B.................	28.6	25.9	35.3	16.7	50	17.7
5A.................	31.3	28.5	5.9	13.3	43.8	10.5
6B.................	11.1	30	20	28.6	35	22.2
6A.................	13.7	72.7		28.2	50	
7B.................	22.5			32.7		
7A.................	34.4			42.1		
8B.................	36.4			27.8		
8A.................	13.3			52.6		

SUMMARY OF TABLE IX

1. In the Central building the per cent of acceleration among the boys is greater than that among the girls in grades 1B, 3B, 3A, 4A, 5B, 5A, 8B.

2. In the McCalla building the per cent of acceleration among the boys is greater than that among the girls in grades 1A, 2B, 4A, 6A.

3. In the Fairview building the per cent of acceleration among the boys is greater than that among the girls in grades 1A, 2B, 2A, 3B, 4B, 5B.

4. Among the boys in grades 1B to 6B inclusive Central has the greatest per cent of acceleration in 5 grades, Fairview in 3, and McCalla in 3. Among the girls Central has the greatest per cent of retardation in 5 grades, McCalla in 5, and Fairview in 1.

5. Among the boys Fairview has the least percentage of acceleration in 5 grades, McCalla in 4, and Central in 2. Among the girls Fairview has the least percentage in acceleration in 6 grades, McCalla in 3, and Central in 2.

6. On the basis of the per cent of acceleration beginning with the greatest per cent of acceleration the various grades rank as follows: 1B, 2A, 1A, 7A, 3A, 8A, 3B, 2B, 6A, 8B, 5B, 4A, 4B, 6B, 5A.

TABLE X

SHOWING BY SEX, GRADE, AND BUILDINGS PERCENTAGES OF NORMAL PROGRESS
ON AGE–GRADE TABLES FOR OCTOBER 4, 1913

Ages as of September 1. Normal age for entering 1B grade, six and one-half years. Normal progress, half year for each half year in school.

GRADE	BOYS			GIRLS		
	CENTRAL	McCALLA	FAIRVIEW	CENTRAL	McCALLA	FAIRVIEW
1B.................	22.6	34.4	12.9	25	32.4	32
1A.................	15.4	22.2	30	12.5	25	26.8
2B.................	4.8	17.6	16.8	20	24.2	13.3
2A.................	16.7	27.8	42.8	30.8	38.4	50
3B.................	25	18.2	17.3	16.7	14.2	15
3A.................	16.7	14.8	25	16.7	17.6	14.2
4B.................	26.3	16.1	9	20	22.2	31.8
4A.................	5.3	4.7	16.6	15.4	28.5	18.7
5B.................	19	11.1	17.7	8.3	25	17.7
5A.................	6.3	7.1	23.5	20	31.2	21.1
6B.................	11.1	25	20	7.1	50	16.6
6A.................	18.2	0		20.5	16.6	
7B.................	30			18.4		
7A.................	15.6			26.3		
8B.................	21.2			22.2		
8A.................	20			10.5		

SUMMARY OF TABLE X

1. In the Central building the per cent of normal progress among the boys is greater than that among the girls in grades 1A, 3B, 4B, 5B, 6B, 7B, 8A. In grade 3A it is the same for boys and girls.

2. In the McCalla building the per cent of normal progress among the boys is greater than that among the girls in grades 1B, 3B.

3. In the Fairview building the per cent of normal progress among the boys is greater than that among the girls in grades 1A, 2B, 3B, 3A, 5A, 6B. In grade 5B it is the same for boys and girls.

4. Among the boys in grades 1B to 6B inclusive Fairview has the greatest percentage of normal progress in 5 grades, McCalla in 3, and Central in 3. Among the girls McCalla has the greatest percentage of normal progress in 7 grades, Fairview in 3, and Central in 1.

5. Among the boys Central has the least percentage of normal progress in 5 grades, Fairview in 3, and McCalla in 3. Among the girls Central has the least percentage of normal progress in 8 grades, Fairview in 2, and McCalla in 1.

6. On the basis of the percentage of normal progress beginning with the greatest percentage of normal progress the various grades rank as follows: 2A, 2B, 1B, 1A, 7B, 8B, 7A, 4B, 5A, 3B, 3A, 5B, 6A, 6B, 4A, 8A.

Tables VIII, IX, and X show that for the Central building the retardation far exceeds the acceleration. The per cent of pupils making normal progress decreases abruptly in the 1A and 2B grades and in the 4A, 5B, 5A, and 6B grades. The decrease in the fourth, fifth, and sixth grades would naturally be expected since the law compelling all children to attend school until sixteen years of age unless they have passed the 5A grade and are at work, operated for the first time during the fall of 1913–14. Before that time children had been compelled to attend school only until the age of fourteen without regard to the grade reached. The boys as a rule show a greater degree of retardation than the girls, while the girls show a greater degree of acceleration.

Retardation in the Fairview school is distinctly higher than in the Central building. This retardation gradually increases with fluctuations until the highest grade in the building, 6B, is reached. There is not the same degree of difference in this building between the boys and the girls.

McCalla building shows the least per cent of retardation of all the buildings. This is to be expected since most of the children of the University professors attend this school through the 6A or 7B grade. Such children are the children of a selected group and are children too that enjoy greater privileges in the home in the way of helpful supplementary material.

The age-grade tables for the years 1909–10, 1910–11, 1911–12 were made out on a slightly different basis from those that precede or follow them. They are not so far different, however, that they may not be used fairly safely for comparison. The necessary allowances can be made when they are used as bases of comparison. All ages for these years, 1909–10, 1910–11, 1911–12, were secured from school records by three advanced students in Indiana University, D. W. Horton, C. A. Davis and Sylvia Cuzzort.

All ages were reckoned from date of birth, year, and month, to September 30, 1909. No account was taken of fractions of a month. To get the age for each of the six semesters after September 30, 1909, one-half year was added. Thus if a child was six years old on entering 6B, his age would be six and one-half for 6A, seven for 7B, seven and one-half for 7A, eight for 8B, eight and one-half for 8A, etc. A pupil was considered six until six and one-half, and six and one-half until seven years old.

Table XI shows a rather uniformly high degree of retardation. The per cent of acceleration fluctuates considerably. The low point for the normals occurs in the 5B grade. The 8A group is incomplete and for that reason unreliable as a basis for drawing conclusions.

TABLE XI — NUMBER AND PER CENT OF ALL WHITE PUPILS IN BLOOMINGTON SCHOOLS, FIRST SEMESTER, 1909–10, THAT WERE NORMAL, ACCELERATED, RETARDED

Normal age for entering 1B grade, six and one-half years. Normal progress, one-half year for each half year in school. Ages as of September 30.

GRADE	1B	1A	2B	2A	3B	3A	4B	4A	5B	5A	6B	6A	7B	7A	8B	8A
Boys	89	23	37	24	17	31	48	25	45	24	34	40	32	29	24	1
Girls	110	22	45	51	26	51	36	35	42	24	23	31	29	16	21	3
Total	199	45	82	75	43	82	84	60	87	48	57	71	61	45	45	4
Normal																
Boys	23	3	10	3	5	6	9	3	3	3	5	11	2	4	3	0
Girls	28	5	11	8	3	10	11	8	2	2	5	4	4	7	4	0
Total	51	8	21	11	8	16	20	11	5	5	10	15	6	11	7	0
Accelerated																
Boys	30	4	7	15	7	11	17	6	20	10	11	9	19	10	8	1
Girls	55	4	14	19	4	13	8	12	16	12	9	9	10	1	7	0
Total	85	8	21	34	11	24	25	18	36	22	20	18	29	11	15	1
Retarded																
Boys	36	16	20	6	5	14	22	16	22	11	18	20	11	15	13	0
Girls	27	13	20	24	19	28	17	15	24	10	9	18	15	8	10	3
Total	63	29	40	30	24	42	39	31	46	21	27	38	26	23	23	3
Per cent Normal																
Boys	25.8	13.1	27.0	12.5	29.4	19.3	18.7	12.0	6.6	12.5	14.7	27.5	6.2	13.7	12.5	0
Girls	25.4	22.7	24.4	15.6	11.5	19.5	30.5	22.8	4.7	8.3	21.7	12.9	13.8	43.7	19.0	0
Total	25.6	17.8	25.6	14.7	18.6	19.5	23.7	18.3	5.7	10.4	17.5	21.1	9.8	24.4	15.6	0
Per cent Accelerated																
Boys	33.7	17.2	18.9	62.5	41.1	35.4	35.4	24.0	44.4	41.6	32.4	22.5	59.3	34.4	33.3	100
Girls	50.0	18.1	31.1	37.2	15.3	25.4	22.2	34.3	38.0	58.0	39.1	29.0	34.5	6.2	33.3	0
Total	42.3	17.8	25.6	45.3	25.6	29.3	29.8	30.0	41.4	45.8	35.0	25.4	47.5	24.4	33.3	25.0
Per cent Retarded																
Boys	40.5	69.5	54.0	25.0	29.4	45.1	45.8	64.0	48.8	45.8	52.8	50.0	34.4	51.7	54.3	0
Girls	24.5	59.0	44.4	47.0	73.1	54.9	47.2	42.8	57.1	41.7	39.1	58.0	51.7	50.0	47.6	100.0
Total	31.7	64.4	48.4	40.0	55.8	51.2	46.4	57.7	52.9	43.7	47.4	53.5	42.6	51.1	51.1	75.0

TABLE XII — NUMBER AND PER CENT OF ALL WHITE PUPILS IN BLOOMINGTON SCHOOLS, SECOND SEMESTER, 1909-10, THAT WERE NORMAL, ACCELERATED, RETARDED

Normal age for entering 1B grade, six and one-half years. Normal progress, one-half year for each half year in school. Ages as of March 30.

GRADE	1B	1A	2B	2A	3B	3A	4B	4A	5B	5A	6B	6A	7B	7A	8B	8A
Boys	61	70	25	38	63	30	41	39	36	39	32	23	25	27	15	17
Girls	61	72	24	39	61	30	41	40	35	38	28	23	25	27	15	17
Total	122	142	49	77	124	60	82	79	71	77	60	46	50	54	30	34
Normal																
Boys	25	19	6	10	11	5	9	7	9	5	0	6	4	5	6	3
Girls	25	19	6	10	11	5	9	8	9	5	6	6	4	5	6	3
Total	50	38	12	20	22	10	18	15	18	10	6	12	8	10	12	6
Accelerated																
Boys	18	26	4	11	22	4	8	13	11	17	8	6	6	9	1	4
Girls	18	27	3	11	21	4	8	13	11	15	8	6	6	9	1	4
Total	36	53	7	22	43	8	16	26	22	32	16	12	12	18	2	8
Retarded																
Boys	18	25	15	17	30	21	24	19	16	17	24	11	15	13	8	10
Girls	18	26	15	18	29	21	24	19	15	18	14	11	15	13	8	10
Total	36	51	30	35	59	42	48	38	31	35	38	22	30	26	16	20
Per cent Normal																
Boys	40.9	27.1	24.0	26.3	17.4	16.6	21.9	17.9	25.0	12.8	0	26.1	16.0	18.6	40.0	17.6
Girls	40.9	26.3	25.0	25.6	18.1	16.6	21.9	20.0	25.7	13.1	21.5	26.1	16.0	18.6	40.0	17.6
Total	41.0	26.8	24.5	26.2	17.7	16.7	22.0	19.0	25.4	13.0	10.0	26.0	16.0	18.5	40.0	17.6
Per cent Accelerated																
Boys	29.5	37.1	16.0	28.9	34.9	13.3	19.5	33.3	30.5	43.7	25.0	26.1	24.0	33.3	6.6	23.5
Girls	29.5	37.5	12.5	28.2	34.4	13.3	19.5	32.5	31.4	39.5	28.6	26.1	24.0	33.3	6.6	23.5
Total	29.5	37.3	14.3	28.6	34.7	13.3	19.5	32.9	31.3	41.6	27.0	26.0	24.0	33.3	6.7	23.5
Per cent Retarded																
Boys	29.5	35.6	60.0	44.7	47.6	70.0	58.5	48.6	44.4	43.6	75.0	47.7	60.0	48.1	53.3	58.8
Girls	29.5	36.1	62.5	46.0	47.5	70.0	58.5	47.5	42.8	47.3	50.0	47.7	60.0	48.1	53.3	58.8
Total	29.5	35.9	61.2	45.5	47.6	70.0	58.5	48.0	43.7	45.6	63.0	48.0	60.0	48.0	53.3	58.8

TABLE XIII — NUMBER AND PER CENT OF ALL WHITE PUPILS IN BLOOMINGTON SCHOOLS, FIRST SEMESTER, 1910–11, THAT WERE NORMAL, ACCELERATED, RETARDED

Normal age for entering 1B grade, six and one-half years. Normal progress, one-half year for each half year in school. Ages as of September 30.

GRADE	1B	1A	2B	2A	3B	3A	4B	4A	5B	5A	6B	6A	7B	7A	8B	8A
Boys	115	48	87	56	56	39	53	39	41	35	32	42	32	31	33	21
Girls	63	57	50	31	56	60	42	39	43	47	40	44	37	23	33	18
Total	178	105	137	87	112	99	95	78	84	82	72	86	69	54	66	39
Normal																
Boys	31	10	25	7	10	7	6	7	5	2	7	8	2	0	6	4
Girls	18	20	11	6	11	11	6	6	13	8	6	10	6	1	6	1
Total	49	30	36	13	21	18	12	13	18	10	13	18	8	1	12	5
Accelerated																
Boys	26	1	18	10	14	9	8	8	11	6	9	8	5	6	14	5
Girls	20	10	19	15	15	23	9	9	9	16	22	19	14	12	20	16
Total	46	11	37	25	29	32	17	17	20	22	31	27	19	18	34	21
Retarded																
Boys	58	37	44	39	32	23	39	24	25	27	16	26	25	25	13	12
Girls	25	27	20	10	30	26	27	24	21	23	12	15	17	10	7	1
Total	83	64	64	49	62	49	66	48	46	50	28	41	42	35	20	13
Per cent Normal																
Boys	26.9	20.8	28.7	12.4	17.9	17.8	11.3	17.9	12.2	5.7	21.8	19.0	6.2		18.1	19.0
Girls	28.5	35.1	22.0	19.3	19.6	18.3	14.3	15.4	30.2	17.0	15.0	22.7	16.2	4.3	18.1	5.5
Total	28.1	28.5	26.2	14.8	18.7	18.2	12.7	17.9	21.4	12.1	18.1	20.9	11.5	1.8	18.1	12.7
Per cent Accelerated																
Boys	22.6	2.0	20.6	17.8	25.0	23.1	15.1	20.5	26.8	17.1	28.1	19.0	15.6	19.3	42.4	23.7
Girls	31.7	17.5	38.0	48.4	26.8	38.3	21.4	23.1	20.9	34.0	55.0	43.2	37.8	52.1	60.6	88.8
Total	25.2	10.4	27.0	28.7	25.9	32.4	17.8	20.5	23.8	26.8	43.0	31.3	27.5	33.3	51.5	53.8
Per cent Retarded																
Boys	50.4	77.1	50.6	69.6	57.1	58.9	73.6	61.5	60.9	77.4	50.0	61.9	78.1	80.6	39.3	57.1
Girls	39.7	47.3	40.0	32.2	53.5	43.3	64.3	61.5	48.8	48.9	30.0	34.0	45.9	43.4	21.2	5.5
Total	46.6	61.0	46.6	56.3	55.3	49.3	69.4	61.5	54.7	60.9	38.8	47.7	60.0	64.8	30.3	33.3

TABLE XIV — NUMBER AND PER CENT OF ALL WHITE PUPILS IN BLOOMINGTON SCHOOLS, SECOND SEMESTER, 1910–11, THAT WERE NORMAL, ACCELERATED, RETARDED

Normal age for entering 1B grade, six and one-half years. Normal progress, one-half year for each half year in school. Ages as of March 30.

GRADE	1B	1A	2B	2A	3B	3A	4B	4A	5B	5A	6B	6A	7B	7A	8B	8A
Boys	49	35	41	32	50	43	53	36	55	45	38	44	35	32	27	35
Girls	50	36	40	32	45	43	55	36	46	46	38	44	35	33	27	36
Total	99	71	81	64	95	86	108	72	101	91	76	88	70	65	54	71
Normal																
Boys	13	9	12	6	16	7	11	4	9	9	8	10	2	5	8	5
Girls	13	9	12	6	6	7	5	7	10	5	7	9	9	4	2	5
Total	26	18	24	12	22	14	16	11	19	14	15	19	11	9	10	10
Accelerated																
Boys	9	5	11	12	16	13	17	4	10	10	12	10	9	4	2	11
Girls	9	5	10	18	27	20	30	8	20	20	20	20	11	9	15	23
Total	18	10	21	30	43	33	47	12	30	30	32	30	20	13	17	34
Retarded																
Boys	27	21	18	14	18	23	25	28	36	26	18	24	24	23	17	19
Girls	28	22	18	8	12	16	20	21	16	21	11	15	15	20	10	8
Total	55	43	36	22	30	39	45	49	52	47	29	39	39	43	27	27
Per cent Normal																
Boys	26.5	25.7	29.2	18.7	32.0	16.3	20.8	11.4	16.4	20.0	21.1	22.7	5.7	15.6	29.6	14.3
Girls	26.0	25.0	30.0	18.7	13.3	16.3	9.1	19.4	21.7	10.9	18.4	20.4	25.7	12.1	7.4	13.9
Total	26.2	25.3	29.8	18.7	23.1	16.3	14.8	15.2	18.8	15.6	19.7	21.6	15.7	13.8	18.5	14.1
Per cent Accelerated																
Boys	18.4	14.3	26.8	37.5	32.0	30.2	32.1	11.1	18.2	22.2	31.6	22.7	25.7	12.5	7.4	31.4
Girls	18.0	13.9	25.0	56.3	60.0	46.5	54.5	22.2	43.5	43.4	52.6	45.5	31.4	27.3	55.6	63.9
Total	18.1	14.0	25.9	46.8	45.2	38.3	43.5	16.6	29.7	32.9	42.1	34.0	28.6	20.0	31.5	47.8
Per cent Retarded																
Boys	55.1	60.0	44.0	43.8	36.0	53.5	47.1	77.8	65.4	57.8	47.3	54.5	68.6	71.9	63.0	54.3
Girls	56.0	61.1	45.0	25.0	26.7	37.2	36.4	58.3	34.8	45.7	29.0	34.1	42.9	60.6	37.0	22.2
Total	55.5	60.5	44.4	34.3	31.5	45.3	41.6	68.1	51.4	51.6	38.1	44.3	55.7	66.1	50.0	38.0

TABLE XV — NUMBER AND PER CENT OF ALL WHITE PUPILS IN BLOOMINGTON SCHOOLS, FIRST SEMESTER, 1911-12, THAT WERE NORMAL, ACCELERATED, RETARDED

Normal age for entering 1B grade, six and one-half years. Normal progress, one-half year for each half year in school. Ages as of September 30.

GRADE	1B	1A	2B	2A	3B	3A	4B	4A	5B	5A	6B	6A	7B	7A	8B	8A
Boys	101	30	36	32	48	31	24	37	46	36	44	23	43	37	38	6
Girls	94	39	61	48	53	47	60	60	44	43	50	41	43	40	24	23
Total	195	69	97	80	101	78	84	97	90	79	94	64	86	77	62	29
Normal																
Boys	26	8	7	2	10	3	4	3	8	9	10	2	10	2	6	1
Girls	22	9	15	14	10	12	11	10	7	9	11	8	7	3	6	5
Total	48	17	22	16	20	15	15	13	15	18	21	10	17	5	12	6
Accelerated																
Boys	39	5	9	6	12	12	5	12	8	9	12	5	13	4	5	3
Girls	35	10	15	12	20	14	13	22	11	11	10	15	10	11	7	4
Total	74	15	24	18	32	26	18	34	19	20	22	20	23	15	12	7
Retarded																
Boys	36	17	20	24	26	16	15	22	30	18	22	16	20	31	27	2
Girls	37	20	31	22	23	21	36	28	26	23	29	18	26	26	11	14
Total	73	37	51	46	49	37	51	50	56	41	51	34	46	57	38	16
Per cent Normal																
Boys	25.7	26.6	19.4	6.2	20.9	9.7	16.7	8.0	17.4	25.0	22.7	8.7	23.3	5.4	15.8	16.7
Girls	23.4	23.0	24.6	29.2	18.9	25.5	18.3	16.7	15.9	20.9	22.0	19.5	16.3	7.5	25.0	21.7
Total	24.6	24.6	22.6	20.0	19.8	19.2	17.8	13.3	16.6	22.8	22.3	15.6	19.7	6.4	19.3	20.6
Per cent Accelerated																
Boys	38.6	16.6	25.0	18.8	25.0	38.7	20.8	32.4	17.4	25.0	27.3	21.8	30.2	10.8	13.2	50.0
Girls	37.2	25.6	24.6	25.0	37.7	29.8	21.7	36.7	25.0	25.6	20.0	36.6	23.3	27.5	29.2	17.4
Total	37.8	21.8	24.6	22.5	31.6	33.3	21.4	35.1	21.1	25.3	23.4	31.2	26.7	19.4	19.3	24.1
Per cent Retarded																
Boys	35.6	56.6	55.5	75.0	54.1	51.6	62.5	59.5	65.2	50.0	50.0	69.6	46.5	83.8	71.0	33.3
Girls	39.3	51.2	50.8	45.9	43.4	44.7	60.0	46.7	59.1	53.5	58.0	43.9	60.4	75.0	45.8	60.9
Total	37.4	53.6	52.7	57.5	48.5	47.5	60.7	51.5	62.2	51.9	54.2	53.1	53.4	74.1	61.2	55.1

TABLE XVI—NUMBER AND PER CENT OF ALL WHITE PUPILS IN BLOOMINGTON SCHOOLS, SECOND SEMESTER, 1911–12, THAT WERE NORMAL, ACCELERATED, RETARDED

Normal age for entrance to 1B grade, six and one-half years. Normal progress, one-half year for each half year in school. Ages as of March 30.

GRADE	1B	1A	2B	2A	3B	3A	4B	4A	5B	5A	6B	6A	7B	7A	8B	8A
Boys	54	68	42	63	48	49	48	55	77	43	43	39	27	44	25	36
Girls	55	67	42	63	48	54	62	55	75	43	43	42	28	45	24	33
Total	109	135	84	126	96	103	110	110	152	86	86	81	55	89	49	69
Normal																
Boys	15	13	11	17	13	11	12	9	12	6	8	10	6	8	1	7
Girls	15	13	11	17	13	11	12	9	12	6	8	10	6	8	1	7
Total	30	26	22	34	26	22	24	18	24	12	16	20	12	16	2	14
Accelerated																
Boys	15	27	8	14	11	21	12	10	26	5	12	5	11	10	6	12
Girls	15	27	8	14	11	21	12	10	26	5	12	7	11	10	6	12
Total	30	54	16	28	22	42	24	20	52	10	24	12	22	20	12	24
Retarded																
Boys	24	28	23	32	24	17	24	36	39	32	23	24	10	26	18	17
Girls	25	27	23	32	24	22	38	36	37	32	23	25	11	27	17	14
Total	49	55	46	64	48	39	62	72	76	64	46	49	21	53	35	31
Per cent Normal																
Boys	27.8	19.1	26.2	27.0	27.0	22.4	25.0	16.4	15.6	14.0	18.6	25.6	22.2	18.2	4.0	19.4
Girls	27.3	19.4	26.2	27.0	27.0	20.4	19.4	16.4	16.0	14.0	18.6	23.8	21.4	17.8	4.2	21.2
Total	27.5	19.2	26.1	27.1	27.1	21.3	21.8	16.3	15.8	13.9	18.6	24.6	21.8	17.9	4.0	20.2
Per cent Accelerated																
Boys	27.8	39.7	19.0	22.2	23.0	42.9	25.0	18.2	36.4	11.6	28.0	12.8	40.8	22.7	24.0	33.3
Girls	27.3	40.3	19.0	22.2	23.0	39.0	19.4	18.2	34.7	11.6	28.0	16.7	39.3	22.2	25.0	36.4
Total	27.5	40.0	19.1	22.2	22.9	40.7	21.8	18.1	34.2	11.6	27.9	14.8	40.0	22.4	24.4	34.8
Per cent Retarded																
Boys	44.4	41.2	54.8	50.8	50.0	34.7	50.0	65.5	50.6	74.4	53.5	61.5	37.0	59.1	72.0	47.2
Girls	45.4	40.3	54.8	50.8	50.0	40.7	61.3	65.5	49.3	74.4	53.5	59.5	39.3	60.0	70.8	42.4
Total	44.9	40.7	54.7	50.7	50.0	37.8	56.3	65.4	50.0	74.3	53.4	60.5	38.1	59.5	71.4	44.9

TABLE XVII — NUMBER AND PER CENT OF ALL WHITE PUPILS IN BLOOMINGTON SCHOOLS, FIRST SEMESTER, 1912–13, THAT WERE NORMAL, ACCELERATED, RETARDED

Ages as of September 1, 1912. Normal age for entering 1B grade, six and one-half years. Normal progress, one-half year of credit for each half year in school

GRADE	1B	1A	2B	2A	3B	3A	4B	4A	5B	5A	6B	6A	7B	7A	8B	8A
Boys.	122	54	82	38	76	60	71	52	41	38	48	35	31	16	38	25
Girls.	97	46	62	37	57	48	49	54	58	60	50	42	35	33	31	30
Total.	219	100	144	75	133	108	120	106	99	98	98	77	66	49	69	55
Normal																
Boys.	28	13	20	15	11	9	8	7	7	3	9	5	6	1	2	6
Girls.	18	13	9	7	14	11	10	8	9	9	9	10	8	4	4	7
Total.	46	26	29	22	25	20	18	15	16	12	18	15	14	5	6	13
Accelerated																
Boys.	47	16	24	7	18	7	24	14	9	12	12	10	10	4	14	7
Girls.	47	14	29	16	16	14	22	14	17	23	6	17	9	13	5	9
Total.	94	30	53	23	34	21	46	28	26	35	18	27	19	17	19	16
Retarded																
Boys.	47	25	38	16	47	44	39	31	25	23	27	20	15	11	22	12
Girls.	32	19	24	14	27	23	17	32	32	28	35	15	18	16	22	14
Total.	79	44	62	30	74	67	56	63	57	51	62	35	33	27	44	26
Per cent Normal																
Boys.	22.9	24.1	24.3	39.6	14.4	15.0	11.2	13.4	17.1	7.9	18.7	14.2	19.3	6.2	5.2	24.0
Girls.	18.6	28.3	14.5	18.9	24.5	22.9	20.4	14.9	15.5	15.0	18.0	23.8	22.9	12.1	12.8	23.3
Total.	21.0	26.0	20.1	29.3	18.8	18.5	15.0	14.1	16.1	12.1	18.3	19.4	21.2	10.2	8.7	23.6
Per cent Accelerated																
Boys.	38.5	29.6	29.2	18.4	23.7	11.6	33.9	26.9	21.9	31.6	25.0	28.5	32.3	25.0	36.9	28.0
Girls.	48.4	30.4	46.7	43.2	28.1	29.1	44.9	25.1	29.3	38.3	12.0	40.5	25.7	39.1	16.1	30.0
Total.	42.9	30.0	36.8	30.6	24.2	19.4	38.3	26.4	26.1	35.7	18.3	35.1	28.8	34.7	27.5	29.1
Per cent Retarded																
Boys.	38.5	46.2	46.5	42.1	61.8	73.3	54.9	59.6	60.9	60.5	56.2	57.2	48.3	68.7	57.9	48.0
Girls.	32.9	41.1	38.7	37.8	47.3	47.9	34.6	60.0	55.1	46.6	70.0	35.6	51.4	48.8	70.9	46.6
Total.	36.2	44.0	43.1	40.0	55.8	62.0	46.6	59.4	57.7	52.0	63.2	45.4	50.0	55.1	63.8	47.2

TABLE XVIII — NUMBER AND PER CENT OF TOTAL WHITE CHILDREN IN BLOOMINGTON SCHOOLS, OCTOBER 4, 1913, THAT WERE NORMAL, ACCELERATED, RETARDED

Entering age in 1B grade, six and one-half years. Normal progress, one-half year of progress for each half year in school. Ages as of September 1.

GRADE	1B	1A	2B	2A	3B	3A	4B	4A	5B	5A	6B	6A	7B	7A	8B	8A
Boys	91	41	73	49	76	51	83	58	65	47	39	33	40	32	33	15
Girls	95	43	63	40	59	43	64	50	53	50	52	51	49	38	36	19
Total	186	84	136	89	135	94	147	108	118	97	91	84	89	70	69	34
Normal																
Boys	21	9	10	12	15	9	13	5	10	6	8	4	12	5	7	3
Girls	28	12	29	16	9	7	16	11	10	12	7	10	9	10	8	2
Total	49	21	39	28	24	16	29	16	20	18	15	14	21	15	15	5
Accelerated																
Boys	38	18	26	21	26	17	20	17	19	10	9	11	9	11	12	2
Girls	44	15	21	16	21	17	19	13	17	11	15	17	16	16	10	10
Total	82	33	47	37	47	34	39	30	36	21	24	28	25	27	22	12
Retarded																
Boys	32	14	37	16	35	25	50	36	36	31	22	18	19	16	14	10
Girls	23	16	13	8	29	19	29	26	26	27	30	24	24	12	18	7
Total	55	30	50	24	64	44	79	62	62	58	52	42	43	28	32	17
Per cent Normal																
Boys	23.1	22.0	13.7	24.5	19.7	17.6	15.7	8.7	15.4	12.8	20.5	12.1	30.0	15.6	21.2	20.0
Girls	29.5	27.9	46.0	40.0	15.3	16.3	25.0	22.0	18.9	24.0	13.5	19.6	18.4	26.3	22.2	10.5
Total	26.3	25.0	28.6	31.4	17.7	17.0	19.7	14.7	16.8	18.5	16.4	16.6	23.6	21.4	21.8	14.7
Per cent Accelerated																
Boys	41.7	43.9	35.6	42.9	34.2	33.3	24.1	29.3	29.1	21.3	23.1	33.3	22.5	34.4	36.4	13.3
Girls	46.3	34.9	33.3	40.0	35.6	39.5	29.7	26.0	32.1	22.0	28.9	33.3	32.6	42.1	27.8	52.6
Total	44.1	39.2	34.5	41.5	34.7	36.1	26.5	27.7	30.4	21.6	26.3	33.3	28.1	38.5	31.9	35.3
Per cent Retarded																
Boys	35.2	34.1	50.7	32.6	46.0	49.0	60.2	52.0	55.4	65.9	56.4	54.5	47.5	50.0	42.2	66.7
Girls	24.2	37.2	20.6	20.0	49.0	44.1	45.3	62.0	49.0	54.0	57.6	47.1	49.0	31.6	50.0	36.8
Total	29.5	35.7	36.7	26.9	47.4	46.8	53.7	57.4	52.6	59.8	57.3	50.0	48.3	40.0	46.3	50.0

TABLE XIX — NUMBER AND PER CENT OF TOTAL WHITE CHILDREN IN BLOOMINGTON SCHOOLS DURING SECOND SEMESTER, 1913-14, LESS WITHDRAWALS, WHO WERE NORMAL, ACCELERATED, RETARDED IN GRADE

Ages as of May 29, 1914 — the day before promotion. Pupils assigned to the grade they were in the day before promotion. Normal age for entering 1B grade, six and one-half years. Normal progress, one-half year for each half year in school.

GRADE	1B	1A	2B	2A	3B	3A	4B	4A	5B	5A	6B	6A	7B	7A	8B	8A
Boys	64	79	44	61	61	70	65	60	55	66	41	30	34	45	19	18
Girls	36	77	39	45	52	50	39	59	44	44	45	57	45	54	33	25
Total	100	156	83	106	113	120	104	119	99	110	86	87	79	99	52	43
Normal																
Boys	25	20	9	21	14	15	11	11	6	10	6	6	5	10	4	3
Girls	16	26	12	8	12	13	6	7	8	11	10	5	8	4	7	7
Total	41	46	21	29	26	28	17	18	14	21	16	11	13	14	11	10
Accelerated																
Boys	0	16	11	11	13	23	13	11	5	14	8	5	8	5	7	7
Girls	0	26	7	16	19	16	9	16	8	16	8	16	15	6	11	5
Total	0	42	18	27	32	39	22	27	13	30	16	21	23	11	18	12
Retarded																
Boys	39	43	24	29	34	32	41	38	44	42	27	19	21	30	8	8
Girls	20	25	20	21	21	21	24	36	28	17	27	36	22	44	15	13
Total	59	68	44	50	55	53	65	74	72	59	54	55	43	74	23	21
Per cent Normal																
Boys	39.0	25.3	20.4	34.4	22.9	21.4	16.9	18.3	10.9	15.1	14.8	20.0	14.7	22.2	12.3	16.7
Girls	44.4	33.7	30.7	17.8	23.1	26.0	15.4	11.9	18.1	25.0	22.2	8.7	17.7	7.3	21.2	28.0
Total	41.0	29.3	25.3	27.3	23.0	23.3	16.3	15.1	14.1	19.1	18.6	12.6	16.4	14.1	21.1	23.2
Per cent Accelerated																
Boys	0.0	20.2	25.0	18.0	21.3	32.8	20.0	18.3	9.1	21.2	19.5	16.6	23.5	11.1	36.7	38.8
Girls	0.0	33.7	17.9	35.5	36.5	32.0	23.1	27.1	18.1	36.3	17.7	28.1	33.3	11.1	33.3	20.0
Total	0.0	26.9	21.6	25.4	28.3	32.5	21.1	22.6	13.1	27.2	18.6	24.1	29.1	11.1	34.6	27.8
Per cent Retarded																
Boys	60.9	54.4	54.5	47.5	55.7	45.9	63.0	63.3	80.0	63.6	65.7	63.3	61.7	66.6	42.1	44.4
Girls	55.5	32.5	51.3	46.6	40.3	42.0	61.5	61.0	63.7	38.6	60.0	63.1	50.0	81.7	45.4	52.0
Total	59.0	43.7	53.0	47.1	48.6	44.1	62.5	62.1	72.7	53.6	62.7	63.2	54.4	74.7	44.2	48.8

TABLE XX — NUMBER AND PER CENT OF TOTAL WHITE CHILDREN IN BLOOMINGTON SCHOOLS DURING SECOND SEMESTER, 1913-14, LESS WITHDRAWALS DURING SEMESTER, WHO WERE NORMAL, ACCELERATED, RETARDED IN GRADE

Ages as of June 1, 1914, the day after promotion. Pupils assigned to the grade they were in the day after promotion. Normal age for entering 1B grade, six and one-half years. Normal progress, one-half year for each half year in school.

GRADE	1B	1A	2B	2A	3B	3A	4B	4A	5B	5A	6B	6A	7B	7A	8B	8A
Boys	13	49	63	61	62	64	70	61	63	57	65	42	36	36	41	14
Girls	1	39	67	45	54	47	50	39	56	43	48	47	56	48	52	29
Total	14	88	130	106	116	111	120	100	119	100	113	89	92	84	93	43
Normal																
Boys	4	13	15	11	8	11	10	10	9	9	5	9	5	7	4	2
Girls	0	9	13	8	9	5	5	5	11	7	4	9	15	9	14	3
Total	4	22	28	19	17	16	15	15	20	16	9	18	20	16	18	5
Accelerated																
Boys	0	19	26	30	30	26	39	18	27	10	24	13	9	14	17	7
Girls	0	17	42	29	28	26	28	15	20	19	25	16	19	19	10	16
Total	0	36	68	59	58	52	67	33	47	29	49	29	28	33	27	23
Retarded																
Boys	9	17	22	20	24	27	21	33	27	38	36	20	22	15	20	5
Girls	1	13	12	8	17	16	17	19	25	17	19	22	22	20	28	10
Total	10	30	34	28	41	43	38	52	52	55	55	42	44	35	48	15
Per cent Normal																
Boys	30.8	26.5	23.8	18.0	12.9	17.2	14.3	16.4	14.3	15.8	7.6	21.4	13.9	19.5	9.7	14.2
Girls	0.0	23.1	19.4	17.8	16.7	10.6	10.0	12.8	19.6	16.3	8.3	19.2	26.8	18.7	26.9	10.3
Total	28.6	25.0	21.5	17.9	14.7	14.4	12.5	15.0	16.8	16.0	8.0	20.2	21.7	19.0	19.4	11.8
Per cent Accelerated																
Boys	0.0	38.7	41.2	49.2	48.4	40.6	55.7	29.5	42.8	17.5	36.9	30.9	25.0	38.8	41.4	50.0
Girls	0.0	43.6	62.7	64.4	51.8	55.3	56.0	38.4	35.7	44.2	52.1	34.0	33.8	39.6	19.2	55.1
Total	0.0	40.9	52.3	55.7	50.0	46.8	55.8	33.0	39.5	29.0	43.4	32.6	30.4	39.3	29.0	53.5
Per cent Retarded																
Boys	69.2	34.7	34.9	32.8	38.8	42.2	30.0	54.1	42.8	66.6	55.4	47.6	61.1	41.6	48.8	35.8
Girls	100.0	33.3	17.9	17.8	31.5	34.0	34.0	48.7	44.6	39.5	39.5	46.7	39.3	41.6	53.8	34.7
Total	71.4	34.1	26.1	26.4	35.3	38.7	31.7	52.0	43.7	55.0	48.7	47.2	47.8	41.7	51.6	34.9

TABLE XXI — NUMBER AND PER CENT OF CHILDREN IN BLOOMINGTON SCHOOLS DURING SECOND SEMESTER, 1914-15, LESS WITHDRAWALS DURING SEMESTER, WHO WERE NORMAL, ACCELERATED, RETARDED IN GRADE

Ages as of June 12, the day after promotion. Pupils assigned to the grade they were in the day after promotion. Normal age for entering 1B, six and one-half years. Normal progress one-half year for each half year in school.

GRADE	1B	1A	2B	2A	3B	3A	4B	4A	5B	5A	6B	6A	7B	7A	8B	8A
Boys	11	39	70	52	61	47	75	61	64	52	79	52	51	30	30	26
Girls	6	39	45	49	61	54	48	39	57	42	59	46	56	39	60	29
Total	17	78	115	101	122	101	123	100	121	94	138	98	107	69	90	55
Normal																
Boys	3	7	18	2	14	7	10	7	15	8	13	11	6	6	5	4
Girls	2	6	12	5	8	9	10	5	6	4	9	8	5	7	10	4
Total	5	13	30	7	22	16	20	12	21	12	22	19	11	13	15	8
Accelerated																
Boys	1	21	36	27	18	17	37	20	27	14	21	9	22	9	10	7
Girls	2	25	22	33	35	31	26	15	31	15	16	20	24	16	20	10
Total	3	46	58	60	53	48	63	35	58	29	37	29	46	25	30	17
Retarded																
Boys	7	11	16	23	29	23	28	34	22	30	45	32	23	15	15	15
Girls	2	8	11	11	18	14	12	19	20	23	34	18	27	16	30	15
Total	9	19	27	34	47	37	40	53	42	53	79	50	50	31	45	30
Per Cent Normal																
Boys	27.3	17.9	25.7	3.8	23	14.9	13.3	11.5	23.4	15.4	16.5	21.2	11.8	20	16.7	15.2
Girls	33.3	15.4	26.7	10.2	13.1	16.7	20.8	12.8	10.5	9.5	15.3	17.4	8.9	17.9	16.7	13.8
Total	29.4	16.7	26.1	6.9	18.	15.8	16.3	12.	17.4	12.8	16.	19.4	10.3	18.8	16.7	14.5
Per Cent Accelerated																
Boys	9.1	53.8	51.4	51.9	29.5	36.2	49.3	32.8	42.2	26.7	26.6	17.3	43.1	30.	33.3	26.9
Girls	33.3	64.1	48.9	67.3	57.4	57.4	54.2	38.4	54.4	35.7	27.1	43.4	42.8	41.	33.3	34.5
Total	17.6	59.	50.4	59.4	43.4	47.5	51.2	35.	48.	30.6	26.8	29.6	43.	36.2	33.3	30.9
Per Cent Retarded																
Boys	63.6	28.2	22.9	44.2	47.5	48.9	37.3	55.7	34.4	57.7	57.	61.5	45.1	50	50	57.7
Girls	33.3	20.5	24.4	22.4	29.5	25.9	25.	48.7	35.1	54.7	57.6	39.1	48.2	41	50	51.7
Total	52.9	24.4	23.5	33.6	38.5	36.6	32.5	53	34.7	56.4	57.2	51.	46.9	45	50	54.5

TABLE XXII — COMPARISON BETWEEN PER CENTS OF NORMAL, ACCELERATED, AND RETARDED PUPILS FOR SECOND SEMESTERS, YEARS 1913–14 AND 1914–15

Ages taken as of day after June promotion. Normal age for entering 1B grade, six and one-half years. Normal progress, one-half year for each half year in school.

GRADE	1B	1A	2B	2A	3B	3A	4B	4A	5B	5A	6B	6A	7B	7A	8B	8A
Per Cent Normal																
Boys 1913–14	30.8	26.5	23.8	18.	12.9	17.2	14.3	16.4	14.3	15.8	7.6	21.4	13.9	19.5	9.7	14.2
Boys 1914–15	27.3	17.9	25.7	3.8	23.	14.9	13.3	11.5	23.4	15.4	16.5	21.2	11.8	20.	16.7	15.2
Girls 1913–14	0.	23.1	19.4	17.8	16.7	10.6	10.	12.8	19.6	16.3	8.3	19.2	26.8	18.7	26.9	10.3
Girls 1914–15	33.3	15.4	26.7	10.2	13.1	16.7	20.8	12.8	10.5	9.5	15.3	17.4	8.9	17.9	16.7	13.8
Total 1913–14	28.6	25.	21.5	17.9	14.7	14.4	12.5	15.	16.8	16.	.8	20.2	21.7	19.	19.4	11.8
Total 1914–15	29.4	16.7	26.1	6.9	18.	15.8	16.3	12.	17.4	12.8	16.	19.4	10.3	18.8	16.7	14.5
Per Cent Accelerated																
Boys 1913–14	0.	38.7	41.2	49.2	48.4	40.6	55.7	29.5	42.8	17.5	36.9	30.9	25.	38.8	41.4	50.
Boys 1914–15	9.1	53.8	51.4	51.9	29.5	36.2	49.3	32.8	42.2	26.7	26.6	17.3	43.1	30.	33.3	26.9
Girls 1913–14	0.	43.6	62.7	64.3	51.8	55.3	56.	38.4	35.7	44.2	52.1	34.	33.8	39.6	19.2	55.1
Girls 1914–15	33.3	64.1	48.9	67.3	57.4	57.4	54.2	38.4	54.4	35.7	27.1	43.4	42.8	41.	33.3	34.5
Total 1913–14	0.	40.9	52.3	55.7	50.	46.8	55.8	33.	39.5	29.	43.4	32.6	30.4	39.3	29.	53.5
Total 1914–15	17.6	59.	50.4	59.4	43.4	47.5	51.2	35.	48.	30.6	26.8	29.6	43.	36.2	33.3	30.9
Per Cent Retarded																
Boys 1913–14	69.2	34.7	34.9	32.8	38.7	42.2	30.	54.1	42.8	66.6	55.4	47.6	61.1	41.6	48.8	35.8
Boys 1914–15	63.6	28.2	22.9	44.2	47.5	48.9	37.3	55.7	34.4	57.7	57.	61.5	45.1	50.	50.	57.7
Girls 1913–14	100.	33.3	17.9	17.8	31.5	34.	34.	48.7	44.6	39.5	39.5	46.7	39.3	41.6	53.8	34.7
Girls 1914–15	33.3	20.5	24.4	22.4	29.5	25.9	25.	48.7	35.6	54.7	57.6	39.1	48.2	41.	50.	51.7
Total 1913–14	71.4	34.1	26.1	26.4	35.3	38.7	31.7	52.	43.7	55.	48.7	47.2	47.8	41.7	51.6	34.9
Total 1914–15	52.9	24.4	23.5	33.6	38.5	36.6	32.5	53.	34.7	56.4	57.2	51.	46.9	45.	50.	54.5

TABLE XXIII — NUMBER AND PER CENT OF CHILDREN IN BLOOMINGTON SCHOOLS DURING SECOND SEMESTER, 1914–15, LESS WITHDRAWALS DURING SEMESTER, WHO WERE NORMAL, ACCELERATED, RETARDED IN GRADE

Ages as of June 12 the day after promotion. Pupils assigned to the grade they were in the day after promotion. Normal age for entering 1B grade, six years. Normal progress, one-half year per each half year in school.

GRADE	1B	1A	2B	2A	3B	3A	4B	4A	5B	5A	6B	6A	7B	7A	8B	8A
Total																
Boys	11	39	70	52	61	47	75	61	64	52	79	52	51	30	30	26
Girls	6	39	45	49	61	54	48	39	57	42	59	46	56	39	60	29
Total	17	78	115	101	122	101	123	100	121	94	138	98	107	69	90	55
Normal																
Boys	1	15	17	10	8	8	22	11	9	3	8	6	10	6	7	3
Girls	2	15	11	15	15	12	6	6	11	5	8	9	12	9	7	3
Total	3	30	28	25	23	20	28	17	20	8	16	15	22	15	14	6
Accelerated																
Boys	0	6	19	17	10	9	15	9	18	11	13	3	12	3	3	4
Girls	0	10	11	18	20	19	20	9	20	10	8	11	12	7	13	7
Total	0	16	30	35	30	28	35	18	38	21	21	14	24	10	16	11
Retarded																
Boys	10	18	34	25	43	30	38	41	37	38	58	43	29	21	20	19
Girls	4	14	23	16	26	23	22	24	26	27	43	26	32	23	40	19
Total	14	32	57	41	69	53	60	65	63	65	101	69	61	44	60	38
Per Cent Normal																
Boys	9.1	38.5	24.3	19.2	13.1	17.	29.3	18.	14.	5.7	10.1	11.5	19.6	20.	23.3	11.5
Girls	33.3	38.5	24.4	30.6	24.6	22.2	12.5	15.4	19.4	11.9	13.6	19.8	21.4	23.1	11.7	10.3
Total	17.6	38.5	24.3	24.8	18.9	19.8	22.7	17.	16.5	8.5	11.6	15.3	20.6	21.7	15.6	10.9
Per Cent Accelerated																
Boys	0	15.4	27.1	32.7	16.4	19.1	20.	14.8	28.1	21.2	16.5	5.8	23.5	10.	10.	15.4
Girls	0	25.6	24.4	36.7	32.9	35.2	41.6	23.	35.	23.8	13.6	23.9	21.4	17.9	21.7	24.1
Total	0	20.5	26.1	34.7	24.6	27.7	28.4	18.	31.4	22.3	15.2	14.5	22.3	14.5	17.8	20.
Per Cent Retarded																
Boys	90.9	46.2	48.6	48.	70.6	63.8	50.6	67.2	57.8	73.	73.4	82.7	56.9	70.	66.7	73.1
Girls	66.7	35.9	51.1	32.6	42.6	42.6	45.8	61.5	45.6	64.2	72.9	56.5	57.1	59.	66.7	65.5
Total	82.4	41.	49.6	40.6	56.6	52.5	48.7	65.	52.	69.	73.2	70.4	57.	63.8	66.7	69.

Tables XVIII, XIX, XX are given to show the wide range of difference in per cents of retardation, acceleration, and normal progress based on age-grade tables computed for varying times of the year. Comparison between cities cannot be intelligently made unless the time of computing the data is taken into consideration. These three tables show that with the exception of 1B, 5A, 7B, and 8B the acceleration is distinctly lower for May 29th, the day before promotion in the spring, than for the close of school in the spring or the opening of school in the fall. With the exception of grades 1B, 6A, 8B, acceleration is distinctly higher just after the second semester promotion than at any other time of the year.

Tables XXI and XXII show the progress made in a single year in eliminating retardation and increasing acceleration and normal progress. In general, some progress was made in the lower grades but not in the upper grades.

There was a larger per cent of acceleration in 1914–15 than in 1913–14 in the following grades: 1B, 1A, 2A, 3A, 4A, 5B, 5A, 7B, 8B, while there was a lower per cent in grades 2B, 3B, 4B, 6B, 6A, 7A, 8A.

In retardation there was a smaller per cent in 1914–15 than in 1913–14 in the following grades: 1B, 1A, 2B, 3A, 5B, 7B, 8B, but a larger per cent in grades 2A, 3B, 4B, 4A, 5A, 6B, 6A, 7A, 8A.

Table XXIII is inserted simply to show per cents of normal progress, acceleration, and retardation based on age six as the normal age for entering school. It will serve as a basis of comparison with those systems that may later figure per cents on the same basis.

Comparing first semester results which are most safely comparable, the summary table of per cent accelerated shows that for the 1B grade there is a gain from 1909–10 to 1913–14 of 1.8 per cent. When the 1914 result is compared with the intervening years, it shows a still greater gain in acceleration. The 1A grade shows an improvement of 21.4 per cent during the four-year period, with the 1913 record distinctly better than any other first semester record. In the 2B grade the improvement is 8.9 per cent, the 1913 record being surpassed only by the 1912 record. In the 2A grade the loss in 1913 over 1909 was 3.8 per cent, though the 1913 record was the second best of all first semester records. In the 3B grade the improvement was 9.1 per cent; in the 3A, 6.8 per cent. A loss of 3.3 per cent occurs in the 4B grade; likewise a loss of 2.3 per cent in the 4A grade, 11 per cent in the 5B grade, 24.2 per cent in the 5A grade, 8.7 per cent in the 6B grade. A gain of 7.9 per cent occurs in the 6A grade but is followed in the 7B grade by a loss of 19.4 per cent. The gain in the 7A grade is 14.1 per cent, falling again in the 8B grade to a loss of 1.4 per cent. In the 8A grade there is a gain of 10.3 per cent. By adding the number of per cent gain in each grade where a gain was made and adding the number of per cent loss in each grade in which a loss occurred we get a total gain of 80.3 per cent and a total loss of 74.1 per cent. In the past four years a good showing has been made in regard to acceleration as far as the first three grades are concerned. The condition in Grades 4, 5, 6, and the first half of the 7th grade indicates that the interests of children in those grades have not been so carefully safeguarded.[1]

As far as retardation is concerned the 1913 record in the 1B grade is 2.2 per cent less than for the same time in 1909; in the 1A grade, 28.7 per cent less; in the 2B grade, 11.7 per cent less; in the 2A grade, 13.1 per cent less; in the 3B grade, 8.4 per cent less; in the 3A grade, 4.4 per cent less; in the 4B grade, 7.3 per cent more; in the 4A grade, 5.7 per cent more; in the 5B grade, .3 per cent less; in the 5A grade, 16.1 per cent more; in the 6B grade, 9.9 per cent more; in the 6A grade, 3.5 per cent less; in the 7B grade, 5.7 per cent more; in the 7A grade, 11.1 per cent less; in the 8B grade, 4.8 per cent less; and in the 8A grade, 25 per cent less. Counting all grades in the same manner in which summaries for acceleration were counted there has been during the period from 1909 to 1913 a total loss of 113.2 points and a total gain of 44.7 points. On the whole, the condition as far as retardation is concerned has been improved during the four-year period. It suggests some spots, though, that need further investigation.

Concerning the per cent making normal progress, the 1913 first semester record as compared with the 1909 first semester record shows in the 1B grade an increase of .7 per cent; in the 1A grade, an increase of 7.2 per cent; in the 2B grade, an increase of 3 per cent; in the 2A grade, an increase of 16.7 per cent; in the 3B grade, a decrease of .9 per cent; in the 3A grade, a decrease of 2.5 per cent; in the 4B grade, a decrease of 4 per cent; in the 4A grade, a decrease of 3.6 per cent; in the 5B grade, an increase of 11.1 per cent; in the 5A grade, an increase of 8.1 per cent; in the 6B grade, a decrease of 1.1 per cent; in the 6A grade, a decrease of 4.5 per cent; in the 7B grade,

---

[1] One factor to keep in mind here, however, is the effect of the more stringent compulsory education law in forcing children to attend school until they pass the 5A grade and until they are sixteen years of age even if they have passed the 5A grade, unless they have positions and are at work.

TABLE XXIV — PER CENT NORMAL

COMPILATION OF PREVIOUS TABLES SHOWING PER CENT OF PUPILS WHO HAVE MADE NORMAL PROGRESS

Normal age of entering grade 1B six and one-half years and normal progress, one-half year in one half year in school. Ages for first semesters, 1909-10, 1910-11, 1911-12, as of September 30; second semesters, 1909-10, 1910-11, 1911-12, as of March 30 and October 4, 1913, as of September 1; May 29, 1914, as of May 29, the day before promotions, and June 1, 1914, as of June 1, the day before promotions, the day after promotions.

GRADE	FIRST SEMESTER 1909–10	SECOND SEMESTER 1909–10	FIRST SEMESTER 1910–11	SECOND SEMESTER 1910–11	FIRST SEMESTER 1911–12	SECOND SEMESTER 1911–12	FIRST SEMESTER 1912–13	OCT. 4, 1913	MAY 29, 1914	JUNE 1, 1914
1B —										
Boys	25.8	40.9	26.9	26.5	25.7	27.8	22.9	23.1	39.0	30.8
Girls	25.4	40.9	28.5	26.0	23.4	27.3	18.6	29.5	44.4	0.0
Total	25.6	41.0	28.1	26.2	24.6	27.5	21.0	26.3	41.0	28.6
1A —										
Boys	13.1	27.1	20.8	25.7	26.6	19.1	24.1	22.0	25.3	26.5
Girls	22.7	26.3	35.1	25.0	23.0	19.4	28.3	27.9	33.7	23.1
Total	17.8	26.8	28.5	25.3	24.6	19.2	26.0	25.0	29.3	25.0
2B —										
Boys	27.0	24.0	28.7	29.2	19.4	26.2	24.3	13.7	20.4	23.8
Girls	24.4	25.0	22.0	30.0	24.6	26.2	14.5	46.0	30.7	19.4
Total	25.6	24.5	26.2	29.8	22.6	26.1	20.1	28.6	25.3	21.5
2A —										
Boys	12.5	26.3	12.4	18.7	6.2	27.0	39.6	24.5	34.4	18.0
Girls	15.6	25.6	19.3	18.7	29.2	27.0	18.9	40.0	17.8	17.8
Total	14.7	26.2	14.8	18.7	20.0	27.1	29.3	31.4	27.3	17.9
3B —										
Boys	29.4	17.4	17.9	32.0	20.9	27.1	14.4	19.7	22.9	12.9
Girls	11.5	18.1	19.6	13.3	18.9	27.1	24.5	15.3	23.1	16.7
Total	18.6	17.7	18.7	23.1	19.8	27.0	18.8	17.7	23.0	14.7
3A —										
Boys	19.3	16.6	17.8	16.3	9.7	22.4	15.0	17.6	21.4	17.2
Girls	19.5	16.6	18.3	16.3	25.5	20.4	22.9	16.3	26.0	10.6
Total	19.5	16.7	18.2	16.4	19.2	21.3	18.5	17.0	23.3	14.4
4B —										
Boys	18.7	21.9	11.3	20.8	16.7	25.0	11.2	15.7	16.9	14.3
Girls	30.5	21.9	14.3	9.1	18.3	19.4	20.4	25.0	15.4	10.0
Total	23.7	22.0	12.7	14.8	17.8	21.8	15.0	19.7	16.3	12.5

4A — Boys	16.4	18.3	8.7	13.4	16.4	8.0	11.1	17.9	17.9	12.0
Girls	12.8	11.9	22.0	14.9	16.4	16.7	19.4	15.4	20.0	22.8
Total	15.0	15.1	14.7	14.1	16.3	13.3	15.2	17.9	19.0	18.3
5B — Boys	14.3	10.9	15.4	17.1	15.6	17.4	16.4	12.2	25.0	6.6
Girls	19.6	18.1	18.9	15.5	16.0	15.9	21.7	30.2	25.7	4.7
Total	16.8	14.1	16.8	16.1	15.8	16.6	18.8	21.4	25.4	5.7
5A — Boys	15.8	15.1	12.8	7.9	14.0	25.0	20.0	5.7	12.8	12.5
Girls	16.3	25.0	24.0	15.0	14.0	20.9	10.9	17.0	13.2	8.3
Total	16.0	19.1	18.5	12.1	13.9	22.8	15.6	12.1	13.0	10.4
6B — Boys	7.6	14.8	20.5	18.7	18.6	22.7	21.1	21.8	0.0	14.7
Girls	8.3	22.2	13.5	18.0	18.6	22.0	18.4	15.0	21.5	21.7
Total	8.0	18.6	16.4	18.3	18.6	22.3	19.7	18.1	10.0	17.5
6A — Boys	21.4	20.0	12.1	14.2	25.6	8.7	22.7	19.0	26.1	27.5
Girls	19.2	8.7	19.6	23.8	23.8	19.5	20.4	22.7	26.1	12.9
Total	20.2	12.6	16.6	19.4	24.6	15.6	21.6	20.9	26.0	21.1
7B — Boys	13.9	14.7	30.0	19.3	22.2	23.3	5.7	6.2	16.0	6.2
Girls	26.8	17.7	18.4	22.9	21.4	16.3	25.7	16.2	16.0	13.8
Total	21.7	16.4	23.6	21.2	21.8	19.7	15.7	11.5	16.0	9.8
7A — Boys	19.5	22.2	15.6	6.2	18.2	5.4	15.6	0.0	18.6	13.7
Girls	18.7	7.3	26.3	12.1	17.8	7.5	12.1	4.3	18.6	43.7
Total	19.0	14.1	21.4	10.2	17.9	6.4	13.8	1.8	18.5	24.4
8B — Boys	9.7	21.3	21.2	5.2	4.0	15.8	29.6	18.1	40.0	12.5
Girls	26.9	21.2	22.2	12.8	4.2	25.0	7.4	18.1	40.0	19.0
Total	19.4	21.1	21.8	8.7	4.0	19.3	18.5	18.1	40.0	15.6
8A — Boys	14.2	16.7	20.0	24.0	19.4	16.7	14.3	19.0	17.6	0.0
Girls	10.3	28.0	10.5	23.3	21.2	21.7	13.9	5.5	17.6	0.0
Total	11.8	23.2	14.7	23.6	20.2	20.6	14.1	12.7	17.6	0.0

TABLE XXV — PER CENT ACCELERATED

COMPILATION OF PREVIOUS TABLES SHOWING PER CENT OF PUPILS WHO HAVE BEEN ACCELERATED

Normal age of entering grade 1B, six and one-half years, normal progress one-half year in one half year in school. Ages for first semesters, 1909–10, 1910–11, 1911–12, as of September 30; second semesters, 1909–10, 1910–11, 1911–12, as of March 30 and October 4, 1913, as of September 1; May 29, 1914, as of May 29, the day before promotions, and June 1, 1914, as of June 1, the day after promotions.

GRADE	FIRST SEMESTER 1909-10	SECOND SEMESTER 1909-10	FIRST SEMESTER 1910-11	SECOND SEMESTER 1910-11	FIRST SEMESTER 1911-12	SECOND SEMESTER 1911-12	FIRST SEMESTER 1912-13	OCT. 4, 1913	MAY 29, 1914	JUNE 1, 1914
1B —										
Boys	33.7	29.5	22.6	18.4	38.6	27.8	38.5	41.7	0.0	0.0
Girls	50.0	29.5	31.7	18.0	37.2	27.3	48.4	46.3	0.0	0.0
Total	42.3	29.5	25.2	18.1	37.8	27.5	42.9	44.1	0.0	0.0
1A —										
Boys	17.2	37.1	2.0	14.3	16.6	39.7	29.6	43.9	20.2	38.7
Girls	18.1	37.5	17.5	13.9	25.6	40.3	30.4	34.9	33.7	43.6
Total	17.8	37.3	10.4	14.0	21.8	40.0	30.0	39.2	29.6	40.9
2B —										
Boys	18.9	16.0	20.6	26.8	25.0	19.0	29.2	35.6	25.0	41.2
Girls	31.1	12.5	38.0	25.0	24.6	19.0	46.7	33.3	17.9	62.7
Total	25.6	14.3	27.0	25.9	24.6	19.1	36.8	34.5	21.6	52.3
2A —										
Boys	62.5	28.9	17.8	37.5	18.8	22.2	18.4	42.9	18.0	49.2
Girls	37.2	28.2	48.4	56.3	25.0	22.2	43.2	40.0	35.5	64.4
Total	45.3	28.6	28.7	46.8	22.5	22.2	30.6	41.5	25.4	55.7
3B —										
Boys	41.1	34.9	25.0	32.0	25.0	23.0	23.7	34.2	21.3	48.4
Girls	15.3	34.4	26.8	60.0	37.7	23.0	28.1	35.6	36.5	51.8
Total	25.6	34.7	25.9	45.2	31.6	22.9	24.2	34.7	28.3	50.0
3A —										
Boys	35.4	13.3	23.1	30.2	38.7	42.9	11.6	33.3	32.8	40.6
Girls	25.4	13.3	38.3	46.5	29.8	39.0	29.1	39.5	32.0	55.3
Total	29.3	13.3	32.4	38.3	33.3	40.7	19.4	36.1	32.5	46.8
4B —										
Boys	35.4	19.5	15.1	32.1	20.8	25.0	33.9	24.1	20.0	55.7
Girls	22.2	19.5	21.4	54.5	21.7	19.4	44.9	29.7	23.1	56.0
Total	29.8	19.5	17.8	43.5	21.4	21.8	38.3	26.5	21.1	55.8

4A —										
Boys	24.0	33.3	20.5	11.1	32.4	18.2	26.9	29.3	18.3	29.5
Girls	34.3	32.5	23.1	22.2	36.7	18.2	25.1	26.0	27.1	38.4
Total	30.0	32.9	20.5	16.6	35.1	18.1	26.4	27.7	22.6	33.0
5B —										
Boys	44.4	30.5	26.8	18.2	17.4	36.4	21.9	29.1	9.1	42.8
Girls	38.0	31.4	20.9	43.5	25.0	34.7	29.3	32.1	18.1	35.7
Total	41.4	31.3	23.8	29.7	21.1	34.2	26.1	30.4	13.1	39.5
5A —										
Boys	41.6	43.7	17.1	22.2	25.0	11.6	31.6	21.3	21.2	17.5
Girls	58.0	39.5	34.0	43.4	25.6	11.6	38.3	22.0	36.3	44.2
Total	45.8	41.6	26.8	32.9	35.3	11.6	35.7	21.6	27.2	29.0
6B —										
Boys	32.4	25.0	28.1	31.6	27.3	28.0	25.0	23.1	19.5	36.9
Girls	39.1	28.6	55.0	52.6	20.0	28.0	12.0	28.9	17.7	52.1
Total	35.0	27.0	43.0	42.1	23.4	27.9	18.3	26.3	18.6	43.4
6A —										
Boys	22.5	26.1	19.0	22.7	21.8	12.8	28.5	33.3	16.6	30.9
Girls	29.0	26.1	43.2	45.5	36.6	16.7	40.5	33.3	28.1	34.0
Total	25.4	26.0	31.3	34.0	31.2	14.8	35.1	33.3	24.1	32.6
7B —										
Boys	59.3	24.0	15.6	25.7	30.2	40.8	32.3	22.5	23.5	25.0
Girls	34.5	24.0	37.8	31.4	23.3	39.3	25.7	32.6	33.3	33.8
Total	47.5	24.0	27.5	28.6	26.7	40.0	28.8	28.1	29.1	30.4
7A —										
Boys	34.4	33.3	19.3	12.5	10.8	22.7	25.0	34.4	11.1	38.8
Girls	6.2	33.3	52.1	27.3	27.5	22.2	39.1	42.1	11.1	39.6
Total	24.4	33.3	33.3	20.0	19.4	22.4	34.7	38.5	11.1	39.3
8B —										
Boys	33.3	6.6	42.4	7.4	13.2	24.0	36.9	36.4	36.7	41.4
Girls	33.3	6.6	60.6	55.6	29.2	25.0	16.1	27.8	33.3	19.2
Total	33.3	6.7	51.5	31.5	19.3	24.4	27.5	31.9	34.6	29.0
8A —										
Boys	100.0	23.5	23.7	31.4	50.0	33.3	28.0	13.3	38.8	50.0
Girls	0.0	23.5	88.8	63.9	17.4	36.4	30.0	52.6	20.0	55.1
Total	25.0	23.5	53.8	47.8	24.1	34.8	29.1	35.3	27.8	53.5

TABLE XXVI — PER CENT RETARDED

COMPILATION OF PREVIOUS TABLES SHOWING PER CENT OF PUPILS WHO HAVE BEEN RETARDED

Normal age of entering 1B, six and one-half years, normal progress one-half year in one half year in school. Ages for first semesters, 1909-10, 1910-11, 1911-12 as of September 30; second semesters, 1909-10, 1910-11, 1911-12, as of March 30 and October 4, 1913, as of September 1; May 29, 1914, as of May 29, the day before promotions, and June 1, 1914, as of June 1, the day after promotions.

GRADE	FIRST SEMESTER 1909-10	SECOND SEMESTER 1909-10	FIRST SEMESTER 1910-11	SECOND SEMESTER 1910-11	FIRST SEMESTER 1911-12	SECOND SEMESTER 1911-12	FIRST SEMESTER 1912-13	OCT. 4, 1913	MAY 29, 1914	JUNE 1, 1914
1B —										
Boys	40.5	29.5	50.4	55.1	35.6	44.4	38.5	35.2	60.9	69.2
Girls	24.5	29.5	39.7	56.0	39.3	45.4	32.9	24.2	55.5	100.0
Total	31.7	29.5	46.6	55.5	37.4	44.9	36.2	29.5	59.0	71.4
1A —										
Boys	69.5	35.6	77.1	60.0	56.6	41.2	46.2	34.1	54.4	34.7
Girls	59.0	36.1	47.3	61.1	51.2	40.3	41.1	37.2	32.5	33.3
Total	64.4	35.9	61.0	60.5	53.6	40.7	44.0	35.7	43.7	34.1
2B —										
Boys	54.0	60.0	50.6	44.0	55.5	54.8	46.5	50.7	54.5	34.9
Girls	44.4	62.5	40.0	45.0	50.8	54.8	38.7	20.6	51.3	17.9
Total	48.4	61.2	46.6	44.4	52.7	54.7	43.1	36.7	53.0	26.1
2A —										
Boys	25.0	44.7	69.6	43.8	75.0	50.8	42.1	32.6	47.5	32.8
Girls	47.0	46.0	32.2	25.0	45.9	50.8	37.8	20.0	46.6	17.8
Total	40.0	45.5	56.3	34.3	57.5	50.7	40.0	26.9	47.1	26.4
3B —										
Boys	29.4	47.6	57.1	36.0	54.1	50.0	61.8	46.0	55.7	38.7
Girls	73.1	47.5	53.5	26.7	43.4	50.0	47.3	49.0	40.3	31.5
Total	55.8	47.6	55.3	31.5	48.5	50.0	55.8	47.4	48.6	35.3
3A —										
Boys	45.1	70.0	58.9	53.5	51.6	34.7	73.3	49.0	45.9	42.2
Girls	54.9	70.0	43.3	37.2	44.7	40.7	47.9	44.1	42.0	34.0
Total	51.2	70.0	49.3	45.3	47.5	37.8	62.0	46.8	44.1	38.7
4B —										
Boys	45.8	58.5	73.6	47.1	62.5	50.0	54.9	60.2	63.0	30.0
Girls	47.2	58.5	64.3	36.4	60.0	61.3	34.6	45.3	61.5	34.0
Total	46.4	58.5	69.4	41.6	60.7	56.3	46.6	53.7	62.5	31.7

4A —										
Boys	64.0	48.6	61.5	77.8	59.5	65.5	59.6	52.0	63.3	54.1
Girls	42.8	47.5	61.5	58.3	46.7	65.5	60.0	62.0	61.0	48.7
Total	51.7	48.0	61.5	68.1	51.5	65.4	59.4	57.4	62.1	52.0
5B —										
Boys	48.8	44.4	60.9	65.4	65.2	50.6	60.9	55.4	80.0	42.8
Girls	57.1	42.8	48.8	34.8	59.1	49.3	55.1	49.0	63.7	44.6
Total	52.9	43.7	54.7	51.4	62.2	50.0	57.7	52.6	72.7	43.7
5A —										
Boys	45.8	43.6	77.4	57.8	50.0	74.4	60.5	65.9	63.6	66.6
Girls	41.7	47.3	48.9	45.7	53.5	74.4	46.6	54.0	38.6	39.5
Total	43.7	45.6	60.9	51.6	51.9	74.3	52.0	59.8	53.6	55.0
6B —										
Boys	52.8	75.0	50.0	47.3	50.0	53.5	56.2	56.4	65.7	55.4
Girls	39.1	50.0	30.0	29.0	58.0	53.5	70.0	57.6	60.0	39.5
Total	47.4	63.0	38.8	38.1	54.2	53.4	63.2	57.3	62.7	48.7
6A —										
Boys	50.0	47.7	61.9	54.5	69.6	61.5	57.2	54.5	63.3	47.6
Girls	58.0	47.7	34.0	34.1	43.9	59.5	35.6	47.1	63.1	46.7
Total	53.5	48.0	47.7	44.3	53.1	60.5	45.4	50.0	63.2	47.2
7B —										
Boys	34.4	60.0	78.1	68.6	46.5	37.0	48.3	47.5	61.7	61.1
Girls	51.7	60.0	45.9	42.9	60.4	39.3	51.4	49.0	50.0	39.3
Total	42.6	60.0	60.9	55.7	53.4	38.1	50.0	48.3	54.4	47.8
7A —										
Boys	51.7	48.1	80.6	71.9	83.8	59.1	68.7	50.0	66.6	41.6
Girls	50.0	48.1	43.4	60.6	75.0	60.0	48.8	31.6	81.7	41.6
Total	51.1	48.0	64.8	66.1	74.1	59.5	55.1	40.0	74.7	41.7
8B —										
Boys	54.2	53.3	39.3	63.0	71.0	72.0	57.9	42.2	42.1	48.8
Girls	47.6	53.3	21.2	37.0	45.8	70.8	70.9	50.0	45.4	53.8
Total	51.1	53.3	30.3	50.0	61.2	71.4	63.8	46.3	44.2	51.6
8A —										
Boys	0.0	58.8	57.1	54.3	33.3	47.2	48.0	66.7	44.4	35.8
Girls	100.0	58.8	5.5	22.2	60.9	42.4	46.6	36.8	52.0	34.7
Total	75.0	58.8	33.3	38.0	55.1	44.9	47.2	50.0	48.8	34.9

an increase of 13.8 per cent; in the 7A grade, a decrease of 3 per cent; in the 8B grade, an increase of 6.2 per cent; in the 8A grade, an increase of 14.7 per cent. Again counting all grades there has been during the period from 1909 to 1913 a total gain of 81.5 points in per cent and a total loss of 19.4 points in per cent in the per cent of children making normal progress.

Using the per cent for the grade as the unit for computing per cents of gain and loss and counting the per cents in all grades for the first semester of 1909–1910 and the first semester of 1913–14, the sum of all the gains in all grades where there was a gain in 1913 over gains in 1909 in per cents of normal progress was 75 per cent, the loss, 25 per cent. In acceleration, gain 60.3 per cent, loss 38.9 per cent. In retardation gain 44.7 per cent, loss 113.2 per cent.

Summarizing, with each grade as a unit, the accumulative gain and loss shown by considering all grades, we find that for normal progress the total gain for the year 1913 over 1909 was 75 points in per cent, the loss 25; for acceleration the gain was 60.3, the loss, 38.9; for retardation the gain was 44.7, the loss 113.2.

The following tables show acceleration, retardation, and normal progress, not on the age-grade basis, but on the basis of years in school and progress made. The study includes every child in school the last semester of the school year 1913–14 whose record could be traced.

TABLE XXVII

RECORD OF YEARS IN SCHOOL AND PROGRESS MADE OF ALL WHITE CHILDREN IN THE GRADES WHO HAVE RECEIVED ALL OR PART OF THEIR TRAINING IN THE BLOOMINGTON SCHOOLS. DATA AFTER PROMOTION AT CLOSE OF THE SCHOOL YEAR 1913–14

	CHILDREN RECEIVING ALL THEIR GRADE WORK IN THE BLOOMINGTON SCHOOLS		CHILDREN RECEIVING ONLY PART OF THEIR GRADE WORK IN THE BLOOMINGTON SCHOOLS		TOTAL
	BOYS	GIRLS	BOYS	GIRLS	
Number of terms gained over normal amount of one-half grade in one half year......	75	99	15	32	221
Number of terms lost........	494	438	225	177	1334
Total number of half years in school....................	3784	3967	1605	1573	10929
Total number of half years' credit made..............	3365	3628	1395	1428	9816
Percentage of terms gained based on total number of terms in school...........	2.0	2.5	1.0	2.0	2.0
Percentage of terms lost based on total number of terms in school....................	13.1	11.0	14.0	11.2	12.2
Percentage of terms made based on total number of terms in school...........	88.9	91.5	87.0	90.8	89.8

TABLE XXVIII

SAME DATA FOR COLORED CHILDREN AS GIVEN IN TABLE XXVII FOR WHITE
CHILDREN

	CHILDREN RECEIVING ALL OF THEIR GRADE WORK IN THE BLOOMINGTON SCHOOLS		CHILDREN RECEIVING ONLY PART OF THEIR GRADE WORK IN THE BLOOMINGTON SCHOOLS		TOTAL
	BOYS	GIRLS	BOYS	GIRLS	
Number of terms gained over normal amount of one-half grade in one half year.........	0	0	0	0	0
Number of terms lost...	23	21	13	21	78
Total number of half years in school.......	135	122	96	152	505
Total number of half years' credit made...	112	101	83	131	427
Percentage of terms gained based on total number of terms in school.............	0	0	0	0	0
Percentage of terms lost based on total number of terms in school....	17	17.2	13.5	13.8	15.4
Percentage of terms made based on total number of terms in school.............	83	82.8	86.5	86.2	84.6

SUMMARY OF TABLES XXVII AND XXVIII

1. The percentage of terms gained by white children on basis of total number of terms in schools is 2.0; colored children 0.

2. Per cent of terms gained by white boys is from ½ to 1 less than the gain made by the girls.

3. Per cent of terms lost is from 2 to 3 more for the white boys than for the white girls, and about the same for colored boys compared with the colored girls.

4. The white boys and girls receiving all of their training in the Bloomington schools make a smaller per cent of loss of terms than do those receiving only a part of their training in the Bloomington schools. With the colored children the situation is reversed.

5. For white children the per cent of terms made based on terms in school is 89.8; for the colored children 84.6.

During the past three years more attention has been given than formerly to providing opportunities for capable children to do the work of the grades in a shorter time than the time regularly allotted. During the second semester of the year 1913–14 from 4 to 5 per cent of all the children in the school system made an extra semester's work.

Table **XXIX** shows normal progress, retardation, and acceleration according to age.

TABLE XXIX

NUMBER AND PER CENT OF TOTAL WHITE PUPILS IN BLOOMINGTON SCHOOLS, END OF FIRST SCHOOL MONTH, OCTOBER 4, 1913, THAT WERE NORMAL, ACCELERATED, RETARDED ACCORDING TO AGE

Normal age for entering 1B grade, six and one-half years. Normal progress, one-half year for each half year in school. Children counted six until six and one-half, seven until seven and one-half, etc. Ages as of September 1, 1913.

AGE	5½	6	6½	7	7½	8	8½	9	9½	10	10½	11	11½	12
Total number...	10	74	94	105	84	105	100	91	100	112	91	88	96	95
Normal.........			49	21	23	28	24	30	29	16	20	18	15	14
Accelerated.....	10	74	45	55	33	42	47	25	35	38	20	25	24	23
Retarded.......				29	28	35	29	36	36	58	51	45	57	58
Per cent Normal.........			52.1	20.0	27.3	26.6	24.0	32.9	29.0	14.2	21.9	20.4	15.6	14.8
Per cent Accelerated.....	100.0	100.0	47.8	52.3	39.2	40.0	47.0	27.4	35.0	83.9	21.9	28.4	25.0	24.2
Per cent Retarded.......				27.6	33.3	33.3	29.0	39.5	36.0	51.7	56.0	51.1	59.3	61.1

AGE	12½	13	13½	14	14½	15	15½	16	16½	17	17½	18	18½	19
Total number...	85	103	72	42	34	29	14	14	2	3	1	0	1	1
Normal........	21	15	15	5										
Accelerated	22	19	5	0										
Retarded	42	69	52	37	34	29	14	14	2	3	1	0	1	1
Per cent Normal........	24.6	14.5	20.8	11.9										
Per cent Accelerated	25.8	18.4	6.9											
Per cent Retarded	49.4	66.9	72.2	88.0	100	100	100	100	100	100	100		100	100

SUMMARY OF TABLE XXIX

1. The various ages with the per cent of retardation for each age are as follows: Ages 19, 18½, 17½, 17, 16½, 16, 15½, 15, 14½ — 100 per cent retardation; age 14, 88 per cent; age 13½, 72.2 per cent; age 13, 66.9 per cent; age 12, 61.1 per cent; age 11½, 59.3 per cent; age 10½, 56 per cent; age 10, 51.7 per cent; age 11, 51.1 per cent; age 12½, 49.4 per cent; age 9, 39.5 per cent; age 9½, 36 per cent; ages 8 and 7½, 33.3 per cent; age 8½, 29 per cent; age 7, 27.6 per cent.

2. The various ages with the per cent of acceleration for each age are as follows: Ages 5½ and 6, 100 per cent; age 10, 83.9 per cent; age 7, 52.3 per cent; age 6½, 47.8 per cent; age 8½, 47 per cent; age 8, 40 per cent; age 7½, 39.2 per cent; age 9½, 35 per cent; age 11, 28.4 per cent; age 9, 27.4 per cent; age 12½, 25.8 per cent; age 11½, 25 per cent; age 12, 24.2 per cent; age 10½, 21.9 per cent; age 13, 18.4 per cent; age 13½, 6.9 per cent.

3. The various ages with the per cent of normal progress for each age are as follows: Age 6½, 52.1 per cent; age 9, 32.9 per cent; age 9½, 29 per cent; age 7½, 27.3 per cent; age 8, 26.6 per cent; age 12½, 24.6 per cent; age 8½, 24 per cent; age 10½, 21.9 per cent; age 13½, 20.8 per cent; age 11, 20.4 per cent; age 7, 20 per cent; age 11½, 15.6 per cent; age 12, 14.8 per cent; age 13, 14.5 per cent; age 10, 14.2 per cent; age 14, 11.9 per cent.

Another approach to normal progress, acceleration, and retardation is through Table XXX (pages 50–51), setting forth average and median ages of children in the various grades at the beginning of the fall semester, 1912–13, the time of year when retardation shows at its greatest.

Using six and one-half years of age as the normal entering age, the following table shows the normal age for each grade:

1B......................	6½– 7	5B......................	10½–11
1A......................	7 – 7½	5A......................	11 –11½
2B......................	7½– 8	6B......................	11½–12
2A......................	8 – 8½	6A......................	12 –12½
3B......................	8½– 9	7B......................	12½–13
3A......................	9 – 9½	7A......................	13 –13½
4B......................	9½–10	8B......................	13½–14
4A......................	10 –10½	8A......................	14 –14½

A comparison of the above table with the table of average and median ages (Table XXX) justifies the following conclusions:

1. On the basis of average ages, total boys and girls, the children in the 1B grade are within the limits of normal age for the grade; those in the 1A grade are 3 months, 28.7 days beyond the upper limit of normal age for their grade; those in the 2B grade 1 month 14.8 days older than the upper normal limit for their grade; those in the 2A grade, 21.6 days older; those in the 3B grade, 4 months 18.4 days older; those in the 3A grade, 7 months 4.7 days older; those in the 4B grade, 5 months 23.6 days older; those in the 4A grade, 5 months 9.2 days older; those in the 5B grade, 6 months 28.6 days older; those in the 5A grade, 3 months 24.1 days older; those in the 6B grade, 6 months 20.1 days older; those in the 6A grade, 2 months 11.2 days older; those in the 7B grade, 1 month 4.2 days older; those in the 7A grade, 4 months 12.7 days older; those in the 8B grade, 8 months 19.9 days older; those in the 8A grade, 1 month 20.4 days older.

2. On the basis of median ages, total boys and girls, the results are: 1B, within normal age limits; 1A, within normal age limits; 2B, within normal age limits; 2A, within limits; 3B, 2 months 17.2 days older; 3A, 5 months 13 days older; 4B, within limits; 4A, 3 months 3 days older; 5B, 3 months 19 days older; 5A, 3 months 18 days older; 6B, 5 months 12 days older; 6A, within limits; 7B, within limits; 7A, 2 months 3 days older; 8B, 5 months 22 days older; 8A, 3 days older.

3. On the basis of median ages grades 3A, 6B, 8B show the greatest retardation.

4. On the whole the McCalla Building shows the least retardation.

5. The girls are distinctly less retarded than the boys.

TABLE XXX

Table Showing Average and Median Ages by Grades, Sex, and Buildings of All White Pupils in Grades, Fall Term Beginning September 9, 1912. Ages as of September 9, 1912

Building	Grade	Number of Boys	Number of Girls	Total Number of Boys and Girls	Average Age of Boys Yr.	Mo.	Da.	Average Age of Girls Yr.	Mo.	Da.	Average Age of Boys and Girls Yr.	Mo.	Da.	Median Age of Boys Yr.	Mo.	Da.	Median Age of Girls Yr.	Mo.	Da.	Median Age of Boys and Girls Yr.	Mo.	Da.
Central	1B	22	21	43	6	8	26.6	6	8	11.5	6	8	19.2	6	5	9	6	5	21	6	5	13
McCalla	1B	39	35	74	6	11	16	6	10	11.6	6	10	29.7	6	7	29	6	5	24	6	7	7
Fairview	1B	27	24	51	7	1	3	6	11	14.6	7	0	10.2	6	8	20	6	6	27	6	8	3
Total	1B	88	80	168	6	11	10.6	6	10	5.7	6	10	24.0	6	7	21	6	6	3.5	6	6	16.5
Central	1A	18	8	26	7	2	23	8	5	23.3	7	7	11.6	7	0	3.5	7	9	25	7	4	25
McCalla	1A	23	8	31	7	8	5.9	8	0	19.	7	9	10.2	7	6	4	7	11	29	7	7	3
Fairview	1A	12	15	27	8	8	20.6	7	7	3.2	8	1	4.2	7	9	12.5	7	4	23	7	7	26
Total	1A	53	31	84	7	9	5.4	7	11	8.6	7	9	28.7	7	5	22	7	6	1	7	5	29
Central	2B	20	16	36	8	0	7.8	7	13	23.7	8	0	28.1	7	6	26	7	9	6	7	7	24.5
McCalla	2B	33	22	55	8	1	21.9	7	7	27.1	7	11	12	8	0	6	7	8	29.2	7	10	8
Fairview	2B	16	18	34	8	8	25	8	2	14.5	8	5	14.1	8	0	10	7	10	16	7	9	19.2
Total	2B	69	56	125	7	14	28.5	7	11	21.0	8	1	14.8	7	11	6	7	8	29.2	7	10	2
Central	2A	11	12	23	8	7	17.6	8	6	2.7	8	6	24.2	8	5	19	8	4	6	8	5	19
McCalla	2A	14	13	27	8	9	14.	8	1	15.6	8	5	19.2	8	7	13	8	0	8	8	1	28
Fairview	2A	17	8	25	8	7	23.	8	7	26.3	8	7	24.1	8	3	14	8	0	0	8	3	15
Total	2A	42	33	75	8	8	8.6	8	4	21.7	8	6	21.6	8	4	14	8	1	28	8	3	25
Central	3B	19	14	33	8	11	19.2	9	9	9.5	9	3	22.4	9	1	7	9	4	2.5	9	9	29
McCalla	3B	20	18	38	9	5	9.6	9	11	23.8	9	2	21.1	9	0	17.2	8	11	4	8	12	20
Fairview	3B	26	21	47	9	9	4.6	9	3	24.6	9	6	23.1	9	5	13	9	2	10	9	7	23
Total	3B	65	53	118	9	5	5.8	9	3	27.1	9	4	18.4	9	2	18	9	2	10	9	2	17.2
Central	3A	29	13	42	10	3	6.	9	7	16.	10	0	24.8	10	10	24	9	2	17	9	10	17
McCalla	3A	15	16	31	10	4	17.4	9	6	14.6	9	11	11.1	10	8	22	9	4	28.5	9	9	3
Fairview	3A	10	11	21	10	10	9.3	9	11	4.4	10	4	13.9	10	6	24	9	5	4	9	8	2
Total	3A	54	40	94	10	4	27.	9	8	3.3	10	1	4.7	10	1	.5	9	5	4	9	11	13

School	Grade	1	2	3	4	5	6	7	8	9	10	11	12	13	14	15	16	17	18	19	20
Central	4B	23	9	32	10	8	29.1	2	14.8	10	7	4.4	10	3	28	10	0	0	10	3	4.5
McCalla	4B	25	24	49	10	5	8.4	3	13.3	10	0	11.4	10	2	3	9	4	8.5	9	7	2
Fairview	4B	20	8	28	10	8	22.4	1	16.0	10	6	20.6	10	10	19	9	7	4	10	7	7
Total	4B	68	41	109	10	7	16.4	2	25.9	10	11	23.6	10	4	0	9	6	12.5	9	11	4
Central	4A	14	16	30	10	6	12.6	5	16.6	11	0	10.7	10	6	16	11	2	8	10	10	8
McCalla	4A	17	19	36	10	9	21.8	3	11.5	10	6	11.3	10	7	24	10	1	8	10	5	10.5
Fairview	4A	11	14	25	11	4	29.6	5	12.6	11	5	6.9	10	10	24	11	2	10	10	10	24
Total	4A	42	49	91	10	10	14.3	0	.6	10	11	9.2	10	8	0	10	9	3	10	9	3
Central	5B	10	15	25	11	7	6.5	0	13.6	11	7	10.9	11	7	9	11	6	1	11	6	1
McCalla	5B	15	21	36	11	5	27.	8	11.3	11	11	10.3	10	11	19	10	7	3	10	10	1.5
Fairview	5B	12	14	26	12	8	10.	6	11.9	12	0	24.9	13	0	15.5	11	5	7.5	11	10	17.5
Total	5B	37	50	87	11	6	5.4	4	.1	11	7	28.6	11	7	24	11	2	1	11	3	19
Central	5A	7	17	24	12	0	18.7	6	6.3	12	9	17.4	11	9	18	12	0	8	12	7	28
McCalla	5A	15	25	40	11	8	7.	2	28.	11	3	27.5	12	3	12	10	8	28	11	10	11
Fairview	5A	13	10	23	11	8	19.	2	18.3	11	0	27	12	0	3	12	3	7.5	12	0	3
Total	5A	35	52	87	11	8	37.7	10	6.9	11	0	24.1	12	0	3	11	8	22.5	11	9	18
Central	6B	22	22	44	12	7	25.4	1	29.5	12	6	27.4	12	6	10.5	12	2	26	12	5	7
McCalla	6B	12	15	27	11	9	25.	1	7.8	11	10	12.1	12	10	9.2	13	6	13	12	5	17
Fairview	6B	11	8	19	12	11	4.9	11	.4	12	7	3	12	7	0	12	11	5	12	5	16
Total	6B	45	45	90	12	5	29.6	7	10.5	12	5	20.1	12	5	5	12	6	5	12	5	12
Central	6A	17	15	32	13	9	24.6	11	3.4	12	8	.6	12	8	14	12	4	12	12	5	13
McCalla	6A	8	17	25	11	7	29.1	2	1.9	11	7	11.8	11	7	28	11	11	1	11	9	4
Fairview	6A	8	9	17	13	7	27.8	0	2.4	12	8	21.4	13	8	15.5	12	8	12	12	11	19
Total	6A	33	41	74	12	10	28.3	6	9.1	12	7	11.2	12	7	18	12	2	21	12	5	6
Central*	7B	26	29	55	13	0	16.4	1	20.2	13	10	4.2	12	10	2	12	8	4	12	8	29
Central	7A	14	23	37	14	1	12.0	8	18.4	13	11	12.7	13	11	24.5	13	3	2	13	8	3
Central	8B	35	26	61	14	9	15.4	6	22.1	14	5	19.9	14	5	18	14	8	7	14	5	22
Central	8A	24	32	56	14	8	17.1	7	.3	14	5	20.4	14	5	17	14	6	3	14	6	3

All 7B's, 7A's, 8B's, and 8A's were in the Central building.

The following four tables show age and grade of high-school pupils as nearly as it is possible to make such a classification where pupils are promoted by subjects rather than by years.

TABLE XXXI

Age–Grade Table of Boys in High School, Second Month of First Semester, School Year 1913–14

Ages taken September 1, 1913. Each pupil is supposed to make 4 credits each semester. Pupils are classified as to grade as follows: 0 credits to $3\frac{3}{4}$ credits inclusive — 9B; 4 to $7\frac{3}{4}$ — 9A; 8 to $11\frac{3}{4}$ — 10B; 12 to $15\frac{3}{4}$ — 10A; 16 to $19\frac{3}{4}$ — 11B; 20 to $23\frac{3}{4}$ — 11A; 24 to $27\frac{3}{4}$ — 12B; 28 to 32 — 12A.

	9B	9A	10B	10A	11B	11A	12B	12A
13	1							
13½	4	1						
14	9	3						
14½	5	1	3					
15	7	8	5	5	1			
15½	4	4	4	1	2			
16	6	2	11	2	6	2		
16½	6	2	3	3	4	2		
17	2	6	3	3	1	1	4	4
17½	2	3	0	1	0	2		
18	1	1	2	1	1	2	2	2
18½			2	1	0	1	2	
19	1		1		1		1	2
19½							1	2
20								1
20½						1		
21						1		
21½						1		
22							1	1
Total	48	31	35	17	16	13	11	12

TABLE XXXII

Age–Grade Table of Girls in High School, Second Month of First Semester, School Year 1913–14

Ages taken September 1, 1913. Each pupil is supposed to make 4 credits each semester. Pupils are classified as to grade as follows: 0 credits to $3\frac{3}{4}$ credits inclusive — 9B; 4 to $7\frac{3}{4}$ — 9A; 8 to $11\frac{3}{4}$ — 10B; 12 to $15\frac{3}{4}$ — 10A; 16 to $19\frac{3}{4}$ — 11B; 20 to $23\frac{3}{4}$ — 11A; 24 to $27\frac{3}{4}$ — 12B; 28 to 32 — 12A.

	9B	9A	10B	10A	11B	11A	12B	12A
13	1							
13½	6	2						
14	3	2						
14½	10	1	7	2				
15	14	3	3	0	3	1		
15½	6	5	5	4	6			
16	4	5	3	3	9	3		
16½	7	2	5	2	4	0	1	
17	1	6	2	3	2	2	3	
17½	5	2	1	3	3	5	5	
18	1	0	1	1	0	3	2	
18½		1				1		3
19					1	2		4
19½					1	1		
20								
20½								
21					1		1	1
21½								
22					1			
Total	58	29	27	18	31	18	12	8

TABLE XXXIII

AGE–GRADE TABLE OF ALL PUPILS IN HIGH SCHOOL, SECOND MONTH OF
FIRST SEMESTER, SCHOOL YEAR 1913–14

Ages taken September 1, 1913. Each pupil is supposed to make 4 credits each semester. Pupils are classified as to grade as follows: o credits to $3\frac{3}{4}$ credits inclusive — 9B; 4 to $7\frac{3}{4}$ — 9A; 8 to $11\frac{3}{4}$ — 10B; 12 to $15\frac{3}{4}$ — 10A; 16 to $19\frac{3}{4}$ — 11B; 20 to $23\frac{3}{4}$ — 11A; 24 to $27\frac{3}{4}$ — 12B; 28 to 32 — 12A.

	9B	9A	10B	10A	11B	11A	12B	12A
13.........	2							
13½........	10	3						
14.........	12	5	1					
14½........	15	2	10	2				
15.........	21	11	8	5	4	1		
15½........	10	9	9	5	8	0		
16.........	10	7	14	5	15	5		
16½........	13	4	8	5	8	2	1	
17.........	3	12	5	6	3	3	7	4
17½........	7	5	1	4	3	7	5	0
18.........	2	1	3	2	1	5	4	2
18½........	0	d	2	1	0	2	2	3
19.........	1		1		2	2	1	6
19½........					1	1	1	2
20.........							1	2
20½........						1		
21.........					1	1	1	1
21½........						1		
22.........					1		1	1
Total......	106	60	62	35	47	31	24	21

TABLE XXXIV

AVERAGE NUMBER OF CREDITS BY GRADES AND SEX OF PUPILS IN HIGH SCHOOL, SECOND MONTH OF FIRST SEMESTER, SCHOOL YEAR 1913–14

GRADE	NUMBER OF BOYS	AVERAGE NUMBER OF CREDITS OF BOYS	NUMBER OF GIRLS	AVERAGE NUMBER OF CREDITS OF GIRLS	TOTAL NUMBER OF BOYS AND GIRLS	AVERAGE TOTAL NUMBER OF CREDITS OF BOYS AND GIRLS
9B.....	46	.4	58	.5	104	.5
9A.....	31	5.4	32	5.0	63	5.2
10B.....	35	8.9	26	8.6	61	8.8
10A.:...	17	12.8	21	13.6	38	13.3
11B.....	20	16.3	29	16.1	49	16.1
11A.....	10	21.3	14	21.4	24	21.4
12B.....	8	25.1	18	25.0	26	25.1
12A.....	9	28.6	11	29.3	20	29.0

The age-grade tables for the Bloomington schools reveal the fact that there are marked individual differences in pupils and suggest that methods should be planned whereby these differences should be quickly recognized and provided for. Up to the present time the following plans have been used in an effort to adjust the work to the varying abilities of pupils and to promote their interest and success in their work.

PLANS USED IN THE GRADES

1. Practically all of the grade pupils are divided into groups according to strength in the subjects. In a single building, for instance, there are frequently three or four divisions of one grade, the most advanced division of the grade being from one to three months ahead of the slowest group. Whenever a child in the advanced group is absent and loses some of his work he drops into the group just below upon his return to school. As soon as he shows strength in that work he is transferred again to the higher group. This plan is sometimes extended even to the grouping of pupils from adjoining grades.

2. Frequently there are classes that cannot be reached satisfactorily by this plan and for them there has been provided in the past individual teachers who pass from building to building, giving such children instruction in the subjects in which they are weakest. As many as five or six such teachers giving from one to two hours each day of their time to individual instruction of this type have been provided at one time. Bloomington is fortunately located in that it is a university town and can secure teachers for this sort of work very reasonably, and sometimes even for the experience.

3. For children who are noticeably defective, there have been organized separate groups who have been taught at centers away from the other children. For these special groups there is provided more handwork and manual training, sewing, etc., than for the normal children of the grades. Much attention is given with these groups also to games, boxing, wrestling, jumping, after which they take a plunge in the swimming pool. The idea back of this practice is that through physical exercise they may be somewhat stimulated to more mental exertion.

4. Summer school work for limited numbers of the grade children has also been offered. These special summer school classes are meant primarily for those who are especially strong and by summer attendance can make an extra grade, and for those who are weak in their work and who need extra attention to insure their being able to carry their work satisfactorily the following year.

5. In the upper grades, where the departmental plan of instruction is used, pupils are now promoted by subjects, the promotion, however, only in rare cases extending by subject from the 8A grade into high school.

6. Opportunity to begin the study of Latin and German in the upper grades is given to the strongest pupils and these are given

advanced standing in this subject upon their entrance to high school.

7. Medical examination and advice are provided for pupils whose physical condition is such as to interfere with their normal progress in their studies. Tests of hearing and eyesight are made by students of the department of education of Indiana University often enough for teachers to keep informed of any defect of these senses on the part of any pupil. This practice applies to high-school pupils also.

PLANS USED IN THE HIGH SCHOOL

All Pupils:

The basis for specific action toward failing pupils and toward pupils of differing abilities is arrived at through two channels directed by the principal of the high school.

1. A blank is filled out by each teacher once a semester for each pupil in his classes. Another blank is filled out by each pupil at the end of each semester. These reports serve as a basis not only for individual action on the part of each teacher, but for concerted action agreed upon in teachers' meetings. In these meetings various devices are suggested for dealing with failing pupils, the devices differing of course with the differing causes of failure.

2. All pupils in classes in English are required to make fifteen points per semester on reading, outside of recitation, standard books of literature from a prescribed list. In history, also, ten points per semester must be made on outside reading. Teachers by their advice and direction do much to help the pupil to read according to his ability.

3. For the past three years there have been classes in algebra and geometry whose study was supervised during one recitation period daily. This plan gave the teacher the best possible opportunity to adapt the work to all abilities in the class.

4. In most departments there is opportunity for pupils to make advance credits under competent teachers during the summer vacation. In this case the pupil pays his own tuition.

5. The first thing in the morning, a thirty-five minute period, from 8.30 to 9.05, is given over for a study period. No recitations whatever are held during that period. All teachers are in their rooms ready to consult with pupils who have questions to ask about their work or to aid pupils with whom they have made an appointment for that period. By this method individual instruction is

offered to every child in the building and is enforced in the case of pupils that the teachers feel need special help. Other conferences with pupils are arranged at the wish of the teacher.

Failing Pupils:

1. If not too far below, failing pupils are passed at the end of the term on condition that they make during the succeeding semester a specific per cent above passing. The amount of this per cent varies for varying circumstances. This plan is being tried to some extent in all subjects but most extensively at present in botany in the high school where pupils with weak or failing grades in one semester, but who give promise of better or more energetic work later on, are passed on the condition that a grade of from five to ten per cent above passing be made during a part or all of the second semester.

2. Certain failing pupils are marked incomplete at the end of a term and given an opportunity to complete the work without repeating. Students whose attitude and effort are good but who cannot make passing grades are marked incomplete on the record but are given special individual work to cover the deficiency if it be specific or to make up for approximate credits lacking if the work is generally low. This special work is carefully outlined and checked up and is done out of school hours by the student, who is thus able to continue in other work with those passing regularly.

3. Special classes are organized during the school term to take care of certain specific weaknesses general with students in different years of the subject. For instance, such classes have been organized in English, composed of pupils from first, second, third, and fourth years, who because of a lack of the knowledge of grammar flounder in literary interpretation and write bunglesome sentences in the composition work. These pupils are temporarily drawn from their regular work and placed in an after-school class that studies practical speaking-grammar. When such a student shows enough language and grammar information to warrant his proceeding with the regular course, he is placed in the term's work in which he would have been had he originally passed successfully or had he not been assigned to the grammar section.

4. Special examinations over the work failed in.

5. Repeating the work.

6. Instead of having the pupils do over work in which low grades have been made, substitutions of related work are occasionally made in which students are given material upon a subject closely related to

facts discussed in the recitation and in which they have shown a particular interest. Evidence of satisfactory completion of such work is obtained from written reports or from oral examinations. In physics one hour each Thursday is set aside for those who are simply slow and fail to complete their experiments in the regular laboratory periods.

7. Reduce the number of subjects that the pupil is permitted to carry. This is done only by the principal of the high school.

Pupils of Different Abilities Within a Single Group:

1. By giving strong members of the class the most difficult work. In the assignment of lessons to mixed classes in mathematics the work is developed enough to place it in reach of the average student and further modification of the assignment is given the poor students during the consultation periods.

2. In laboratory work slow pupils are allowed to devote extra time to the subject.

3. A minimum requirement is made of all and the stronger pupils are kept up to their maximum through additional assignments or through experimental work. How this is taken care of in such subjects as botany and mathematics, has already been indicated. In Latin this same end has been attained through the following methods: (a) Having the strong pupils throw the Latin into drama form in a written translation, thus correlating with English. (b) Having them write Latin poems and editorials for high-school publications.

4. Weaker pupils are encouraged by being given some particular thing to do along certain lines of special interest that are not required of other members of the class. For instance, one boy who was weak in the regular Latin work was encouraged to construct a catapult and other of Cæsar's war instruments, and he thus commanded the respect of the class.

5. Dividing classes into weak and strong sections. This plan has been followed to a limited extent in each of the following subjects: mathematics, Latin, German, English, and physics. It has already been indicated how the work is made more difficult for the stronger sections. In English not only are the assignments longer and more difficult, but in one strong class the materials dealt with were totally different from those coming in the regular course. This division in the strong and weak sections in German has been limited to Freshmen classes.

6. The following is a detailed account of a method rather thoroughly tried out during 1912–13, of dealing with those of different abilities in the subject of physics. This account is given as it was submitted by the teacher of physics:

(*a*) During the second semester, the two sections of physics are divided according to ability in the subject. Up until the present time, the assigned text-book has been the same for each class. In the more advanced section, excursions are made into more difficult fields. Topics not discussed in the text-book are presented. In the other section, each student usually has sufficient exercise in mastering the text itself. The class discussions are confined to the assigned topics. The examinations for the two sections have not always been the same.

(*b*) In experimental work, the entire class works on the same experiment at the regular laboratory period during the first six weeks of the semester. At this time, differences in experimental ability become very marked. From this point, students are allowed to work in groups of two and three, the groups being chosen with respect to ability shown in the previous work. Each group has a different experiment. When this is mastered another exercise is assigned. (The best possible results for any given set of apparatus are known by the instructor.) The plan takes care of the slow student and allows the individual with ability to do more difficult work.

(*c*) With one student of exceptional ability, a different plan is used. This student recites with the class but does the laboratory work alone, at a different time, under the direction of the instructor. This student is usually from four to five weeks ahead of the class in laboratory work, and has done twice the number of experiments outlined for the regular work. He has devised many interesting experiments himself. He has made an induction coil, electric tourniquet, cartesian diver (special form blown from glass), a half dozen commutators, electrolytic cell for projection, coherer for wireless outfit, apparatus for determining frequency of a tuning fork, apparatus for distillation of water, and many other pieces of apparatus, and has gained skill in glass blowing, use of the lathe, and the use of the principles of chemistry. This student could have graduated in one half year.

7. In physics last year there were four groups of students. One section was for those who were noticeably weak in that particular subject. Pupils in the weak section enjoyed the advantage of being in a small group and also of work only on the simpler and most important things in the subject. The third group was composed of girls of average ability, and the fourth of boys of average ability. The illustrative material used in the girls' class was taken almost wholly from the machinery in the home; whereas, the illustrative material for the boys' group was taken from machinery on the farm, in the industrial plants, on the streets and roads. The fourth group was a mixed group of boys and girls, the strongest pupils in the whole group.

8. In science and in mathematics the strongest pupils are often employed as laboratory or class-room helpers.

Summary of Chapter II

1. The approximate age of children on entering the 1B grade in the Bloomington schools is six and one-half years; hence in most of the age-grade tables this age is considered normal for entrance to the 1B grade, and normal progress is interpreted as meaning one half year's progress for every half year in school.

2. For the sake of comparison with other cities, a few age-grade tables are made out on the basis of a two-year leeway in each grade to represent pupils of normal progress. Comparison on this basis shows that Bloomington has a very low percentage of retardation, a high percentage of normal progress, and a very low percentage of acceleration.

3. The boys are more retarded than the girls.

4. The greatest retardation is in the Fairview building and the least is in the McCalla building.

5. The greatest retardation is in grades 5A, 4A, 6B, 4B, and 5B; whereas the least retardation is in grades 1B, 2A, 1A, 2B, and 7A.

6. The greatest acceleration is in grades 1B, 2A, 1A, 7A, and 3A; whereas the least acceleration is in grades 5A, 6B, 4B, 4A, and 5B.

7. The greatest percentage of normal progress is in grades 2A, 2B, 1B, 1A, and 7B; whereas the least is in grades 8A, 4A, 6B, 6A, and 5B.

8. There has been a gradual improvement for several years in the Bloomington schools as far as retardation, normal progress, and acceleration is concerned.

9. Years in school and progress made data show the following conditions:

(*a*) The percentage of terms of school work gained over the normal amount is for white children 2, colored 0.

(*b*) Per cent of terms gained by white boys is from $\frac{1}{2}$ to 1 less than the gain made by girls.

(*c*) Per cent of terms lost is from 2 to 3 more for the white boys than for the white girls, and about the same for colored boys compared with colored girls.

(*d*) The white boys and girls receiving all their training in the Bloomington schools make a smaller per cent of loss of terms than do those receiving only a part of their training in the Bloomington schools. With the colored children the situation is reversed.

(*e*) For the white children the percentage of terms made based on terms in school is 89.8; for the colored children, 84.6.

10. The greatest percentage of retardation in the grades is for ages 14½ to 19 inclusive, which is 100 per cent. For age 14 it is 88 per cent; age 13½, 72.2 per cent; age 13, 66.9 per cent. The least retardation is for age 7, 27.6 per cent. For age 8½ it is 29 per cent; ages 7½ and 8, 33.3 per cent; 9½, 36 per cent; 9, 39.5 per cent.

11. The greatest percentage of acceleration in the grades is for the ages 5½ and 6 which is 100 per cent. For age 10 it is 83.9 per cent; age 7, 52.3 per cent; age 6½, 47.8 per cent; age 8½, 47 per cent. The least acceleration is in age 13½ with 6.9 per cent; age 13 with 18.4 per cent; age 10½ with 21.9 per cent; age 12 with 24.2 per cent.

12. On the basis of median ages grades 3A, 6B, and 8B show the greatest retardation.

CHAPTER III

CENSUS, ENROLLMENT, PROMOTIONS, FAILURES, WITHDRAWALS, REPETITIONS

Table **XXXV** shows a fairly even distribution of children through the whole range of ages from six to twenty inclusive.

TABLE XXXV, CENSUS

DISTRIBUTION OF CHILDREN WITHIN SCHOOL AGE BETWEEN SIX AND TWENTY-ONE, SCHOOL CENSUS, SPRING, 1914, ACCORDING TO AGE AT TIME OF ENUMERATION, APRIL 10 TO 30

AGE IN YEARS AT TIME OF ENUMERATION	NUMBER OF CHILDREN OF EACH AGE			PERCENTAGE OF CHILDREN OF EACH AGE	FOR COMPARISON	
					NUMBER ACCORDING TO ENUMERATION 1913	PERCENTAGE ACCORDING TO ENUMERATION 1913
	WHITE	COLORED	TOTAL			
6........	160	8	168	5.9	193	7.1
7........	208	11	219	7.7	194	7.2
8........	196	10	206	7.2	170	6.3
9........	179	10	189	6.6	203	7.5
10........	191	5	196	6.9	202	7.4
11........	198	8	206	7.2	180	6.6
12........	174	10	184	6.4	191	7.0
13........	184	6	190	6.6	187	6.9
14........	178	7	185	6.5	170	6.3
15........	167	7	174	6.1	201	7.4
16........	198	14	212	7.4	182	6.7
17........	185	7	192	6.7	185	6.8
18........	190	6	196	6.9	155	5.7
19........	160	11	171	6.0	172	6.3
20........	161	10	171	6.0	127	4.7
Total......	2729	130	2859	100.1	2712	99.9

TABLE XXXVI

DISTRIBUTION OF ALL CHILDREN OF SCHOOL AGE ENUMERATED, SPRING, 1914, AMONG FAMILIES OF VARIOUS SIZES

Only children from 6 to 20 years of age, inclusive, are considered in the enumeration and in determining number of children of school age in family. Children are counted as twenty until their twenty-first birthday.

NUMBER OF CHILDREN OF SCHOOL AGE IN FAMILY	NUMBER OF FAMILIES OF EACH SIZE				
	FIRST WARD	WHITE SECOND WARD	THIRD WARD	COLORED	TOTAL
1.........	190	188	197	21	596
2.........	126	109	138	22	395
3.........	65	50	72	8	195
4.........	28	30	34	5	97
5.........	17	19	17	3	56
6.........	6	9	10	1	26
7.........	1	6	1		8
8.........	1				1
Total......	434	411	469	60	1374

NUMBER OF CHILDREN OF SCHOOL AGE IN FAMILY	NUMBER OF CHILDREN IN EACH FAMILY SIZE			PERCENTAGE OF CHILDREN IN EACH SIZE
	WHITE	COLORED	TOTAL	
1.........	575	21	596	20.8
2.........	746	44	790	27.6
3.........	561	24	585	20.5
4.........	368	20	388	13.6
5.........	265	15	280	9.8
6.........	150	6	156	5.5
7.........	56		56	2.3
8.........	8		8	.3
TOTAL.....	2729	130	2859	

SUMMARY OF TABLE XXXVI

1. 43.4 per cent of the families having children of school age have only one such child, and 20.8 per cent of all children of school age belong to families having only one child of school age.

2. 28.7 per cent of the families having children of school age have two such children each, and 27.6 per cent of all children of school age belong to families having only two children of school age.

3. 14.2 per cent of the families having children of school age have three such children each, and 20.5 per cent of the children of school age belong to families having only three children of school age.

4. 7.1 per cent of the families have four children each and 13.6 per cent of the children belong to such families.

5. With families of five children the per cents are 4.1 per cent for families and 9.8 per cent for children. Families of six children, 1.9 per cent for families and 5.5 per cent for children. Families of seven children, .6 per cent for families and 2.3 per cent for children. Families of 8 children, .1 per cent for families and .3 per cent for children.

6. 86.2 per cent of all families having children of school age have either one, two, or three of such children, while 68.9 per cent of all children of school age belong to families of only one, two, or three of such children.

7. On 13.8 per cent of the families the burden of educating their families is extremely heavy, while 31.1 per cent of all children of school age belong to families carrying this heavy burden. It is understood of course that not all of the children of school age in any of the above families are necessarily in school.

TABLE XXXVII

DISTRIBUTION BY BUILDINGS SHOWING PLACES OF BIRTH WHERE KNOWN OF CHILDREN IN SCHOOL IN THE FIRST EIGHT GRADES DURING THE YEAR 1913–14

PLACE OF BIRTH	SCHOOL					PERCENTAGE IN EACH GROUP
	CENTRAL	McCALLA	FAIRVIEW	COLORED	TOTAL	
Bloomington.......	338	247	171	40	796	47.4
Monroe County outside of Bloomington..............	121	63	67		251	14.9
Indiana outside of Monroe County...	190	125	115	19	449	26.7
Alabama...........	1	2			3	
Arizona............		1			1	
Arkansas..........	1	3	1		5	
Colorado..........	1				1	
Georgia............		1			1	
Illinois.............	21	17	8	1	47	
Kansas............	4	1			5	
Kentucky..........	23	11	4	17	55	

TABLE XXXVII (*Continued*)

Massachusetts......	3				3
Michigan...........	1	1			2
Minnesota.........		1			1
Missouri..........	3	2	2	2	9
New York.........	1				1
Ohio.............	5	10		4	19
Oklahoma.........	1		1	1	3
Pennsylvania.......	2	1	1		4
Rhode Island......	1				1
Tennessee.........	1	5	1	8	15
Texas............	1	1			2
Wisconsin.........	1	1			2
Foreign:					
Scotland........		4	1		5
Total.............					1681
Total outside Indiana					185	11

SUMMARY OF TABLE XXXVII

1. There are practically no foreign-born children of school age in the city, hence no problem of the foreign-born child to deal with.
2. Only 11 per cent of the children in the first eight grades of school last year were born outside of Indiana.
3. 26.7 per cent were born in Indiana outside of Monroe County.
4. 14.9 per cent were born in Monroe County outside of Bloomington.
5. 47.4 per cent were born in Bloomington.
6. Kentucky still contributes largely, as it has done from the earliest history of the state, to the school population of the city.
7. Illinois is second to Kentucky as a source of school population for Bloomington.

TABLE XXXVIII

NUMBER ENROLLED IN GRADES AND HIGH SCHOOL IN THE BLOOMINGTON SCHOOLS DURING LAST FIVE YEARS

	1910	1911	1912	1913	1914
First Grade................	322	326	281	326	318
Second Grade.............	117	198	236	254	251
Third Grade..............	260	215	261	248	306
Fourth Grade.............	233	252	205	253	284
Fifth Grade...............	181	197	208	222	249
Sixth Grade...............	170	169	190	197	213
Seventh Grade............	158	157	161	156	216
Eighth Grade.............	89	142	137	124	130
Total for Grades.........	1,530	1,656	1,679	1,780	1,967
First Year (High School)....	162	129	174	167	176
Second Year..............	93	113	92	113	100
Third Year...............	70	80	90	60	84
Fourth Year..............	61	52	58	106	68
Total for High School.....	386	374	414	446	428
Grand Total for both Grades and High School........	1,916	2,030	2,093	2,226	2,395
Number of High School Graduates..............	44	47	36	37	45
Total High School Graduates........					209

During the past five years 19.2 per cent of the total enrollment both in grades and in high school has been in the high school, and 70.8 per cent of all the graduates from the high school during the past seven years have entered a college or university.

Of the 548,497 children enrolled in the public schools of the State of Indiana during the year 1913–14, 89 per cent were found in the elementary schools and 11 per cent in the high schools.[1]

TABLE XXXIX

NUMBER AND PER CENT OF EIGHTH GRADE GRADUATES FROM THE BLOOMINGTON COMMON SCHOOLS WHO ENTER THE BLOOMINGTON HIGH SCHOOL

DATE OF GRADUATION FROM GRADES	NUMBER IN CLASS	NUMBER ENTERING HIGH SCHOOL	PER CENT ENTERING HIGH SCHOOL
January, 1907	36	32	88.9
May, 1907	29	25	86.2
January, 1908	34	31	91.2
May, 1908	39	34	87.2
January, 1909	31	28	90.3
May, 1909	46	42	91.3
January, 1910	25	20	80.0
June, 1910	17	16	94.1
January, 1911	31	29	93.5
June, 1911	62	58	93.5
January, 1912	36	35	97.2
June, 1912	55	48	87.3
January, 1913	39	36	92.3
June, 1913	51	41	80.4
January, 1914	30	26	86.7
Total	561	501	89.3

TABLE XL

SHOWING NUMBER AND PER CENT OF PUPILS ENTERING THE BLOOMINGTON HIGH SCHOOL WHO COMPLETED THEIR HIGH SCHOOL COURSE

CLASS ENTERING	NUMBER IN CLASS	NUMBER GRADUATED FROM BLOOMINGTON HIGH SCHOOL	NUMBER GRADUATED FROM HIGH SCHOOL ELSEWHERE	PER CENT OF ENTERING CLASS THAT GRADUATED
January, 1904	22	15	3	81.8
January, 1905	36	15	1	44.4
January, 1906	22	10	2	54.5
January, 1907	37	17	3	54.1
January, 1908	30	14	1	50.0
January, 1909	25	12	2	56.0
Total	172	83	12	55.8
September, 1905	96	47	2	51.0
September, 1906	63	33	2	55.6
September, 1907	73	43	2	61.6
September, 1908	55	10	5	27.3
September, 1909	105	49	1	47.6
Total	392	182	12	49.5
Grand Total, January and September	564	265	24	51.2

[1] Report of Superintendent of Public Instruction, Indiana, 1913–14.

TABLE XLI

Enrollment, Withdrawals, and Promotions by Sex and Grade, Central Building, Second Semester, School Year 1913–14

	Number Enrolled in Grade During Term			To Leave City			Number Dropped — To Enter Lower Grade			To Enter Higher Grade			To Quit School			Number Remaining at End of Term			Number Remaining Failed			Number Remaining Promoted on Trial			Number Remaining Irregularly Promoted			Number Remaining Regularly Promoted		
	B	G	T	B	G	T	B	G	T	B	G	T	B	G	T	B	G	T	B	G	T	B	G	T	B	G	T	B	G	T
1B	26	20	46	2	1	3							1	0	1	23	19	42	5	2	7	0	3	3				18	14	32
1A	24	25	49	3	2	5							0	3	3	21	20	41	0	1	1	0	2	2				21	17	38
2B	14	14	28	3	2	5				1	1	2	1	0	1	10	11	21	0	1	1							10	10	20
2A	21	14	35	1	1	2				2	1	3	1	0	1	17	12	29	1	0	1							16	12	28
3B	26	22	48	2	3	5							0	1	1	23	19	42	2	3	5	4	0	4				17	16	33
3A	26	20	46	2	6	8	1	1	2				1	0	1	23	13	36	2	1	3	1	0	1				20	12	32
4B	15	11	26	4	1	5				0	5	5	0	2	2	10	10	20	2	0	2							8	10	18
4A	18	21	39	4	2	6										14	12	26	1	1	2	4	1	5				9	10	19
5B	19	12	31	0	1	1							1	1	2	19	12	31	2	0	2	1	1	2				16	11	27
5A	21	12	33	0	1	1				1	0	1	1	1	2	19	10	29	2	0	2	2	2	4				15	8	23
6B	18	14	32	3	0	3							2	0	2	17	12	29	3	1	4	4	1	5	1	0	1	9	10	19
6A	25	48	73	1	4	5							3	5	8	20	48	68	3	4	7	2	11	13				15	33	48
7B	37	53	90	4	4	8	1	1	2				5	2	7	32	43	75	8	4	12	10	8	18				14	31	45
7A	54	61	115	2	1	3	1	0	1				2	0	2	44	55	99	9	10	19	14	7	21				21	38	59
8B	25	36	61	1	1	2	0	1	1							21	34	55	4	7	11	0	4	4				17	23	40
8A	24	28	52	0	2	2	4	0	4				1	0	1	19	25	44	3	4	7							16	21	37
	393	411	804	31	31	62	7	3	10	4	7	11	19	15	34	332	355	687	47	39	86	42	40	82	1	0	1	242	276	518

TABLE XLII

Enrollment, Withdrawals, and Promotions by Sex and Grade, McCalla Building, Second Semester, School Year 1913–14

	Number Enrolled in Grade During Term			To Leave School			Number Dropped To Enter Lower Grade			Number Dropped To Enter Higher Grade			To Quit School			Number Remaining at End of Term			Number of Remaining Failed			Number of Remaining Promoted on Trial			Number of Remaining Irregularly Promoted			Number of Remaining Regularly Promoted		
	B	G	T	B	G	T	B	G	T	B	G	T	B	G	T	B	G	T	B	G	T	B	G	T	B	G	T	B	G	T
1B	26	8	34	1	0	1							2	0	2	23	8	31	3	1	4							20	7	27
1A	26	33	59	1	3	4										25	30	55	1	1	2							24	29	53
2B	20	17	37	2	1	3				0	2	2	0	1	1	18	13	31	3	1	4							14	12	26
2A	28	34	62	3	6	9							0	1	1	25	27	52	1	0	1	1	0	1				24	27	51
3B	35	22	57	7	4	11										28	18	46	3	3	6							25	14	39
3A	28	33	61	2	8	10	0	2	2				0	1	1	26	22	48	4	0	4	0	1	1				22	22	44
4B	36	18	54	3	2	5	1	0	1				1	1	2	31	15	46	4	0	4							27	15	42
4A	32	25	57	3	6	9										29	19	48	6	2	8	2	1	3				21	16	37
5B	22	20	42										2	0	2	20	20	40	0	2	2							20	18	38
5A	27	25	52	2	3	5							1	0	1	24	22	46	1	1	2	3	0	3				20	21	41
6B	16	18	34	1	0	1							3	0	3	12	18	30	1	0	1	1	1	2				11	18	29
6A	8	9	17													8	9	17	0	1	1							7	7	14
	304	262	566	25	33	58	1	2	3	0	2	2	9	4	13	269	221	490	27	12	39	7	3	10				235	206	441

TABLE XLIII

ENROLLMENT, WITHDRAWALS, AND PROMOTIONS BY SEX AND GRADE, FAIRVIEW BUILDING, SECOND SEMESTER, SCHOOL YEAR 1913–14

	Number Enrolled in Grade During Term			To Leave City			Number To Enter Lower Grade			Dropped To Enter Higher Grade			To Quit School			Number Remaining at End of Term			Number of Remaining Failed			Number of Remaining Promoted on Trial			Number of Remaining Irregularly Promoted			Number of Remaining Regularly Promoted		
	B	G	T	B	G	T	B	G	T	B	G	T	B	G	T	B	G	T	B	G	T	B	G	T	B	G	T	B	G	T
1B	25	12	37	3	3	6	0	1	1	1	0	1	1	0	1	21	9	30	3	0	3	5	1	6				13	8	21
1A	25	25	50	3	1	4	0	1	1	1	1	2				21	23	44				1	1	2				20	22	42
2B	18	20	38	1	4	5										17	15	32	0	3	3	4	0	4				13	12	25
2A	19	12	31	2	1	3										16	10	26	1	0	1	1	2	3				14	8	22
3B	16	19	35	6	5	11							0	1	1	10	13	23	1	0	1	2	3	5				7	10	17
3A	25	21	46	3	4	7							0	1	1	22	16	38	1	1	2	2	1	3				19	14	33
4B	24	16	40	4	4	8	0	1	1							20	11	31	0	2	2	7	1	8				13	8	21
4A	21	27	48	1	3	4	2	0	2				0	1	1	18	23	41	1	1	2	1	3	4				16	19	35
5B	20	17	37	1	2	3							1	2	3	18	13	31	0	3	3							18	10	28
5A	22	15	37	0	2	2	1	1	2				3	1	4	18	11	29	4	0	4	0	1	1				14	10	24
6B	18	18	36	3	0	3							2	3	5	13	15	28	1	4	5	2	3	5				10	8	18
	233	202	435	27	29	56	3	4	7	2	1	3	7	9	16	194	159	353	12	14	26	25	16	41				157	129	286

TABLE XLIV

ENROLLMENT, WITHDRAWALS, AND PROMOTIONS BY SEX AND GRADE, COLORED BUILDING, SECOND SEMESTER, SCHOOL YEAR 1913–14

	Number Enrolled in Grade During Term			To Leave City			Number To Enter Lower Grade			Dropped To Enter Higher Grade			To Quit School			Number Remaining At End Of Term			Number Of Remaining Failed			Number Of Remaining Promoted On Trial			Number Of Remaining Irregularly Promoted			Number Of Remaining Regularly Promoted		
	B	G	T	B	G	T	B	G	T	B	G	T	B	G	T	B	G	T	B	G	T	B	G	T	B	G	T	B	G	T
1A	7	13	20	1	1	2										7	13	20	2	0	2	1	1	2				4	12	16
2A	9	9	18										1	0	1	7	8	15				2	1	3				5	7	12
3A	11	6	17	0	1	1							1	0	1	10	6	16	2	2	4	3	0	3				5	4	9
4A	3	5	8													3	4	7	1	2	3	0	1	1				2	1	3
5A	5	5	10													5	5	10	0	4	4	1	0	1	1	0	1	2	3	5
6A	1	6	7										0	1	1	1	5	6										1	1	2
7A	5	3	8	0	1	1							1	0	1	4	2	6				0	1	1	0	1	1	4	2	6
8A	3	3	6										1	0	1	2	3	5				0	1	1				2	1	3
	44	50	94	1	3	4							4	1	5	39	46	85	6	10	16	7	4	11	1	1	2	25	31	56

TABLE XLV

Enrollment, Withdrawals, and Promotions by Sex and Grade, All Grade Schools, Second Semester, School Year 1913–14

	Number Enrolled in Grade During Term			To Leave City			Number To Enter Lower Grade			Dropped To Enter Higher Grade			To Quit School			Number Remaining at End of Term			Number of Remaining Failed			Number of Remaining Promoted on Trial			Number of Remaining Irregularly Promoted			Number of Remaining Regularly Promoted		
	B	G	T	B	G	T	B	G	T	B	G	T	B	G	T	B	G	T	B	G	T	B	G	T	B	G	T	B	G	T
1B	77	40	117	6	4	10	0	1	1	1	0	1	4	0	4	67	36	103	13	1	14	5	4	9				51	29	80
1A	82	96	178	7	6	13	0	1	1	1	3	4	0	3	3	74	86	160	3	2	5	2	4	6				69	80	149
2B	52	51	103	6	7	13							0	1	1	45	39	84	3	5	8	5	0	5				37	34	71
2A	77	69	146	7	9	16				3	2	5	2	1	3	65	57	122	3	0	3	3	3	6				59	54	113
3B	77	63	140	15	12	27	1	3	4				1	1	2	61	50	111	6	6	12	6	4	10				49	40	89
3A	90	80	170	7	18	25	1	1	2				1	3	4	81	57	138	9	4	13	6	1	7				66	52	118
4B	75	45	120	11	7	18	2	0	2	0	5	5	2	1	3	61	36	97	6	2	8	7	1	8				48	33	81
4A	74	78	152	8	12	20							0	3	3	64	58	122	9	6	15	7	6	13				48	46	94
5B	61	49	110	1	2	3	1	1	2				3	2	5	57	45	102	2	5	7	1	1	2	1	0	1	54	39	93
5A	75	57	132	2	6	8				1	0	1	5	2	7	66	48	114	6	5	11	6	3	9	1	0	1	51	42	93
6B	52	50	102	4	1	5							6	4	10	42	45	87	5	5	10	6	4	10				30	36	66
6A	34	63	97	3	0	3	1	1	2				2	1	3	29	62	91	3	9	12	3	12	15				23	41	64
7B	37	53	90	1	4	5	1	0	1				3	5	8	32	43	75	8	4	12	10	8	18				14	31	45
7A	59	64	123	4	5	9	0	1	1				6	2	8	48	57	105	9	10	19	14	7	21				25	40	65
8B	25	36	61	2	1	3	4	0	4				2	0	2	21	34	55	4	7	11	0	4	4				17	23	40
8A	27	31	58	0	2	2							2	0	2	21	28	49	3	4	7	0	1	1	0	1	1	18	22	40
	974	925	1899	84	96	180	11	9	20	6	10	16	39	29	68	834	781	1615	92	75	167	81	63	144	2	1	3	659	642	1301

SUMMARY OF TABLE XLV — 1. The per cent of withdrawals that withdrew: (a) To enter another school system was 63.4: (b) To enter a lower or a higher grade, 12.7: (c) To quit school, 23.9

2. The withdrawals to quit school represent 3.6 per cent of the total net enrollment for the year.

3. Of those remaining in school to the end of the year 10.3 per cent failed to be promoted.

4. Based on the returns for the Central building, the only absolutely accurate data of the kind compiled for Bloomington, 4½ per cent of those remaining to the end of the semester made a double promotion during the semester.

5. Counting as failures all those who withdrew before the end of the term to quit school, the per cent of failures was 13.9. Some of those who withdrew will return again and some were promoted in spite of withdrawal.

6. Failures based on number remaining to end of term:

	Per Cent		Per Cent		Per Cent		Per Cent		Per Cent		Per Cent		Per Cent		Per Cent
1B....	13.6	2B....	9.5	3B....	10.8	4B....	8.2	5B....	6.8	6B....	11.5	7B....	16	8B....	20
1A....	3.1	2A....	2.3	3A....	9.4	4A....	12.3	5A....	9.7	6A....	13.2	7A....	18.1	8A....	14.3

TABLE XLVI

Enrollment, Withdrawals, Promotions by Sex, Subject, and Grade, High School, Second Semester, School Year 1913–1914

Subject	Number Enrolled in Subject During Term			Number To Leave City			Dropped To Quit School			Number Remaining At End of Term			Number Remaining Pupils Failed			Total Failures and Dropped To Quit School			Number Remaining Pupils Conditioned			Per Cent of Failures of Those Remaining			Per Cent of Total Failures and Dropped To Quit School of Those Enrolled		
	B	G	T	B	G	T	B	G	T	B	G	T	B	G	T	B	G	T	B	G	T	B	G	T	B	G	T
English 9B	28	23	51				7	4	11	16	24	40	5	0	5	12	4	16	2	0	2	31.3	0	12.5	42.8	17.4	31.4
English 9A	22	28	50	1	1	2	6	1	7	15	27	42	3	2	5	9	3	12				20	7.4	11.9	40.9	10.7	24
English 10B	21	21	42	1	0	1	1	3	4	19	17	36	2	0	2	3	3	6				10.5	0	5.6	14.3	14.3	14.3
English 10A	25	32	57	1	0	1				24	32	56	2	1	3	2	1	3	3	1	4	8.3	3.1	5.4	8	3.1	5.3
English 11B	13	15	28							12	15	27							0	1	1						
English 11A	20	40	60	0	1	1	1	3	4	19	35	54	3	2	5	4	5	9	0	2	2	15.8	5.7	9.3	20	12.5	15
English 12B	5	9	14							5	8	13															
English 12A	7	5	12							7	15	22															
TOTAL	141	173	314	3	2	5	15	11	26	117	173	290	15	5	20	30	16	46	5	4	9	12.8	2.9	6.9	21.3	9.2	14.7
Math. 9B	19	19	38				10	0	10	9	19	28	2	1	3	12	1	13				22.2	5.2	10.7	63.2	5.3	34.2
Math. 9A	37	49	86	0	1	1	3	3	6	34	46	80	6	1	7	9	4	13				17.6	2.2	8.8	24.3	8.2	15.1
Math. 10B	23	32	55				1	1	2	22	29	51	4	4	8	4	2	6				18.2	13.8	15.7	17.4	6.3	10.9
Math. 10A	17	17	34	4	2	6				16	17	33	2	2	4	1	1	2				12.5	11.8	12.1	5.9	5.9	5.9
Math. 11B	22	21	43	0	1	1	0	1	1	19	17	36	1	1	2	4	1	5				5.3	5.9	5.6	18.2	4.8	11.6
Math. 11A	7	15	22	1	0	1				7	14	21	0	2	2	0	2	2				0	14.3	9.5	0	13.3	9.1
TOTAL	125	153	278	5	4	9	14	5	19	107	142	249	15	11	26	30	11	41				14	7.7	10.4	24	7.2	14.6
Botany 9B	7	8	15	1	0	1	3	0	3	3	8	11	1	1	2	4	1	5				33.3	12.5	18.2	57.1	12.5	33.3
Botany 9A	11	14	25				1	0	1	10	24	34	2	4	6	3	4	7				20	16.7	17.6	27.3	28.6	28
TOTAL	18	22	40	1	0	1	4	0	4	13	32	45	3	5	8	7	5	12				23.1	15.6	17.8	38.9	22.7	30
German 9B	11	14	25				5	2	7	6	12	18	2	1	3	7	3	10				33.3	8.3	16.7	63.4	21.5	40
German 9A	31	34	65	1	0	1	6	4	10	25	30	55	1	0	1	7	4	11	3	1	4	4	0	1.8	22.6	11.8	17
German 10B	21	18	39	1	0	1	1	2	3	19	16	35	3	0	3	4	2	6				15.8	0	8.6	19	11.1	15.4
German 10A	13	20	33				0	1	1	12	19	31	0	1	1	0	2	2				0	5.3	3.2	0	10	6.1
German 11B	4	6	10							4	6	10										0	0	0	0	0	0
German 11A	13	10	23				0	1	1	11	8	19	1	0	1	1	1	2	0	1	1	9	0	5.3	7.7	10	8.7
German 12B	4	10	14				0	1	1	4	9	13				0	1	1							0	10	7.1
German 12A	2	8	10							1	8	9													0	0	0
TOTAL	99	120	219	2	0	2	12	11	23	82	108	190	7	2	9	19	13	32				8.5	1.9	4.7	19.2	10.8	14.6

	Census B	Census G	Census T	En. B	En. G	En. T	Enr. B	Enr. G	Enr. T	Fail. B	Fail. G	Fail. T	Wd. B	Wd. G	Wd. T	%F B	%F G	%F T	%W B	%W G	%W T
Com. 9B	16	11	27							0	1	1	6	3	13	40	22.2	31.6	62.5	27.3	48.1
Com. 9A	20	10	30							1		1	6	4	10	6.7		4.8	30	40	33.3
Com. 10B	8	8	16										1		1				12.5		6.3
Com. 10A	7	7	14										2	2	2				20	28.6	14.3
Com. 11B	15	3	18	1	1								3	2	5	7.6	50	13.3	20	66.7	27.8
Com. 11A	11	10	21													0	0	0	0	0	0
Com. 12B	5	4	9	1		1							3	2	5	0	0	0	20	0	11.1
Com. 12A	7	2	9										2		4	0	0	0	0	0	0
TOTAL	89	55	144	0	2	2	74	46	120	6	3	9	21	11	32	8.1	6.5	7.5	23.6	20	22.2
Physical Geography	9	21	30				8	20	28	1		3	2	1	3	12.5	0	3.5	22.2	4.8	10
Hist. 9B	11	15	26				7	12	19	4	2	6	8	3	11	57.1	16.7	31.5	72.8	20	42.3
Hist. 9A	28	27	55				27	26	53	5	3	8	6	4	10	18.5	11.5	15.1	21.4	14.8	18.2
Hist. 10B	11	11	17				4	11	15	3	1	4	3	1	3	50	20	20	50	9.1	23.5
Hist. 10A	6	11	17				11	30	41	2	1	1	1	1	1	0	0	0	0	8.3	2.3
Hist. 11B	11	30	41				4	9	13		1	1		1	1	0	0	0	0	10	5.3
Hist. 11A	9	10	19				6	14	18					1	1	0	0	0	0	7.1	5.3
Hist. 12B	6	14	20	1			9	13	20	1		1	1		1	0	7.1	5	7.1		5
Hist. 12A																					
TOTAL	72	109	181	2	3	5	64	102	166	11	7	18	18	10	28	17.2	6.9	10.8	25	9.2	15.5
Latin 9B	11	14	25	1	1	2	9	12	21	3	2	5	4	2	6	33.3	16.7	23.8	36.4	14.3	24
Latin 9A	10	14	24		1		10	14	24	1	1	2	1	1	6	10	7.1	8.3	10	7.1	8.3
Latin 10B	11	23	34	1	2	3	8	20	28			3	1	1	3	0	0	0	18.2	4.4	8.8
Latin 10A	8	7	15				7	8	15		1	1	2		1	0	12.5	6.7	12.5	0	6.7
Latin 11B	8	9	17				4	6	10	1	1	2	1			12.5	5.9	5.9	12.5	0	5.9
Latin 11A	5	8	13		1		5	12	10			4		2	3	25	0	10	40	25	30.8
Latin 12B	5	12	17		2	3	9	13	17			2				0	0	0	0	0	0
Latin 12A	9	13	22				13	13	22		1	1	1		1	11.1	0	4.5	11.1	0	4.5
TOTAL	66	101	167	2	3	7	60	94	154	7	4	11	11	7	18	11.7	4.3	7.1	16.7	6.9	10.8
Physics 12B & 12A	23	35	58	0	2	2	23	33	56	1	3	4	1	5	6	4.3	9.1	7.1	4.3	14.3	10.3

TABLE XLVIa

SUMMARY OF TABLE XLVI, ENROLLMENT, FAILURES, WITHDRAWALS, SECOND SEMESTER, SCHOOL YEAR 1913–14

PER CENT OF FAILURES OF THOSE REMAINING

Grade	Group	English	Mathematics	Botany	History	Latin	Physics	German	Physical Geography	Commercial Geography
9B	Boys	31.3	22.2	33.3	33.3			33.3	40	¹12.5
9B	Girls	0	5.2	12.5	16.7			8.3	22.2	0
9B	Total	12.5	10.7	18.2	23.8			16.7	31.6	3.5
9A	Boys	20	17.6	20	10			4	6.7	
9A	Girls	7.4	2.2	16.7	7.1			0	0	
9A	Total	11.9	8.8	17.6	8.3			1.8	4.8	
10B	Boys	10.5	18.2	57.1	0			15.8	0	
10B	Girls	0	13.8	16.7	0			0	0	
10B	Total	5.6	15.7	31.5	0			8.6	0	
10A	Boys	8.3	12.5		18.5	0		0	0	
10A	Girls	3.1	11.8		11.5	12.5		5.3	0	
10A	Total	5.4	12.1		15.1	6.7		3.2	0	
11B	Boys	0	5.3		50	12.5		0		7.6
11B	Girls	0	5.9		9	0		0		50
11B	Total	0	5.6		20	5.9		0		13.3
11A	Boys	15.8	0		0	25		9		0
11A	Girls	5.7	14.3		0	0		0		0
11A	Total	9.3	9.5		0	10		5.3		0
12B	Boys	0			0	0	²4.3	0		0
12B	Girls	0			0	0	9.1	0		0
12B	Total	0			0	0	7.1	0		0
12A	Boys	0			0	11.1		0		0
12A	Girls	0			7.1	0		0		0
12A	Total	0			5	4.5		0		0

PER CENT OF FAILURES AND DROPPED TO QUIT SCHOOL TO THOSE ENROLLED

Grade	Group	English	Mathematics	Botany	History	Latin	Physics	German	Physical Geography	Commercial Geography
9B	Boys	42.8	63.2	57.1	36.4			63.4	62.5	22.2
9B	Girls	17.4	5.3	12.5	14.3			21.5	27.3	4.8
9B	Total	31.4	34.2	33.3	24			40	48.1	10
9A	Boys	40.9	24.3	27.3	10			22.6	30	
9A	Girls	10.7	8.2	28.6	7.1			11.8	40	
9A	Total	24	15.1	28	8.3			17	33.3	
10B	Boys	14.3	17.4	72.8	18.2			19	12.5	
10B	Girls	14.3	6.3	20	4.4			11.1	0	
10B	Total	14.3	10.9	42.3	8.8			15.4	6.3	
10A	Boys	8	5.9		21.4	0		0	0	
10A	Girls	3.1	5.9		14.8	12.5		10	28.6	
10A	Total	5.3	5.9		18.2	6.7		6.1	14.3	
11B	Boys	0	18.2		50	12.5		0		20
11B	Girls	0	4.8		9.1	0		0		66.7
11B	Total	0	11.6		23.5	5.9		0		27.8
11A	Boys	20	0		8.3	40		7.7		0
11A	Girls	12.5	13.3		0	25		10		0
11A	Total	15	9.1		2.3	30.8		8.7		0
12B	Boys	0			0	0	4.3	0		20
12B	Girls	0			10	0	14.3	10		0
12B	Total	0			5.3	0	10.3	7.1		11.1
12A	Boys	0			0	11.1		0		0
12A	Girls	0			7.1	0		0		0
12A	Total	0			5	4.5		0		0

¹ 9B and 9A combined in one class.   ² 12B and 12A combined.

Tables XLV and XLVI show that the great mortality occurs in the early part of the high school course. The average per cents of failures are:

	FAILURES BASED ON NUMBER REMAINING	FAILURES AND QUITTING BASED ON ENROLLMENT
9B	16.7	31.6
9A	8.9	21
10B	10.2	16.3
10A	7.1	9.4
11B	7.5	11.5
11A	5.7	11
12B	1.2	5.6
12A	1.9	1.9

A further analysis of failures and withdrawals is contained in Tables XLVII to LXV inclusive. The data for Table XLVII were compiled by P. C. Emmons, Superintentent of Schools, Kendallville, Indiana, and are based on reports for the first semester, 1913–14.

Responses were received from seven Indiana cities with population and high school enrollment as follows:

No. OF CITY	POPULATION	H. S. ENROLLMENT
1	8838	385
2	8634	324
3	10272	325
4	4891	180
5	11886	200
6	6987	179
7	8687	243

Pupils who left city are not counted enrolled.
City No. 1 is Bloomington.

In the following subjects the mortality in the Bloomington schools is evidently comparatively high: botany, first-year English, first-year Latin, Cæsar, and Virgil. It is about average in first-year German, second-year German, physics, second-year English, fourth-year English, Cicero, first-year algebra, second-year algebra, plane geometry, mediæval and modern history, and comparatively low in third-year English, solid geometry, United States history, and Civics.

The mortality would seem to be too high in beginning English, in botany, and in all of the Latin except Cicero.

TABLE XLVII

COMPARISON OF FAILURES IN SEVEN INDIANA CITIES

Numbers in first column under subject represent the various cities.

SUBJECT	ENROLLED IN SUBJECT	NUMBER DROPPED	NUMBER REMAINING	FAILURES	TOTAL FAILURES AND DROPPED	PER CENT OF FAILURES OF THOSE REMAINING	PER CENT OF TOTAL FAILURES AND DROPPED OF THOSE ENROLLED
German I							
4.......	22	1	21	5	6	23.8	27.2
3.......	31	5	76	13	18	17.1	22.2
5.......	29	1	28	4	5	14.3	17.1
1.......	79	6	73	11	17	15.0	21.5
2.......	69	7	62	6	13	9.7	17.4
7.......	44	0	44	3	3	6.8	6.8
German II							
1.......	79	6	73	11	17	15.0	21.5
2.......	24	3	21	1	4	4.8	16.7
5.......	21	0	21	1	1	5.0	5.0
7.......	25	1	24	1	2	4.0	8.0
4.......	21	0	21	0	0	0	0
3.......	26	0	26	0	0	0	0

Three schools reported third-year classes in German.

SUBJECT							
Botany:							
1.........	56	8	48	9	17	18.8	30.1
6.........	47	1	46	7	8	15.2	17
4.........	18	2	16	2	4	12.5	22.2
2.........	70	8	62	5	13	8.1	18.5
7.........	24	3	21	0	3	0	12.5
Physics:							
6.........	12	0	12	1	1	8.3	8.3
1.........	55	1	54	4	5	7.4	9.1

SCHOOLS 3, 7, 2, 5, 4 — REPORT NO FAILURES IN PHYSICS

Reports show that it is not customary to fail pupils in Domestic Science or Manual Training.

SUBJECT							
English I:							
1.........	150	21	129	19	40	14.7	26.7
4.........	57	2	55	6	8	10.9	14
5.........	44	1	43	4	5	9	11
6.........	61	3	58	5	8	8.3	13.1
2.........	113	12	101	6	18	5.9	15.9
3.........	115	0	115	2	2	1.7	1.7
7.........	69	3	66	0	3	0	4
English II:							
4.........	48	4	44	5	9	11.3	18.7
2.........	84	6	78	8	14	10.3	16.6
1.........	96	5	91	7	12	7.7	12.5
6.........	54	3	51	2	5	3.9	9.3
5.........	75	10	65	2	12	3	16
3.........	48	2	46	1	3	2.2	6.2
7.........	72	7	65	1	8	1	11.1

TABLE XLVII (*Continued*)

Subject	Enrolled in Subject	Number Dropped	Number Remaining	Failures	Total Failures and Dropped	Per Cent of Failures of those Remaining	Per Cent of Total Failures and Dropped of those Enrolled
English III:							
2.........	74	2	72	10	12	13.9	16.2
6.........	36	0	36	3	3	8.3	8.3
5.........	31	3	28	2	5	7.1	16.1
3.........	65	4	61	3	7	4.9	10.7
1.........	79	1	78	2	3	2.6	3.8
4.........	41	0	41	1	1	2.4	2.4
7.........	37	2	35	0	2	0	5.4
English IV:							
4.........	25	1	24	4	5	16.6	20
5.........	26	2	24	2	4	8.3	15.4
1.........	39	1	38	2	3	5.3	7.7
2.........	66	4	62	1	5	1.6	7.6
3.........	40	3	37	0	3	0	7.5
6.........	22	1	21	0	1	0	4.5
7.........	29	1	28	0	1	0	3.5
Latin I:							
1.........	49	3	46	9	12	19.6	24.5
3.........	56	0	56	9	9	16	16
4........	49	11	38	6	17	15.7	34.7
2.........	83	9	74	6	15	8.1	18.1
6.........	42	2	40	2	4	5	9.5
7.........	40	3	37	4	7	1.1	18
5.........	24	2	22	0	2	0	8.3
Cæsar:							
1.........	34	1	33	5	6	15.2	17.6
3.........	37	0	37	5	5	13.5	13.5
7.........	22	0	22	3	3	13.7	13.7
6.........	41	5	36	4	9	11.1	21.9
2.........	52	1	51	5	6	9.8	11.5
4.........	38	0	38	1	1	2.8	2.8
5.........	18	0	18	0	0	0	0
Cicero:							
7.........	15	1	14	1	2	7.1	13.3
4.........	15	0	15	1	1	6.7	6.7
1.........	37	1	36	2	3	5.6	8.1
		6, 2, 3, 5 — No Failures					
Virgil:							
1.........	25	1	24	1	2	4.2	8
		6, 7, 4, 2 — No Failures					
Algebra I:							
4.........	58	3	55	20	23	36.3	39.6
6.........	43	0	43	9	9	20.9	20.9
1.........	124	16	108	13	29	12	25.4
7.........	44	0	44	3	3	6.8	6.8
2.........	107	12	95	4	16	4.2	14.9
3.........	110	3	107	1	4	.9	3.6
5.........	50	5	45	0	5	0	10

TABLE XLVII (*Continued*)

Subject	Enrolled in Subject	Number Dropped	Number Remaining	Failures	Total Failure and Dropped	Per Cent of Failures of those Remaining	Per Cent of Failures and Dropped of those Enrolled
Algebra II:							
4	25	0	25	7	7	28	28
7	19	1	18	2	3	11.1	16
2	62	6	56	6	12	10.7	19.3
1	66	4	62	6	10	9.7	15.2
6	48	0	48	3	3	6.3	6.3
3	19	0	19	0	0	0	0
Pl. Geom.:							
4	46	2	44	9	11	20.4	23.9
7	35	5	30	5	10	16.7	28
1	84	5	79	9	14	11.4	16.7
2	78	7	71	6	13	8.4	16.7
3	97	0	97	3	3	3	3
6	25	0	25	6	6	2.4	2.4
5	34	2	32	0	2	0	6
Sol. Geom.:							
5	18	0	18	2	2	11.1	11.1
7	11	0	11	1	1	9.9	9.9
6	31	3	28	2	5	9.7	16.1
1	8	0	8	0	0	0	0
3	20	1	19	0	1	0	5
Gr. History:							
4	28	3	25	3	6	12	21.4
6	34	0	34	3	3	8.8	8.8
2	70	6	64	4	10	6.2	14.3
5	17	0	17	1	1	6	6
3	78	3	75	2	5	2.6	6.4
7	58	0	58	0	0	0	0
Rom. History:							
6	22	1	21	2	3	9.5	13.6
7	34	0	34	0	0	0	0
4	20	2	18	0	2	0	10
2	45	2	43	0	2	0	4.4
Med. and Mod. History:							
1	53	0	53	2	2	3.8	3.8
6	29	0	29	1	1	3.5	3.5
2	25	4	21	0	4	0	16
4	13	1	12	0	1	0	7.1
7	20	1	19	0	1	0	5
5	13	0	13	0	0	0	0
U. S. History and Civics:							
6	34	0	34	4	4	11.6	11.6
4	17	0	17	1	1	5.8	5.8
2	67	5	62	3	8	4.8	11.9
1	38	1	37	1	2	2.4	5.3
5	23	1	22	0	1	0	4.3
3	35	1	34	0	1	0	2.8

In the following tables, Tables XLVIII and XLIX, promotions are worked out on four bases:

Basis No. 1. Percentage that number of promotions plus number of conditions is of number of pupils remaining until close of the semester.

Basis No. 2. Percentage that number of promotions plus number of conditions is of the number of pupils remaining to end of semester plus the number that withdrew during the semester to quit school.

Basis No. 3. Percentage that the number of promotions is of the number of pupils remaining until close of the semester.

Basis No. 4. Percentage that the number of promotions is of the number of pupils remaining to end of semester plus those who withdrew to quit school.

TABLE XLVIII

PERCENTAGE OF PROMOTIONS IN THE GRADE SCHOOLS AT THE CLOSE OF THE FIRST SEMESTER, 1914–15. (ALL CHILDREN IN THE SYSTEM INCLUDED)

GRADE	PROMOTIONS ON BASIS No. 1	PROMOTIONS ON BASIS No. 2	PROMOTIONS ON BASIS No. 3	PROMOTIONS ON BASIS No. 4
1B	82.5	80.2	79.0	76.7
1A	90.4	90.4	89.4	89.4
2B	95.3	95.3	93.6	93.6
2A	97.1	97.1	94.3	94.3
3B	89.6	89.6	84.3	84.3
3A	96.7	96.7	93.7	93.7
4B	88.9	88.9	76.8	76.8
4A	88.0	88.0	86.0	86.0
5B	93.8	91.9	86.2	85.7
5A	91.7	89.0	89.7	89.0
6B	88.3	85.0	68.9	66.3
6A	88.8	84.5	53.8	51.2
7B	90.4	85.2	53.0	50.0
7A	88.9	82.1	58.3	53.8
8B	84.3	80.5	65.1	62.1
8A	97.8	95.7	97.8	95.7
9B	88.2	76.7	87.0	75.6
9A	88.0	76.1	80.1	69.7
10B	96.1	87.0	89.8	81.2
10A	86.8	80.7	78.7	73.1
11B	94.2	90.6	86.4	83.1
11A	92.7	87.7	88.6	83.8
12B	98.0	92.3	95.4	90.0
12A	95.5	91.3	93.2	89.1

Results in Table XLVIII prove the necessity of clearly stating the basis upon which failures or promotions are figured. Without such a statement comparisons are valueless.

TABLE XLIX

PERCENTAGE OF PROMOTIONS BY SUBJECTS IN THE BLOOMINGTON HIGH SCHOOL
AT THE CLOSE OF THE FIRST SEMESTER, 1914–15

GRADE	PROMOTIONS ON BASIS No. 1	PROMOTIONS ON BASIS No. 2	PROMOTIONS ON BASIS No. 3	PROMOTIONS ON BASIS No. 4
English	90.7	82.2	84.3	76.4
Latin	91.5	87.8	88.0	84.5
German	86.7	79.6	84.7	77.8
Mathematics	87.5	79.6	80.6	73.3
History	92.2	85.2	86.3	79.7
Commercial	92.5	80.4	88.7	77.1
Physical Geography	94.1	84.2	94.1	84.2
Physics	100.0	95.5	98.4	94.0
Botany	86.4	76.0	77.3	68.0

TABLE L

WITHDRAWALS FROM HIGH SCHOOL BY SEX AND NUMBER OF CREDITS AT
TIME OF WITHDRAWAL

The number of credits required to graduate is 32. The period covered began with the second semester, 1903–04, and closed with the second semester, 1914.

NUMBER OF CREDITS AT TIME OF WITHDRAWAL	BOYS	GIRLS	TOTAL	PER CENT OF TOTAL WITHDRAWALS
0	1	4	5	1.0
1	14	4	18	3.6
2	10	12	22	4.5
3	19	12	31	6.3
4	27	28	55	11.1
5	12	13	25	5.1
6	9	16	25	5.1
7	14	16	30	6.1
8	17	29	46	9.3
9	6	14	20	4.0
10	5	11	16	3.2
11	7	9	16	3.2
12	8	12	20	4.0
13	5	8	13	2.6
14	9	10	19	3.8
15	6	10	16	3.2
16	10	11	21	4.2
17	9	4	13	2.6
18	1	8	9	1.8
19	5	6	11	2.2
20	1	6	7	1.4
21	4	3	7	1.4
22	7	6	13	2.6
23	0	2	2	.4
24	5	6	11	2.2
25	2	1	3	.6
26	1	2	3	.6
27	2	3	5	1.0
28	4	0	4	.8
29	0	2	2	.4
30	2	3	5	1.0
31	1	0	1	.2
Total	223	271	494	99.5

TABLE LI — Number Withdrawing as a Result of Removal from City
(Based on Table L)

Number of Credits at Time of Withdrawal	Boys	Girls	Number of Credits at Time of Withdrawal	Boys	Girls
0	..	..	7	2	1
1	..	..	8	1	5
2	..	..	9	..	1
3	..	..	10	..	6
4	4	2	11	1	2
5	..	..	12	1	..
6	1	..	13	1	..

TABLE LII — Withdrawals from High School According to Age Since
the Year 1904–05

In many cases age records were not available.

Age at Time of Withdrawal	Boys	Girls	Total
14	3	6	9
15	18	15	33
16	25	28	53
17	44	48	92
18	25	27	52
19	16	27	43
20	11	13	24
21	1	1	2
22	4	1	5
23	1	1	2
24	1	0	1
Total	149	167	316

TABLE LIII — Withdrawals from Bloomington High School by
Semesters. All Withdrawals for any Cause Whatever

Year	Semester	Withdrawals in Semester	Withdrawals in Year
1903–1904	First	3	
	Second	9	12
1904–1905	First	10	
	Second	23	33
1905–1906	First	12	
	Second	37	49
1906–1907	First	10	
	Second	28	38
1907–1908	First	17	
	Second	17	34
1908–1909	First	18	
	Second	29	47
1909–1910	First	22	
	Second	34	56
1910–1911	First	18	
	Second	29	47
1911–1912	First	15	
	Second	42	57
1912–1913	First	23	
	Second	36	59
1913–1914	First	12	
	Second	39	51

Of the total number of withdrawals from high school the largest per cent, 11.1, withdrew with only four credits completed. The second largest per cent, 9.3, withdrew with only eight credits completed; 6.3 per cent withdrew with three credits; 6.1 per cent with seven credits; 5.1 per cent with five credits; 5.1 per cent with six credits. Comparatively few withdrew after the completion of sixteen credits or the equivalent of two complete years of school work.   52.1 per cent withdrew before completing more than eight credits or the equivalent of the first year's work.   28.2 per cent more withdrew before completing more than the equivalent of two complete-years of work.   14.6 per cent more withdrew before completing more than three years of work.   4.6 per cent more withdrew before completing the full four years' course.

As a result of the discovery of the above condition arrangements have been made to devote thirty minutes each day the first thing after school begins in the morning to individual consultation.   Each teacher is free at that period to give help to those that seek her help or to those that she thinks need her help.

An additional forty-five minute period each day is devoted by the teacher appointed as adviser to the girls in the high school, in an effort to find out and supply the needs of the girls particularly in the first and second years.   It is hoped that these provisions may have some effect in reducing the mortality in the early period of the high school course.

Of all the withdrawals from high school during the ten-year period from 1903–04, 21.6 per cent were doing less than passing work in one or more subjects; 78.4 per cent were doing passing work in all subjects at the time of withdrawal.   Of the boys that withdrew, 27.4 per cent were doing less than passing work in one or more subjects, while 72.6 per cent were doing passing work in all subjects. Of the girls that withdrew 17.1 per cent were doing less than passing work at the time of withdrawal, while 82.9 per cent were doing passing work in all subjects.

Causes of Children Leaving School without Graduation and Their Employment After Leaving

A study by Belvia Cuzzort, a graduate student of Indiana University

The study included 187 pupils, the number whose homes were finally located in Bloomington and concerning whom information was received either from the pupils themselves or from their parents.

These 187 were all that could be located out of over 500 who had dropped out of the Bloomington schools during the years 1906 and 1907 to 1910–11, inclusive, and who had withdrawn from the common school after reaching the fifth grade, but before graduation, or had withdrawn from high school before graduation. These 187 pupils were classified according to age, sex, and progress in school at the time of withdrawal.

Table LIV is a summary of the classification as to sex, grade, and age:

TABLE LIV

SEX

SCHOOL	GIRLS	BOYS
Common School	40	61
High School	43	43
Common School and High School	83	104

GRADE DISTRIBUTION

GRADE	GIRLS	BOYS	TOTAL	GRADE	GIRLS	BOYS	TOTAL
5	9	7	16	9	18	16	34
6	8	17	25	10	16	17	33
7	13	21	34	11	8	6	14
8	10	16	26	12	1	4	5

AGE

AGE	COMMON SCHOOL			HIGH SCHOOL			COMMON SCHOOL AND HIGH SCHOOL		
	GIRLS	TOTAL	BOYS	GIRLS	TOTAL	BOYS	GIRLS	TOTAL	BOYS
12......	3	4	1	0	0	0	3	4	1
13......	6	13	7	0	0	0	6	13	7
14......	13	31	18	1	6	5	14	37	23
15......	10	24	14	7	9	2	17	33	16
16......	4	19	15	10	23	13	14	42	28
17......	3	5	2	12	21	9	15	26	11
18......	0	2	2	7	13	6	7	15	8
19......	0	0	0	3	8	5	3	8	5
20......	0	0	0	1	3	2	1	3	2

The following table shows the relation between withdrawal from school and the school training of the parents and should be read as follows: Of those pupils who withdrew from school in the fifth grade there were 14 mothers, 21.42 per cent of whom left school after completing the common school and 78.6 per cent before completing the common school course.

TABLE LV

School Training of Parents

Grade of Pupils at Time of Leaving School	Total Cases of Parents	COMMON SCHOOL TRAINING	
		Per Cent Completing the Course	Per Cent not Completing the Course
5..............	Mother 14	21.42	78.6
	Father 14	14.3	85.7
	Both 14	7	64
6.............	Mother 23	13	87
	Father 21	9.5	90.5
	Both 21	4.8	76
7.............	Mother 32	31	68.8
	Father 31	22.9	87.1
	Both 31	19	48.4
8.............	Mother 23	30.4	69.6
	Father 22	13.6	83.4
	Both 22	13.6	68
Totals.......	Mother 92	25	75
	Father 88	17	83
	Both 88	12.5	62.5
9.............	Mother 32	47.5	32.5
	Father 34	41	38.9
	Both 32	37.5	47.5
10............	Mother 32	61.2	38.8
	Father 32	59	40.6
	Both 32	50	28
11............	Mother 13	61.5	38.5
	Father 13	54	46
	Both 13	46	30.8
12............	Mother 5	60	40
	Father 5	40	60
	Both 5	40	36.4
Totals.......	Mother 82	56	46.9
	Father 84	52.4	47.6
	Both 82	43.9	35.4
Final Totals.......	Mother 174	39.7	60.4
	Father 172	24	65.7
	Both 170	27.3	48.9

Seven and five-tenths per cent of the mothers and 9.3 per cent of the fathers had some school training beyond the common school.

Grade of Pupils at Time of Leaving School	Total Cases of Parents	HIGH SCHOOL		COLLEGE TRAINING	
		Per Cent Completing the Course	Per Cent In H. S. but not Graduating	Per Cent Completing the Course	Per Cent In College but not Graduating
5......	Mother 14				
	Father 14				
	Both 14				
6.......	Mother 23				
	Father 21				
	Both 21				

TABLE LV (*Continued*)

7.......	Mother	32	3.12			
	Father	31	3.12		3.12	
	Both	31	3.03			
8.......	Mother	23	4.35	13		
	Father	22				
	Both	22				
TOTALS.	Mother	92	2.06	3.1		
	Father	88	1.13		1.13	
	Both	88	1.11			
9.......	Mother	32		6.3		3.12
	Father	34		8.8		
	Both	32				
10.......	Mother	32		9.4		3.12
	Father	32		12.5	3.12	3.12
	Both	32				
11.......	Mother	13		7.8		
	Father	13		3.1		7.8
	Both	13				
12.......	Mother	5				20
	Father	5				
	Both	5				
TOTALS.	Mother	82		7.3		3.7
	Father	84		13.1	1.19	2.4
	Both	82				
FINAL TOTALS.	Mother	174	1.15	5.18		1.72
	Father	172	.58	6.4	1.16	1.16
	Both	170	.58	.58		

SUMMARY OF TABLE LV

1. Whatever the degree of school advancement of the pupil leaving school, a greater per cent of mothers have completed the common-school course than of fathers, i.e., 40 per cent of the mothers and 34 per cent of the fathers have completed the common-school course.

2. If the pupils continue in school until the high school is reached, dropping out during the high-school course, 56 per cent of the mothers and 52 per cent of the fathers have completed the common-school course. In other words, twice as many mothers and three times as many fathers have completed a common-school course as when the pupils drop out of school in the grades, suggesting that the school training of the father is more influential than that of the mother.

3. Thirty and four-tenths per cent of the mothers and 13.64 per cent of the fathers completed the common-school course when pupils dropped out of school from Grade 8, and 47.5 per cent of the mothers and 41.4 per cent of the fathers completed the common-school course where the pupils dropped out of school from the high school. This is suggestive of the influence of the school training of the parents on the length of time which the pupil remains in high school.

4. Only 7.5 per cent of the mothers and 9.3 per cent of the fathers had some training beyond the common schools. Most of this school training consisted in partially completing a high-school course.

It therefore appears that the school training of the parent, especially the school training of the father, is important in causing the pupil to withdraw from school. As more of the parents have completed the common-school course there is a tendency for the pupils to be higher advanced in the high-school course at the time of withdrawal. It also happens that few parents whose children withdraw from school without graduation have any school training beyond the common schools. This is especially true where pupils withdrew during the common-school course.

The occupation of the father as a factor in the withdrawal of pupils from school is indicated in Table LVI. The table shows three classes: (1) those who had a regular vocation, including business owner, farmer, and professional man; (2) those who had regular employment, including both the skilled and unskilled laborer; (3) those who had irregular employment, i.e., those who worked at job work and were not fortunate enough to find regular employment.

TABLE LVI

OCCUPATION OF FATHER AND SEX AND AGE OF ELIMINATION OF CHILDREN

AGE	CASES		REGULAR VOCATION	REGULAR EMPLOYMENT	IRREGULAR EMPLOYMENT
12..........	Girls	1			100
	Boys				
	Both				
13..........	Girls	2			100
	Boys	5	40	40	20
	Both	7	28.55	28.55	42.90
14..........	Girls	8	25	37.5	37.5
	Boys	5	26.66	13.34	66
	Both	13	26.09	21.74	52.17
15..........	Girls	12	16.67	50.00	33.33
	Boys	10	10	70.00	20.00
	Both	22	13.64	59.09	27.27
16..........	Girls	9	44.44	14.11	44.44
	Boys	27	29.63	22.22	48.15
	Both	36	33.33	19.44	47.22
17..........	Girls	15	26.67	53.33	20.00
	Boys	5	80.00	0	20
	Both	20	40	40	20
18..........	Girls	6	50	33.33	16.67
	Boys	7	42.86	28.57	28.57
	Both	13	46.54	30.77	22.69
19..........	Girls	5	60	40	0
	Boys	2	100	0	0
	Both	7	71.43	28.57	0
20..........	Girls	1	100	0	0
	Boys	2	100	0	0
	Both	3	100	0	0
TOTAL......	Girls	59	32.2	40.68	27.12
	Boys	63	35.66	26.03	38.36
	Both	122	54.04	52.58	33.38

Table LVI should be interpreted as follows: Of the fathers of the 8 girls who withdrew from school at the age of fourteen 25 per cent had a regular vocation, 37.5 per cent had regular employment and 37.5 had irregular employment.

This table gives the per cent of fathers in each group of occupation for the different ages of withdrawal. It is evident that there is a rather definite correlation between the regular vocation of the fathers and continuation in school. That is to say, a greater per cent of the fathers of pupils who remain in school until they are sixteen years or more of age have regular vocations. There is no sex differences in regard to the correlation of the father's occupation and the age of the pupil at the time of withdrawal from school. On the whole, the table shows that more of the fathers have either regular or irregular employment than have regular vocations, if the pupils withdraw before the sixteenth year, and that a greater per cent of the fathers have regular vocations if the pupil remains in school until he is sixteen years old or more.

TABLE LVII

EFFECT OF RETARDATION ON WITHDRAWAL

The ages here considered as normal are 6 and 7 for first grade, 7 and 8 for second, etc.

TOTAL NUMBER OF NORMALS, ACCELERATES, AND RETARDS BY YEARS

		COMMON SCHOOL	HIGH SCHOOL	COMMON AND HIGH SCHOOL
Normals.......	Girls........	1	6	7
	Boys........	1	5	6
	Both........	2	11	13
Accelerates....	Girls........	0		0
	Boys........	1		1
	Both........	1		1
Retards.......	Girls........	38	35	73
	Boys........	57	37	94
	Total........	95	72	167
Totals......	Girls........	39	41	80
	Boys........	59	42	101
	Both........	98	83	181

PER CENT OF NORMALS, ACCELERATES, AND RETARDS BY YEARS

		COMMON SCHOOL	HIGH SCHOOL	COMMON AND HIGH SCHOOL
Normals......	Girls........	2.56	14.64	8.75
	Boys........	1.695	11.9	5.94
	Both........	2.04	13.2	7.17
Accelerates....	Girls........			
	Boys........	1.695		.99
	Both........	1.02		.552
Retards.......	Girls........	97.44	85.36	91.25
	Boys........	96.61	88.1	93.07
	Both........	96.94	86.8	92.28

Summary tables for total number of normals, accelerates, and retards by years show that 91.25 per cent of the girls and 93.07 per cent of the boys were retarded. The retardation for the pupils withdrawing from the common school is 10 per cent greater than for the pupils withdrawing from the high school.

Following is a comparison of retardation of withdrawals with retardation of all pupils in the system.

CENTRAL TENDENCY OF RETARDATION OF 101 PUPILS WITHDRAWING AND OF 3067 RECORDS OF THE PUPILS IN THE SYSTEM

		MEDIAN	MEAN VARIATION	MODE
101 pupils withdrawing.	Girls.....	2.375	.956	12 retarded 3 years
(Grades 5 to 8 inclusive)	Boys.....	3	1.0	16 retarded 4 years
	Both.....	2.7	1.43	26 retarded 4 years
3067 records of the sys-	Girls.....,	1.2	.91	410 retarded 1 year
tem..............	Boys.....	1.34	.96	381 retarded 1 year
(Grades 5 to 8 inclusive)	Both.....	1.26	.95	791 retarded 1 year

The proportion of retardation for the group that withdrew is nearly twice as great as for the system as a whole: 64 per cent of the 101 pupils were retarded three years or more as against 28.8 per cent of the pupils for the system taken as a whole. This means that if a pupil is retarded three years or more, the chances for his withdrawal are two and one-eighth times as great as the chances for the average pupil in the school. These tables also indicate that pupils retarded three years or more do not enter the high school. One year of retardation does not seem to be very influential in causing pupils to withdraw from school.

TABLE LVIII

TABLE SHOWING THE PER CENT OF PUPILS LEAVING SCHOOL FROM FOUR CAUSES, 178 CASES

CAUSES OF WITHDRAWAL	PER CENT OF PUPILS WITHDRAWING	
	GIRLS	BOYS
Did not like school.......................	30.5	34
Ill health................................	36	18
Desire to become self-supporting............	10.3	23
Need for helping the family................	8	18.84
Per cent of total number leaving from one or more of these causes.....................	91.82	73.5

TABLE LIX

Occupation of Boys During the First and Second Years after Leaving School

Grade	Cases	Per Cent Learning a Trade	Per Cent in Occupations which Lead Directly to Skilled Labor	Per Cent in Occupations which might Lead to Skilled Labor but in these Instances no such Provision is made	Per Cent Doing Common Labor	Per Cent Doing Odd Jobs or Un-employed	Per Cent Unclassified
5......	7	Yr. 1 14.3			71.3	14.3	
	7	Yr. 2 14.3			57	24.6	
6.....	17	Yr. 1	11.8	29.4	35.3	23.6	
	17	Yr. 2	23.6	23.6	41.3	11.8	
7......	21	Yr. 1	4.8	24	57	14.3	
	19	Yr. 2 5.3	10.5	30.5	47.3	5.3	
8......	16	Yr. 1 12.5	18.75	12.5	43.75	12.5	
	15	Yr. 2 13.3	46.6		33.3	6.7	
Average for four grades..	61	Yr. 1 4.92	9.84	19.7	49.3	16.4	
	58	Yr. 2 6.9	22	17	42.6	10.4	
9......		Yr. 1 12.5		43.75	37.5		6.25
		Yr. 2 18.75	12.5	31.25	31.25		6.25
10.....		Yr. 1 14.3	21.4	7.1	43	7.1	7.1
		Yr. 2 23	44	7.7		7.7	14.4
11......		Yr 1 20		40	40		
		Yr. 2 20			40		40
12......		Yr. 1 25		50		25	
		Yr. 2 25		50	25		
Average for High School..		Yr. 1 15.4	7.7	30.8	36	5.1	5.1
		Yr. 2 21	21	21	21	2.6	13

Table LIX should read as follows: of the 19 cases of boys who withdrew from school in the seventh grade 5.3 per cent during their second year out of school were learning a trade, 10.5 per cent were in occupations which led directly to skilled labor, etc.

Summary of Table LIX

1. A greater per cent of the boys were employed in doing common labor than in any other kind of work. This is true whether the pupils withdrew from the common school or the high school. The per cent doing common labor is less in the second year after withdrawal than in the first.

2. Three times as many boys are employed in learning a trade if they withdrew from the high school than if they withdrew before completing the common-school course. From this table it appears that 83 per cent of the boys leaving the common school and 72 per cent of the boys leaving high school did work that offered little opportunity for promotion. In the second year after withdrawal the number thus employed was 70 per cent in case of withdrawal from grades and 44.6 per cent in case of withdrawal from high school. That indicates that there is an advantage so far as the kind of employment is concerned in completing the common school and doing high-school work.

Of the boys 81.1 per cent who withdrew from the common school received $5 or less per week during the first year after leaving school, and 58.2 per cent of the boys received this amount during the second year. In case of withdrawal from the high school $60.9 per cent of the boys received $5 or less per week during the first year after withdrawal, and 38 per cent received this amount in the second year after leaving. This would indicate that there is a relationship between the degree of school advancement and the salary received after leaving school.

TABLE LX

OCCUPATION OF GIRLS DURING THE FIRST AND SECOND YEARS AFTER LEAVING SCHOOL

GRADES	CASES		PER CENT NOT EMPLOYED OTHER THAN IN THE HOME	PER CENT DOING DOMESTIC WORK	PER CENT CLERKING	PER CENT WORKING IN FACTORY	PER CENT DOING OFFICE WORK	PER CENT WORKING IN TELEPHONE EXCHANGE	PER CENT SEWING OR LEARNING MILLINERY TRADE
5....	7	Yr. 1	28.5	28.5		28.5			14.3
	6	Yr. 2	16.6			50			33.33
6....	7	Yr. 1	42.4			28.5		14.3	14.3
	7	Yr. 2	42.4	14.3		28.5			14.3
7....	13	Yr. 1	77		7.7	7.7		7.7	
	11	Yr. 2	73.6	18				9	
8....	10	Yr. 1	10	30	20		20	10	10
	10	Yr. 2	10	10	20	20	20	10	10
Average for four grades..	37	Yr. 1	43.2	13.5	8	13.5	5.4	8	8
	34	Yr. 2	40	11.9	6	20.6	6	6	3
9.....	18	Yr. 1	66.6		5.55		22.22	5.55	
	15	Yr. 2	53.33		20		6.7	13.33	6.7
10.....	12	Yr. 1	58.33	8.33	16.67		8.33	8.33	
	12	Yr. 2	58.33		16.67		16.67		8.33
11.....	8	Yr. 1	37.5		37.5		12.5		12.5
	6	Yr. 2	33.33		50		16.67		
12.....	1	Yr. 1			100				
	0	Yr. 2							
Average for H. S.	39	Yr. 1	51.3	2.56	19		16.2	5.13	
	33	Yr. 2	51.4		24		12	9	3

Four of the girls doing office work were taking business courses at the same time.

SUMMARY OF TABLE LX

1. Forty-three and two-tenths per cent of the girls leaving the grades and 51.4 per cent leaving the high school were not employed other than in the home during the first year after leaving. These per cents are about the same for the second year after withdrawal.

2. No girls leaving the high school did work in a factory, while 13.5 per cent of the girls leaving the grades worked in a factory the first year after leaving and 20.6 per cent the second year.

3. A majority of the girls withdrawing from the high school were clerks or office girls in case they were employed outside the home.

Comparison of the salaries of girls with the degree of advancement in the school course shows that a large per cent of the girls received no salary, i.e., they were not employed for wages, and that if receiving a salary there seemed to be a slight advantage so far as weekly salary is concerned if the withdrawal took place from the high school.

For this table it would appear that for the girls who work outside the home those farther advanced in the school course get the more desirable positions.

REPEATERS

One method of determining the value to a child of repetition of school work is to work out a comparison between the grade on repetition and the grade made in the succeeding term's work. Of the eighty-seven graduates from the Bloomington high school forming the basis of Mr. Bruner's study [1] already referred to, twenty-five cases were found among nineteen pupils of repetition of a term's work from the fourth grade to the eighth inclusive. These twenty-five cases had done all of their school work in the Bloomington system. The following table gives the results of a study of these twenty-five cases. In the first column is given the number identifying the pupil whose record is studied. The numbers marked 1^1, 4^1 indicate that the pupil failed a second time in his school course. The first group of columns, marked 1, 2, 3, gives the averages of three successive terms' work, column 1 representing the failing grade; 2, the repeating grade; and 3, the grade made in the first term in advance. The second group of three columns gives the grades of the particular subjects in which the pupils failed, the order of the grades being the same as for the preceding columns.

For example, pupil 19 made an average of 69 in all of his work the first time the work was taken, 85 when work was repeated, and 85 for the succeeding term's work. In reading, the grades were 63 for the first time over the work, 87 when work was repeated, and 87 for the succeeding term's work. In grammar the grades were 54 for the first time over the work, 81 when work was repeated, and 81 for the succeeding term's work.

[1] See also pages 219 and 239.

TABLE LXI — Total Averages and Subject Averages

Number of Pupils	1	2	3	1	2	3
19	69	85	85	63	87	87
				61	80	80
				67	85	85
				54	81	81
8	72	87	76	60	88	73
				71	83	73
				66	88	x
1¹	73	80	H. S. 82	73	77	83
				73	83	83
4¹	75	81	H. S. 80	73	83	83
				73	78	78
				73	83	
8¹	76	88	H. S. 79	73	93	78
				73	78	78
				73	93	83
				73	88	x
14	76	84	H. S. 95	73	83	98
				73	93	98
				73	83	x
18	76	86	83	73	88	88
15¹	78	81	85	73	78	83
				73	88	93
11	80	87	89	73	83	83
				83	88	88
15	80	87	87	69	84	80
17	80	88	85	61	85	77
				68	83	80
3	81	90	86	71	89	87
4	81	84	75	73	83	73
5	81	86	85	73	83	78
				73	83	78
7	81	86	83	73	83	83
				73	83	84
10	81	83	87	73	78	78
13	81	87	90	73	88	93
				73	83	88
16	81	88	88	76	89	82
				76	89	83
3¹	82	80	85	77	78	83
2¹	82	83	81	77	88	78
				77	88	80
12	83	84	89	73	78	93
2	83	85	82	73	83	77
				73	83	77
1	83	90	81	71	88	78
6	83	84	83	78	79	83
9	85	86	82	78	83	88
				73	83	78
				78	78	78

TABLE LXI (*Continued*)

FIRST TERM	DEPORTMENT SECOND TERM	THIRD TERM	GRADE AT TIME OF FAILURE	SUBJECTS FAILED IN	AGE AT TIME OF FAILURE
75......	85	80	5A	Reading Arithmetic Geography Grammar	11
93.....	93	93	8B	Arithmetic History Physiology	13
78.....	78	88	8	Arithmetic Grammar	16
88.....	88	98	8A	Reading Arithmetic History	14
93.....	93		8A	Reading Arithmetic Grammar History	14
93.....	93	93	8A	Arithmetic Grammar History	15
83.....	83	88	8B	History	14
88.....	88	83	8B	Grammar History	
88.....	88		7A	Arithmetic History	13
87.....	93	93	7B	Arithmetic	
88.....	93	93	6A	Arithmetic Geography	13
91.....	89	88	4th yr.	Arithmetic	11
98.....	98	93	8B	History	13
88.....	88	93	7A	History Physiology	13
73.....	88	83	8B	Arithmetic History	12
88.....	88		7A	Arithmetic	13
88.....	88	88	8B	Grammar History	13
84.....	87	88	6A	Geography Arithmetic	
88.....	88	83	8B	History	16
78.....	78	88	7B	Arithmetic History	12
93.....	93	88	7A	History	13
78.....	78	78	6A	Arithmetic History	11
90.....	91	88	4th yr.	Arithmetic	10
93.....	93	88	6A	Arithmetic	11
93.....	93	93	7A	Writing Arithmetic History	13

SUMMARY OF TABLE LXI

AVERAGE SCHOLARSHIP IN ALL SUBJECTS			AVERAGE SCHOLARSHIP IN SUBJECTS FAILED IN			DEPORTMENT		
FAILING TERM	REPEATING TERM	SUCCEEDING TERM	FAILING TERM	REPEATING TERM	SUCCEEDING TERM	FAILING TERM	REPEATING TERM	SUCCEEDING TERM
79	85	84	72	84	83	87	89	89

Considering average scholarship in all subjects, the average gain per cent due to repeating a term's work over the average scholarship made the first term is 7.6. During the succeeding term not all of the gain is held but the grade is still 6.3 per cent higher. When just-failing grades are considered the difference is still greater. The per cent gained the second term over the first is 16.6, dropping in the third term to 15.3.

Not only was there improvement in the subjects in which failures were made but improvement was made in subjects that were being repeated but in which passing grades were made the first time the work was taken.

The average scholarship gain, all subjects considered, due to gain in subjects that pupils had failed in the first time was 3.3 per cent. The average gain due to gain in all subjects was 7.6 per cent, thus clearly showing that the subjects in which the pupils passed the first time were done better when they were repeated. Considering individual cases the average scholarship was improved in nineteen cases, remained the same in one case, and became worse in five cases. The grades for the failing subjects were improved in forty-one cases, remained the same in three cases, and went lower in none.

The following tables show distribution of school years, subjects and ages according to their toll of failures:

TABLE LXII

FREQUENCY TABLE SHOWING YEARS IN WHICH FAILURES WERE MADE AND THE SUBJECTS IN WHICH THE FAILURES OCCURRED

YEAR OF SCHOOL	CASES OF FAILURE	FAILING SUBJECTS	FREQUENCY OF FAILURES
4.............	2	Writing	1
5.............	1	Physiology	2
6.............	4	Reading	3
7.............	7	Geography	3
8.............	11	Grammar	6
		History	16
		Arithmetic	18

TABLE LXIII

NUMBER OF PUPILS FAILING IN VARIOUS SUBJECTS

ONE SUBJECT	TWO SUBJECTS	THREE SUBJECTS	FOUR SUBJECTS
9	9	5	2

TABLE LXIV — AGE-FREQUENCY TABLE FOR PUPILS WHO FAILED

AGE	NUMBER OF PUPILS	AGE	NUMBER OF PUPILS
10	1	14	3
11	4	15	1
12	2	16	2
13	9		

The above tables show that the number of failures occurred most in the eighth grade and least in the fifth.

The subject that caused the most failures was arithmetic, with history running a close second. Eighteen failures occurred in arithmetic and sixteen in history.

Of the twenty-five failures, nine failed in one subject, nine in two subjects, five in three subjects, and two in four subjects.

The age-frequency table shows that of twenty-two pupils nine were thirteen years old, the others ranging from ten to sixteen.

A further study of these failing pupils shows that fourteen of them failed a second time before they completed the high-school course and twenty-six did not fail any more.

A more recent study of the effect of repetition of work covers all cases of repetition in all grades from the first to the eighth inclusive for the second semester of the school year 1913–14. The table setting forth the results of this study follows:

TABLE LXV — COMPARISON OF QUALITY OF WORK DONE BY REPEATERS DURING SECOND TIME WORK WAS TAKEN WITH THE QUALITY OF WORK DONE THE FIRST TIME THE WORK WAS TAKEN. ALL WHITE CHILDREN IN FIRST EIGHT GRADES

ALL SUBJECTS

GRADE	NUMBER OF RE-PEATERS SECOND SEMESTER SCHOOL YEAR 1913–14	NUMBER OF RE-PEATERS DOING BETTER WORK SECOND TIME THAN FIRST TIME WORK WAS TAKEN	NUMBER OF RE-PEATERS DOING SAME QUALITY OF WORK SECOND TIME AS FIRST TIME WORK WAS TAKEN	NUMBER OF RE-PEATERS DOING POORER WORK SECOND TIME THAN FIRST TIME WORK WAS TAKEN
1B........	111	82	24	5
1A........	23	16	7	
2B........	33	24	8	1
2A........	13	7	5	1
3B........	65	29	31	5
3A........	44	32	11	1
4B........	124	77	33	14
4A........	88	53	29	6
5B........	45	20	19	6
5A........	46	34	8	4
6B........	42	26	13	3
6A........	14	5	6	3
7B........	36	20	14	2
7A........	45	28	16	1
8B........	32	16	15	1
8A........	21	12	7	2
TOTAL......	782	481	246	55
Per Cent....	100	61.5	31.4	7

TABLE LXVI — COMPARISON OF QUALITY OF WORK DONE BY REPEATERS DUR-
ING THE SECOND TIME WORK WAS TAKEN WITH THE QUALITY OF WORK DONE
THE FIRST TIME THE WORK WAS TAKEN. ALL PUPILS IN FIRST EIGHT GRADES
OF SCHOOL FOR WHITE CHILDREN

SUBJECT — SPELLING

GRADE	NUMBER OF RE-PEATERS SECOND SEMESTER SCHOOL YEAR 1913–14	NUMBER OF RE-PEATERS DOING BETTER WORK SECOND TIME than FIRST TIME WORK WAS TAKEN	NUMBER OF RE-PEATERS DOING SAME QUALITY OF WORK SECOND TIME AS FIRST TIME WORK WAS TAKEN	NUMBER OF RE-PEATERS DOING POORER WORK SECOND TIME than FIRST TIME WORK WAS TAKEN
1B	30	25	4	1
1A	7	5	2	
2B	9	8	1	
2A	4	2	2	
3B	12	7	4	1
3A	8	7	1	
4B	18	11	5	2
4A	13	7	5	1
5B	6	2	3	1
5A	7	5	2	
6B	6	5	1	
6A	2	1	1	
7B	5	1	4	
7A	8	5	3	
8B	6	1	5	
8A	4	0	4	
TOTAL	145	92	47	6
Per Cent	100	63.4	32.4	4.1

TABLE LXVII — COMPARISON OF QUALITY OF WORK DONE BY REPEATERS
DURING SECOND TIME WORK WAS TAKEN WITH THE QUALITY OF WORK DONE
THE FIRST TIME THE WORK WAS TAKEN. ALL PUPILS IN FIRST EIGHT GRADES
OF SCHOOLS FOR WHITE CHILDREN

SUBJECT — HISTORY

GRADE	NUMBER OF RE-PEATERS SECOND SEMESTER SCHOOL YEAR 1913–14	NUMBER OF RE-PEATERS DOING BETTER WORK SECOND TIME than FIRST TIME WORK WAS TAKEN	NUMBER OF RE-PEATERS DOING SAME QUALITY OF WORK SECOND TIME AS FIRST TIME WORK WAS TAKEN	NUMBER OF RE-PEATERS DOING POORER WORK SECOND TIME than FIRST TIME WORK WAS TAKEN
1B				
1A				
2B				
2A				
3B	7	2	5	
3A	4	3	1	
4B	17	9	7	1
4A	13	8	4	1
5B	6	2	2	2
5A	7	7		
6B	6	6		
6A	2			2
7B	5	5		
7A	8	4	4	
8B	6	4	2	
8A	4	3	1	
TOTAL	85	53	26	6
Per Cent	100	62.4	30.6	7.1

TABLE LXVIII — COMPARISON OF QUALITY OF WORK DONE BY REPEATERS DURING SECOND TIME WORK WAS TAKEN WITH THE QUALITY OF WORK DONE THE FIRST TIME THE WORK WAS TAKEN. ALL PUPILS IN THE FIRST EIGHT GRADES OF SCHOOL FOR WHITE CHILDREN

SUBJECT — ARITHMETIC

GRADE	NUMBER OF RE-PEATERS SECOND SEMESTER SCHOOL YEAR 1913–14	NUMBER OF RE-PEATERS DOING BETTER WORK SECOND TIME THAN FIRST TIME WORK WAS TAKEN	NUMBER OF RE-PEATERS DOING SAME QUALITY OF WORK SECOND TIME AS FIRST TIME WORK WAS TAKEN	NUMBER OF RE-PEATERS DOING POORER WORK SECOND TIME THAN FIRST TIME WORK WAS TAKEN
1B				
1A				
2B				
2A				
3B........	12	11	1	
3A........	8	6	2	
4B........	18	14	1	3
4A........	10	8	2	
5B........	6	3	2	1
5A........	7	7		
6B........	6	5	1	
6A:........	2	1	1	
7B........	5	2	2	1
7A........	8	5	3	
8B........	7	4	2	1
8A........	4	3		1
TOTAL....	93	69	17	7
Per Cent...	100	74.2	18.3	7.5

TABLE LXIX — COMPARISON OF QUALITY OF WORK DONE BY REPEATERS SECOND TIME WORK WAS TAKEN WITH THE QUALITY OF WORK DONE THE FIRST TIME THE WORK WAS TAKEN. ALL PUPILS IN THE FIRST EIGHT GRADES OF SCHOOLS FOR WHITE CHILDREN

SUBJECT — GEOGRAPHY

GRADE	NUMBER OF RE-PEATERS SECOND SEMESTER SCHOOL YEAR 1913–14	NUMBER OF RE-PEATERS DOING BETTER WORK SECOND TIME THAN FIRST TIME WORK WAS TAKEN	NUMBER OF RE-PEATERS DOING SAME QUALITY OF WORK SECOND TIME AS FIRST TIME WORK WAS TAKEN	NUMBER OF RE-PEATERS DOING POORER WORK SECOND TIME THAN FIRST TIME WORK WAS TAKEN
1B				
1A				
2B				
2A				
3B				
3A				
4B........	17	15	2	
4A........	13	13		
5B........	6	5		1
5A........	7	7		
6B........	5	3	1	1
6A........	2	1	1	
7B........	5	2	3	
7A........	4	3	1	
8B				
8A				
TOTAL.....	59	49	8	2
Per Cent...	100	83.1	13.5	3.4

TABLE LXX — Comparison of Quality of Work Done by Repeaters During Second Time Work was Taken with the Quality of Work Done the First Time the Work was Taken. All Pupils in the First Eight Grades of Schools for White Children

SUBJECT — LANGUAGE AND GRAMMAR

Grade	Number of Repeaters Second Semester School Year 1913-14	Number of Repeaters Doing Better Work Second Time than First Time Work was Taken	Number of Repeaters Doing Same Quality of Work Second Time as First Time Work was Taken	Number of Repeaters Doing Poorer Work Second Time than First Time Work was Taken
1B				
1A........	2	0	2	
2B........	6	5	1	
2A.........	1	0	1	
3B........	10	3	6	1
3A........	8	5	3	
4B........	18	13	3	2
4A........	13	5	8	
5B........	6	3	3	
5A........	7	3	2	2
6B........	7	6	1	
6A........	2	1	1	
7B........	5	4	1	
7A........	9	5	4	
8B........	7	2	5	
8A........	5	3	1	1
TOTAL.....	106	58	42	6
Per Cent...	100	54.7	39.6	5.7

TABLE LXXI — Comparison of Quality of Work Done by Repeaters During Second Time Work was Taken with the Quality of Work Done the First Time the Work was Taken. All Pupils in the First Eight Grades in Schools for White Children

SUBJECT — WRITING

Grade	Number of Repeaters Second Semester School Year 1913-14	Number of Repeaters Doing Better Work Second Time than First Time Work was Taken	Number of Repeaters Doing Same Quality of Work Second Time as First Time Work was Taken	Number of Repeaters Doing Poorer Work Second Time than First Time Work was Taken
1B........	42	25	14	3
1A........	7	5	2	
2B........	9	3	6	
2A........	4	2	1	1
3B........	12	2	10	
3A........	8	4	3	1
4B........	18	7	10	1
4A........	13	5	7	1
5B........	9	3	6	
5A........	4	1	2	1
6B........	6		5	1
6A........	2	1	1	
7B........	5		4	1
TOTAL.....	139	58	71	10
Per Cent...	100	41.7	51.1	7.1

TABLE LXXII

COMPARISON OF QUALITY OF WORK DONE BY REPEATERS DURING SECOND TIME
WORK WAS TAKEN WITH THE QUALITY OF WORK DONE THE FIRST TIME THE
WORK WAS TAKEN. ALL PUPILS IN FIRST EIGHT GRADES OF SCHOOLS FOR
WHITE CHILDREN

SUBJECT — READING

GRADE	NUMBER OF REPEATERS SECOND SEMESTER SCHOOL YEAR 1913–14	NUMBER OF REPEATERS DOING BETTER WORK SECOND TIME THAN FIRST TIME WORK WAS TAKEN	NUMBER OF REPEATERS DOING SAME QUALITY OF WORK SECOND TIME AS FIRST TIME WORK WAS TAKEN	NUMBER OF REPEATERS DOING POORER WORK SECOND TIME THAN FIRST TIME WORK WAS TAKEN
1B	39	32	6	1
1A	7	6	1	0
2B	9	8	0	1
2A	4	3	1	0
3B	12	4	5	3
3A	8	7	1	0
4B	18	8	5	5
4A	13	7	3	3
5B	6	2	3	1
5A	7	4	2	1
6B	6	1	4	1
6A	2	0	1	1
7B	6	6	0	0
7A	8	6	1	1
8B	6	5	1	0
8A	4	3	1	0
TOTAL	155	102	35	18
Per Cent	100	65.8	22.6	11.6

The tables show that 38.4 per cent of the grades given repeaters during the second semester of the school year 1913–14 were either no better or were poorer than the grades made by these same pupils the first time they took the work. If the grades given by the teachers are reliable measures of what pupils are doing, the conclusion is self-evident that as far as efficiency in subject matter is concerned there was a great waste of time in a large part of the repetition work. Especially is this waste noticeable in the subjects of writing, with 58.2 per cent of the grades no better than the grades of the first term, language and grammar with 45.3 per cent, history with 37.8 per cent, spelling with 36.5 per cent, reading 34.2 per cent. In geography and in arithmetic doing the work over seems to be of more benefit to the child than in other subjects.

These conditions should be remedied either through the exercise of greater care in sentencing pupils to a repetition of the work or to such an organization that repeaters can get more individual attention than they now receive.

The Benefit of Repetition

Extracts from Paper by J. W. Holdeman, Principal of the Central School, 1914–15

The purpose of this study is to determine the instances of "gain," "loss," or "neither gain nor loss" where pupils need to repeat their work.

The pupils in this study include those enrolled in the Central School during the months of February and March, who some time in their course in the Bloomington schools were compelled to repeat. Since there was no grade above the fifth, this study will cover only the work done during the earlier period of the pupils' courses as students.

In computing ages only years and months were counted. Less than a half month was ignored, while a half month or more was counted a full month.

The "gain," "loss," and "neither gain nor loss" are computed (1) for all repetitions whether failures or not; (2) for all repetitions of failures, (a) total, (b) by subjects; (3) for all repetitions of passed work, (a) total, (b) by subjects.

The subjects considered were those taught in the grades from first to fifth, inclusive, namely: arithmetic, spelling — designated phonics in the first and second grades — reading, language, history, geography, hygiene, and writing — a total of eight.

The number of pupils included was eighty-seven.

The computations are as follows:

(1) Total Number of Repetitions 511
    With "gain"................................... 347 or 67.9%
    With "loss"................................... 22 or 4.3
    With "neither gain nor loss".................. 142 or 27.8

Using a repetition with "neither gain nor loss" as a loss, which it really is, the loss becomes, 164 or 32.1 per cent.

(2) Total Number of Failures Repeated........................ 217
    With "gain"................................... 186 or 85.7%
    With "loss"................................... 2 or   .9
    With "neither gain nor loss".................. 29 or 13.4

Repetition of failures by subjects:
  (a) Arithmetic, total. 31
        With "gain"............................... 25 or 80.6%
        With "loss"............................... 1 or 3.3
        With "neither gain nor loss".............. 5 or 16.1

  (b) Spelling, total. 58
        With "gain"............................... 49 or 84.5%
        With "loss"............................... 0 or 0
        With "neither gain nor loss".............. 9 or 15.5

(c) Reading, total... 65
  With "gain"................................... 57 or 87.7%
  With "loss"................................... 0 or   0
  With "neither gain nor loss".................. 8 or   12.3

(d) Language or grammar, total............................. 8
  With "gain"................................... 8 or 100.0%
  With "loss"................................... 0 or   0
  With "neither gain nor loss".................. 0

(e) History, total... 5
  With "gain"................................... 5 or 100.0%
  With "loss"................................... 0 or   0
  With "neither gain nor loss".................. 0 or   0

(f) Geography, total....................................... 14
  With "gain"................................... 13 or 93.0%
  With "loss"................................... 0 or   0
  With "neither gain nor loss".................. 1 or   7

(g) Hygiene, total... 0

(h) Writing, total... 36
  With "gain"................................... 29 or 80.6%
  With "loss"................................... 1 or   2.8
  With "neither gain nor loss".................. 6 or   16.6

(3) TOTAL NUMBER OF REPETITIONS IN NON-FAILING WORK............. 294
  With "gain"................................... 160 or 54.4%
  With "loss"................................... 21 or   7.2
  With "neither gain nor loss".................. 113 or 38.4

Repetitions of non-failures by subjects
(a) Arithmetic, total...................................... 8
  With "gain"................................... 8 or 100 %

(b) Spelling, total.. 67
  With "gain"................................... 36 or 53.7%
  With "loss".................................. 4 or   6
  With "neither gain nor loss" .... 27 or 40.3

(c) Reading, total... 62
  With "gain" .... 34 or 54.8%
  With "loss"................................... 5 or   8.1
  With "neither gain nor loss" .... 23 or 37.1

(d) Grammar, total... 30
  With "gain".................................. 17 or 56.7%
  With "loss"................................... 2 or   6.7
  With "neither gain nor loss".................. 11 or 36.7

(e) History, total... 17
  With "gain " .... 8 or   47.7%
  With "loss "................................. 2 or   11.8
  With "neither gain nor loss " .... 7 or   41.2

(f) Geography, total 4
  With "gain " .... 4 or 100.0%

(g) Hygiene, total.. 16

    With "gain"...................................... 8 or 50.0%

    With "loss"...................................... 2 or 12.5

    With "neither gain nor loss"...................... 6 or 37.5

(h) Writing, total... 90

    With "gain"...................................... 45 or 50.0%

    With "loss"...................................... 6 or 6.7

    With "neither gain nor loss".................... 39 or 43.3

From (2) it will be noticed that 85.7 per cent of the failures were repeated with "gain." In only one case was a failure repeated with distinct loss; so one must conclude that, if a pupil's scholarship is very low in a subject, his knowledge will be strengthened sufficiently, other things being equal, to justify his repeating the subject.

The repetition is justified even further when we remember that 68 per cent of all repetitions are made with increase and that 54.4 per cent of the passing grades are benefited.

There may be elements of waste in the present plan that need to be considered, but, from the side of scholarship alone, the repetitions seem to be justified.

The following table is taken from the study by A. C. Burgin, which deals with the records of all children entering the grades in any classes beginning September, 1900, January, 1901, September, 1901, January, 1902, September, 1902, January, 1903, September, 1903, and January, 1904, and graduating June, 1908, January, 1909, June, 1909, January, 1910, June, 1910, January, 1911, June, 1911, January, 1912. All children entering these classes, regardless of the year of entering and of the grade entered, make up the cases serving as a basis for this table.

TABLE LXXIII

REPEATERS

Taken from study worked out by A. C. Burgin, graduate student in Indiana University.

YEARS OF REPETITION

GRADES	.5		1		1.5		2.		2.5		3	
	B	G	B	G	B	G	B	G	B	G	B	G
1..........	21	23	42	37	9	4	7	3	1	0	1	1
2..........	31	22	19	15	2	3	1					
3..........	66	30	18	13	2	2	1	1				
4..........	57	44	20	10	5	3	1	1				
5..........	42	36	15	10	0	1						
6..........	28	31	8	5	3	2	0	1	1			
7..........	52	48	23	21	7	5	1	2				
8..........	27	36	5	7	1	0	0	0	0	0	1	
	324	270	150	118	29	20	11	8	2	0	2	1
TOTAL	594		268		49		19		2		3	
PER CENTS	65		27		5		2		.2		.3	

Table LXXIII reads as follows: In grade 1, 21 boys and 23 girls repeated .5 of a year, 42 boys and 37 girls repeated one full year each, etc.

It will be seen that the greatest range of repetition in point of length of repetition comes in the first and eighth grades; the shortest range in the fifth grade. Reducing the periods of repetition to semesters, or half years, we find that 21.7 per cent of repetition occurred in the first grade; 10.2 per cent in the second grade; 12.9 per cent in the third grade; 14.1 per cent in the fourth grade; 9.5 per cent in the fifth grade; 7.9 per cent in the sixth grade; 17.2 per cent in the seventh grade; and 6.5 per cent in the eighth grade. It may be seen at a glance that the first and seventh grades are by far the most prolific in promoting repetition.

TABLE LXXIV — REPEATERS DURING SECOND SEMESTER, SCHOOL YEAR, 1913–14, BY AGE, GRADE, AND SEX

GRADE	NUMBER OF REPEATERS	PER CENT OF ALL REPEATERS IN EACH GRADE	AGE AT TIME OF REPETITION	NUMBER OF REPEATERS OF EACH AGE	PER CENT OF REPEATERS OF EACH AGE
1B........	89	25.6	5	4	1.1
1A........	13	3.4	6	46	13.2
2B........	19	5.5	7	50	14.4
2A........	7	2.0	8	20	5.7
3B........	35	10.1	9	41	11.8
3A........	16	4.6	10	48	13.8
4B........	42	12.1	11	25	7.2
4A........	26	7.5	12	28	8.0
5B........	15	4.3	13	51	14.7
5A........	14	4.0	14	18	5.2
6B........	14	4.0	15	14	4.0
6A........	5	1.4	16	3	.9
7B........	12	3.4			
7A........	21	6.0			
8B........	20	5.7			
8A........					
TOTALS	348			348	

Total boys repeating............................	228
Per cent of repeaters that were boys................	65.5
Total girls repeating.............................	120
Per cent of repeaters that were girls................	34.5

It is clear from Table LXXIV that grades 1B, 3B, 4B need special attention since they are taking the largest toll in failures.

Ages 6, 9, 10, and 13 are drawing more than their share of the failures.

The boys are far more liable to failure than the girls and should therefore receive special attention.

Grades 6A, 2A, 7B, 1A, 5A, and 6B have the fewest failures.

TABLE LXXV

School Subjects as They Contributed to Repetition: Accumulative Distribution in Numbers of the Part Played by the Different Subjects in Contributing to Retardation Without Regard to what Combinations with other Subjects Existed

Subject	Individuals Boys	Girls	Totals
Reading	116	76	192
Arithmetic	232	188	420
Writing	39	7	46
History	128	113	241
Grammar	173	122	295
Geography	112	92	204
Spelling	108	35	143
Physiology	26	14	40
Music	66	15	81
Drawing	22	5	27
Industrial Training	1	1	2

Retardation depends somewhat also on the changing character of the population. Pupils entering the system for the first time are handicapped in their work and do not always immediately adjust themselves satisfactorily to the requirements of the new conditions.

As the result of an examination of 1463 children entering any of the classes beginning September, 1900, January, 1901, September, 1901, January, 1902, September, 1902, January, 1903, September, 1903, January, 1904, and graduating June, 1908, January, 1909, June, 1909, January, 1910, June, 1910, January, 1911, June, 1911, and January, 1912, Mr. Burgin found that only forty-five — twenty-one boys and twenty-four girls — did the work of the entire eight grades in the Bloomington schools. In his complete study Mr. Burgin considered every child that had entered any of the above classes regardless of the year of entering and of the grade entered.

The following statement shows the percentage of the total group that did work in each grade.

	Per Cent		Per Cent
1	40	5	42
2	35	6	36
3	44	7	30
4	51	8	21

Table LXXVI shows the wide range of records as regards time spent in the Bloomington schools.

TABLE LXXVI
RANGE OF RECORDS

NUMBER OF YEARS IN SYSTEM	NUMBER OF INDIVIDUALS		
	BOYS	GIRLS	TOTALS
.5	64	64	128
1	135	78	213
1.5	74	50	124
2	69	53	122
2.5	45	49	94
3	56	40	96
3.5	24	36	60
4	69	95	164
4.5	25	38	63
5	55	34	89
5.5	28	27	55
6	32	31	63
6.5	19	22	41
7	26	16	42
7.5	20	15	35
8	17	19	36
8.5	8	2	10
9	10	10	20
9.5	3	1	4
10	1	0	1
10.5	2	2	4
TOTAL	782	682	1464

During the year 1913–14 there entered the first eight grades of the Bloomington schools from outside systems of schools 321 pupils, of whom 109 entered the McCalla building, 122 the Central, 80 the Fairview, and 10 the colored.

TABLE LXXVII
DISTRIBUTION TABLE SHOWING ABSENCES MADE BY PUPILS IN THE WHITE SCHOOLS, SECOND SEMESTER OF THE YEAR 1913–14. ABSENCES NOT CHARGED TO PUPILS WITHDRAWN PERMANENTLY FROM SCHOOL THROUGH MOVING OR QUITTING TO GO TO WORK, ETC.

NUMBER OF DAYS ABSENT	McCALLA	FAIRVIEW	CENTRAL	NUMBER OF DAYS ABSENT	McCALLA	FAIRVIEW	CENTRAL
0	87	25	79	8.5	7	6	11
.5	36	9	40	9	10	3	14
1	39	17	40	9.5	7	6	9
1.5	25	15	35	10	6	6	11
2	30	17	48	10.5	6	6	6
2.5	24	12	21	11	6	3	8
3	25	10	32	11.5	6	8	13
3.5	21	13	24	12	5	2	8
4	13	17	25	12.5	3	2	7
4.5	14	18	24	13	6	1	9
5	23	11	24	13.5	2	4	2
5.5	12	10	14	14	2	5	8
6	20	16	27	14.5	9	3	7
6.5	13	12	16	15	7	5	3
7	6	8	15	15.5	3	1	10
7.5	6	4	16	16	6	3	9
8	7	13	15	16.5	1	5	3

TABLE LXXVII (*Continued*)

Number of Days Absent	McCalla	Fairview	Central
17	2	6	1
17.5	1	1	3
18	2	1	3
18.5		1	4
19	2	3	5
19.5			1
20	3	5	3
20.5	1	1	1
21	3	2	2
21.5	4	1	2
22	3	4	8
22.5		1	1
23	2	1	2
23.5	2		
24	1	3	
24.5		1	2
25	1	3	3
25.5		1	3
26		1	1
26.5	3	1	1
27	2	3	
27.5	1	1	5
28	1		
28.5	2		
29	1	3	1
29.5		1	2
30	1		1
30.5	2	1	1
31		1	1
31.5			
32		1	4
32.5	1		1
33	1		
33.5	1		
34			3
34.5		2	
35		1	2
35.5			1
36			3
36.5			
37		2	1
37.5			1
38			
38.5			
39		1	1
39.5	1		
40			
40.5		1	
41			
41.5		1	
42			1
42.5			
43	1	1	
43.5		1	
44			
44.5			
45			
45.5			1
46			
46.5			
47			
47.5		1	1
48			
48.5			
49		1	1
49.5			
50		1	
50.5			
51			
51.5			
52		1	
52.5			1
53	1		1
53.5			
54			
54.5			
55			
55.5			
56		1	1
56.5			
57			
57.5			
58			
58.5			
59			
59.5			
60			
61.5		1	
62			1
62.5			
63			

Approximately 10 per cent of the pupils that were absent were absent more than 20 days. Previous studies indicate that an absence of more than 20 days in one semester usually means failure. Ten per cent of the failures can be charged therefore to absence.

CAUSES OF RETARDATION

One study made in the Bloomington schools during the fall of 1912 has a bearing on the causes of retardation. This study was a limited one connected with the smokers in the schools. The pupils who smoked as well as the grade in which they first learned to smoke were ascertained through statements of the pupils to the teachers. While this method of gathering information is not a scientific one, nevertheless, the principals of buildings had the feeling, which they expressed at the conclusion of the study, that the directions for getting the information, worked out carefully as they were beforehand in principals' and teachers' meetings, and the checks the principals and teachers were enabled to use on their information from their own personal knowledge, together formed a fairly good safeguard against any great degree of error in the study. These results are therefore believed to have a great enough degree of reliability to suggest fairly accurately one of the probable causes of retardation among the boys of the school. The summary of findings is embodied in the following resolution of the School Board addressed to the Common Council of the City of Bloomington.

December 30, 1912

To THE COMMON COUNCIL OF THE CITY OF BLOOMINGTON, INDIANA

Gentlemen:

Whereas, the result of a recent investigation in the Public Schools of Bloomington, Indiana, based upon the statements of pupils themselves as to whether or not they are users of tobacco, reveals a high correlation between the degree to which tobacco is used and the degree to which pupils are over age for their grade, poor in their school work, and subjects of punishment for serious infractions of school rules — all of which is clearly set forth in the following tables compiled from data collected in the McCalla, Central, and High School Buildings:

I. RETARDATION:

The following table gives the present average age of smokers and non-smokers:

GRADE	SMOKERS AVERAGE AGE	NON-SMOKERS AVERAGE AGE	EXCESS AGE OF SMOKERS OVER NON-SMOKERS
First	9.17	7.58	1.59
Second	9.96	8.51	1.45
Third	10.68	9.36	1.32
Fourth	12.6	10.55	2.05
Fifth	14.22	12.21	2.01
Sixth	13.62	12.42	1.20
Seventh	14.67	13.32	1.35
Eighth	15.12	14.65	.47
Ninth	16.47	15.55	.92
Tenth	16.75	16.17	.58
Eleventh	18.00	17.27	.73
Twelfth	17.55	17.22	.33

II. PRESENT SCHOLARSHIP:

High School — last semester:

1. Non-smokers failed in 10 per cent of their work.
2. Occasional smokers failed in 18.7 per cent of their work.
3. Habitual smokers failed in 29 per cent of their work.

Central and McCalla buildings:

1. Average grade of non-smokers — Good.
2. Average grade of smokers — Barely passing.

III. Discipline:

High School:

(No data were collected on this point from the grades)

	Number	Number Disciplined	Per Cent of Number Disciplined
Habitual smokers..........	17	12	70
Occasional smokers.........	29	8	27
Non-smokers..............	109	9	8.2

IV. Conclusions:

1. Smokers are distinctly older than non-smokers, having been failed in their work much more frequently.
2. Smokers are doing distinctly poorer work than non-smokers.
3. Smokers are disciplined much more frequently and for far more serious offences than are non-smokers.

Therefore, the undersigned School Trustees of the City of Bloomington, Indiana, respectfully petition your Honorable Body to direct the police officers of said City to use special efforts in the enforcement of the laws of the state respecting the sale, and the giving of tobacco to children under sixteen years of age, and also to make a specified number of daily rounds to all the Pool Rooms to see that the law in regard to admitting minors is lived up to, and to prevent gambling in these places by the use of slot machines or by games for money.

Signed:

W. A. Rawles
J. R. McDaniel
J. D. Showers
Trustees of the School City
of Bloomington, Indiana

Summary of Chapter III

1. 43.4 per cent of the families in Bloomington having children of school age have only one such child, and 20.8 per cent of all children of school age belong to families having only one child of school age.

2. 86.2 per cent of all families having children of school age have either one, two, or three such children; while 68.9 per cent of all children of school age belong to families of only one, two, or three of such children.

3. On 13.8 per cent of the families in Bloomington having children of school age, the burden of educating their children is extremely heavy; while 31.1 per cent of all children of school age belong to families carrying this heavy burden.

4. There is in Bloomington no problem of the foreign-born child.

5. Only 11 per cent of the children of the first eight grades, 1913–14, were born outside of Indiana.

6. 47.4 per cent of the children in the Bloomington schools 1913–14 were born in Bloomington.

7. During the past five years 19.2 per cent of the total enrollment both in the grades and the high school has been in the high school. For the whole state of Indiana, during the year 1913–14, only 11 per cent were in the high school.

8. 70.8 per cent of all the graduates from the high school during the past seven years have entered a college or a university.

9. During the past seven years 89.3 per cent of the eighth grade graduates in Bloomington have entered high school.

10. 51.2 per cent of all pupils who enter the Bloomington high school remain to graduate.

11. For the second semester of the school year 1913–14, of the withdrawals 63.4 per cent withdrew to enter another school system, 12.7 per cent to enter a lower or a higher grade, and 23.9 per cent to quit school.

12. The number withdrawing during the second semester of the school year 1913–14 to quit school represented 3.6 per cent of the total enrollment for the year.

13. For the second semester of the school year 1913–14, of those remaining in school to the end of the term 10.3 per cent failed to be promoted, and, counting as failures also those who withdrew to quit school, 13.9 per cent failed of promotion.

14. The grades in their order claiming the greatest toll of failures during the second semester, 1913–14, were 8B, 7A, 7B, 8A, 1B, 6A, and 4A. Those taking the least toll were in their order grades 2A, 1A, 5B, 4B, 3A, 2B, 5A, 3B, 6B.

15. For the second semester, 1913–14, the greatest mortality in the high school in the form of failures was in the 9B grade with the 10B, 9A, 11B, and 10A following in order. In the 12A grade only 1.9 per cent failed.

16. For the first semester, 1913–14, compared with seven other Indiana towns Bloomington high school has a high percentage of failures in beginning English, botany, and Latin and a low percentage of failures in third-year English, solid geometry, United States history, and civics. In other subjects the percentage of failures was about the same as the averages of the seven Indiana towns.

17. 52.1 per cent of the withdrawals from the Bloomington high school withdraw before completing one year's work; 28.2 per cent more withdraw before completing the second year's work.

18. Of all the withdrawals from the Bloomington high school 21.6 per cent were doing less than passing work in one or more subjects; 78.4 per cent were doing passing work in all subjects at time of withdrawal.

19. There is a close correlation between the failure of the fathers and mothers of withdrawals to get far in school and the advancement withdrawals made before leaving school.

20. There is a close correlation between the regularity of work of the fathers and continuation in school of the children.

21. The retardation of withdrawals is almost twice as much as that for the school system as a whole.

22. 30.5 per cent of the girls withdrew and 34 per cent of the boys withdrew because they did not like school.

23. Of the boys that withdraw before reaching the high school 65.7 per cent are either unemployed during their first year out of school or employed at common labor or at odd jobs.

24. 43.2 per cent of the girls leaving the grades were not employed other than in the home the first year after leaving school.

25. 38.4 per cent of the grades given repeaters during the second semester of the school year, 1913–14; were either no better or poorer than the grades made by these same pupils the first time they took the work.

26. A study of the repetitions during their whole school course of all the pupils enrolled in the Central building during the months of February and March, 1914–15, shows that 85.7 per cent of all the failures were repeated with gain. 54.4 per cent of the repetitions of subjects in which passing grades were made resulted in better grades the second time the work was taken.

27. With classes entering the grades in any classes beginning anywhere from September, 1900, to January, 1904, and graduating from June, 1908, to January, 1912, 21.7 per cent of all the repetition occurred in the first grade, 10.2 per cent in the second, 12.9 per cent in the third, 14.1 per cent in the fourth, 9.5 per cent in the fifth, 7.9 per cent in the sixth, 17.2 per cent in the seventh, and 6.5 per cent in the eighth.

28. For the second semester, 1913–14, 65.5 per cent of the repeaters were boys and 34.5 per cent girls. Grades 1B, 3B, 4B and ages 9, 10, 13 drew the largest percentages of failures.

29. Arithmetic, grammar, history, geography, reading, and spelling in this order seem to be the subjects that cause failures.

30. Approximately 10 per cent of the failures can be attributed to absence.

31. A study of the school work done by boys who smoke reveals the following facts:

(*a*) Smokers are distinctly older than non-smokers, having failed in their work much more frequently.

(*b*) Smokers are doing distinctly poorer work than non-smokers.

(*c*) Smokers are disciplined much more frequently and for far more serious offences than are non-smokers.

CHAPTER IV

FINANCES

Table LXXVIII, below, gives a summary of receipts and expenditures of all school moneys by years and funds from the year 1900–01 to 1913–14 inclusive.

The table of expenses, on p. 110, was compiled from warrant stubs and the expenses are charged to the school year in which the warrant was issued and not necessarily, therefore, in all cases to the year the expense was incurred. For this same reason also the yearly expenditure shown in this table does not agree with the yearly expenditure as shown in the table compiled by charging warrants to the year in which they were presented to the bank for payment. The following form for compiling expenditures is essentially the form worked out and approved by the National Education Association and adopted by the Commissioner of Education of the United States.

TABLE LXXVIII

Total Receipts and Disbursements by Years and Funds, 1900–14

Years	Special Fund Receipts	Special Fund Disbursements	Special Building Fund Receipts	Special Building Fund Disbursements	Local Receipts
1900–01......	$14,617.50	$19,886.16			$ 9,787.49
1901–02......	9,483.73	7,736.25			11,069.26
1902–03......	12,882.24	8,584.44			11,050.23
1903–04......	14,004.58	12,091.70			11,339.70
1904–05......	13,894.82	13,965.58			11,670.00
1905–06......	14,381.93	14,734.91			15,827.24
1906–07......	17,490.20	14,238.12			19,368.92
1907–08......	22,566.16	20,711.68	$16,028.59	$16,028.59	18,557.50
1908–09......	23,647.12	18,878.69			23,573.15
1909–10......	24,143.51	30,871.38			24,884.41
1910–11......	24,252.03	19,381.08			24,789.66
1911–12......	24,823.00	17,376.26			26,025.90
1912–13......	24,801.21	31,493.78	78,918.98	22,034.24	27,028.97
1913–14*.....	28,067.63	33,180.62	10,760.67	16,604.39	29,855.86

Years	Tuition Fund Disbursements	Common School Fund Receipts	Common School Fund Disbursements	Totals Receipts	Totals Disbursements
1900–01......	$ 9,630.17	$ 4,811.66	$ 4,808.83	$29,216.65	$34,325.16
1901–02......	10,234.57	5,182.08	5,038.18	25,735.07	23,009.00
1902–03......	11,911.86	5,377.74	5,312.32	29,310.21	25,808.62
1903–04......	12,713.99	5,811.25	5,641.23	31,155.53	30,446.92
1904–05......	13,802.20	6,690.28	6,120.62	32,255.10	33,888.40
1905–06......	14,321.56	6,676.70	6,704.18	36,885.87	35,760.65
1906–07......	16,764.32	7,185.68	6,640.36	44,044.80	37,642.80
1907–08......	21,307.58	10,334.33	7,543.50	67,486.58	65,591.35
1908–09......	21,811.09	9,280.86	10,996.24	56,501.13	51,686.02
1909–10......	19,058.30	9,023.70	9,450.69	58,051.62	49,380.37
1910–11......	25,913.93	9,910.27	9,334.69	58,951.96	54,629.70
1911–12......	25,110.02	11,272.37	10,675.81	62,121.27	53,162.09
1912–13......	23,624.49	11,860.32	11,217.53	142,609.48	88,370.04
1913–14*.....	26,666.92	12,554.81	12,037.51	81,238.97	138,489.44

* Special School Fund for year 1913–14 is incorrectly credited with $3,335.85 which properly belongs to the Sanitary Fund, and with $1,111.95 which properly belongs to the Vocational Fund.

TABLE LXXIX

EXPENDITURES IN BLOOMINGTON SCHOOLS IN YEARS:

A. PAYMENTS:

I. EXPENSES

   a. Expenses of General Control:
   1. Board of Education (office expenses and salaries)...............................
   2. School census.....................
   3. Expenses keeping bank deposit account..........................
   4. Janitor for Supt. office........................
   5. Office of Supt. of Schools { Salaries of Supt. and Clerk.......................
      { Office supplies..........................
   6. Commencement exercises { Diplomas and seals........................
      { Other expenses. ....
   7. Expenses for lecturer.....................
      (*a*) Traveling expenses of applicants for positions....................
   8. (*b*) Superintendent's traveling expenses.............................
      Total.........................

   b. Expenses for Instruction:
   1. Salaries Supervisors of special subjects.....................
   2. Salaries of Principals and their Clerks { High School...........................
      { Grades.............................
   3. Other expenses of Principals { High School.......................
      { Grades.....................
   4. Salaries of Teachers......................
   5. Text-books for poor children......................
   6. Supplementary text-books.....................
   7. Stationery and supplies used in instruction.......................
   8. Sewing materials......................
   9. Manual training supplies......................
      Total.........................

   c. Expenses of Operation of School Plant:
   1. Wages of janitors and other employees.......................
   2. Fuel......................
   3. Light......................
   4. Water......................
   5. Janitors' supplies......................
   6. Telephone calls and telegrams.......................
      Total.........................

   d. Expenses of Maintenance of School Plant:
   1. Oiling streets......................
   2. Repairs of buildings and upkeep of grounds......................
   3. Repair of equipment ....
   4. Replacement of equipment ....
   5. Insurance......................
      Total ....

   e. Books for Library......................
      Total ....

   f. Promotion of Health......................
      Total......................

   g. Miscellaneous Expenses
   1. Rent......................
   2. Printing......................
   3. Care of children in institutions......................
   4. Express, drayage, and freight......................
   5. Transfers......................
   6. Commission for selling books......................
      Total ....

II. OUTLAYS:
   a. New buildings......................
   b. Alteration of old buildings......................
   c. Equipment of buildings, exclusive of replacements......................
      Total......................

III. OTHER PAYMENTS:
   a. Redemption of bonds ....
   b. Interest......................
   c. Text-books to be sold to pupils......................
   d. Refund to County Treasurer......................
      Total......................
      Grand Total......................

Finances

Cost per pupil based on average daily attendance.

1913–1914		1912–1913		1910–1911	
To Amt.					
232.05	.122	449.80	.253	529.89	.33
119.05	.062	108.00	.061	92.96	.058
		(6) 120.00	.067	50.00	.031
52.00	.027				
3,048.70	1.599	(1) 3,385.50	1.902		
30.95	.016	125.80	.07?	3,059.66	1.905
37.85	.019	41.96	.024	29.05	.018
		37.63	.021	15.40	.01
25.00	.013				
		8.95	.005		
60.00	.031				
3,605.60	$1.89	$4,277.64	$2.403	$3,776.96	$2.352
1,710.00	.897	1,620.00	.91	1,512.00	.941
		(2) 1,483.58	.833		
(4) 4,724.81	2.478	3,097.00	1.74	4,410.25	2.745
13.80	.007	34.76	.02	34.15	.021
(5) 31,491.28	16.514	(3) 33,850.46	19.017	31,678.05	19.725
17.10	.009	2.98	.002	76.44	.048
42.52	.023	131.13	.074	427.69	.266
298.59	.151	464.98	.261	406.69	.253
10.52	.006	3.88	.002		
178.54	.094	145.41	.081	125.12	.078
$38,487.16	$20.179	$40,834.18	$22.94	$38,670.39	$24.078
2,521.50	1.322	3,166.95	1.779	2,985.66	1.859
1,095.78	.575	1,250.79	.703	1,322.17	.823
279.45	.147	218.39	.123	144.60	.09
52.80	.028				
195.02	.102	289.54	.163	252.62	.157
123.68	.065	124.60	.07	96.40	.06
$4,268.23	$2.238	$5,050.27	$2.837	$4,801.45	$2.989
		68.00	.038		
217.42	.114	853.24	.479	423.74	.264
8.50	.004	96.50	.054	802.71	.499
1,354.00	.71	325.50	.183	264.75	.164
$1,579.92	$.828	$1,343.24	$0.75	$1,491.20	$0.928
164.01	.086	352.50	.198		
164.01	.086	352.50	.198		
105.00	.055	145.00	.081	367.00	.229
102.58	.054	113.58	.064	112.21	.07
		27.54	.015	31.26	.019
104.14	.055	63.78	.036	51.70	.032
				210.00	.131
				19.16	.012
$311.72	.164	$349.90	.197	$791.33	.492
85,639.83	44.908	25,536.49	14.346		
				1,685.30	1.049
1,198.28	.628	925.16	.52		
$86,838.11	$45.536	$26,461.65	$14.88	$1,685.30	$1.049
7,000.00	3.671	5,500.00	3.09	3,000.00	1.868
3,572.50	1.873	1,402.50	.788	980.00	.61
1,846.36	.968	1,293.91	.727		
1.00		2,139.83	1.202		
$12,419.86	$6.512	$10,336.24	$5.807	$3,980.00	$2.478
$147,674.61	$77.438	$89,005.62	$50.002	$55,196.63	$34.368

(1) $244.00 of this amount was for services rendered the year before.
(2) High school principal received $625.00 from another source.
(3) Other high school teachers got additional $1,916.50; counting this the teaching cost was $20.093.
(4) High school principal received additional $625.00 for teaching from another source.
(5) Other high school teachers received additional from another source for teaching, $1,250.00.
(6) Sixty dollars ($60.00) of this amount belongs to the year 1911–12. The 1913–14 amount was not paid until after July 1st, the end of the fiscal year.

The average daily attendance, which is the basis for the Per Capita Cost calculations, follows:

1910–1911 — 1606
1912–1913 — 1780
1913–1914 — 1907

Conclusions Based on Table LXXVIII

1. Expenditures for maintenance and operation increase slightly from 1910–11 to 1912–13 and decrease noticeably in the year 1913–14 over what they were in 1912–13. The explanation of this decrease is twofold:

   a. Retrenchment in order to conserve funds for building purposes.
   b. Absence on leave of one supervisor and two high-salaried teachers. The supervisorship was not filled during the year.

2. Per capita expenditures for general control have remained about the same for the three years considering the fact that 1912–13 has charged to it approximately $350.00 that should in reality be charged to the year 1913–14.

3. Per capita cost for instruction decreased in 1913–14 due largely to these factors:

   a. Reduction of gross amount spent for supplies of a supplementary nature in an effort to conserve funds for building purposes.
   b. Decrease in salaries paid to teachers explained above.
   c. Crowded condition of practically all the grades.
   d. Absence of an epidemic of contagious diseases. The average daily attendance was 92.2 per cent of the Monthly Enrollment and 83.2 per cent of the Total Yearly Enrollment for the year 1910–11; 91.6 per cent and 84.1 per cent respectively for the year 1912–13; and 96.8 per cent and 84.4 per cent for the year 1913–14.

4. An exceptionally large outlay of funds for new buildings was made during the years 1912–13 and 1913–14. Retrenchment along other lines was thus necessitated.

TABLE LXXX

Comparison of Cost per Pupil Expended in Dollars and Cents Based on Average Daily Attendance. Fifty–seven Cities for the School Year 1902–03 and Bloomington for the School Years 1910–11, 1912–13, 1913–14

Data for fifty-seven cities taken from Strayer and Thorndike, Educational Administration, pages 283, 284, 285, and 286.

Number of City	Total	Teaching	Janitors	Janitors' Supplies	Fuel	Light and Power
1............	35.64	22.30	2.35	.31	1.63	.17
2............	28	17.60		.14	4.70	.13
3............	28.06	19.10	1.98	.28	1.32	
4............	31.90	20.35	2.27	.22	1.53	.07
5............	33.27	24.41	2.19	.06	2.03	.16

TABLE LXXX (*Continued*)

6..............	27.65	20.10	1.45	.05	1.14	.07
7..............	21.61	12.91	2.05	.18	.80	
8..............	31.16	18.1C	1.89	.05	1.82	.C5
9..............	31.C1	2C.63	2.32		2.91	
10.............	43.23	31.91	2.56	.12	1.84	.11
11.............	29.01	14.42	2.65		1.77	.18
12.............	29.20	18.75	2.21	1.09	2.05	
13.............	29.56	15.9C	2.03	.07	1.95	.05
14.............	28.75	17.89	1.95	.08		
15.............	25.35	17.91	1.53	.07	1.71	.07
16.............	28.41	19.17	1.82		1.44	
17.............	36	22.60	2.53		2.64	.29
18.............	35.70	25.17	2.43		2.30	
19.............	28.90	18.16	1.97		2.08	
20.............	23.16	16.58	1.19	.04	2.29	.03
21.............	24.50	16.9C	1.44	.09	.94	.05
22.............	8.94	6.63	.37	.13	.37	.03
23.............	12.85	3.69	1.92		1.27	
24.............	15.26	9.87	.96	.01	1.03	.C7
25.............	31	21.67	1.53	.03	2.C4	.04
26.............	32.67	18.37	1.92	.04	1.45	.05
27.............	26.96	15.11	1.95	.48	1.25	
28.............	30.30	19.77	2.19	.00	2.28	
29.............	29.50	18.21	2.06	.33	1.51	.01
30.............	37.32	25.25	2.36	.26	1.85	.07
31.............	27.90	15.75	1.84		3.49	.09
32.............	34.49	19.07	1.93	.13	2.25	.25
33.............	24.85	16.78	1.52	.04	1.24	.04
34.............	35.96	23.15	2.92	.22	3.61	.08
35.............	24.52	17.87	1.60	.10	1.39	.07
36.............	31.94	18.88	1.11	.07	1.66	.22
37.............	19.26	11.40	1.01		1.15	
38.............	23.56	15.21	.91	.15	1.30	
39.............	32.01	19.94	1.67	.25		
40.............	34.79	21.90	1.38	.11		
41.............	24.65	15.99	1.13	.04	1.49	.12
42.............	28.50	15.47	1.49	.16		
43.............	26.09	17.00	1.73	.18	2.31	.10
44.............	26.18	16.69	1.58	.03	2.62	.13
45.............	28.53	19.14	1.53	.08	1.08	.26
46.............	41.52	25.53	1.91	.39	1.63	.05
47.............	2C.71	5.78	1.75	.57	3.34	.12
48.............	22.75	13.29	1.36	.05	1.39	.05
49.............	22.20	14.20	.89	.15	1.22	.00
50.............	32.05	21.05	1.76	.15	1.79	.04
51.............	26.39	13.81	1.84	.16		
52.............	30.61	20.49	2.11			
53.............	54.72	30.60	3.05	.43	2.72	.58
54.............	20.50	12.61	1.C9		1.14	.11
55.............	28.01	15.33	2.35	.33	1.22	.11
56.............	51.25	33.20	2.42	.11	2.01	.22
57.............	21.51	13.55	1.17	.28	.69	.06
1910–11—Bloomington	34.37	19.73	1.86	.16	1.86	.09
1912–13—Bloomington	50.00	19.02	1.78	.16	1.78	.12
1913–14—Bloomington	73.58	15.69	1.26	.10	1.26	.14

TABLE LXXX (*Continued*)

Number of City	Repairs	Rent	School Census	Insurance	Printing and Advertising
1.	1.88	.01	.25		.11
2.	1.50	.05	.05		
3.	1,09				
4.	1.06	.05	.02		.04
5.	.33		.11		
6.	1.09		.00		.04
7.	1.43		.02	.19	.11
8.	1.17		.05	.19	.08
9.	.05		.05		
10.	2.29		.05		.10
11.	1.24	.14		.26	.04
12.	1.03	.07	.04		
13.	.77	.04	.03	.48	.05
14.	2.02	.03	.03		.05
15.	.69	.17	.03		.06
16.	1.14		.05		
17.	1.43		.03		.12
18.	.98		.05		.08
19.	1.64		.07		.05
20.	.85	.09			.05
21.	.94			.14	.01
22.	.59	.01	.02		.06
23.	.90		.06	.40	
24.	.45		.03	.32	.05
25.	1.83		.08	.25	.25
26.	1.12	.19	.10	.44	.10
27.	.63	.54	.10	.03	.08
28.		.14	.13		
29.		3.15	.07		11
30.	2.75		.02		.22
31.	1.79	.10	.11	.08	.15
32.	3.67		.13	.18	.27
33.	1.17		.07	.06	.06
34.	.52		.19	.52	.44
35.	.68		.04	.09	.16
36.	.72		.10	.33	.02
37.	.45			.04	.11
38.	2.32		.05	.27	.14
39.	1.36			.06	
40.	1.21		.05	.51	.70
41.	.04	.45	.06	.17	.06
42.	.80			.32	.08
43.	.65	.04	.11	.01	.13
44.	1.12	.60		.32	.07
45.	1.98			.32	.25
46.	1.07	1.49			.22
47.	2.03	.14		.37	.23
48.	.34	.56	.06	.11	.36
49.	.29		.05	.13	.03
50.	.59		.02	.29	.06

TABLE LXXX (*Continued*)

51....................	3.95			.31	.21
52....................	1.00				
53....................	2.30			.43	.25
54....................	.57				
55....................	1.50			.16	.08
56....................	2.23			.11	.13
57....................	1.12	.24		.03	.03
1910–11 — Bloomington.....	.76	.23	.06	.16	.07
1912–13 — Bloomington.....	.53	.08	.06	.18	.06
1913–14 — Bloomington.....	.11	.05	.06	.68	.05

TABLE LXXXI

THE PER CENT OF TOTAL EXPENDITURE FOR MAINTENANCE AND OPERATION
WHICH IS SPENT FOR TEACHING, SUPERVISION, JANITORS, SALARIES, AND
FUEL. AVERAGE FOR TWO YEARS 1902–03 AND 1903–04, THIRTY CITIES AND
BLOOMINGTON FOR SCHOOL YEARS 1910–1911, 1912–1913, AND 1913–14

Data for thirty cities taken from Strayer and Thorndike, Educational Administration, page 297.

	TEACHING		JANITORS' SALARIES		FUEL	
	PER CENT	FREQUENCY	PER CENT	FREQUENCY	PER CENT	FREQUENCY
	54	3	3	2	3	4
	55	2	4	1	4	3
	56	1	5	10	5	8
	57	2	6	11	6	9
	58	0	7	4	7	2
	59	2	8	1	8	2
	60	2	9	1	9	0
	61	1			10	0
	62	3			11	1
	63	1				
	64	4				
	65	2				
	66	2				
	67	2				
	68	1				
	69	0				
	70	0				
	71	0				
	72	2				
	73	1				
Bloomington, 1910–11.	64		6		2.6	
Bloomington, 1912–13.	64		6		2.4	
Bloomington, 1913–14.	65		5.2		2.3	

CONCLUSIONS BASED ON TABLES LXXX AND LXXXI

1. Bloomington compares favorably with other cities in the per
cent of total expenditure for maintenance and operation that is expended for teaching and janitors' salaries. The per cent of expenditure for coal is very small comparatively, suggesting either economy
in purchasing or economy in consumption or both.

2. The decrease in the per cent of maintenance during the year
1913–14 is due largely to the abnormal expenditure during that

year for new buildings and equipment. The decrease per child in average daily attendance is due largely to a conscious effort to retrench along certain lines in order to provide building funds.

3. In repairs, printing, and advertising Bloomington is distinctly lower than the average of the fifty-seven cities.

4. Since in the matter of fuel Bloomington has a noticeable advantage over other cities an additional amount might profitably be added to teachers' salaries.

5. In all of these conclusions it must be remembered that the figures for the 30 cities were taken ten years earlier than those for Bloomington.

Other Sources of Income

Each building has raised some money each year for several years by giving entertainments of various sorts. The funds from these entertainments have been used at the discretion of the principal and the teachers of the building.

Fairview Building

Since 1900 the sum of $568.00 has been raised for Fairview, $90.00 through donations and the rest by entertainments such as candy sales, picture show benefits, etc. This amount has been expended as follows:

Expenditures:

Twelve (12) pictures, 1900–02	$ 35.00
Piano, 1901 (second-hand)	125.00
Piano, 1909	300.00
Victor machine, 1912	68.50
Victor records	18.00
Victor cabinet	8.50
Total expenditures	$555.00
Balance on hand	13.00
	$568.00

McCalla Building

Since 1908 the receipts and expenditures in the McCalla Building including the school year of 1913–14 were as follows:

Receipts:	*Expenditures:*	
$1,386.33	Victor machine	$ 75.00
	Victor records	130.00
	Piano	300.00
	Portable organ	25.00
	Playground apparatus	456.33
	Pictures	370.00
	Program clock	30.00
		$1,386.33

Colored School

From the beginning of school in the fall of 1909 to the close of school in the spring of 1913 the receipts in the Colored School were $52.84, and the expenditures $51.81, leaving a balance of $1.03.

Central Building

Receipts and expenditures in the Central Building have been carried in two funds since 1912–13: General Fund and Department Fund. The record extends from 1906 to June, 1914.

Receipts in General Fund :

I. Cash Donations

1. Toward buying piano, 1906, Patrons..........	$ 17.50
2. Toward playground, 1910, Patrons............	110.00
3. Toward Grafonola, 1912, Friday Musical Club .	24.50

$152.00

II. Class Memorials, since June 1906
1. Contributed by classes leaving the Department........... 136.27

III. School Entertainments, since 1905–06
1. Old Curiosity Shop....................
2. Thanksgiving entertainments..........................
3. Candy sales...
4. Rubber sales..
5. Lawn fêtes... 1,117.09

Total... $1,405.36

Receipts in Department Fund :

Lawn fête, 1912–13............................	$ 44.59
Musical, May 1913............................	41.80
Musical, May 1914............................	53.20
Pen money, 1914 (Profit on sale of pens)	5.41

Total.. $145.00

Expenditures from General Fund:

I. For Permanent Fixtures

1. Musical

a. Old piano, 1906.......................	$ 40.00
b. New piano, 1906......................	190.00
c. Drum, 1909..........................	11.25
d. Grafonola, 1912.......................	100.00
e. Organ, 1913..........................	25.50
f. Records and needles, 1912–13–14........	32.47

Total.. $399.22

2. Playground

a. Work on yard, 1910, grading and surfacing.	$221.70
b. Equipment	
Giant strides (2).....................	34.65
Swings and climbing poles............	81.63
Volley ball........................	11.00
Slide..............................	55.60
Basket-ball court....................	15.00
Horizontal bars.....................	6.00
Cement, gravel, and sand for concrete..	19.12

Total.. $444.70

3. Class Memorials
   1. Sir Galahad, June 1906................ $ 8.00
   2. Head of Christ, Jan. 1907..............   8.00
   3. Morning — cast, June 1907............   10.00
   4. Night — cast, Jan. 1908...............   10.00
   5. Slides — Lady of the Lake, June 1908...   15.00
   6. Gettysburg Address, Tablet, Jan. 1909...   20.00
   7. Longfellow, bust, June 1909............   13.34
   8. Longfellow, pedestal, Jan. 1910........   7.50
   9. Hedge Fund, June 1910................   4.00
   10. Lincoln, bust, June 1911...............   13.34
   11. Riley Picture, Jan. 1911..............   5.70
   12. Records, Jan. 1912....................   13.89
   13. Lincoln, pedestal, June 1912...........   7.50

   Total....................................... $ 136.27

4. Stereopticon and equipment
   1. Machine and screen, 1908.............. $ 72.56
   2. Blinds, 1908........................   5.C0
   3. Slides, 1908, 1909...................   26.85

   Total....................................... $ 104.41

5. Stage equipment
   1. Stage............................... $ 19.17
   2. Cover and curtains...................   7.37

   Total....................................... $ 26.54

6. Pictures (other than class memorials)
   1. Dance of the Nymphs................. $ 5.00
   2. Aurora.............................   6.00
   3. Sea picture........................   4.50
   4. Sistine Madonna....................   8.50
   5. Old Swimmin' Hole and Riley and Bust   12.50
   6. Glass for pictures...................   2.65

   Total....................................... $ 39.15

Total Expenditures for Permanent Fixtures
   1. Musical............................. $399.22
   2. Playground.........................   444.70
   3. Class Memorials....................   136.27
   4. Stereopticon and equipment...........   104.41
   5. Stage and equipment................   26.54
   6. Pictures...........................   39.15
   7. Miscellaneous......................   9.20

   Total..... .... $1,159.49
For Entertainment Expenses...........................   217.57
Total... $1,377.06

SUMMARY STATEMENT

I. *Central School General Fund*
   Total Receipts since 1905–06.......................... $1,405.36
   Total Expenditures
      Permanent fixtures......................... $1,159.49
      Entertainment expenses.....................   217.57

                                                          1,377.06
   Balance in Citizens Loan and Trust Co.................... $ 28.30

II. *Department Fund*
    Started 1912–13... $ 145.00
    Total Receipts in both General and Department Funds 1,610.36
    Balance in Citizens Loan and Trust Co., June 1, 1914
      1. In Central School General Fund..................... 88.30
      2. In Department Fund.............................. 145.00

TABLE LXXXII

STATEMENT OF ASSETS AND LIABILITIES SEPTEMBER 1, 1914

Assets:

BUILDINGS AND GROUNDS

BUILDING	ORIGINAL COST	PRESENT VALUE OF GROUNDS	PRESENT VALUE OF BUILDINGS
High School.............	$135.000.00	$ 10,000.00	$135,000.00
Department.............	35,000.00	10,0C0.00	20,000.00
Central.................	75,000.00	12,000.00	78,000.00
McCalla................	32,00C.00	14,000.00	32,000.00
Fairview...............	17,000.00	6,000.00	25,000.00
McDoel................		2,000.00	1,500.00
Colored................	3,500.00	10,000.00	1,C00.00
Annex..................	1,000.0C		1,000.00
Total..................	$298,500.00	$ 64,000.00	$293,500.00

Liabilities:

Bonds outstanding.......	$ 75,000.00	
Interest coupons........	15,722.50	
Total assets over liabilities		$286,325.00
Total..................		$377,047.50

TABLE LXXXIII

STATEMENT OF ASSETS AND LIABILITIES JUNE 30, 1914

Assets:

EQUIPMENT

	NUMBER OF PUPILS' DESKS	VALUE	OTHER FURNITURE AND FIXTURES	VALUE	HIGH SCHOOL DEPARTMENTS	VALUE
High School..	844	$1,899.00		$ 533.00		$4,120.50
Central......	799	1,957.75		640.00		
McCalla.....	523	1,206.00		573.00		
Fairview.....	406	913.50		666.00		
Colored.....	83	166.C0		100.00		
Superintendent's office..				195.00		
Total........	2655	$6,142.25		$2,707.00		$4,120.50

	NUMBER OF VOLUMES IN LIBRARY	VALUE	NUMBER OF SUPPLEMENTARY BOOKS COMMON TO ALL	VALUE	NUMBER OF WALL MAPS	VALUE
High School..	3077	$1,206.00			10	$ 50.00
Central......	1474	737.00	1357	$339.25	11	55.C0
McCalla.....	88	60.00	677	169.25	13	65.00
Fairview.....	99	90.00	640	160.00	8	40.00
Colored......	259	64.75	6	3.00	10	30.00
Total........	4997	$2,157.75	2680	$671.50	52	$240.00

	Number of Framed Pictures	Value	Number of Pieces of Sheet Music	Value	Number of Victrola Records	Value
High School..	7	$ 300.00				
Central......	75	350.00	570	$28.50	86	$175.00
McCalla.....	79	370.C0			65	130.00
Fairview.....	59	200.00			15	25.00
Colored......	13	30.00				
Total........	233	$1,250.00	570	$28.50	166	$330.00

Since the year 1911–12 the superintendent of the Bloomington schools has made frequent school budget estimates as a basis for recommendations to the school board. Upon these budget estimates the board depended for its decisions regarding expansion and improvement. The practice of budget making has the virtue of forcing all school officials to look into the future, to compare costs from year to year, to check up on judgments from time to time and thus develop judgment in the line of estimated expenditures. It has the virtue, also, of leaving in the minds of the school officials a feeling of confidence as to where they stand financially.

The following report is an example of the estimates made from time to time by the superintendent.

FINANCIAL REPORT

January 14, 1914

Funds on hand now and to be received before the close of the present school year:

Funds on Hand:

Special Building Fund....................................	$12,331.71
Common School Fund....................................	2,295.39
Local Tuition Fund.....................................	15,976.07
Special School Fund.....................................	12,828.26
Total on hand..	$43,431.43

Funds Yet to be Received During Present School Year Estimated:

Common School Fund....................................	$ 5,392.44
High school text-books.................................	600.00
Tuition from pupils.....................................	5,000.00
Total yet to be received................................	$10,992.44
Total on hand..	43,431.43
Total available funds for remainder of current school year....	$54,423.87

Estimated Expenses for Remainder of Current School Year:

Salaries from Tuition Fund.	$22,387.08
Salaries from Special Fund.	4,795.00
Remaining on Mr. Colvin's contract.	32,534.00
Architects' fees.	720.35
Remaining on electric wiring contract.	1,847.35
Coal.	600.00
Manual training.	150.00
Supplies.	200.00
Telephones.	70.00
Lighting.	150.00
Rent.	100.00
Insurance.	54.00
Taking enumeration.	110.C0
Payment of bonds and interest on bonds.	5,5C0.00
Interest on $27,000 heating and plumbing contract.	750.00
Total expenses current year.	$69,967.78
Total available funds for current year.	54,423.87
Deficit June 30, 1914.	$15,543.91

Estimated Income, 1914–15:

From $1.45 tax levy.	$63,601.45
From tuition from pupils.	5,000.00
Common School Fund.	12,000.00
Sale of bonds, December 1914.	16,0C0.00
Total Income, 1914–15.	$96,601.45

Estimated Expenditures, 1914–15:

Deficit from preceding year.	$15,543.91
Running expenses outside of payment of bonds and interest on bonds.	52,927.80
Equipment of new high school building.	4,000.C0
Additional teachers.	4,C00.0C
Additional janitors.	1,500.00
Interest on $27,C0C heating and plumbing investment.	1,000.00
Heat regulation.	650.00
Payment of bonds.	8,000.00
Interest on bonds.	3,300.00
Additional coal.	1,000.00
Total expenses, 1914–15.	$91,921.71
Total Income, 1914–15.	96,601.45
Balance at end of year, 1914–15.	$ 4,679.74

Estimated Income, 1915–16:

Balance from preceding year.	$ 4,679.74
From $1.45 tax levy (same as for year 1914–15).	63,601.45
From transfers.	5,000.00
Common School Fund.	12,000.00
Total estimated income, 1915–16.	$85,281.19

Estimated Expenses, 1915–16:

Estimated running expenses outside of payment of bonds and interest on bonds.	$60,000.00
Payment of bonds.	8,000.00
Payment of interest on bonds.	3,240.00
Interest on $27,000 heating and plumbing contract.	5,000.00
Heat regulation interest.	65C.00
Total estimated expenses.	$76,890.00
Estimated Income, 1915–16.	$85,281.19
Estimated Expenses, 1915–16.	76,890.00
Balance at end of year, 1915–16.	$ 8,391.19

The unforeseen sale, during the year 1914–15, of the colored school lot and building and the erection of a new colored school building caused the 1914–15 income and expenditure figures to vary materially from the estimates. The unexpected retirement of some outstanding obligations during the year likewise widened the gap between estimated and real expenditures for the year 1914–15.

Summary of Chapter IV

1. School corporation assets June 30, 1914, were:

Building and grounds, present value	$358,000.00
Pupils' desks, present value	6,142.25
Other furniture and fixtures, present value	2,607.00
Department supplies, present value	4,120.50
Library books, present value	3,657.75
Supplementary books, present value	671.50
Wall maps, present value	240.00
Framed pictures, present value	1,250.00
Sheet music, present value	28.50
Victrola records, present value	330.00
Playground equipment, present value	901.03
Total	$377,948.53

2. The outstanding indebtedness September 1, 1914, was $90,722.50.

3. The assessed valuation of property within the city has increased from $4,088,384 in 1907 to 4,728,505 in 1915.

4. The tax rate has increased from $1.10 in 1907 to $1.45 on the hundred dollars in 1915.

5. From 1911 to 1915 improvements to the extent of approximately $150,000 were contracted for.

6. In 1915 the school city was up to its legal limit in its bond issues and its general indebtedness, and it lacked only five cents on the hundred dollars of being to its legal limit in the tax rate for school purposes.

7. Bloomington compares favorably with cities of 30,000 inhabitants and more in the per cent of the whole school expenditure that goes for salaries of teachers and supervisors. The per cent that goes for general control is somewhat higher in Bloomington than in cities of 30,000 or more.

8. The teachers, pupils, and principals have to assume too large a responsibility for the equipment of buildings with pictures, pianos, etc., and for playground equipment. A much larger part of that responsibility should be assumed by the board.

CHAPTER V

THE COURSE OF STUDY

The course of study has been worked out in detail in all subjects. Only in history and geography, however, has there been recent systematic revision of the courses in the grades. Certain modifications have been made in all the courses from time to time, but reading, language, grammar, physiology, and arithmetic need special attention from the point of view of eliminations, additions, and new methods of treatment, with a view to vitalizing the work more thoroughly as well as from the point of view of more nearly meeting the needs of individual pupils.

The course of study is not printed but is issued in typewritten form. Pages that are modified from time to time are thus easily replaced.

Courses of study exist at present in the grades in agriculture, arithmetic, domestic art, domestic science, drawing, geography, grammar, history, manual training, music, physiology, reading, spelling, and writing. In the high school, courses are worked out in botany, commercial lines, English, German, history, civics, Latin, manual training, algebra, geometry, music, physical geography, and physics.

The method now being pursued in the development of the course of study is best illustrated by the subject of history.

PROCEDURE IN DEVELOPING A COURSE OF STUDY, ILLUSTRATED BY THE SUBJECT OF HISTORY

In making the course of study in history the principle that the best results can be obtained by "pooling" the efforts of teachers, scholars in the special subject, and school administrators has been followed. The following committee was appointed in the fall of 1910 by the superintendent to work out the course of study in history:

O. H. WILLIAMS, Head of the History Department in the Bloomington High School, and Critic Teacher in History in Indiana University, *Chairman*

MARY A. KERR, Principal of the Department School Sixth, Seventh, and Eighth Grades and Teacher of History in the Eighth Grade

NEVA CARTER, Teacher of History in the Sixth and Seventh Grades

ELLA WILSON, Principal of the Fairview Building and Teacher of History in the Fourth and Fifth Grades

MARGARET SNODGRASS, Teacher of History in High School

ELIZABETH GOURLEY and ALMA BUNDY, Teachers of Geography in the Fifth, Sixth, and Seventh Grades

H. L. SMITH, Superintendent of Schools

This committee met at regular intervals for one year, 1910–11, and at called meetings during the second year, 1911–12. The plan of procedure at the meetings is illustrated by the following sample programs.

In connection with the first meeting, typewritten extracts as follows were put into the hands of all members of the committee and discussed in a general way.

THE ELEMENTARY COURSE OF STUDY

From Dutton & Snedden, "The Administration of Public Education in the United States." *

Principles applicable to the making of courses for elementary schools. The course of study should be:

a. Related to life — the study, exercise, experience, habit, etc., sought should function in some physical, vocational, cultural, or social result that is worth while.

b. Flexible, according to the characteristics of groups to be educated.

c. Capable of utilizing the social and natural environment of the child which should be drawn upon for concrete materials, illustrations, and opportunities for expression and experience. Recognition of this principle will tend to magnify the tentative and suggestive features of the course and will cause it to put a premium on resourcefulness and initiative.

d. Adjusted so as to provide that education which is complementary to the educative influences of other agencies. What home, church, playground, shop, press, street, etc., do positively the school must supplement where desirable. What they do negatively the school must correct.

e. Integrated in its final effects. Pupils must necessarily get information and skill piece at a time, but in the end each pupil's education should be integral in character.

f. So detailed and flexible as to permit the teacher much freedom while giving fullest guidance. It should indicate prescribed, alternative, and optional work and in connection with each unit of division specify by pages both the texts and the supplementary reading which may be followed. Value of topics should be suggested by stating the approximate time of the term that each should receive. Some will be major subjects and some minor.

g. Dynamic or progressive. It should be changing from time to time in the light of experience with it.

h. Adjusted so as to reflect local initiative and central control and approval.

From Teachers College, Columbia University, Extension Syllabi, Series A, No. 23.*

Aims Commonly Proposed

a. Discipline — training of the memory, the imagination, the judgment.

b. Culture — "Enriching the humanity of the pupil."

c. Inspiration — furnishing ideals of conduct, patriotism, social service.

d. Practical knowledge — teaching pupils how to act in the present.

e. Illumination of other studies, especially literature and geography.

f. The cultivation of a taste for historical reading.

g. The exploration of the present — nothing in the world to-day really intelligible apart from its history.   •

Special Modern Emphasis upon the Social Value of History

a. An application of a general point of view in education.

b. Special demands upon history.

1. Must show in the form of concrete examples what society is and how it works.

2. Must give a "vivid and intense realization of social duties and obligation."

* Reprinted by permission.

THE HISTORY PROGRAM FOR THE ELEMENTARY SCHOOL

1. The Preparatory Period — the First Three or Four Years
   a. Myths, fairy tales, fables, Oriental, Greek, Roman, later European. Some use of American folk lore.
   b. Simple biographies from American or world history. May or may not be arranged chronologically.
   c. Stories connected with anniversaries, birthdays, Thanksgiving, Christmas.
   d. Stories from the Bible.
   e. Stories from primitive life.
   f. Stories of invention.
   g. Stories from local history.
   h. Various studies of a geographical or sociological character.
   i. Several of these types of material may be represented in a single program.
   j. Some schools carry this kind of work into higher grades.

2. The Intermediate Stage — Fifth and Sixth Years
   a. Beginning of text-book instruction.
   b. More attention to chronological order and geological setting.
   c. Subject: Ancient history, the Middle Ages, English history, American history. Chief emphasis on American history.
   d. Material usually biographical.
   e. Some schools begin this stage of work in the fourth year.

3. The Last Two Years
   a. Subject usually the United States.
   b. The subject often divided:
      1. Colonial period for the seventh year.
      2. Later period for the eighth year.
   c. Some schools have English history in the seventh year.
   d. Civics frequently combined with history, especially in the eighth year.
   e. Occasionally some Greek and Roman or general European history in one or both of these years.

From abstract by J. W. Riddle on History in the Elementary School Curriculum.

I. The Problem Stated
   1. To have the child amass a store of historical data, so arranged and classified as to show causal relationship.
   2. To have the child on leaving the elementary school feel something of the spirit of history, and have a deep and sympathetic instinct in human progress and development.
   3. To adapt the material of history to the child in such way that he may acquire the historical sense and perspective.

II. Some popular views concerning method, and the organization of material
   1. The Herbartian views — In history teaching character building is to be the direct aim rather than patriotism, as the latter is sure to follow the former.
   2. The Culture Epoch theory — That there is a parallelism of general physical traits and functions between racial and individual development.
   3. The Source Method — History is based upon documents; and the teaching which does not raise this fact into prominence in the mind of the student is as radically defective as the teaching of literature would be, if it ignored the masterpieces.
   4. Chronological development — This method begins with the primitive race, and follows the development of civilization through the successive stops which it has actually taken.

III. Conclusions made from an examination of forty courses of study. The concensus of opinion among schools seems to be:
   1. That primitive life, national holidays, and legend and story should be the dominant factors in making the course of study for the first and second years.

2. That pioneer stories, tales of adventure, classic and Norse myths and biography should constitute the work provided for third, fourth, fifth, and possibly the sixth grade.
3. That European history, if introduced at all, should be in the sixth year.
4. That the time of the seventh and eighth grades should be given to a serious study of American history

At this first meeting also there was distributed to each member of the committee a copy of the following outline of points that would have to be decided in connection with the making of a course of study in history:

1. Aim
2. Definition or concept
3. Organizing principles
4. Place in course, where begin? end? Per cent of time given to the subject
5. Extent of directions to teachers
   a. Outlines of topics
   b. Problems suggested
   c. Amount of work
      (1) Prescribed
      (2) Alternative
      (3) Optional

6. Correlation
   a. With literature — continuous or differentiated
   b. Geography — sequences
      (1) Determined by
      (2) Preceded by
      (3) Parallel with
   c. Language
   d. Arithmetic
   e. Constructive activities
   f. Civics
   g. Music — national songs, etc.

7. Content
   a. Local history
      (1) Content
      (2) Approach to world history
   b. World history
   c. United States history
   d. Current events

8. Civics
   a. Content
   b. Place in course

9. Methods
   a. Concentric circle
   b. Chronological
   c. Culture epoch
   d. Spiral method
   e. Biographical
   f. Type study
   g. Laboratory (source book)
   h. Problem

10. Books
    a. Text
    b. Supplemental
    c. Reference
11. Sources
12. Aids to teachers
    a. What should they be?
    b. Should they be catalogued?
13. Maps and charts

With the work of the first meeting as a background, a second meeting was called for December 15th. The work of that meeting was outlined as follows:

The committee on the course in History and Civics will meet with the superintendent at the Central Building on Thursday, December 15th, at four o'clock. Topic:

PRINCIPLES UNDERLYING THE HISTORY COURSE

I. Special discussion of recent attempts to solve the problem
    1. Recommendations of the Committee of Eight on History in the Elementary Schools.
        a. Grades One to Four   Miss WILSON
        b. Grades Five and Six   Miss GOURLEY
        c. Grade Seven   Miss CARTER
        d. Grade Eight   Miss KERR
    2. Tentative Report of the Committee of Five on History in the Secondary Schools.
        a. Ancient and Mediæval Europe   Miss SNODGRASS
        b. Mediæval Europe and America   Mr. WILLIAMS

II. General discussion of "Aims in History Teaching." Helpful suggestions will be found in the printed Courses for City Schools in Educational Seminar Room, Library, Indiana University.

The following will be found especially suggestive:
    a. Minneapolis, 1905
    b. Lincoln, Nebr.
    c. Hartford, Conn. (good for reference)
    d. Philadelphia, Pa.
    e. Portland, Ore.
    f. Speyer School, New York City
    g. San Francisco, Cal.
    h. Indianapolis, Ind.
    i. Oakland City, Ind.
    j. Clinton, Ind. (good for local history)
    k. Salt Lake City, Utah (for dramatization in history)

The following courses of study give references in history:
    a. Louisville, Ky.
    b. Superior, Wis.
    c. Baltimore, Md.
    d. Leadville, Colo.
    e. Indianapolis, Ind.
    f. Dekalb Normal School, Illinois, good example of working History and Geography together
    g. Butler, Pa.
    h. New Haven, Conn.
    i. Richmond, Ind.

At the close of this second meeting the essence of the discussion was briefly summarized in the following statement which was later typewritten and distributed to each member of the committee for future reference.

A CONCENSUS UPON SOME FUNDAMENTAL CONCEPTIONS UNDERLYING THE
COURSE IN HISTORY

1. *The Aim.* — Stated broadly, the aim in history instruction is to furnish the pupil with equipment for completer living. More narrowly, the aim is to socialize the child by bringing him into sympathetic and intelligent appreciation of the best elements of our civilization.
2. *The Definition or Concept.* — Our concept of history is necessarily complex. It includes the idea of the unity of mankind, of evolution or development, and comprehends all phases of human activity, whether social, political, industrial, religious, or intellectual. In its method, at least, history is scientific, a science, not of observation, not of experiment, but of criticism. A good working definition is that of Bernheim's: "History is the science of the development of men in their activity as social beings."
3. *Organizing Principles.* — The principle underlying the selection, subordination, and arrangement of historical facts is the growth of men in institutional ideas, of which there are five dominant ones.
4. *Place of History in the Course.* — Some history instruction is given in all the eight grades and in three of the four years of the high school. In Grades One and Two it deals with primitive life, myths, folklore; in Grades Three and Four, with heroic characters; in Grade Five with Greek and Roman life; Grade Six, European, with English as the core; Grades Seven and Eight, American history and elementary civics.

The work of the third meeting is illustrated as follows:

The Teachers' Committee on Course of Study in History will meet at the Superintendent's office at 4:00 P.M., on Friday, January 23d. Continuation of the topic, "Fundamental Conceptions Underlying the Course in History."

The following plan of discussion will be adhered to:

1. Discussion of problems of adapting history to children in the elementary schools.
   - *a.* Degrees of difficulty found in historical facts and its application to History for children   Miss CARTER
   - *b.* History as determined by text-books for upper grades   Miss KERR

Reference: *Teachers College Record*, November, 1908

2. Round-table discussion of "Some things that need to be decided in the making of a course of study in history."
   - *a.* The aim   Miss BUNDY
   - *b.* Definition of concept   Miss SNODGRASS
   - *c.* Organizing principles   Miss WILSON
   - *d.* Place in course   Miss GOURLEY
   - *e.* Extent of directions to teachers   Mr. SMITH

Reference:
Courses of Study for City Schools — Educational Seminar, Library, Indiana University
Columbia University Extension Syllabus, Series A, No. 23
Report of Committee of Eight

3. Brief discussion of report of Committee on Local History in the Public Schools. (Ohio Valley Historical Association)   Mr. WILLIAMS

The following summary of the first part of the meeting of January 23d illustrates the working agreement reached by the committee:

Problem of Adapting History to Children in the Elementary School:

1. Gradation of historical facts based upon the degree of difficulty in apprehending them.
    a. Simplest facts are material — how men looked, what their environment was like.
    b. More difficult facts are deeds and actions — what men did in the past.
    c. Still more difficult are the thoughts, feelings and motives that moved men to act.
    d. More difficult still are collective facts — those relating to social conditions and activities, to men acting together in institutions.
    e. Facts of cause and effect — of how one event led to another — present in some aspects the greatest degree of difficulty.

   A common characteristic of historical facts is that they are localized — in time and place. Just how definitely a fact is to be localized presents another difficulty.

2. Application of this progression in degree of difficulty to history for children·
    a. Material aspects of the past must furnish the foundation. Impressions of men's appearance and surroundings may be created by means of:
        (1) Material remains of neighborhood (local history);
        (2) Pictures, casts, models, and the like.
    b. Particular acts (of their own or of their elders) must furnish the basis for impressions of what men did. These may be supplemented by word-pictures and stories concretely told.
    c. Similarly, children must be led to think and feel of particular men and actions as those men themselves did; e.g., by
        (1) Dramatization of history;
        (2) Writing imaginary letters;
        (3) Keeping fictitious diaries;
        (4) Reciting famous speeches;
        (5) Writing papers giving personal preferences.
    d. Collective facts can only be presented by similar use of details, of particular instances:
        (1) Actual examples of such facts;
        (2) Statistical tables or tabulations.

3. History as determined by text-books in upper grades. Chief defects of these text-books is evident dread of "leaving something out sufficiently to afford space to put something in." Other notable defects.
    a. Full treatment of relatively simple topic, brief mention of more difficult facts. "The principle is that the way to make a thing elementary is not to say much about it."
    b. Mere collections of names and dates, — generalized statements with no basis in concrete detail.

   Proposed remedies: "The text-book for the average elementary school should be a repository of concrete examples." The teacher is to supplement the text by filling in the background. Other books are to supplement the text. Duplicates for class supply should always be furnished.

Later in the year members of the committee were made chairmen for larger committees, each committee having for its work the detailed outline for some one special grade. As a guiding reference each chairman had a complete file of all the preliminary work accomplished by the original committee. The outlines completed by these several committees were finally reviewed by the original committee. An outline of the course as finally adopted follows:

History in the Elementary Grades

GRADES I–III:

Aim:
1. To teach the facts which supply an imaginative background for a later interpretation of history.
2. To develop the power to imagine events in the past.

Methods:
1. Story telling by the teacher.
2. Oral reproduction by the pupil. Teacher should first
   a. Present the story continuously;
   b. Have children express its thoughts; question and stimulate children's questions;
   c. Follow with children's oral reproductions.
3. Simple dramatization of stories.

Outline of Course:
Material suitable for the grade that supplies an imaginative background for the later interpretation of historical material:
1. Fables, fairy tales, folk stories, nature myths.
2. Stories of pioneer life and the Indians.
3. Simple stories of local pioneer history.
4. Stories and simpler facts connected with holidays and anniversaries.
5. Bible stories from patriarchal times.

GRADES IV–V:

Aim:
1. To teach the facts and stimulate interest in the achievements of individual leaders.
2. To develop an understanding of the significance of individual achievements in relation to great historical events.

Methods:
1. Story telling by the teacher.
2. Reading of stories by the teacher and by the class.
3. Oral and written reproduction by the pupils.
4. Silent reading from supplementary texts by pupils.
5. Simple dramatization.
6. Location of countries and important cities in relation to pupils' homes, and simple placing in time periods of heroes and places. Study development of sequence of time.

Outline of Course:
1. Material of the grades preceding, the treatment being extended, especially as regards holidays and anniversaries.
2. Stories from myths and legends and leaders of Greece and Rome.
3. Stories of explorers, discoverers, inventors, chiefly from American history.
4. Bible heroes and characters (from the Old Testament).

GRADE VI:

Aim:
1. To teach the simple facts of English history, particularly those connected with early American history and institutions.
2. To develop the idea of connected historical events ; the power to comprehend historical growth.

Methods:
1. Oral and silent reading by pupils from text-books.
2. Organization of facts by topical outlines by pupils with help of teacher.

    a. Recitation from topics made by teacher and pupils working together.
    b. Oral and written review by topics.

3. Development of place and time sense by use of maps and dates.

Outline of Course:
1. Material from Grades IV and V enlarged and extended.
2. Stories from English history from Roman days to middle of the 18th century, supplemented by stories of the Middle Ages which emphasize continental relations.
3. Local history by topics.

GRADE VII:

Aim:
1. To teach the facts connected with the early colonial and pre-revolutionary period in America, the establishment of the national government, and the beginning of national growth.
2. To develop the power to see cause and effect in history; the ability to appreciate international relations in history.

Methods:
1. Independent study by topics and making of topical outlines developed gradually.
2. Recitation in class:

    a. Chiefly continuous topical recitations from daily lessons.
    b. Supplemented by brief recitations in response to questions by teacher.
    c. Longitudinal review of special topics.
    d. Written treatment of selected topics.

3. Sketching maps and charts and frequent reference to them in class. Data taken from text and printed maps.
4. Reference reading to supplement the text.
5. Drill on dates and events.

Outline of Course:
1. Review Grade VI by topics. Very brief treatment.
2. Significant facts in American history from Columbus to 1815, and related events in European history.
3. Local history by special assignment to groups.
4. Civil government:

    a. Beginning of local, state, and national government. Declaration of Independence, Articles of Confederation and Constitution.
    b. Discussion of elections in city, state, and nation.

GRADE VIII:

Aim:
1. To teach facts in United States history with special reference to development along certain lines: political, economic, educational, international, industrial, commercial, and scientific.
2. To develop the power to see cause and effect as related to growth of institutions; a knowledge of the growth of the United States as a World power.

Methods:
1. Similar to Grade VII.
2. Systematic longitudinal review of related events and growth of institutions in American history, tracing each movement from earliest beginnings and developing effect on present-day conditions.

Outline of Course:
1. Review Grade VII by topics. Emphasis upon longitudinal treatment.
2. Significant facts in economic, social, intellectual, political, and religious life from 1815 to the present day.

3. Current events from newspapers and magazines.
4. Civil government:
    a. Discussion of election returns in city, state, and national elections and duties of officers chosen.
5. Civics: The Community and the Citizen.

HISTORY AND CIVICS IN THE HIGH SCHOOL

Aims:

Second Year: *The Ancient World and Mediæval History to 1648*
1. To teach scientifically the basic facts in the civilization of the Ancient World and in the life and institutions of the Middle Ages and early Modern History.
2. To develop an understanding of fundamental ideas in government, religion, art, industry, and social life; to acquaint the student with the beginnings of human institutions as embodied in simple forms; to discover and properly evaluate specific contributions of the Ancient and Mediæval Worlds to modern life; to familiarize the student with human personality and its part in human progress; to develop the power to gather and organize historical facts and to reason from them to definite conclusions.

Methods:
1. Topical treatment of subject. Historical narrative analyzed into movements, accounts of institutions, features of civilization, and the like. Each aspect of a movement or institution forms a separate topic and a topic constitutes a lesson unit.
2. Full outline of topic given by teacher together with references for reading and map work.
3. Special oral report by students upon special assigned subjects closely related to the topic for the day.
4. Half-page written theme on a concrete subject.
5. Permanent note-book exercises:
    a. Topical or chronological outlines.
    b. Tabulations of groups of related facts.
    c. Summarizations of periods and movements.
    d. Biographical sketches of type characters.
6. Daily supplementary reading in the library:
    a. One parallel account.
    b. One specialized treatment.
7. Report upon reading by outline in temporary note-book.
8. Outline maps filled in:
    a. Physical.
    b. Colonization.
    c. Territorial expansion.
    d. Roads and military defenses.
    e. Routes of invasions and marches.
    f. Centers of art and culture, religious life, and industry.
9. Reading of historical fiction. Report outside the class hour.
10. Current history at intervals.

Outline of Course:

History I. Civilization of the Ancient World to 800 A.D.
1. Brief sketches of primitive men.
2. Oriental beginnings. Chief contributions to the Ancient World of the following people: Babylonians and Assyrians, Egyptians, Hebrews, Phœnicians, and Persians.
3. The civilization of Ancient Greece.
    a. The land of the Greeks.
    b. The Greeks in Homeric times.

     c. Mycenean culture.
• *d.* Greek colonization.
     e. Athens under Pericles.
     f. Spread of Hellenism to the East.
4. Roman life and culture.
     a. Land of Italy.
     b. Roman origins and early institutions.
     c. Roman expansion through the Mediterranean World.
     d. Decline of the Republic.
     e. The Early Empire: first two centuries.
     f. Christianity and the Empire.
     g. Contributions of Greece and Rome to civilization.
5. Transition to the Middle Ages.

History II. Mediæval Europe 800 to 1648
1. Review of what the Middle Ages started with.
2. Origin and development of characteristic mediæval institutions:
     a. The Church.
     b. Feudalism.
     c. Empire and papacy.
3. The life of the Middle Ages: the peasants, the nobles, the townsmen.
4. Origin and influence of continental movements:
     a. The Crusades.
     b. The rise of monarchic states (emphasis upon England).
     c. The Hundred Years' War.
     d. The Renaissance.
     e. The Reformation.
5. The wars of religion: the struggle for control.

Aims:
   Third Year: Modern Europe and Modern England
1. To teach in a scientific way the facts of the history of Western Europe and of Great Britain in the seventeenth, eighteenth, nineteenth, and twentieth centuries.
2. To develop an understanding of the forces and factors in the making of modern Europe, especially of Great Britain, with stress on the growth of the British Empire; to give a background for an intelligent understanding of American life and institutions; to familiarize the student with the use of books, and to cultivate a taste for historical reading; to train in the ability to do simple and elementary research, and to express the results in clear, simple, and forceful language.

Methods:
1. Topical treatment as before. More extended topics.
2. Oral reports by pupils upon special aspects of modern life and institutions.
3. Written themes upon topics connected with the origin and growth of institutions. Independent judgment to be encouraged in stating conclusions.
4. Note-book work of previous grades enlarged and extended.
5. Daily supplementary reading in library:
     a. Fuller parallel account.
     b. Sources and specialized treatment.
6. Map work of previous year continued.
7. Reading of historical fiction appropriate to the field.
8. Constant and regular use of current history.

Outline of Course:
   History III. Modern Europe. 1648 to date
1. International epochs and relations.
     a. Age of Louis XIV, 1643–1715.
     b. Colonial expansion and rivalry, 1715–1763.
     c. Age of Frederick the Great, 1740–1786.
     d. French Revolution and Napoleonic Era, 1789–1815.

2. Reaction, revolution, and growth of democracy in the 19th century.
3. Expansion of Europe in the 19th century.
4. The Near East and the Far East.
5. Revolution in the Twentieth Century.
6. Advance in science and social organization.

History IV. Modern England. 1603 to date
1. Struggle for constitutional government in the 17th century.
2. Growth of the British Empire.
    a. English settlements in America.
    b. French and English struggle for control.
    c. System of colonial administration.
    d. Movement for federation of Empire.
3. Growth of Parliamentary and cabinet government.
4. The American Revolution and French Revolution.
5. The Industrial Revolution.
6. The Reform Movement of the 19th century.
7. The growth of democracy in the 19th century.
8. Social and industrial problems of to-day.

Aims:

Fourth Year: American History and Civics
1. To teach truthfully the facts in the growth of the American nation and the fundamentals in state and national civics.
2. To develop an understanding and an appreciation of the elements in the making of the American nation; to awaken civic consciousness and create and promote civic ideals.

Methods of Work:
1. Topical treatment continued. Emphasis upon longitudinal topics.
2. Extended oral reports by students upon topics related to American life and institutions.
3. Brief preliminary survey of narrative history; more intensive study of the field by topical treatment.
4. Written theme expositions of some length upon topics requiring independent judgment:
    a. Materials gathered and organized.
    b. Outline and bibliography submitted for approval.
    c. Theme written from outline and from notes.
5. Map work and note-books continued and extended.
6. Term thesis upon Civics Topic.
7. Constant and regular study and use of Current History for illustration and application. Based upon reading of newspaper and magazine.
8. Further reading of historical fiction.

Outline of Course:

History V. The Making of the American Nation, 1760 to 1786
1. The struggle for independence.
2. The Confederation and the critical period.
3. The formation of a Federal Union; the Constitution.
4. Beginning of national life, 1789–1815:
    a. Organization of the government.
    b. Relations of the new nation with foreign powers.
    c. Jeffersonian democracy.
    d. Second war with Great Britain.
5. National development and expansion, 1815–1876:
    a. Economic and political reorganization, 1815–1837.
    b. Slavery and sectionalism, 1837–1856.
    c. Secession and Civil War, 1856–1865.
    d. Reconstruction and reunion, 1865–1876.

6. Structure and organization of state and federal government and relations between the two spheres of government.

History VI. Economic, Social, and Civic Problems 1876 to date
I. American Nation.
    1. Industrial expansion since the Civil War.
    2. Economic problems growing out of this expansion.
        a. The tariff: attempts to reduce the tariff.
        b. Currency and banking.
        c. Combinations of labor and capital.
            (1) The labor unions.
            (2) The growth of trusts.
            (3) Contests between labor and capital.
    3. Political problems since the Civil War.
        a. Party contests: growth of opposition.
        b. Civil service reform.
        c. Relations with foreign powers.
II. Civics.
    1. Separate study of civic problems after the study of the history of the nation.
        a. Problems of municipal government.
        b. Problems of suffrage and the ballot.
        c. Industrial problems.
        d. Taxation and monetary problems.
        e. Conservation of national resources.
    2. Close study of current history in state and nation.

OUTSIDE READING IN HISTORICAL FICTION

Choice of Books. — An approved list of books in historical fiction follows. Each student is required to read the books in the field of history carried. A minimum of sixty (60) points is required for graduation in history.

Examination of the Reading. — Students may pass an oral examination on the books read by previous arrangement with the teacher in charge.

Approved List of Books. — The following books are on the rental list. The list may be extended at the option of the teachers.

History I. Greek

	POINTS
Church, Story of the Iliad	4
Church, Story of the Odyssey	4
Church, Three Greek Children	3
Ebers, Uarda (Egypt)	5
Ellen Palmer, Three Greek Children	2
Homer, The Iliad	10
Homer, The Odyssey	10

History II. Roman

Church, Roman Life and Story	7
Davis, A Friend of Cæsar	5
Kingsley, Hypatia	10
Lytton, Last Days of Pompeii	5
Macaulay, Lays of Ancient Rome	2
Wallace, Ben Hur	9

History III. Mediæval

Crawford, Via Crucis	5
Davis, God Wills It	5
Hewlett, Richard Yea and Nay	4
Reade, The Cloister and the Hearth	15
Scheffel, Ekkehard	5
Scott, The Talisman	4

History IV. Modern Europe

Charles, The Chronicles of the Schonberg-Cotta Family........... 8
Davis, The Friar of Wittenberg...................... 5
Dumas, The Three Musketeers....................... 8
Hugo, L'An '93........................... 5
Muhlbach, Frederick the Great and his Family.................. 5
Porter, Scottish Chiefs.......................... 5

History V. American Colonial

Alden, Betty Alden..................................... 7
Alden, Standish of Standish....................... 6
Caruthers, Cavaliers of Old Virginia......................... 4
Churchill, Richard Carvel......................... 4
Doyle, The Refugees............................. 4
Hawthorne, In Colonial Days......................... 5
Johnston, Prisoners of Hope........................ 4
Johnston, To Have and To Hold...................... 4
Kingsley, Westward Ho!........................ 10
Madison, Colonial Maid of Old Virginia...................... 4
Stoddard, On the Old Frontier...................... 4
Thompson, Green Mountain Boys..................... 5
Wallace, The Fair God........................... 5

History VI. American Nation

Bachellor, D'Ri and I........................... 3
Carleton, One Way Out........................... 4
Churchill, The Crossing.......................... 4
Churchill, The Crisis............................ 4
Civil War Stories from St. Nicholas........................ 3
Ford, Honorable Peter Sterling...................... 3
Fox, Little Shepherd from Kingdom Come...................... 4
Page, Red Rock............................. 4
Sewell, Little Jarvis............................ 2
Stowe, Uncle Tom's Cabin........................... 3
Washington, Up from Slavery...................... 3
Wright, Winning of Barbara Worth........................ 4

The course was completed during the year 1910–11. During the following year some of the weak points in it were strengthened. By the opening of the school year 1912–13 it was felt that the course should be in pretty good working order. Consequently it was thought advisable for the critic teacher in history and the superintendent of schools to visit all classes in history in the fifth, sixth, seventh, and eighth grades in the city. After these visitations the work observed was discussed between the critic teacher and the superintendent and a program for a general meeting of all the teachers observed was prepared. After this general meeting individual meetings were arranged whereby each teacher observed was informed both concerning the strong points and the weak points of her work.

The formal report made by Mr. Williams somewhat later is as follows:

Supt. H. L. Smith
  Bloomington Public Schools
  Bloomington, Indiana

Bloomington, Indiana,
December 31, 1913

My dear Mr. Smith:

Our visitation of your departmental teachers of history and civics was so planned as to render possible a more thorough and intensive study of the work than is often practicable in such surveys. As you know, we observed every teacher in these grades through an entire recitation period, and in some cases through two or more such periods. It was understood by the teachers, I believe, that the work during these visits should be the regular and usual class work. Accordingly, the teaching observed was taken to be typical of the kind done in the field by this group of teachers.

On the whole, the teaching observed is marked by a high degree of efficiency. An atmosphere of cheerful and helpful work is everywhere in evidence. Sympathy and hearty co-operation characterize the relations of teachers and pupils. The responses of the latter are natural and free and show little of the conventional school-room attitude. History is properly made an instrumentality in the preparation of these boys and girls for "social efficiency."

At the general or group conference, held at the close of the visiting, a discussion of values and aims which should dominate the teaching of history preceded a "round table" on proper methods of teaching the subject. An exchange of viewpoint and experience proved mutually helpful to every teacher present. Many questions relating to the problems of the teaching of history were proposed and discussed informally. The teachers, in this conference, manifested an alertness and receptivity which indicate a fine professional attitude. To my mind, this sort of exchange teems with possibilities of fruitful suggestion. In the main, I regard this conference as the most helpful feature of the visitation.

As a basis for further work along this line and to make more tangible the results of the survey I respectfully submit herewith a summary of impressions and recommendations bearing upon the history work in these grades.

In making suggestions with a view to strengthening the work, even where it is already done well, one needs always to bear in mind fundamental assumptions as to values and aims in teaching a subject. Without entering minutely into this point, or undertaking a full analysis of the educative value of history, we may say that the central aim of history teaching is now recognized as social. "We believe that a leading aim in history teaching is to help the child to appreciate what his fellows are doing and to help him to intelligent voluntary action in agreement or disagreement with them," says the Committee of Eight. McMurry voices the opinion, when he says, "To give a vivid and intense realization of social duties and obligations is the essence of the best history instruction." In a word, our task as teachers of history is to develop an appreciative understanding of the organized society of which the pupil is a part and so to help him that he may perform with honesty and intelligence his duties as a citizen.

The organized society of which the child is a part is a highly complex thing. Its institutions, its movements and tendencies, its problems of growth, all have their roots far back in the past. To understand these the child must be led over the path of their earlier development, for no mind can comprehend a thing in its entirety by viewing it in its most advanced stage. Moreover, to help the child so he may ultimately perform adequately his duties as a citizen, he must be trained in those processes which a vital citizenship involves. In brief, these are the power to analyze social situations, to "reduce them to their simpler and typical elements," to determine with some degree of definiteness the factors which enter into them and the probable consequences flowing from them.

This gives the cue to the fundamentals of method in teaching history. First, there must be a certain amount of drill on subject matter, through primary presentation, review, and written work. Second, there should be training in the art of gathering data from books and other sources at hand. Third, there should be constant weighing of facts, balancing of arguments for and against a policy, and passing judgment upon the soundness of a policy or viewpoint. The last is the more vital and fundamental operation in good history teaching.

If I were to attempt to summarize the problems of teaching history in these grades, I should wish to emphasize the following points:

1. History teaching is primarily concerned with training the judgment in dealing with social data, and only secondarily with mere fact-gathering, as such. This is its peculiar discipline. From the peculiarly human character of its material, its conclusions are always approximations, never the exact, logical inferences of mathematical reasoning. They are not to be clothed in technical phraseology, as in natural science, or in terms of fine distinction in meaning, as in a language study. The teacher should avoid straining for answers in terms of his own thinking; rather he should allow the pupil to find his own words to clothe his ideas.

2. History teaching should aim to deal with economic and social aspects, and not political alone, for these are more potent factors in the life of the present than are political or religious phases. Hence, the teacher will need to go beyond the text for much of her material. Gleaning from supplementary accounts needs to be constantly encouraged.

3. History teaching in the grammar grades should be made as concrete as the facilities will allow. At best, the material is abstract and remote from experience. Concrete examples should be given to illustrate facts of growth, movement, settlement, agreement. Where possible the material should be visualized. The blackboard for diagrams, outlines by main heads, sketch maps, crude drawings; the wall map for locations, position of boundaries, physical features; pictures for vivid impressions of costume, weapons and armor, buildings, walls, art creations; all are to be manipulated skillfully and at every turn.

4. History teaching should center itself about certain focal points in every lesson. The lesson should not only have unity but close organization as well. The main facts should stand out prominently in the presentation, so that children may carry away definite ideas and a true perspective. A good way to accomplish this is by use of the "topical" treatment. A pupil develops the topic, others adding to or commenting upon the treatment. Discussions follow upon questions of policy, worth, wisdom, truthfulness, and so on of the issue under view. The teacher leads and directs the thinking by skillful questioning. Simple problems may be set in assigning the lesson.

These are a few of the more important and central aspects of the problem of efficient history instruction. Some of them are common to other studies, perhaps, but all are vital to this great socializing subject.

If I were to add, by way of supplementing the foregoing statement, an analysis of the weak points in the actual teaching of history in your departmental grades, I should wish to sum it up in this way:

First, there is a noticeable tendency to ignore the concrete and visualized elements in teaching the subject. Maps, pictures, charts, diagrams, reference to sources, except in the advanced eighth grade, are conspicuous by their absence.

Second, the emphasis is too often placed upon the facts as such, rather than with the exercise of the judgment in dealing with the facts. Effective drill and review are in evidence, but the more valuable aspects of analyzing situations and drawing conclusions are slighted. Here again, I must make exception of the advanced class in eighth grade history and civics.

Third, some formalistic teaching, emphasis upon form of expression and mode of thinking, is observable in a few cases. The rich content is thereby lightly treated or neglected.

Finally, more attention to the social and economic factors in the nation's growth is needed. Of course the teacher is limited to a degree by the material of the text-book, and text-book writers have so far neglected these important phases. But the teacher should seek at all times to supplement the text-book with other books.

In conclusion, I cannot refrain from conveying something of my sense of gratitude for the uniform courtesy and kindness extended me in this work by the teachers and principals, as well as the superintendent. Truly, it was a work of mutual stimulation and suggestiveness. Sincerely yours,

O. H. WILLIAMS, *Critic Teacher in History*

TABLE LXXXIV

SHOWING BY GRADES AND SUBJECTS THE NUMBER OF MINUTES SPENT PER WEEK BY EACH PUPIL DURING REGULAR SCHOOL HOURS IN STUDY AND IN RECITATION

In column headed "R" is recorded the total number of minutes per week devoted to recitations in the particular subjects. In column headed "s" is a total record regarding time spent in study in all subjects combined.

SUBJECT	IB	IA	2B	2A	3B	3A	4B	4A	5B	5A	6B	6A	7B	7A	8B	8A	TOTAL R	PER CENT SCHOOL HOURS GIVEN TO EACH SUBJECT FOR RECITATION
Opening exercises	75	75	75	75	75	75	50	50	50	50	50	50	50	50	50	50	950	6.7
Arithmetic					100	100	125	125	125	125	125	125	125	125	125	125	1450	10.2
Reading	200	200	200	200	200	200	125	125	125	125	125	125	150	150	150	125	2525	17.8
Spelling			75	75	50	50	75	75	75	75	75	75	50	50	50	50	900	6.4
Phonics	75	75	75	75	25												325	2.3
Language	75	75	75	75	100	100	100	100	75	75							925	6.5
History					50	50	60	75	100	100	125	125	125	125	125	75	1135	8.0
Geography					50	50	60	75	100	100	125	125	125	125	75		1010	7.1
Physiology									75	75	50	50	25	25	25	50	400	2.8
Writing	75	75	75	75	75	75	75	75	50	50	50	50	25	25	50	50	960	6.8
Freehand drawing	60	60	60	60	60	60	60	60	60	60	60	60	60	60	60	60	940	6.6
Mechanical "									60[2]	60[2]	60[2]	60[2]	60[2]	60[2]	60[2]	60[2]		
Music	75	75	75	75	75	75	60	60	60	60	60	60	60	60	60	60	1070	7.6
Manual training			75	75	75	75			60[1]	60[1]	60[1]	60[1]	60[1]	60[1]	60[1]	60[1]	420	3.0
Sewing									60[1]	60[1]	60[1]	60[1]	60[1]	60[1]	60[1]	60[1]	900	6.4
Grammar												150[4]	150[4]	150[4]	150[4]	150[4]	240	1.7
Cooking													60[3]	60[3]	60[3]	60[3]		
Agriculture											150[4]	60[3]	60[3]	60[3]	60[3]	60[3]		
Total (R)	635	635	710	785	835	790	845	705	885	1035	1070	1105	1090	1090	965	965	14150	99.9
Total (s)	565	565	590	515	515	610	705	885	565	415	430	395	410	410	535	535		
Recitation and study combined	1200	1200	1300	1300	1350	1350	1400	1400	1450	1450	1500	1500	1500	1500	1500	1500		

[1] Boys take manual training and the girls take sewing.
[2] Boys take mechanical drawing and girls take freehand drawing.
[3] Girls take cooking and boys take agriculture, though as now arranged only a limited number of the boys can be accommodated in agriculture classes.
[4] Grammar and composition combined; grammar three days in the week and composition two days in the week.

CHAPTER VI

ACHIEVEMENT OF PUPILS

1. Arithmetic. Indianapolis Tests

Abstract Arithmetic Tests

The problems used for these tests were problems made out by the supervising principals in the Indianapolis schools seven, eight, and nine years ago. Considerable thought was given to the grading of the problems, and they consequently serve as a good basis for comparison. The different tests were given in Bloomington at various times from the fall of 1909 to the spring of 1914. Some of the tests were given by the superintendent and some by the teachers. Comparisons are made of the results obtained under both conditions of giving the tests. The papers were corrected by the teachers and the results and original papers were handed in to the principals for checking and comparing. No credit was given for answers unless every figure in the answer was exactly right.

The following set of problems was dictated by the superintendent October 15, 1909, and November 7, 1913, according to the directions indicated.

Abstract Arithmetic

October 15, 1909

Grade 3a

Read *once* slowly and distinctly.

1. Write in figures one hundred ten.
2. Add: (Time, 2 minutes.)

    13
    65
    82
    37
    12

3. 21¢ less 5¢ (Answers only).
4. 4 and 9.
5. 9 times 3. 3 times 7.

GRADE 4B

Read *once* slowly and distinctly.
1. Write in figures forty thousand, four hundred.
2. Add: (Time, 3 minutes.)

```
        7
       39
       82
       38
       83
       38
       69
       29
       53
       89
```

3. From 902 take 327. (Time, 2 minutes.)
4. Multiply 6,859 by 4. (Time, 3 minutes.)
5. Divide 23,906 by 3. (Time, 3 minutes.)

GRADE 4A

Read *once* slowly and distinctly.
1. Write in figures twenty-three dollars and seven cents.
   Write in figures two hundred eight thousand four.
2. Add: (Time, 3 minutes.)

```
      182
      359
      423
      229
      259
      732
      992
      224
      856
      698
```

3. From 111,086 take 10,877. (Time, 2 minutes.)
4. Multiply 93,874 by 56. (Time, 3 minutes.)
5. Divide 37,632 by 49. (Time, 3 minutes.)

GRADES 5B AND 5A

Read *once* slowly and distinctly.
1. Write in figures twenty-three million seven thousand fifteen
2. Add: (Time, 2 minutes.)

```
      634
      476
      574
      337
      784
      369
      992
      738
      697
      275
```

3. Multiply 73,869 by 870. (Time, 3 minutes.)
4. Divide 1,731,388 by 186. (Time, 4 minutes.)
5. $\{\frac{2}{3} + \frac{1}{5}\} - \frac{5}{12} = ?$ (Time, 3 minutes.)

GRADES 6B AND 6A

1. Add: (Time, 3 minutes.)
                9367
                8888
                9768
                7998
                8876
                6669
                5998
                9747
                6959

2. From 604.0906 take 206.10386. (Time, 2 minutes.)

3. Multiply 690.78 by 7.098. (Time, 3 minutes.)

4. Divide 1257.0373 by 1.97. (Time, 4 minutes.)

5. $(\frac{7}{8} \times \frac{4}{5}) \div (2\frac{1}{3} - 1\frac{3}{5})$. (Time, 4 minutes. Write on board.)

GRADES 6B AND 6A

1. Write in figures nine million seven hundred thousand three hundred
   and two and five ten-thousandths.

2. Add: (Time, 3 minutes.)
                4989
                7589
                6779
                4788
                8598
                8955
                9399
                5787
                9908
                5679

3. Multiply 908.04 by 706.375. (Time, 4 minutes.)

4. Divide 319,703.3 by .69. Carry to two places. (Time, 4 minutes.)

5. $(3\frac{1}{3} \times 2\frac{3}{4}) \div (7\frac{1}{5} - 4\frac{4}{15}) = ?$ (Time, 4 minutes. Write on the board.)

TABLE LXXXV

RESULTS OF ABSTRACT ARITHMETIC TESTS GIVEN BY THE SUPERINTENDENT,
OCTOBER 15, 1909, AND NOVEMBER 7, 1913

BUILDING	GRADE	GRADE AVERAGE 1909	GRADE AVERAGE 1913	1913 GAIN OVER 1909	1913 LOSS OVER 1909
Fairview.............	3A	73	68		5
McCalla.............	3A	67	83	16	
Central.............	3A	75	72.5		2.5
All buildings combined..	3A	71	75.7	4.7	
Fairview.............	4B	77.6	71.6		6
McCalla.............	4B	38	71.7	33.7	
Central.............	4B	58.8	82	23.2	
All buildings combined.	4B	57.7	74.3	16.6	
Fairview.............	4A	59	51.6		7.4
McCalla.............	4A	36	66	30	
Central.............	4A	21	49	28	
All buildings combined..	4A	36.7	56.7	20	

TABLE LXXXV *(Continued)*

Fairview.............	5B	40	47	7
McCalla.............	5B	26	49	23
Central.............	5B	20	41	21
All buildings combined..	5B	28.6	46.2	17.6
Fairview.............	5A	46	63.3	17.3
McCalla.............	5A	36.3	51.8	15.5
Central.............	5A	Missing	44.9	
All buildings combined..	5A	41.2	53.4	12.2
Fairview.............	6B	20	60	40
McCalla.............	6B	Missing	35.3	
Central.............	6B	21	34.5	
All buildings combined..	6B	20.4	42.5	22.1
Fairview.............	6A	31	Missing	
McCalla.............	6A	30	46	16
Central.............	6A	35	Missing	
All buildings combined..	6A	31.8	45.8	14
Fairview.............	7B ⎫			
McCalla.............	7B ⎬ Reports by separate buildings missing			
Central.............	7B ⎭			
All buildings combined..	7B	31.2	42.4	11.2
Fairview.............	7A ⎫			
McCalla.............	7A ⎪ All summaries missing for 1909			
Central.............	7A ⎬			
All buildings combined..	⎭			

SUMMARY OF TABLE LXXXV

1. The teaching of the fundamentals seems not to have improved much during the four years in the 3A grade, where the results were good in 1909.

2. In all grades except the 3A there was a marked improvement during the four years.

3. The loss in the Fairview 4B and 4A grades is accounted for by the transfer of the 4B and 4A teacher, an excellent arithmetic teacher, to the 6B and 6A grades. The increase from 20 to 60 per cent in the 6B grade is accounted for in the same way.

4. The McCalla building, which made distinctly the poorest showing of all the buildings in 1909, came to the front rapidly under the stimulus of comparative grades, as shown by the measurement of the results.

The following abstract arithmetic test was given September 28, 1909, and December 22, 1911, and December 17, 1913. September 28, 1909 was the first time an examination had been given in the schools by the superintendent. The low grades made at that time can be explained partially from that fact. Since the 1909 test was given at the beginning of the term, the test for the preceding grade was used in every case. That is, the 6A test, as it appears in the accompanying list, was given September 28, 1909, to the 7B's, while the same set of questions was given December 1911, and December 1913, to the 6A's. This fact makes the comparison of results fairer. The grades as recorded for 1909 in the following results will be pushed down one grade. Results obtained from the 7B's, for instance, will be recorded as results from 6A's because the 7B pupils in September, 1909, were 6A's the previous term and were given the 6A test as 7B's in 1909.

Abstract Arithmetic
Grade 3A

December 22, 1911

1. Write in numbers, two thousand one hundred ten; five dollars and five cents.
2. Add: (Time, 3 minutes.)

    51
    34
    72
    14
    19

3. Multiply 3789 by 4. (Time, 3 minutes.)
4. From 382 take 293. (Time, 2 minutes.)
5. Divide 46,893 by 3. (Time, 3 minutes.)

Grade 4B

1. Write in numbers, eight hundred seven thousand six.
2. Add: (Time, 3 minutes.)

    363
    639
    813
    335
    963
    235
    976

3. From 32,907 take 6,958. (Time, 2 minutes.)
4. Multiply 68,790 by 48. (Time, 3 minutes.)
5. Divide 612,637 by 7. (Time, 3 minutes.)

Grade 4A

1. Write in numbers, forty dollars and seventy cents; forty-three dollars and eight cents.
2. Add: (Time, 3 minutes.)

    797
    276
    765
    656
    255
    646
    762
    437
    768

3. From 91,111 take 8,927. (Time, 2 minutes.)
4. Multiply 29,478 by 79. (Time, 3 minutes.)
5. Divide 75,639 by 24. (Time, 4 minutes.)

GRADES 5B AND 5A

1. Add: (Time, 3 minutes.)
   987
   849
   894
   789
   683
   979
   996
   895
   787
   999
2. Multiply 96,087 by 478.   (Time, 4 minutes.)
3. From 904,215 take 764,408.   (Time, 2 minutes.)
4. Divide 139,059 by 196.   (Time, 5 minutes.)
5. $\frac{2}{3} + \frac{1}{6} - \frac{5}{12} = ?$ (Time, 2 minutes.)

GRADES 6B AND 6A

1. Add: (Time, 3 minutes.)
   6847
   9879
   5568
   4896
   7455
   3978
   8607
   6793
   2387
   7677
2. From 508.069 take 99.1596.   (Time, 3 minutes.)
3. Multiply 97.86 by .8709.   (Time, 3 minutes.)
4. Divide 7165.985 by 7.9.   (Time, 3 minutes.)
5. $(1\frac{2}{5} - \frac{2}{3}) + (1\frac{5}{6} \times \frac{3}{4}) = ?$ (Time, 5 minutes after problem is written on board.)

GRADES 7B, 7A, 8B AND 8A

1. Add: (Time, 3 minutes.)
   9478
   6589
   4037
   7089
   6908
   4007
   7987
   6897
   8989
   4397
2. From 80,091.25 take 8,099.067.   (Time, 3 minutes.)
3. Multiply 890.75 by 107.035.   (Time, 3 minutes.)
4. Divide 2438.690 by 27.4.   (Time, 4 minutes.)
5. $(5\frac{1}{5} + 6\frac{1}{3}) \times (6\frac{1}{3} + 9\frac{1}{2}) = ?$ (Time, 5 minutes after problem is written on board.)

TABLE LXXXVI

RESULTS OF ABSTRACT ARITHMETIC TESTS GIVEN SEPTEMBER 28, 1909,
DECEMBER 22, 1911, AND DECEMBER 17, 1913

1909 tests given by superintendent and 1911 and 1913 tests by teachers. All pupils, white and colored, included in 1911 and 1913 tests. Only white children included in 1909 test.

GRADE	1909	1911	1913
3A		77.9	84.7
4B		74.3	72.4
4A	46.6	78	76.6
5B	37.5	67.4	66.1
5A	28.6	64.3	70.2
6B	20.3	59.7	56.4
6A	29.4	51.6	59.3
7B	29.4	50.3	48.1
7A	26	51	51.2
8B	25.4	54.6	56
8A	29.3	64.5	66.8

The following abstract arithmetic test was given by the superintendent October 27, 1910, and March 19, 1914.

GRADE 3A

October 27, 1910

Read *once* slowly and distinctly.

1. Write in figures one hundred nine.
2. Add: (Time, 2 minutes.)

       36
       65
       53
       44
       67
       52

3. From 987 take 453.
4. Multiply 859 by 4.
5. Divide 1296 by 3.

GRADE 4B

Read *once* slowly and distinctly.

1. Write in figures forty thousand, four hundred nine.
2. Add: (Time, 3 minutes.)

       97
       39
       82
       38
       69
       29
       53
       89

3. From 902 take 427.   (Time 1½ minutes.)
4. Multiply 6,859 by 6.   (Time 2½ minutes.)
5. Divide 23,906 by 3.   (Time, 3 minutes.)

Grade 4a

Read *once* slowly and distinctly.

1. Write in figures, four hundred two thousand seventy.
2. Add: (Time, 4 minutes.)

```
897
276
765
656
255
646
762
437
768
```

3. From 111,086 take 10,877.   (Time, 1½ minutes.)
4. Multiply 93,874 by 76.   (Time, 4 minutes.)
5. Divide 37,632 by 42.   (Time, 5 minutes.)

Grades 5b and 5a

1. Add: (Time, 4 minutes.)

```
987
849
894
789
683
979
996
895
787
999
```

2. Multiply 65,048 by 546.   (Time, 4 minutes.)
3. Write in figures twenty-three million, seventy thousand five.
4. From 82,311,024 take 46,973,687.   (Time 1½ minutes.)
5. Divide 2,753,296 by 364.   (Time, 6 minutes.)

Grade 6b

1. Add: (Time, 3 minutes.)

```
8989
8589
6779
4788
8598
8955
9399
5787
9908
5679
```

2. Multiply 96,587 by 478.   (Time, 4 minutes.)
3. Divide 139,059 by 196.   (Time, 4 minutes.)
4. $5\frac{2}{3} - 1\frac{3}{4} + 7\frac{5}{8}$.   Reduce fraction to lowest terms in answer.   (Time, 5 minutes.)

GRADES 6A, 7B, 7A, 8B AND 8A

1. Add: (Time, 3 minutes.)
                 65,843
                 76,868
                 66,989
                 58,393
                 79,656
                 57,866
                 38,575
                 75,967
2. Divide 763.6399 by 9.67. (Time, 5 minutes.)
3. Multiply 98.756 by 76.8. (Time, 4 minutes.)
4. $(3\frac{1}{3} \times 2\frac{3}{4}) \div (7\frac{1}{5} - 4\frac{4}{15}) = ?$ (Time, 6 minutes. Write on board.)

All of these tests show clearly the effects of systematic drill in the fundamentals. Since the fall of 1909, special attention has been given to the work. Tests have been given, teachers' meetings have been held, and the best teachers of arithmetic have been visited by all teachers of the system. As a result, both teachers and pupils have taken a pride in trying to improve the arithmetic work. During the past year the emphasis was shifted slightly from the fundamentals to the reasoning processes.

TABLE LXXXVII

RESULTS OF ABSTRACT ARITHMETIC TESTS GIVEN BY THE SUPERINTENDENT OCTOBER 27, 1910 AND MARCH 19, 1914

BUILDING	GRADE	GRADE AVERAGE 1910	GRADE AVERAGE 1914	1914 GAIN OVER 1910	1914 LOSS OVER 1910
Fairview	3A	74	92.6	18.6	
McCalla	3A	73.1	76	2.9	
Central	3A	81	80.6		.4
All buildings combined	3A	70.6	83	12.4	
Fairview	4B	76.8	65.8		11
McCalla	4B	60	87	27	
Central	4B	66.3	85.7	19.4	
All buildings combined	4B	69.2	80.3	11.1	
Fairview	4A	52.5	71.4	18.9	
McCalla	4A	45	64.4	19.4	
Central	4A	33	38.4	5.4	
All buildings combined	4A	43.5	60.2	16.7	
Fairview	5B	50	58	.8	
McCalla	5B	40.6	74	33.4	
Central	5B	37	51.6	14.6	
All buildings combined	5B	44.1	61.8	17.7	
Fairview	5A	52	79.6	27.6	
McCalla	5A	41.8	81	39.2	
Central	5A	52	55	3	
All buildings combined	5A	47.3	73.6	26.3	

Fairview..............	6B	46	62.5	16.5
McCalla..............	6B	40	56	16
Central..............	6B	29	31	2
All buildings combined..	6B	37.8	50	12.2
Fairview..............	6A	46	No 6A's	
McCalla..............	6A	21	36.7	35.7
Central..............	6A	31	Test not given	
All buildings combined..	6A	33.4	56.7	23.3

SUMMARY OF TABLE LXXXVII

1. Maximum improvement in the fundamentals cannot be gained in a year. The 1910 tests were given after a year of emphasis on fundamentals. The 1914 tests show marked improvement over the 1910 tests.

2. Considering the system as a whole, there was marked improvement in all grades during the four years, though an occasional loss occurred in individual buildings.

2. STONE TESTS IN ARITHMETIC [1]

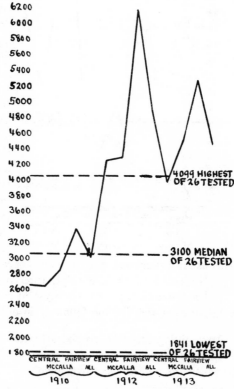

FIG. 1. — SCORES IN FUNDAMENTALS. 1910–1913.

The Stone tests were given to sixth-grade pupils in Bloomington three different times. First, during the second semester of the school year 1909–10; second, about the same time of year 1911–12; third, spring of 1912–13. The tests were given the first time by Dr. Stone himself. The second and third times the tests were given by Dr. E. E. Jones, of the department of education, Indiana University. The papers were graded and the results tabulated each time by Dr. Stone. Table LXXXVIII*a* gives a summary of standings for the three years. Graphs 1, 2, 3, 4 show accomplishment and per cent of inaccuracy of Bloomington's sixth grade com-

[1] For the problems used and the method of scoring, see Arithmetical Abilities, C. W. Stone, published by Bureau of Publications, Teachers College, Columbia University.

pared with the original twenty-six school systems included in Dr. Stone's tests and study.

The Stone test was first given at the conclusion of one half year of drill to overcome the defects revealed by the tests given early the first semester of the year 1909–10. The first Stone test shows the Bloomington sixth grade:

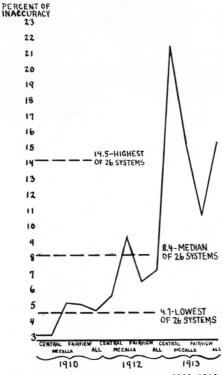

1. Slightly above the median for the twenty-six systems tested by Dr. Stone in amount done both in reasoning and in fundamentals.

2. Well toward the top in per cent of accuracy. In reasoning the per cent of inaccuracy was 17.6, only two other systems of the twenty-six making a lower per cent. In fundamentals the per cent of inaccuracy was greater, ranking Bloomington near the bottom of the first third of the twenty-six systems as far as per cent of accuracy is concerned.

FIG. 2. MISTAKES IN ADDITION. 1910–1913.

3. Noticeably weak in multiplication and division.

4. On the accuracy side, strongest in subtraction, with addition, multiplication and division following in order.

After giving this test, special attention was given to weaknesses exhibited in fundamentals. The 1912 summary indicates the degree to which the defects were overcome.

The principal conclusions drawn from the second test are:

1. Total scores in fundamentals increased to an unlooked-for high score; better, in fact, than the highest of the original twenty-six systems.

2. Total scores in reasoning increased only slightly.

3. Inaccuracy increased noticeably both in fundamentals and in reasoning.

The following year considerably less attention was given to the fundamentals and more to reasoning. The third test shows the results as follows:

1. Decrease in amount attempted in fundamentals, but still a relatively high score.

2. Slight increase in total scores in reasoning.

3. Alarming increase in inaccuracy both in fundamentals and in reasoning.

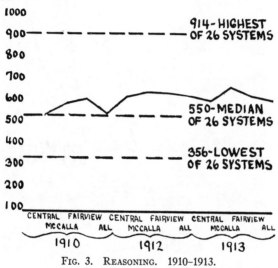

Fig. 3. Reasoning. 1910–1913.

TABLE LXXXVIIIA

Date of Test	Schools	Scores in Fundamentals [1]					Accuracy Per Cent of Addition Incorrect	Scores in Reasoning	Accuracy Per Cent of Problems in Correct Reasoning
		Add.	Sub.	Mult.	Div.	Total			
Feb. 1910	Central					2656	2.3	550	6.8
	McCalla					2863	5.4	600	14.1
	Fairview					3400	5.3	616	23.2
	All Schools					3066	4.9	599	17.6
Feb. 1912	Central	1527	611	1466	811	4316	5.9	630.0	25.0
	McCalla	1490	503	1509	809	4342	9.4	667.9	30.5
	Fairview	2140	720	2180	1160	6200	6.8	643.6	29.5
	All Schools	1719	611	1722	927	4962	7.4	647.2	28.3
May 1913	Central	1433	458	1368	761	4020	21.9	612	43.5
	McCalla	1567	537	1590	866	4561	15.2	688	35.1
	Fairview	1816	619	1826	992	5314	10.9	634	43.2
	All Schools	1569	525	1570	853	4518	16.7	611	40.6

[1] All scores recorded on basis of 100 pupils.

The Courtis tests given the latter part of May, 1913, to the 6A grade also show a greater per cent of inaccuracy than is shown for the years 1911 and 1914. The results for those three years in Tests

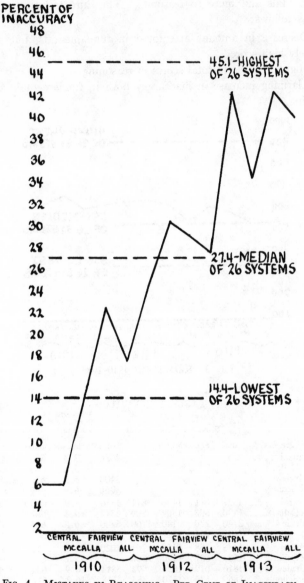

FIG. 4.   MISTAKES IN REASONING.   PER CENT OF INACCURACY.
1910–1913.

6, 7, and 8 in Series A are as follows for the 6A grade, the latter half of the sixth year:

TABLE LXXXVIIIb

RESULTS OF COURTIS TESTS 6, 7 AND 8, SERIES A, IN SIXTH GRADE

Test 6

	NUMBER ATTEMPTED	NUMBER RIGHT	PER CENT OF ACCURACY
1911...................	4.5	3.9	86.7
1913...................	3.8	2.7	71.5
1914...................	4.7	4.4	93.6

Test 7

	NUMBER ATTEMPTED	NUMBER RIGHT	PER CENT OF ACCURACY
1911...................	11.0	8.3	75.5
1913...................	11.2	7.9	70.5
1914...................	11.7	8.1	69.2

Test 8

	NUMBER ATTEMPTED	NUMBER RIGHT	PER CENT OF ACCURACY
1911...................	3.0	1.8	60.0
1913...................	2.8	1.3	46.4
1914...................	3.0	2.1	70.0

The results in Table LXXXVIIIb indicate that the 6A grade in 1913 was somewhat below normal in per cent of accuracy, but they show up considerably better in the Courtis tests than in the Stone tests. I am unable to explain the great difference shown. No other tests given during the past five years show the degree of increase of inaccuracy that the Stone tests show.

3. COLUMN ADDITION — HAGGERTY AND SMITH TEST

The following test in addition was given as a preliminary test to serve as a basis from which to figure improvement in skill in addition resulting from daily five-minute practice periods, a problem undertaken in the Bloomington schools by M. E. Haggerty and H. L. Smith in the fall of 1912. Different groups of children were practiced five minutes a day for twenty days under varying directions, some being urged to work for accuracy alone, others for speed alone, still others for general efficiency. This complete study will probably be published ultimately. Here is given only that portion of it which shows the ability by grades, at the beginning of the term, of children in the Bloomington schools to add problems of this particular type.

The following are the problems as given to the various grades. Children began work at a given signal and worked for five minutes.

The test was given by the superintendent of schools. In most cases, the children were not seated in their own rooms for the test, but were grouped together in large groups in an assembly room. The children were carefully instructed beforehand as to the directions so that they were not confused over that point. When the signal to stop was

GRADES 4B AND 4A

(15)	(14)	(13)	(12)	(11)	(10)	(9)	(8)	(7)	(6)	(5)	(4)	(3)	(2)	(1)
59	18	54	97	25	51	65	84	45	97	30	79	44	83	48
65	75	07	04	59	33	63	22	54	58	87	37	74	76	24
43	92	94	58	07	81	66	07	42	32	29	12	53	62	39
24	35	24	39	97	50	42	96	54	16	03	11	55	55	28
72	86	13	38	28	98	17	33	21	08	66	63	68	14	57
41	83	54	16	56	32	08	18	97	11	47	12	73	27	94
30	72	64	67	42	19	16	79	91	23	16	49	62	55	32
26	86	61	21	89	02	52	33	77	16	86	62	96	38	74

GRADES 5B, 5A, 6B AND 6A

(15)	(14)	(13)	(12)	(11)	(10)	(9)	(8)	(7)	(6)	(5)	(4)	(3)	(2)	(1)
34	05	53	71	78	16	78	69	99	23	47	36	46	95	82
67	98	55	65	18	04	25	79	85	67	76	27	12	91	77
85	49	12	32	36	41	79	88	76	05	83	31	47	81	09
03	47	40	61	42	65	70	73	15	87	12	73	87	33	67
54	91	29	25	82	93	19	86	53	64	30	85	99	29	53
28	63	76	43	44	75	50	05	84	21	36	40	03	18	48
19	14	80	06	01	98	97	91	43	24	20	68	56	59	75
71	03	69	89	23	76	71	92	66	41	09	75	37	85	16
32	61	47	37	53	35	08	05	75	58	57	47	26	97	65
32	35	54	12	07	43	26	84	63	27	15	16	68	08	89
81	40	32	24	95	03	35	52	92	69	18	63	44	28	70
62	18	11	16	83	94	22	06	41	30	94	04	42	19	69
17	48	25	78	03	80	20	78	38	27	00	41	24	27	54

GRADES 7B, 7A, 8B AND 8A

(15)	(14)	(13)	(12)	(11)	(10)	(9)	(8)	(7)	(6)	(5)	(4)	(3)	(2)	(1)
79	19	24	00	57	99	59	15	04	63	70	22	40	70	08
76	79	02	13	41	93	49	17	53	22	84	30	33	52	19
57	86	51	01	07	55	18	36	64	18	22	67	76	75	77
25	76	68	59	36	48	12	80	33	39	04	62	10	61	86
80	51	95	96	10	23	03	32	79	76	89	34	86	85	44
69	06	23	80	75	17	13	27	41	12	91	50	18	87	77
75	93	25	95	87	18	85	74	50	51	23	53	52	28	61
80	16	90	07	31	59	43	02	24	05	12	14	09	12	22
54	67	04	83	51	26	06	53	24	19	50	35	90	45	75
43	81	48	32	23	24	86	71	18	34	61	65	42	74	69
49	84	79	74	49	67	30	65	28	47	95	74	36	05	00
15	77	28	81	87	08	62	01	43	08	19	83	90	94	93
98	58	51	02	76	48	45	18	82	30	78	76	91	28	22
62	37	42	14	41	29	76	17	02	51	06	12	95	45	43
72	65	90	21	62	19	92	46	49	13	74	41	83	40	56
90	53	47	00	30	05	36	08	15	26	74	65	76	71	30
83	42	34	32	63	21	96	23	50	18	00	60	13	82	39
42	36	64	57	50	48	24	32	76	93	85	13	35	92	04

given, each child indicated by a short horizontal line the point which he had reached in the unfinished column. This mark served as a guide in determining the number of combinations made by each pupil. The per cent of accuracy was determined by dividing the whole number of columns completely added into the number of columns correctly added. Pupils worked as many problems as they could in five minutes' time, working at their normal rate. Not all pupils in each grade are represented in this test. Representative pupils from all grades are included, however. Each building is also represented, though not all grades in each building. The following table shows the results in this addition test.

TABLE LXXXIX

AVERAGE NUMBER OF COMBINATIONS IN ADDITION WITH PER CENT OF ACCURACY, BY GRADES

GRADE	NUMBER TAKING TEST	AVERAGE PER CENT OF ACCURACY ATTAINED	AVERAGE NUMBER OF COMBINATIONS MADE IN FIVE MINUTES
4B	51	68.5	88.5
4A	36	76.0	120.8
5B	27	54.0	119.4
5A	33	57.5	161.4
6B	31	58.4	148.5
6A	41	58.5	134.2
7B	58	57.2	150.4
7A	36	54.2	164.5
8B	52	53.2	165.5
8A	52	67.6	178.0

A noticeable fact about these results is that even within the grades tested on the same list of problems, there is not, as we would expect to find, a steady increase either in speed or accuracy from lower to higher grades although the general tendency is upward. The per cent of accuracy hovers around 60 and is therefore in reasonable accord with the findings of Courtis in his addition tests.

4. COURTIS TESTS IN ARITHMETIC

Table XC gives a double comparison. It gives a comparison between the achievement of the Bloomington schools in the years 1911 and 1914 with the Courtis standard of achievement. It also furnishes a comparison of Bloomington achievement in 1911 with its own achievement in 1914. The Courtis standards are for both halves of the sixth grade combined. Bloomington results are given by half years separately. The Courtis tests were given for the first time in the Bloomington schools in 1911 a little less than two years after the special emphasis began to be placed on the fundamentals in Arithmetic.

TABLE XC

Results in Courtis Test in Arithmetic, Series A, Eight Tests

Grade	Test No. 1 Attempts			Test No. 2 Attempts			Test No. 3 Attempts			Test No. 4 Attempts			Test No. 5 Attempts		
	Bloom-ington 1911	Bloom-ington 1914	Courtis Stand-ard	Bloom-ington 1911	Bloom-ington 1914	Courtis Stand-ard	Bloom-ington 1911	Bloom-ington 1914	Courtis Stand-ard	Bloom-ington 1911	Bloom-ington 1914	Courtis Stand-ard	Bloom-ington 1911	Bloom-ington 1914	Courtis Stand-ard
4B	32.6	30.9		27.7	25.1		25.0	22.0		25.0	21.0		72.0	68.0	
4A	42.8	35.0		33.0	31.0		29.1	27.0		29.0	26.0		82.2	77.0	
All of 4th Grade			34			25			23			23			75
5B	36.0	39.0		31.0	31.2		28.0	28.3		28.8	28.7		72.4	79.0	
5A	42.8	38.7		37.5	33.0		31.7	28.5		36.2	31.3		89.8	84.1	
All of 5th Grade			42			31			30			30			84
6B	46.4	43.5		39.4	36.8		34.6	30.0		37.6	34.2		91.6	90.5	
6A	44.6	47.0		37.8	38.7		34.3	33.3		35.0	36.1		94.7	91.8	
All of 6th Grade			50			38			37			37			92
7B	50.0	47.5		39.0	39.0		35.3	33.3		37.4	37.6		98.3	95.6	
7A	51.0	51.3		41.8	42.8		34.2	34.2		37.2	41.0		99.7	98.4	
All of 7th Grade			58			44			41			44			100
8B	53.0	56.2		44.0	46.0		37.0	37.6		41.0	44.8		107.0	101.7	
8A	57.2	59.0		46.8	50.0		39.8	40.0		46.1	49.6		109.9	105.0	
All of 8th Grade			63			49			45			49			108

TABLE XC (*Continued*)

RESULTS IN COURTIS TEST IN ARITHMETIC, SERIES A, EIGHT TESTS

GRADE	TEST No. 6 ATTEMPTS Bloomington 1911	Bloomington 1914	Courtis Standard	TEST No. 6 RIGHTS Bloomington 1911	Bloomington 1914	Courtis Standard	TEST No. 7 ATTEMPTS Bloomington 1911	Bloomington 1914	Courtis Standard	TEST No. 7 RIGHTS Bloomington 1911	Bloomington 1914	Courtis Standard	TEST No. 8 ATTEMPTS Bloomington 1911	Bloomington 1914	Courtis Standard	TEST No. 8 RIGHTS Bloomington 1911	Bloomington 1914	Courtis Standard
4B	3.2	3.0		2.2	2.5		7.2	6.7		4.1	3.8			2.3			.3	
4A	3.4	3.8		2.6	3.2		7.8	8.0		5.9	5.3		2.3	2.5		1.1	1.0	
All of 4th Grade			3.5			1.8			7.0			3.5			2.9			.7
5B	3.8	3.8		2.8	2.4		7.6	9.2		6.2	6.1		2.9	2.3		1.2	1.3	
5A	4.3	3.7		3.4	3.3		10.3	9.7		6.6	6.7		3.3	2.4		1.0	1.4	
All of 5th Grade			4.2			2.6			9.0			5.2			3.1			1.0
6B	4.7	4.4		3.9	4.1		11.5	10.5		8.0	7.6		3.3	2.9		1.7	1.6	
6A	4.5	4.7		3.9	4.4		11.0	11.7		8.3	8.1		3.0	3.0		1.8	2.1	
All of 6th Grade			4.9			3.5			11.0			6.7			3.4			1.4
7B	4.6	4.9		4.3	4.5		11.0	12.1		9.1	8.1		3.5	3.6		2.3	2.1	
7A	4.9	5.1		4.5	4.8		11.8	12.8		8.1	9.0		3.3	3.9		2.4	2.7	
All of 7th Grade			5.6			4.5			12.5			8.2			3.7			1.9
8B	5.8	5.9		5.4	5.6		13.1	13.0		9.2	10.2		4.2	4.4		2.9	3.1	
8A	6.4	5.8		6.1	5.6		14.2	15.1		10.4	11.5		4.7	4.7		3.5	3.1	
All of 8th Grade			6.4			5.7			14.0			9.4			4.0			2.5

1. The 1911 results in Test 1, single combinations in addition show grades 4B, 4A approximately equal to the Courtis standard, whereas all other grades are below, the greatest difference being in the 7B and 7A grades.

2. The 1911 results in Test 2, single combinations in subtraction, show grades 4B, 4A, 5B, 5A, distinctly above Courtis standard, whereas in the 6B and 6A grades they are approximately the same and in all other grades they are lower.

3. The 1911 results in Test 3, single combinations in multiplication, show grades 4B, 4A higher than Courtis standards, 5B and 5A approximately the same and the other grades lower.

4. The 1911 results in Test 4, simple division problems, show grades 4B, 4A, 5B, 5A, higher than Courtis standards, 6B, 6A, approximately the same and the other grades lower.

5. The 1911 results in Test 5, copying figures, show all grades in Bloomington approximately even with Courtis standards.

6. The 1911 results in Test 6, speed reasoning, show grades 4B to 6A inclusive slightly lower than Courtis standards and other grades noticeably lower.

7. The 1911 results in Test 7, fundamentals, show grades 4B, 4A, 5B, 5A, 6A, higher or equal to Courtis standards in number of problems attempted, while remaining grades are slightly lower. In number of problems right, Bloomington ranks distinctly above Courtis standard in practically all grades.

8. The 1911 results in Test 8, reasoning, show grades 4A, 6A, 7B, and 7A lower in attempts than Courtis standard. In all other grades, higher. In number of problems right, Bloomington schools ranked better than Courtis standards.

In a comparison of Bloomington results for the two years 1911 and 1914, the following facts are noticeable:

1. The 1914 results in Test 1 show a slight loss in grades 4B, 4A, 5A, 6B, 7B; in other grades a gain is shown.

2. The 1914 results in Test 2 show a loss in grades 4B, 4A, 5A, 6B; in other grades a gain is shown.

3. The 1914 results in Test 3 show a slight loss in grades 4B, 4A, 5A, 6B, 6A, 7B, and slight gains in the other grades.

4. The 1914 results in Test 4 show slight losses in grades 4B, 4A, 5B, 5A, 6B, and gains in other grades.

5. The 1914 results in Test 5 show slight losses in grades 4B, 4A, 5A, 6B, 6A, 7B, 7A, 8B, 8A.

6. The 1914 results in Test 6 show in number of problems attempted, losses in grades 4B, 5A, 6B, 8A, and gains in the other grades. In number of problems right, 1914 results show losses in grades 5B, 5A, 8A, and gains in the other grades.

7. The 1914 results in Test 7 show in problems attempted losses in grades 4B, 5A, 6B, 8B, and gains in the other grades. In number of problems right, 1914 results show losses in grades 4B, 4A, 5B, 5A, 6B, 6A, 7B, though losses are all slight.

8. The 1914 results in Test 8 show losses in number of problems attempted in grades 5B, 5A, 6B. In other grades, the 1914 results were equal to or better than the 1911 results. In number of problems right, the 1914 results show loss in grades 4A, 6B, 7B, 8A.

Altogether, the results show slight loss in fundamentals in the lower grades and gains in the higher grades, whereas in reasoning problems there is rather general improvement shown in the 1914 results over results in 1911, which indicates that the shift of emphasis from fundamentals to reasoning brought up the results in reasoning.

TABLE XCI

Per Cent of Accuracy of Bloomington Children in Courtis Tests
6, 7, 8, Series a, Years 1911 and 1914

Grade	Test 6	Test 7	Test 8
4b, 1911	68.8	57.0	
1914	83.3	56.7	13.0
4a, 1911	76.5	75.6	47.8
1914	84.2	66.3	40.0
5b, 1911	85.0	57.4	46.7
1914	63.2	66.3	56.5
5a, 1911	79.1	64.1	30.3
1914	89.2	69.1	58.3
6b, 1911	83.0	69.6	51.5
1914	93.2	72.4	55.2
6a, 1911	86.7	75.5	60.0
1914	93.6	69.2	70.0
7b, 1911	93.5	82.7	65.7
1914	91.8	66.9	58.3
7a, 1911	91.8	68.6	72.7
1914	94.1	70.3	69.2
8b, 1911	93.1	70.2	69.0
1914	94.9	78.5	70.5
8a, 1911	95.3	73.2	74.5
1914	96.6	76.2	66.0

Summary of Table XCI

Table XCI shows that in Test 6, losses were made in per cent of accuracy in 1914 as compared with 1911 in grades 5b, 7b. In all other grades, the per cent of accuracy in 1914 was distinctly greater than in 1911.

In Test 7, the 1914 results show a loss in per cent of accuracy in grades 4b, 4a, 6a, 7b, and a gain in all other grades.

In Test 8, the 1914 results show a loss in per cent of accuracy in grades 4a, 7b, 7a, 8a, and a gain in the other grades.

These results bear out the statement made in connection with the discussion of the Stone tests that in the matter of accuracy, the 6b and 6a grades in the spring of 1913 were somewhat below average, because the 7b and 7a grades show a comparatively low per cent in accuracy in the spring of 1914.

Tables XCII–XCIX give comparisons of the scores made by the Bloomington schools in Series b of the Courtis tests in arithmetic with scores made by the following school systems in Indiana: Wabash, LaPorte, Columbia City, East Chicago, Alexandria, Elwood, Decatur, Noblesville, Michigan City, Bluffton, Crown Point, Kendallville, Frankfort, Princeton, Rochester, Hartford City, Crawfordsville, and Plymouth. These tests were given in all cases during the latter part of the school year 1913–14.

TABLE XCII

COMPARISON OF SCORES MADE IN COURTIS ARITHMETIC TESTS, SERIES B, PROBLEM 1, BY BLOOMINGTON SCHOOLS WITH SCORES MADE BY 20 INDIANA SCHOOL SYSTEMS[1]

GRADE	MEDIAN ATTEMPTS BLOOMINGTON	MEDIAN ATTEMPTS OF 20 INDIANA CITIES	MEDIAN ATTEMPTS COURTIS STANDARD	MEDIAN RIGHTS BLOOMINGTON	MEDIAN RIGHTS OF 20 INDIANA CITIES	MEDIAN RIGHTS COURTIS STANDARD	PER CENT ACCURACY BLOOMINGTON	PER CENT ACCURACY OF 20 INDIANA CITIES	PER CENT ACCURACY COURTIS STANDARD APPROXIMATE
4A	7.5			4.7			62.7		
All 4th Grade			5.0						65.0
5B	.9.2			5.9			64.1		
5A	8.8			5.1			58.0		
All 5th Grade		6.6	7.1		3.6	3.9	54.5	54.5	55.0
6B	10.1			5.5			54.5		
6A	9.9			6.2			62.6		
All 6th Grade		7.4	8.0		4.4	4.4	67.0	59.0	55.0
7B	11.5			7.7			67.0		
7A	10.6			6.3			59.4		
All 7th Grade		8.0	8.9		5.0	4.7	61.8	62.5	52.8
8B	11.0			6.8			61.8		
8A	11.0			8.0			72.7		
All 8th Grade		9.0	9.7		5.8	5.6		63.7	57.7

[1] Data for twenty Indiana school systems and Courtis Standard Tests taken from M. E. Haggerty's study, Arithmetic: A Co-operative Study in Educational Measurements, page 439, published by Indiana University.

TABLE XCIII

Comparison of Scores made in Courtis Arithmetic Tests, Series B, Problem 2, by Bloomington Schools, with Scores made by 20 Indiana School Systems

Grade	Median Attempts Bloomington	Median Attempts of Group of 20 Indiana Cities	Median Attempts Courtis Standard	Median Rights Bloomington	Median Rights of Group of 20 Indiana Cities	Median Rights Courtis Standard	Per Cent Accuracy Bloomington	Per Cent Accuracy 20 Indiana Cities	Per Cent Accuracy Courtis Standard
4A	7.0			4.8			68.6		
All 4th Grade			6.0						
5B	8.4			5.4			64.3		
5A	8.3			5.9			71.1		
All 5th Grade		7.3	6.5		5.0	4.5		68.5	69.2
6B	8.9			6.4			71.9		
6A	9.7			6.7			69.1		
All 6th Grade		8.9	8.9		6.5	6.1		73.0	68.5
7B	11.0			7.7			70.0		
7A	11.2			8.0			71.4		
All 7th Grade		10.1	10.2		7.8	7.8		77.2	76.5
8B	10.7			9.0			84.1		
8A	12.6			10.3			81.7		
All 8th Grade		11.2	11.7		8.9	8.4		79.5	71.8

TABLE XCIV

COMPARISON OF SCORES MADE IN COURTIS ARITHMETIC TESTS, SERIES B, PROBLEM 3, BY BLOOMINGTON SCHOOLS WITH SCORES MADE BY 20 INDIANA SCHOOL SYSTEMS

GRADE	MEDIAN ATTEMPTS BLOOMINGTON	MEDIAN ATTEMPTS OF GROUP OF 20 INDIANA CITIES	MEDIAN ATTEMPTS COURTIS STANDARD	MEDIAN RIGHTS BLOOMINGTON	MEDIAN RIGHTS OF GROUP OF 20 INDIANA CITIES	MEDIAN RIGHTS COURTIS STANDARD	PER CENT ACCURACY BLOOMINGTON	PER CENT ACCURACY 20 INDIANA CITIES	PER CENT ACCURACY COURTIS STANDARD
4A.									
All 4th Grade	6.3		5.0	4.3			68.3		
5B.	7.4			5.2			70.3		
5A.	6.8			4.5			66.2		
All 5th Grade		6.3	6.0		3.9	2.6		62.0	43.3
6B.	8.1			5.4			66.7		
6A.	8.9			5.2			58.4		
All 6th Grade		7.6	7.2		5.1	4.5		67.1	62.5
7B.	10.0			5.5			55.0		
7A.	9.2			5.9			64.1		
All 7th Grade		8.6	8.4		5.9	5.2		68.6	61.9
8B.	9.7			6.7			69.1		
8A.	10.5			7.3			69.5		
All 8th Grade		10.2	9.9		7.3	6.4		71.6	64.6

TABLE XCV

COMPARISON OF SCORES MADE IN COURTIS ARITHMETIC TESTS, SERIES B, PROBLEM 4, BY BLOOMINGTON SCHOOLS WITH SCORES MADE BY 20 INDIANA SCHOOL SYSTEMS

GRADE	MEDIAN ATTEMPTS BLOOMINGTON	MEDIAN ATTEMPTS OF GROUP OF 20 INDIANA CITIES	MEDIAN ATTEMPTS COURTIS STANDARD	MEDIAN RIGHTS BLOOMINGTON	MEDIAN RIGHTS OF GROUP OF 20 INDIANA CITIES	MEDIAN RIGHTS COURTIS STANDARD	PER CENT ACCURACY BLOOMINGTON	PER CENT ACCURACY 20 INDIANA CITIES	PER CENT ACCURACY COURTIS STANDARD
4A									
All 4th Grade	5.2			4.1			78.8		
5B	7.1			5.1			71.8		
5A	6.9			5.0			72.5		
All 5th Grade		4.5	4.5		2.6	2.3		57.8	51.1
6B	8.5			6.7			78.8		
6A	8.5			7.0			82.4		
All 6th Grade		5.7	5.8		4.8	4.3		84.2	74.1
7B	10.3			8.3			80.6		
7A	10.2			8.6			84.3		
All 7th Grade		8.5	7.6		6.7	5.8		78.8	78.9
8B	11.3			8.9			78.8		
8A	12.7			11.3			89.0		
All 8th Grade		10.6	9.2		9.0	6.3		84.9	68.5

TABLE XCVI

COMPARISON OF VARIABILITY IN SCORES MADE IN COURTIS ARITHMETIC TESTS, SERIES B, PROBLEM 1, BY BLOOMINGTON SCHOOLS WITH SCORES MADE BY 20 INDIANA SCHOOL SYSTEMS

GRADE	VARIABILITY IN ATTEMPTS BLOOMINGTON	VARIABILITY IN ATTEMPTS 20 INDIANA CITIES	VARIABILITY IN RIGHTS BLOOMINGTON	VARIABILITY IN RIGHTS 20 INDIANA CITIES
4A	29		53	
All 4th Grade				
5B	25		41	
5A	27		59	
All 5th Grade		29		58
6B	29		56	
6A	22		48	
All 6th Grade		26		52
7B	26		43	
7A	27		46	
All 7th Grade		26		46
8B	31		50	
8A	29		45	
All 8th Grade		24		41

TABLE XCVII

COMPARISON OF VARIABILITY IN SCORES MADE IN COURTIS ARITHMETIC TESTS, SERIES B, PROBLEM 2, BY BLOOMINGTON SCHOOLS WITH SCORES MADE BY 20 INDIANA SCHOOL SYSTEMS

GRADE	VARIABILITY IN ATTEMPTS BLOOMINGTON	VARIABILITY IN ATTEMPTS 20 INDIANA CITIES	VARIABILITY IN RIGHTS BLOOMINGTON	VARIABILITY IN RIGHTS 20 INDIANA CITIES
4A	27		38	
All 4th Grade				
5B	21		48	
5A	25		41	
All 5th Grade		25		46
6B	21		41	
6A	20		39	
All 6th Grade		22		37
7B	30		39	
7A	23		31	
All 7th Grade		22		32
8B	22		33	
8A	28		31	
All 8th Grade		22		31

TABLE XCVIII

COMPARISON OF VARIABILITY IN SCORES MADE IN COURTIS ARITHMETIC TESTS, SERIES B, PROBLEM 3, BY BLOOMINGTON SCHOOLS WITH SCORES MADE BY 20 INDIANA SCHOOL SYSTEMS

GRADE	VARIABILITY IN ATTEMPTS BLOOMINGTON	VARIABILITY IN ATTEMPTS 20 INDIANA CITIES	VARIABILITY IN RIGHTS BLOOMINGTON	VARIABILITY IN RIGHTS 20 INDIANA CITIES
4A........................	27		44	
All 4th Grade..............				
5B........................	24		44	
5A........................	28		22	
All 5th Grade..............		30		56
6B........................	30		37	
6A........................	25		42	
All 6th Grade..............		28		47
7B........................	33		42	
7A........................	26		41	
All 7th Grade..............		27		41
8B........................	27		39	
8A........................	25		30	
All 8th Grade..............		25		34

TABLE XCIX

COMPARISON OF VARIABILITY IN SCORES MADE IN COURTIS ARITHMETIC TESTS, SERIES B, PROBLEM 4, BY BLOOMINGTON SCHOOLS WITH SCORES MADE BY 20 INDIANA SCHOOL SYSTEMS

GRADE	VARIABILITY IN ATTEMPTS BLOOMINGTON	VARIABILITY IN ATTEMPTS 20 INDIANA CITIES	VARIABILITY IN RIGHTS BLOOMINGTON	VARIABILITY IN RIGHTS 20 INDIANA CITIES
4A........................	42		71	
All 4th Grade..............				
5B........................	34		45	
5A........................	38		60	
All 5th Grade..............		42		81
6B........................	31		42	
6A........................	28		39	
All 6th Grade..............		46		60
7B........................	32		41	
7A........................	26		30	
All 7th Grade..............		35		46
8B........................	28		34	
8A........................	25		27	
All 8th Grade..............		30		40

Table C gives a comparison of the scores made by the Bloomington schools in Series A of the Courtis Arithmetic Tests with scores made by fourteen school systems in Indiana. This test was given in the Bloomington schools the latter part of the first semester of the school year 1913–14 and in all of the other systems the latter part of the second semester of the school year 1913–14.

TABLE C

COMPARISON OF SCORES MADE IN COURTIS ARITHMETIC TESTS, SERIES A, PROBLEM 7, BY BLOOMINGTON SCHOOLS WITH SCORES MADE BY 14 OTHER INDIANA SCHOOL SYSTEMS

GRADE	Average Attempts Bloomington	Average Attempts Fourteen Other Cities	Average Attempts Courtis Standards	Average Rights Bloomington	Average Rights Fourteen Other Cities	Average Rights Courtis Standards	Per Cent of Rights Bloomington	Per Cent of Rights Fourteen Other Cities	Per Cent of Rights Courtis Standards
4B	6.7			3.8			56.7		
4A	8.0			5.3			66.3		
All 4th Grade			7.0			3.5			50.0
5B	9.2			6.1			66.3		
5A	9.7			6.7			69.1		
All 5th Grade		7.4	9.0		4.7	5.2		63.5	47.8
6B	10.5			7.6			72.4		
6A	11.7			8.1			69.2		
All 6th Grade		9.0	11.0		6.0	6.7		66.7	60.9
7B	12.1			8.1			67.0		
7A	12.8			9.0			70.3		
All 7th Grade		10.5	12.5		7.2	8.2		68.6	65.6
8B	13.0			10.2			78.5		
8A	15.1			11.5			76.2		
All 8th Grade		11.8	14.0		8.6	9.4		72.9	67.1

RESULTS OF TABLE C

1. Bloomington results in attempts are higher than the average in the fourteen other Indiana systems of schools in all grades and equal to or higher than the Courtis standard in all grades except seventh and eighth, which are slightly lower.

2. Bloomington results in number right are higher than the average of the fourteen other Indiana systems of schools in all grades in which comparisons are possible, and higher than the Courtis standard in all grades.

3. Bloomington results in per cent of accuracy are higher than the average for the fourteen other Indiana school systems in all grades except the seventh, in which it is approximately the same and higher than the Courtis standard in all grades.

Table XCII shows that in Problem 1 the Bloomington scores for number of problems attempted are higher than scores of twenty Indiana city systems in all grades and higher than the Courtis standard in all grades. In problems right Bloomington scores were higher than scores from twenty city systems. In per cent of accuracy the Bloomington results are higher than those of the twenty cities except in the sixth grade, and in all grades they are all higher than the Courtis approximate statement of standard accuracy except in the 4A grade.

Table XCIII shows that in Problem 2 the Bloomington scores for problems attempted are higher for all grades than the scores of the twenty cities and higher than the Courtis standards in all grades. In number of problems right Bloomington scores are equal to or greater than the scores of the twenty cities.

Table XCIV shows that in Problem 3 the Bloomington scores for problems attempted are higher for all grades except the 8B than the scores of the twenty cities, and are slightly higher than the Courtis standards. In number of problems right the Bloomington scores are equal to or higher than the scores for the twenty cities except in the eighth year in which they are slightly lower.

Table XCV shows that in Problem 4 the Bloomington scores in number of problems attempted are higher in all grades than the scores of the twenty cities and higher than the Courtis standard in all grades. In number of problems right the Bloomington scores are also higher.

Table XCVI shows that in Test 1 in number of problems attempted the variability was approximately the same in the Bloomington schools as in the twenty other systems except in the eighth grade in which it was distinctly higher in the Bloomington schools. In variability in rights the twenty other systems show better than the Bloomington schools except in the fifth and seventh grade.

Table XCVII shows that in Test 2 in number of problems attempted the variability was slightly lower in the fifth and sixth grades and noticeably higher in the seventh and eighth grades in Bloomington than in the other systems. In variability in rights the twenty systems make a much better showing than Bloomington does.

Table XCVIII shows that in Test 3 in number of problems attempted the variability was slightly lower in grades 5B, 5A, 6A, 7A, and higher in the other grades in Bloomington than in the twenty other systems. In the matter of variability in the number of problems right the Bloomington record is on the whole better than that of the other twenty systems.

Table XCIX shows that in Test 4 in number of problems attempted the variability was as low or lower in all grades in the Bloomington schools as in the twenty systems. In the matter of variability in number of problems right the advantage is wholly with the Bloomington scores.

There has been practically no improvement made as far as better grading is concerned since the 1911 tests. The problem for grading is being attacked during the year 1914–15 in two ways. First, by an effort to have teachers regrade as often as they think advisable in an effort to maintain as nearly equal ability as possible on the part of each member of the group. Second, by using the Courtis practice pads in an effort to provide an opportunity for taking proper care of varying differences in ability within the group. By these two methods we hope to be able to get better results during the present school year.

Efficiency is measured not only by average amount achieved by a group in quantity, but also by the individual variability within the group. Table CI shows the variability according to Courtis' method of working it out, in Series A, Arithmetic Test, for the years 1911 and 1914. The lower the variability, the better the grading.

TABLE CI

COMPARISON OF VARIABILITY IN RESULTS, COURTIS ARITHMETIC TESTS, SERIES A, BLOOMINGTON SCHOOLS FOR THE YEARS 1911 AND 1914

Grade	No. 1 Variability in Attempts Bloomington 1911	1914	No. 2 Variability in Attempts Bloomington 1911	1914	No. 3 Variability in Attempts Bloomington 1911	1914	No. 4 Variability in Attempts Bloomington 1911	1914	No. 5 Variability in Attempts Bloomington 1911	1914	No. 6 Variability in Attempts Bloomington 1911	1914	No. 6 Variability in Rights Bloomington 1911	1914	No. 7 Variability in Attempts Bloomington 1911	1914	No. 7 Variability in Rights Bloomington 1911	1914	No. 8 Variability in Attempts Bloomington 1911	1914	No. 8 Variability in Rights Bloomington 1911	1914
4B	26	21	23	17	15	21	17	26	14	18	25	27	40	32	19	25	39	44	.	39		10
4A	21	17	20	24	22	16	26	22	14	18	18	21	27	25	26	18	34	26	52	28	54	70
5B	24	19	22	22	20	18	15	22	14	15	29	21	43	38	21	14	27	31	31	43	50	46
5A	21	21	11	22	24	22	20	24	13	14	21	22	24	24	19	12	32	27	36	42	80	35
6B	17	21	16	19	17	27	15	18	13	14	21	23	31	27	17	17	26	23	33	31	39	44
6A	14	19	16	19	17	19	19	18	9	12	20	23	28	30	19	22	24	32	33	30	56	38
7B	20	18	18	18	16	18	18	21	10	14	18	18	19	22	16	22	24	24	33	30	39	48
7A	20	20	16	22	18	23	18	21	23	15	19	19	18	23	17	16	23	27	33	20	42	30
8B	15	20	16	22	19	22	15	19	9	14	24	24	20	24	14	22	22	28	21	23	27	42
8A	16	19	16	14	20	20	16	18	11	10	22	17	23	16	14	15	16	26	19	19	29	29

TABLE CII

RESULTS OF COURTIS TESTS IN ARITHMETIC, SERIES B, JUNE 3, 1915

GRADE	NO. TAKING TESTS	ADDITION PER CENT				SUBTRACTION PER CENT				MULTIPLICATION PER CENT				DIVISION PER CENT			
		AT-TEMPTS	ACCU-RACY	RIGHTS	EFFI-CIENCY	AT-TEMPTS	ACCU-RACY	RIGHTS	EFFI-CIENCY	AT-TEMPTS	ACCU-RACY	RIGHTS	EFFI-CIENCY	AT-TEMPTS	ACCU-RACY	RIGHTS	EFFI-CIENCY
4B	104	7.9	51.5	4.06	6.7	6.4	70.0	4.48	10.6	5.8	55.0	3.19	5.8	4.4	49.0	2.15	8.7
4A	[1]116	7.7	55.6	4.28	3.4	6.6	68.0	4.48	12.1	6.1	61.8	3.76	5.2	4.9	63.3	2.59	6.9
5B	86	8.3	56.7	4.7	7.0	7.8	67.8	5.28	3.5	6.8	53.7	3.65	2.3	5.5	59.2	3.25	4.6
5A	123	8.2	60.5	4.96	4.9	8.0	66.3	5.3	7.3	7.0	61.2	4.28	3.2	6.0	71.2	4.27	9.0
6B	90	9.7	71.2	6.9	5.5	8.5	76.0	6.46	1.1	6.6	65.0	4.29	1.1	5.7	73.6	4.19	4.4
6A	102	10.1	69.5	7.02	3.9	9.0	79.5	7.15	3.9	7.2	63.1	4.54	0.0	6.6	80.4	5.3	8.8
7B	69	10.8	74.0	7.99	0.0	9.1	79.4	7.22	0.0	7.6	60.8	4.62	2.6	7.4	87.0	6.43	10.1
7A	76	11.4	71.8	8.18	3.9	10.1	71.7	7.24	5.3	8.8	63.1	5.55	2.6	8.8	85.5	7.52	13.1
8B	72	12.0	77.1	9.25	2.8	10.7	76.7	8.2	2.8	9.3	65.8	6.12	0.0	9.0	86.7	7.8	16.7
8A	68	13.2	77.5	10.23	4.4	11.8	82.0	9.67	7.4	10.9	67.2	7.32	0.0	11.2	90.0	10.00	20.6

[1]In division there were only 74. Forty-two children did not have a chance to try division.

SUMMARY OF TABLE CI

1. The 1914 results for Test 1 show a decrease or an equality in variability as compared with the 1911 results in grades 4B, 4A, 5B, 5A, 7B, 7A, and an increase in the other grades.

2. The 1914 results for Test 2 show a decrease or an equality in variability as compared with the 1911 results in grades 4B, 5B, 7B, 7A, 8A, and an increase in the other grades.

3. The 1914 results for Test 3 show a decrease or an equality in variability as compared with the 1911 results in grades 4A, 5B, 5A, 8A, and an increase in the other grades.

4. The 1914 results for Test 4 show a decrease or an equality in variability as compared with the 1911 results in grades 4A, 6A, and an increase in the other grades.

5. The 1914 results for Test 5 show a decrease or an equality in variability as compared with the 1911 results in grades 7A and 8A. In all other grades the variability increased.

6. The 1914 results for Test 6 in number of problems attempted show a decrease or an equality in variability as compared with the 1911 results in grades 5B, 7B, 8A, and an increase in the other grades.

7. The 1914 results for Test 7 in number of problems attempted show a decrease or an equality in variability as compared with the results 1911 in grades 4A, 5B, 5A, 6B, 6A, 7A, and greater in other grades.

8. The 1914 results for Test 8 in number of problems attempted show a decrease or an equality in variability as compared with 1911 results in grades 4A, 6B, 6A, 7B, 7A, 8A, and an increase in the other grades.

5. WRITING

The following directions were given out to the teachers near the beginning of the first semester of the school year 1913–14 to govern their collection of writing samples.

1. Distribute printed slips and have blanks at top filled out by pupils before announcing the purpose of the exercise.

2. Then have papers turned face down, after which explain to pupils that we want to get samples of their handwriting. Tell them to be ready at a given signal to turn their papers over and begin to copy the paragraph immediately below the printed matter and in the upper part of the blank space.

3. Copy with pen and ink at natural rate of speed, and in your best handwriting.

4. At second signal everybody should stop writing. (The second signal will be given at the end of two minutes.)

5. If anyone finishes the paragraph before the signal to stop is given, he should begin recopying the paragraph.

6. At the close the papers should be collected, fastened together, and turned over to the principal to be held until further notice.

The heading of each sheet containing the selection to be copied by the pupil was as follows:

NAME   SCHOOL   GRADE

DATE   TIME OF DAY   AGE

(September 1, 1913)

Samples of writing were taken October 1, 1913. The following table gives the median number of letters written by the various grades in two minutes' time at normal rate of speed from printed copy. All pupils, white and colored, are represented in the table.

TABLE CIII

GRADE	MEDIAN NUMBER OF LETTERS WRITTEN IN TWO MINUTES' TIME
4A	85.0
5B	76.5
5A	93.0
6B	114.0
6A	125.5
7B	145.5
7A	182.0
8B	154.0
8A	143.0
5B and 5A combined	87.0
6B and 6A combined	117.0
7B and 7A combined	180.0
8B and 8A combined	149.

The median number of letters written by the 5B grade in the two minutes' time was 76.5, and by the 5B and 5A together the median number was 87.

With the exception of the 5B, 8B, and 8A grades there is, as would be expected, a gradual increase in speed evidenced as we go higher in the grades.

Table CIV gives a comparison of the grading as done by the teachers and the superintendent separately.

Table CIV interpreted means, for example, that according to the teachers' markings ten 8A pupils did writing of quality 8 on the Thorndike Scale, whereas according to the superintendent's markings only three of the 8A pupils did writing of quality 8.

The striking conclusion to be drawn from this table is that there is very little improvement shown from grade to grade. The largest group of pupils in the 4A grade did writing of quality 9 whether marked by teacher or by superintendent. Practically all the way up through the grades quality 9 has the largest representations of any quality. On either side of quality 9 the distribution of grades is largely the same in all grades. The discovery of the failure of the schools to make steady progress from grade to grade in writing led to the formation of a class of teachers in writing. This class contained all of the teachers from the 4A grade up through the 8A grade who taught writing as one of their subjects. The class met for one hour every two weeks and was taught by the head of the commercial department in the high school. The teachers took lessons in writing as well as lessons in the teaching of writing. Soon after the class had started it was decided to substitute the free arm movement for the finger movement in teaching writing to children. This substitution was

TABLE CIV

DISTRIBUTION OF GRADES ON HANDWRITING AS MEASURED BY THE THORNDIKE SCALE. SPECIMENS OF WRITING TAKEN OCTOBER 1, 1913, MEASUREMENTS MADE BY TEACHERS AND SUPERINTENDENT SEPARATELY

QUALITY OF WRITING	4	5	6	7	8	9	10	11	12	13	14	15	16	17	18	TOTAL	PER CENT OF EACH GRADE MAKING A MARK OF 12 OR ABOVE
8A Teachers' grades				2	10	9	2	4	1	2	1					31	13.0
Superintendent's grades				2	3	7	12	3	3	0	0	1				31	13.0
8B Teachers' grades			5	2	10	26	4	10	6	1	1					67	14.9
Superintendent's grades				4	14	20	16	7	3	3		0	2			67	9.0
7A Teachers' grades			2	8	16	31	4	7	3	1						72	5.6
Superintendent's grades				4	9	28	14	8	5	4						72	12.5
7B Teachers' grades			7	9	24	27	3	9	3	4	7	0	1			94	16.0
Superintendent's grades			1	12	27	32	7	7	3	4	0	1				94	8.5
6A Teachers' grades				4	21	34	5	7	5	5	1	1				83	14.5
Superintendent's grades				9	17	25	16	9	6	0	1					83	8.4
6B Teachers' grades			2	7	22	39	1	17	5	3	1					97	9.3
Superintendent's grades				7	25	31	21	12	1							97	1.0
5A Teachers' grades				6	21	33	5	19	1	4	1	1				91	7.7
Superintendent's grades			1	8	25	24	18	11	3	1						91	4.4
5B Teachers' grades			2	17	22	52	6	5	4	9	3					120	13.3
Superintendent's grades			1	12	43	42	16	5	0	1						120	1.0
4A Teachers' grades	1		3	7	7	25	6	11	2	24 }¹	1					87	31.0
Superintendent's grades				14	19	31	13	8	0	2 }						87	2.3

¹ This large difference is due to the grading of one teacher who was far more liberal in her grading than any other teacher.

TABLE CV

DISTRIBUTION OF GRADES ON HANDWRITING AS MEASURED BY THE THORNDIKE SCALE. SPECIMENS OF WRITING TAKEN OCTOBER 1, 1913, AND MAY 1, 1914. MEASUREMENTS MADE BY TEACHERS

QUALITY OF WRITING	4	5	6	7	8	9	10	11	12	13	14	15	16	17	18	TOTAL	PER CENT OF EACH GRADE MAKING A MARK OF 12 OR ABOVE
4A																	
October 1, 1913...		1	3	7	7	25	6	11	2	24	1					87	10.3
May 1, 1914.......		2	8	24	17	29	7	9	6	5						107	
5B																	
October 1, 1913...			2	17	22	52	6	5	4	9	3					120	17.0
May 1, 1914.......			3	4	13	32	7	14	9	6						88	
5A																	
October 1, 1913...				6	21	33	5	19	1	4	1	1				91	13.3
May 1, 1914.......				8	31	37	3	12	7	7		1				105	
6B																	
October 1, 1913...			2	7	22	39	1	17	5	3	1					97	8.4
May 1, 1914.......				3	15	34	6	18	2	5						83	
6A																	
October 1, 1913...		1		4	21	34	5	7	5	5	1	1				83	16.8
May 1, 1914.......			2	9	23	20	7	7	6	8						83	
7B																	
October 1, 1913...		1	7	9	24	27	3	9	3	4	7	0				94	10.4
May 1, 1914.......			0	4	19	25	5	6	5	2			1			67	
7A																	
October 1, 1913...				8	16	31	4	7	3	1						72	22.4
May 1, 1914.......			2	9	25	28	3	11	12	7	3					98	
8B																	
October 1, 1913...			5	2	10	26	4	10	6	1	1	0				67	38.0
May 1, 1914.......				14	21	6	0	10	0	1	1		2			53	
8A																	
October 1, 1913...		2	1	2	10	9	2	4	1	2	1	2				31	22.2
May 1, 1914.......		1		1	8	12	0	11	5	3	2					45	
TOTAL, October 1, 1913			21	62	153	276	36	89	30	53	16		3			742	14.0
TOTAL, May 1, 1914		6	14	76	172	223	38	98	52	44	6					729	16.2

made under the direction of the commercial teacher. The result was that the writing throughout the system suddenly became poorer. The free arm movement was insisted on though in the hope that ultimately it would result not only in better writing but in more rapid writing.

A second sample of writing was taken on May 1, 1914, under the same conditions governing the taking of samples as on October 1, 1913. Table CV shows the results as well as a comparison by grades of the two sets of markings.

On the whole, the markings of May 1, 1914 showed no great improvement over those of October 1, 1913. That condition was expected, however, and the free arm movement is being tried out further during the year 1914–15.

Table CVI shows the gains or losses of individual pupils during the second test as compared with the first test. In both cases each child is classified as to grade in the grade he was in when the first test was made.

To illustrate the interpretation of Table CVI take the 5A grade as an example. There were twenty pupils tested in writing in May who were classified as 5A's in October and received the same mark

TABLE CVI

GAINS AND LOSSES MADE BY PUPILS TESTED IN WRITING OCTOBER 1, 1913, AND MAY 1, 1914, THORNDIKE SCALE. THE INTERVENING TIME HAVING BEEN GIVEN TO INTRODUCTION OF FREE ARM MOVEMENT IN WRITING

	POINTS GAINED ON THORNDIKE SCALE							
	0	1	2	3	4	5	6	7
4A..........................								
5B..........................	16	8	6					
5A..........................	20	16	12	2	1	1	0	7
6B..........................	26	11	8	2	1	1		
6A..........................	17	14	6	1	4			
7B..........................	15	15	6	2	0			
7A..........................	23	12	11	5	4	4		
8B..........................	8	7	7	0	0	2	•	
8A..........................	10	5	5	3				
TOTAL..................	135	88	61	15	10	8		7

	POINTS LOST ON THE THORNDIKE SCALE					
	1	2	3	4	5	6
4A..........................						
5B..........................	12	7	4	2	1	1
5A..........................	19	4	0	2	1	
6B..........................	9	15	3	3	1	
6A..........................	15	10	6	2		
7B..........................	13	5	1	5		
7A..........................	18	3	3	3	1	
8B..........................	16	5	5	1		
8A..........................	7	5	3	0	1	
TOTAL..................	109	54	25	18	5	1

according to the Thorndike Scale in May as they had received in October. There were sixteen pupils who received a mark one step higher in May than in October while seven pupils received a mark seven points higher than in May. At the same time there were nineteen cases in which there was a loss of one point and one case in which the quality of writing dropped in May five points below what it was in October.

In 135 cases there was neither gain nor loss. On the whole, there were 384 points gained and 395 points lost.

In the spring of 1915 Professor W. W. Black, dean of the School of Education, Indiana University, made a study of handwriting in the public schools of Indiana. The test was given in the Bloomington schools according to the accompanying directions which he sent out. The results are embodied in Table CVII. These results do not show an improvement in writing that there had been reason to hope for.

TABLE CVII

SHOWING BY GRADE AND SEX RESULT OF WRITING TEST GIVEN APRIL 8, 1915, AND SCORED ACCORDING TO THE AYRES SCALE [1]

			Average No. Letters per Minute	Average Scale Grade	Number of Individuals Receiving Each of the Grades on the Scale 20, 30, 40, 50, 60, 70, 80, 90							
GRADE	SEX	No.			20	30	40	50	60	70	80	90
2B	Boys	54	9.3	37.4	6	20	16	8	2	2		
2B	Girls	41	11.8	46.6		3	4	8	15	11		
2A	Boys	48	15.1	41.3	4	14	13	9	5	3		
2A	Girls	60	16.3	44.5	2	12	19	14	11	1	1	
3B	Boys	55	17.7	36.7	4	26	13	9	2	1		
3B	Girls	52	18.9	41.2	5	15	12	11	7	2		
3A	Boys	57	26.6	36.7	13	19	9	9	4	3		
3A	Girls	48	29.3	42.3	1	16	13	11	4	2	1	
4B	Boys	60	32.1	35.2	14	26	6	8	2	3	1	
4B	Girls	39	34.5	42.1	4	11	10	5	6	2	1	
4A	Boys	59	37.1	37.3	7	25	11	10	5	1		
4A	Girls	43	37.7	45.8	2	9	9	10	11	2		
5B	Boys	51	47.0	33.3	10	26	7	4	4			
5B	Girls	35	48.3	38.6	3	14	8	7	2		1	
5A	Boys	56	43.3	35.0	9	29	8	3	5	2		
5A	Girls	49	45.1	44.7	2	13	14	8	6	5		1
6B	Boys	57	44.7	29.5	25	19	7	4	1	1		
6B	Girls	40	54.6	39.5	4	14	11	5	4	1	1	
6A	Boys	45	52.8	34.4	9	17	11	7		1		
6A	Girls	42	60.4	38.8	6	11	13	7	4	11		
7B	Boys	32	52.0	40.3	3	8	11	5	5			
7B	Girls	36	53.0	49.2		4	8	12	11	1		
7A	Boys	25	58.0	34.4	7	7	7	2	1	1		
7A	Girls	52	67.0	47.3	2	7	16	13	8	5		1
8B	Boys	25	59.7	41.2		8	8	8		1		
8B	Girls	34	59.3	64.4	0	1	2	4	10	10	5	2
8A	Boys	23	58.6	46.5	1	3	6	8	3	2		
8A	Girls	38	52.1	58.9		2	3	8	14	8	1	2

[1] Papers scored by Superintendent of Schools.

Table CVII reads thus: 54 boys in the 2B grade took the test. The average number of letters written by them per minute was 9.3; six of the 54 boys received a grade of 20 on their writing; twenty a grade of 30; sixteen a grade of 40, etc. The average scale grade for all 54 boys was 37.4.

INSTRUCTIONS

TAKING SAMPLES

1. Take samples from second grade through high school, regardless of where the teaching of writing ends.

2. Select for each grade, from pupils' readers (or other sources in the upper grades and high school), some selection with which pupils of the grade are familiar. Have pupils write (copying the selection from the book) for *just five minutes*.

It is necessary that pupils be *timed accurately* in order that the rate of speed may be obtained.

3. Have pupils write on paper such as they commonly use, either ruled or unruled.

4. Have pupils use pen and ink. If pupils in primary grades are not accustomed to use pens, pencils may be used in these grades.

5. As nearly as possible, samples should be secured without the pupil's being conscious that his writing is being tested.

6. Before taking sample, have pupil write his name, and indicate the grade to which he belongs (2B, 2A, etc.) on the back of his paper.

If promotions are made annually instead of semi-annually, indicate the grade to which the pupil belongs on the principle that the first half of the year is to be classed as B, and the second half as A.

Express all grades by numbers and letters, as 2B, 2A . . . 12B, 12A.

7. Include all pupils of same grade in one report. Do not report by buildings.

8. Keep boys' and girls' samples separate.

GRADING SAMPLES

1. Select a committee of two persons to scale samples, the two to work together on each sample.

Where the number of pupils in a system is considered too large to be graded by a single committee, two or more committees may be appointed. In the latter case, each committee should scale its proportion of samples in *all* grades, including the high school.

2. Indicate the style of the handwriting on the face of the sample, and record in report, using the letters V (vertical), M (medium slant), S (full slant), X (not classifiable under V, M, or S).

3. The grade and style as shown by the Scale should be marked on the face of the sample.

4. Committees should study carefully the Ayres Report and Scale before beginning the work of scaling samples.

RECORDING SCALE GRADES

1. Make a separate report for each grade (2B, 2A, 3B, etc.).

2. As the grade for each sample is recorded, give it a number, and write the number on the face of the sample and also in the column indicated in the report blank.

NOTE. — As grades are recorded place samples in numerical order, for convenience of those who determine the speed.

3. Record grades of boys and girls in separate groups. Write Boys or Girls at the head of each group of grades.

4. Fill in all the blanks at the head of the first page of the report for each grade.

DETERMINING AND RECORDING SPEED

1. Divide the number of letters in the sample by (5) to find the number of letters per minute written by the pupil. Write this number of letters per minute on the face of the sample.

The rate may be made out by the room teacher.

NOTE. — The number of letters in a given sample can be determined quickly if the one who makes out the rate of speed will write under each word in the selection copied the total number of letters preceding it and included in it. If, for illustration, this note were copied by the pupil as a sample, the teacher could write in the printed copy used for counting "4" under the word "note," "7" under the word "the," "13" under the word "number," etc. The total number of letters in a given sample can then be seen at a glance by finding the place (in the printed selection) of the last word in the sample.

2. Record the number of letters per minute in the proper column, and opposite the sample number.

Preserve samples for use in case further data should be needed.

Send reports to Wm. W. Black, Bloomington, Indiana.

During the latter part of the first semester of the year 1913–14 the superintendent of schools gave the Courtis Tests in Reading, Composition, Spelling, and Writing and sent the papers to Mr. Courtis to be graded under his direction and by skilled graders. The results of the Writing test as reported by Mr. Courtis are here given.

HANDWRITING

TABLE CVIII

GRADE ACCORDING TO THORNDIKE SCALE

GRADE	TEST 1 MEDIAN	VARIABILITY	TEST 2 MEDIAN	VARIABILITY	TEST 3 MEDIAN	VARIABILITY
4B	11.8	14	8.8	20	10.6	18
4A	11.4	15	8.4	23	9.8	19
5B	11.5	15	8.8	19	10.3	16
5A	12.0	14	8.7	17	10.3	16
6B	11.6	15	8.9	20	10.2	19
6A	11.5	17	8.8	21	10.0	22
7B	11.9	13	9.6	28	11.2	15
7A	11.7	18	9.3	18	10.2	16
8B	12.1	12	9.5	22	10.4	18
8A	12.0	22	10.6	20	11.2	16

GRADE ACCORDING TO AYRES SCALE

GRADE	TEST 1 MEDIAN	VARIABILITY	TEST 2 MEDIAN	VARIABILITY	TEST 3 MEDIAN	VARIABILITY
4B	62	22	45	32	54	24
4A	58	22	42	33	51	27
5B	57	24	41	34	53	24
5A	59	24	43	30	50	26
6B	61	23	45	27	50	26
6A	57	24	44	34	50	30
7B	63	22	47	28	55	25
7A	61	24	43	28	48	29
8B	60	23	45	27	51	25
8A	56	27	49	26	54	28

TABLE CIX

EFFICIENCY IN WRITING OBTAINED BY FINDING PER CENT OF CLASS ABLE TO
WRITE AS WELL AS QUALITY TWELVE OR BETTER ON THE THORNDIKE SCALE

	TEST 1	TEST 2	TEST 3
4B	45	7	18
4A	32	1	15
5B	38	4	16
5A	51	1	17
6B	42	2	10
6A	40	4	19
7B	46	5	42
7A	42	5	10
8B	51	10	17
8A	48	15	26

The Courtis tests provide for samples of handwriting taken under three different conditions. In Test 1 the children were given a copy to follow and were not only allowed to choose their own rate, but were told it was a handwriting test. In Test 2 the material was dictated to them at adult rate, about twenty-two words or one hundred letters a minute. In Test 3 the children were unconscious of their writing, the main activity being the composition of an original story. "Test 3 then," as Mr. Courtis says, "should really be used to measure the quality of the product in handwriting, as in this test the handwriting was serving its normal purpose of expressing thought."

Reference to Table CVIII or to Graph 5 shows what was clearly shown in the October and May tests in handwriting, namely, that the achievement of pupils is practically uniform throughout the grades. Teaching should do two things — maintain proficiency gained in lower grades and add to that proficiency. The latter has not been done in the Bloomington schools, as the tests clearly indicate. Courtis in his comments says, "In comparison with other cities Bloomington rises early to the common level, and holds this position throughout." On the graph the figures for Madison, Wisconsin, are given for comparison in Test 3. The eighth-grade score for many school systems is between ten and eleven on the Thorndike Scale and with this figure the Bloomington schools agree. In every

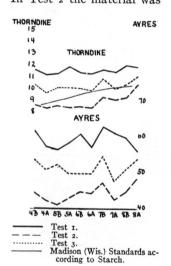

— Test 1.
— — Test 2.
.... Test 3.
——— Madison (Wis.) Standards according to Starch.

FIG. 5. GRADE AVERAGES.

grade, however, there are many poor writers and the proportion of good to poor is fairly constant. For the system as a whole about one child in five can make his handwriting as good as quality twelve or better in writing an original story. In other words, the efficiency of handwriting instruction on the basis of the final product is not over 20 per cent. The results show plainly that handwriting in the Bloomington schools offers a good field for work looking toward the improvement of the efficiency of the instruction.

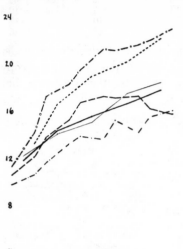

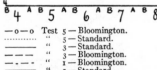

—o—o Test 5 — Bloomington.
....   "   5 — Standard.
————   "   3 — Standard.
— — —   "   3 — Bloomington.
— · — ·   "   1 — Bloomington.
————   "   1 — Standard.

FIG. 6. RATES OF WRITING.
BLOOMINGTON AND STANDARD.

"A number of interesting points stand out in Table CX in connection with the results already reported. In Test 1 the rate was much slower and the quality better than in any other test. The effect of warning the children to give a good specimen of their handwriting was to retard the speed by an amount equal to that of the effort of composing an original story. On the other hand, the speed of Test 2 was too great for most of the children, and the handwriting correspondingly poor. On the basis of grade averages, the relative values in the different tests are about the same except, with ncreasing maturity, the curves for Tests 2 and 3 approach each other more closely, as was to be expected. In the different classes, however, the relative value in the three tests shows wide variations.

"It will be noted that the results by the Thorndike Scale seem more consistent and uniform than with the Ayres Scale, and this probably means that the Thorndike Scale is better. It permits of finer gradations, but the effect noted may be due wholly to the fact that the larger number of samples simply increases the number of factors entering into a judgment, so that the real differences smooth themselves out. Nothing final can be said on this point.

"As all these papers were scored by one person with frequent checks upon her first training, the results are as consistent as it is possible to obtain at this time. In this connection it should be noted that of seventy-two judgments in one class, by the Thorndike Scale 50 per cent were exactly the same, 45 per cent within one unit, and 5 per cent within two units. In another class, by the Ayres Scale 73 per cent were the same, 26 per cent within one unit, and 1 per cent within two units. As one unit on the Ayres Scale is about equal to two units on the Thorndike Scale, the differences between the two scales is not as great as it seems. In both cases, however, the variations in judgment did not affect the average score of the class. The class averages are perfectly reliable, therefore, and the individual scores nearly so. How the standard of the judge compares with that of other judges is another question, but in view of the uniformity of the 8th grade scores, there is probably not a great error from this source."

Proficiency in writing is determined not only by the quality of the writing but by the quantity or by the speed at which the writing is done.

TABLE CX

RATE OF WRITING, BLOOMINGTON SCHOOLS, COMPARED WITH COURTIS STANDARD

| | MEDIAN NUMBER OF WORDS PER MINUTE | | | NUMBER OF LETTERS PER MINUTE |
GRADE	COPYING LETTERS TEST 1	ORIGINAL STORY TEST 3	REPRODUCTION TEST 5	TEST 1
4B, Bloomington.........	10.0	10.9	11.8	46
4A, Bloomington.........	10.9	12.5	14.6	47
Fourth Standard............	12.6	12.0	13.6	55
5B, Bloomington.........	11.9	13.7	17.1	51
5A, Bloomington.........	13.1	15.3	18.3	57
Fifth Standard.............	14.1	14.3	16.5	61
6B, Bloomington.........	14.0	16.8	19.5	61
6A, Bloomington.........	13.7	17.1	21.3	60
Sixth Standard.............	15.6	15.8	19.2	59
7B, Bloomington.........	15.4	16.8	20.9	67
7A, Bloomington......:....	14.3	16.9	21.3	62
Seventh Standard...........	17.1	16.9	20.7	75
8B, Bloomington.........	15.8	16.6	22.6	69
8A, Bloomington.........	16.5	16.0	23.2	72
Eighth Standard............	18.1	17.5	22.3	79

I quote from Mr. Courtis' report in regard to the speed of the writing in the Bloomington schools. "In the tables will be found (1) rate of copying letters, Test 1; (2) rate of writing an original story, Test 3; and (3) rate of reproduction, Test 5. The first measures the rate at which letters can be written by a child when he has nothing to think except that he must make his handwriting as perfect as possible. As the children chose their own rates these results furnish a means of determining at what rate children should be given their writing practice. The development from grade to grade shows something of the development that comes with maturity. The results should be judged from this point of view.

"The second is influenced by two factors: (1) ease of thinking; (2) ease of expression. That is, a child that has a vivid imagination and that can readily think up an original story writes a larger number of words per minute than a child without the ability to do such thinking. But the actual number of words written per minute may also be determined by the ease of expression. For the child that is master of English composition will put his thoughts into words more readily than one who has not learned to choose words to express his thoughts, or to construct a sentence rapidly. Further a child's rate may be influenced by the rate of motor activity.

"For all these reasons the rate of reproduction becomes important. In reproduction tests the words and ideas are supplied, and even the sentence structure is largely determined. For everyone, the rate of reproduction is higher than the rate of composition, but a child that has a greater or less difference than the average is having trouble at some point.

"If his rate of reproduction is equal to his rate of composition and his scores are high, he is an exceptional child.

"If his scores are low, he is probably having trouble with expression, and needs work in which deas are supplied but words are not, that he may learn to put ideas into words.

"If his rate of reproduction is normal, but his rate of composition is low, he probably needs work to stimulate his imagination and imagery; help on the content side rather than the mechanical side.

Rate of Copying Letters

"In Table CX a summary will be found by grades. It is given in letters per minute rather than words, in spite of the fact that the record sheet is prepared the other way, because at a late hour it was found that the conversion to words had been made on a false assumption. For adults, one word on the average equals 4.5 letters. For fourth-grade children, however, the number ranges from 3.2 to 4, averaging about 3.5. At the eighth grade the average value is 4.1 according to a rather limited count. For this reason any conclusions made by comparing the scores in Test 1 with those in the other tests would be wrong. The scores are therefore given in letters per minute. This change would not affect the graph, and this is drawn in words. The difference needs to be kept in mind only when making comparisons on an absolute basis.

Development Curves

"In Graph 6 are given the development curves for the rates of writing; also for comparison the median scores derived from the general tabulations from 2800 children in six states. These last are called standard scores. The curve for copying letters shows a steady development except at the 7A grade. The absolute value of this curve for Bloomington falls below the similar general curve (1S). This means either that the Bloomington children have slower habits of response, or that the admonition to make their handwriting as legible as possible made them take more pains than most children. For the general tabulations the curves for copying letters and for rate of writing an original story closely agree, but in Bloomington this is not true. In other words, most children show a retardation in rate of writing while trying to make good penmanship about equal to that caused by trying to compose an original story, but the Bloomington children show a greater retardation. It is hard to tell how this should be interpreted. It probably means that more attention has been given to handwriting in the Bloomington schools than elsewhere, so that the children paid attention to the directions for legible writing. But whatever the real meaning, one thing is certain. The child that writes at but 15.7 words per minute when it is preparing "samples" of handwriting and 24 words per minute when reproducing a story it has read, is likely to find that its skill in handwriting will not stand the strain of the more rapid work. In other words, more attention should be paid to attaining handwriting of say quality 60 on the Ayres Scale at a speed equal to that of the greatest demands made by the life of the child. The Detroit schools have adopted standards of speed in conformity with this idea, and it is probable that the Bloomington schools would benefit by similar standards.

"The curve for rate of writing in Test 3, the Original Story, agrees with the general tabulations at the fourth grade, is higher up to 7B, and then falls below. The curves show that conditions are very good up to 6A and increasingly poorer from that grade on until the final product falls below that of other cities. The dotted line shows the probably final curve if the work in the upper grades was on a par with that in the lower.

"The curve for reproduction shows the rate at which children write when there is no effort for words or ideas. It is the rate of free writing, and both the Bloomington and the general curves which closely agree (the differences are all in favor of Bloomington) show that while the curve is approaching a maximum, adult ability in this line will not be reached for several years more. It suggests that the tests should be continued through the high school and college until the maximum is determined."

6. SPELLING

Two tests in spelling are included in this study. The tests used by B. R. Buckingham in "Spelling Ability — Its Measurement and Distribution," published by Teachers College, Columbia University, were given the latter part of the first semester of the year 1913–14. These tests include Mr. Buckingham's own list and the list used by Mr. Rice a few years ago. The second spelling tests, the Courtis Tests, were given the latter part of the second semester of the year 1913–14. All the pupils in all the grades are represented except in the Rice Tests in the 4B grade, in which through an error of the teacher eight colored 4B's included in the total of 122 failed to take the test on the following words: because, thought, writing, language, feather, light, surface, rough, smooth.

BUCKINGHAM TESTS IN SPELLING

TABLE CXI

DISTRIBUTION TABLE — BUCKINGHAM FIFTY-WORD TEST IN SPELLING [1]

GRADE	2B				2A			
NUMBER IN GRADE	93				71			
	FALLING IN EACH GROUP				FALLING IN EACH GROUP			
	BLOOMINGTON		BUCKINGHAM		BLOOMINGTON		BUCKINGHAM	
GRADE ON TEST	No.	PER CENT	No.	PER CENT	No.	PER CENT	No.	PER CENT
0–10.......			39	22.0				
11–20.......	1	1.1	32	18.0			5	3.0
21–30.......	13	14.0	37	21.0			9	5.0
31–40.......	11	11.8	27	16.0	4	5.6	29	17.0
41–50.......	9	9.7	18	10.0	15	21.1	26	15.0
51–60.......	10	10.8	14	18.0			47	28.0
61–70.......	19	20.4	5	3.0	3	4.2	31	18.0
71–80.......	21	22.6	2	1.0	12	16.9	14	18.0
81–90.......	9	9.7	1	.6	24	33.8	7	4.0
91–100......					13	18.3	1	.6
TOTALS....	93		175		71		169	
MEDIANS..		56.6		26.5		75.4		56.17

[1] For Buckingham results see "Spelling Ability — Its Measurement and Distribution," B. R. Buckingham, page 57.

TABLE CXI (*Continued*)

DISTRIBUTION TABLE — BUCKINGHAM FIFTY-WORD TEST IN SPELLING

GRADE	3B AND 3A				4B AND 4A			
NUMBER IN GRADE	186				195			
	FALLING IN EACH GROUP				FALLING IN EACH GROUP			
	BLOOMINGTON		BUCKINGHAM		BLOOMINGTON		BUCKINGHAM	
GRADE ON TEST	No.	PER CENT	No.	PER CENT	No.	PER CENT	No.	PER CENT
0–10								
11–20			1	.6				
21–30	1	5.0	4	2.0				
31–40	10	5.4	7	4.0	4	2.1		
41–50	39	21.0	11	7.0	12	6.2	4	1.0
51–60	3	1.6	25	15.0			13	4.0
61–70	3	1.6	33	20.0	1	.5	29	9.0
71–80	9	4.8	36	21.0	9	4.6	50	16.0
81–90	24	12.9	30	18.0	33	16.9	86	27.0
91–100	97	52.2	21	13.0	136	69.7	134	42.0
TOTALS	186		168		195		316	
MEDIANS		85.5		72.5		86.5		88.12

TABLE CXII

DISTRIBUTION TABLE — BUCKINGHAM ONE-HUNDRED WORD TEST IN SPELLING [1]

GRADE	THIRD				FOURTH			
NUMBER IN GRADE	181				210			
	FALLING IN EACH GROUP				FALLING IN EACH GROUP			
	BLOOMINGTON		BUCKINGHAM [1]		BLOOMINGTON		BUCKINGHAM	
GRADE ON TEST	No.	PER CENT	No.	PER CENT	No.	PER CENT	No.	PER CENT
0–5	1	.6	9	2.0			1	.2
6–10	3	1.7	22	4.9			1	.2
11–15	7	3.9	30	6.7			10	2.1
16–20	4	2.2	38	8.5	2	1.0	12	2.6
21–25	14	7.7	44	9.9	1	.5	13	2.8
26–30	16	8.8	47	10.1	2	1.0	23	4.9
31–35	11	6.1	34	7.6	6	2.9	29	6.2
36–40	10	5.5	38	8.5	7	3.3	27	5.8
41–45	8	4.4	24	5.4	8	3.8	30	6.4
46–50	16	8.8	34	7.6	9	4.3	33	7.1
51–55	16	8.8	26	5.8	9	4.3	27	5.8
56–60	12	6.6	24	5.4	17	8.1	31	6.6
61–65	10	5.5	26	5.8	20	10.0	39	8.4
66–70	17	9.4	17	3.8	17	8.1	29	6.2
71–75	6	3.3	13	2.9	24	11.4	45	9.6
76–80	10	5.5	8	1.8	25	11.9	35	7.5
81–85	6	3.3	4	.9	25	11.9	33	7.1
86–90	10	5.5	4	.9	20	10.0	26	5.6
91–95	2	1.1	3	.7	14	6.7	19	4.1
96–100	2	1.1			4	1.9	4	.9
TOTALS	181		445		210		467	
MEDIANS		54.5		35.8		71.5		60.7

[1] See "Spelling Ability — Its Measurement and Distribution," B. R. Buckingham, page 27.

TABLE CXII (*Continued*)

DISTRIBUTION TABLE — BUCKINGHAM ONE-HUNDRED WORD TEST IN SPELLING

GRADE NUMBER IN GROUP	FIFTH 192				SIXTH 157			
	FALLING IN EACH GROUP				FALLING IN EACH GROUP			
	BLOOMINGTON		BUCKINGHAM		BLOOMINGTON		BUCKINGHAM	
GRADE ON TEST	No.	PER CENT	No.	PER CENT	No.	PER CENT	No.	PER CENT
0–5	1	.5	1	.2				
6–10			2	.4				
11–15			1	.2	1	.6		
16–20			2	.4				
21–25			6	1.2			2	.5
26–30	1	.5	12	2.3				
31–35	1	.5	13	2.5			2	.5
36–40			11	2.1				
41–45			18	3.5	1	.6	6	1.4
46–50	2	1.0	28	5.4	1	.6	4	1.0
51–55	2	1.0	20	3.9	1	.6	6	1.4
56–60	5	2.6	32	6.2	1	.6	15	3.6
61–65	11	5.7	44	8.5	3	1.9	12	2.9
66–70	11	5.7	48	9.3	3	1.9	23	5.5
71–75	22	11.5	49	9.5	3	1.9	30	7.2
76–80	16	8.3	59	11.5	13	8.3	52	12.4
81–85	17	8.9	37	7.2	9	5.7	67	16.0
86–90	37	19.2	64	12.4	26	16.6	61	14.6
91–95	37	19.2	50	9.7	40	25.5	101	24.2
96–100	29	15.1	18	3.5	55	35.0	37	8.9
TOTALS	192		515		157		418	
MEDIANS		86.0		73.1		92.1		84.9

DISTRIBUTION TABLE — BUCKINGHAM ONE-HUNDRED WORD TEST IN SPELLING

GRADE NUMBER IN GRADE	SEVENTH 147				EIGHTH 87			
	FALLING IN EACH GROUP				FALLING IN EACH GROUP			
	BLOOMINGTON		BUCKINGHAM		BLOOMINGTON		BUCKINGHAM	
GRADE ON TEST	No.	PER CENT	No.	PER CENT	No.	PER CENT	No.	PER CENT
0–5								
6–10								
11–15								
16–20								
21–25								
26–30								
31–35			2	.5				
36–40								
41–45			2	.5				
46–50			1	.3				
51–55	1	.7	3	.8				
56–60	1	.7	5	1.4	1	1.1	1	.4
61–65	4	2.7	6	1.6			1	.4
66–70	5	3.4	8	2.2			3	1.1
71–75	4	2.7	18	4.9			8	2.9
76–80	4	2.7	31	8.5			11	4.0
81–85	3	2.0	38	10.4			9	6.9
86–90	18	12.2	79	21.6	3	3.4	41	14.8
91–95	39	26.5	93	25.5	15	17.2	80	28.9
96–100	68	46.2	79	21.6	68	78.2	113	40.8
TOTALS	147		365		87		268	
MEDIANS		94.4		90.5		96.4		94.68

Tables CXI and CXII read as follows: The first horizontal line below the title indicates the grades. Beneath this line is a row of figures indicating the number of pupils in each grade taking the test. The horizontal line beginning 0–10 indicates for each grade both the absolute number of cases and the per cent that such cases are of the whole number in that grade taking the test that made grades falling within the limits of nothing up to ten.

The table shows that the Bloomington schools are more proficient in the second and third grade spelling than in the fourth grade according to comparative results. The median grade for Bloomington in the 2B group is 56.6 while the Buckingham standard is 26.5. For Bloomington 2A's the median is 75.4 as against 56.17 according to Buckingham. In the third grade Bloomington shows a median grade of 85.5, Buckingham 72.5. In the fourth grade Bloomington 86.5, Buckingham 88.12.

Table CXI shows, as does Table CXII, that Bloomington gets comparatively better results in the lower than in the higher grades. In the lower grades the results are distinctly better than the Buckingham results. In the seventh and eighth grades the differences become slight, though there the advantage is slightly in favor of Bloomington.

TABLE CXIII

NUMBER OF WORDS MISSED PER HUNDRED WRITTEN, AND PER CENT OF EACH
GRADE MAKING LESS THAN ONE MISTAKE PER HUNDRED WORDS

GRADE	AVERAGE NUMBER OF WORDS MISSED PER HUNDRED WRITTEN IN DICTATION EXERCISE	AVERAGE NUMBER OF WORDS MISSED PER HUNDRED WRITTEN, ORIGINAL STORY EXERCISE	PER CENT OF GRADE MAKING LESS THAN ONE MISTAKE PER HUNDRED WORDS WRITTEN IN ORIGINAL STORY EXERCISE
4B		4.9	16
4A		4.1	12
5B		4.0	20
5A		3.6	24
6B		2.3	22
6A		2.5	24
7B	5.0	1.6	35
7A	3.2	1.5	39
8B	2.8	.9	59
8A	2.8	1.0	52

COURTIS TESTS IN SPELLING

Mr. Courtis determines proficiency in spelling by the degree of accuracy in spelling in the written work of the pupils. For the Bloomington schools he scored the papers of all seventh and eighth grade pupils on the dictation exercise and all the grades from the 4B to the 8A inclusive on the original story exercise. Table CXIII shows the number of words misspelled per hundred written, as well as the per cent of each grade making less than one mistake per hundred words written.

Mr. Courtis comments as follows on Table CXIII: "The general development of spelling ability in Bloomington is of the same general character as that in other cities but as far as can be judged from these results much better."

RICE SPELLING TESTS AS USED IN BUCKINGHAM STUDY

Buckingham's study shows results by full years while the Bloomington study is by half years. For Bloomington, therefore, is shown separately the per cent of all 4B and 4A pupils spelling each word correctly. Buckingham combines 4B and 4A grades in fourth-grade results. The results in the Rice test point in the same direction as the results in the Buckingham proper tests, namely, that Bloomington gets fairly good results in spelling early in the grades and throughout the grades gets a higher degree of accuracy than do those systems tested by Buckingham.

TABLE CXIV

RICE SENTENCE TEST IN SPELLING USED BY BUCKINGHAM[1]

GRADE		4B 122			4A 87	
		CORRECT			CORRECT	
		BLOOMINGTON	BUCKINGHAM		BLOOMINGTON	
	No.	PER CENT	No.	PER CENT	No.	PER CENT
Running.....	68	55.7		48.0	53	60.9
Slipped......	36	29.5		30.0	60	68.9
Listened.....	58	47.5		29.6	40	46.0
Queer.......	62	50.9		56.9	52	59.8
Speech......	42	34.4		45.3	36	41.4
Believe......	76	62.3		37.2	44	50.6
Weather.....	95	77.9		70.9	79	90.8
Changeable...	22	18.0		27.7	17	19.5
Whistling....	34	27.9		27.3	46	52.8
Frightened...	38	31.1		17.8	42	48.3
Always......	95	77.9		53.8	81	93.1
Changing....	78	63.9		58.5	69	79.3
Chain.......	38	31.1		57.8	50	57.5
Loose.......	34	27.9		24.7	44	50.6
Baking......	100	82.0		63.4	64	73.6
Piece........	49	40.2		58.5	40	46.0
Receive......	32	26.2		21.1	35	40.2
Laughter....	72	59.0		59.9	70	80.5
Distance.....	64	52.5		35.6	60	69.0

[1] See "Spelling Ability — Its Measurement and Distribution," B. R. Buckingham, pp. 78–79.

TABLE CXIV (*Continued*)

RICE SENTENCE TEST IN SPELLING USED BY BUCKINGHAM [1]

GRADE		4B			4A	
NUMBER IN GRADE		122			87	
		CORRECT			CORRECT	
		BLOOMINGTON	BUCKINGHAM		BLOOMINGTON	
	No.	PER CENT	PER CENT	No.	PER CENT	
Choose......	32	26.2	41.7	33	37.9	
Strange......	85	69.7	57.7	76	87.4	
Picture......	78	63.9	69.6	81	93.1	
Because.....	91	74.6	66.2	80	91.9	
Thought	89	73.0	58.7	77	88.5	
Purpose.....	25	20.5	21.7	42	48.2	
Learn.......	87	71.3	70.1	76	87.4	
Lose........	69	56.6	46.4	44	50.6	
Almanac.....	6	4.9	10.1	11	12.6	
Neighbor....	22	18.0	27.5	70	80.5	
Writing......	72	63.1	56.3	74	85.1	
Language....	60	52.6	40.3	74	85.1	
Careful......	62	50.8	54.3	61	70.1	
Enough......	64	52.5	54.9	66	75.9	
Necessary....	7	5.8	4.5	25	28.7	
Waiting.....	77	63.1	55.9	69	79.3	
Disappoint...	6	4.9	11.7	1	1.1	
Often........	101	82.8	51.6	71	81.6	
Covered.....	72	63.1	42.1	56	64.4	
Mixture.....	45	36.9	33.6	47	54.0	
Getting......	60	49.1	57.5	53	60.9	
Better.......	101	82.8	80.6	77	88.5	
Feather......	75	65.8	77.1	80	91.9	
Light........	88	77.8	77.5	81	93.1	
Deceive......	21	17.2	18.4	22	25.3	
Driving......	104	85.2	59.7	82	94.3	
Surface......	46	40.4	48.4	44	50.6	
Rough.......	73	64.0	64.2	65	74.7	
Smooth......	42	36.8	47.2	44	50.6	
Hopping.....	86	70.5	58.1	69	79.3	
Certainly....	18	14.8	16.8	30	34.5	

RICE SENTENCE TEST IN SPELLING USED BY BUCKINGHAM [1]

GRADE		5B			5A	
NUMBER IN GRADE		110			89	
		CORRECT			CORRECT	
		BLOOMINGTON	BUCKINGHAM 5TH GRADE		BLOOMINGTON	
	No.	PER CENT	PER CENT	No.	PER CENT	
Running...........	64	58.2	66.0	81	91.0	
Slipped............	63	57.3	34.8	49	55.1	
Listened...........	79	71.8	40.4	58	65.2	
Queer.............	72	65.5	58.8	54	60.7	
Speech............	42	38.2	41.4	43	48.3	
Believe............	84	76.4	49.7	71	49.8	
Weather...........	107	97.3	57.5	83	93.3	
Changeable........	43	39.1	31.3	35	39.3	
Whistling..........	73	66.4	40.0	57	64.0	
Frightened.........	76	69.1	42.7	59	66.3	
Always............	102	92.7	68.7	83	93.3	

[1] See "Spelling Ability — Its Measurement and Distribution," B. R. Buckingham, pp. 78–79.

TABLE CXIV (*Continued*)

RICE SENTENCE TEST IN SPELLING USED BY BUCKINGHAM

GRADE		5B			5A	
NUMBER IN GRADE		110			89	
		CORRECT			CORRECT	
	BLOOMINGTON		BUCKINGHAM 5TH GRADE		BLOOMINGTON	
	No.	PER CENT	PER CENT		No.	PER CENT
Changing..........	87	79.1	69.2		72	80.9
Chain.............	76	69.1	59.8		74	83.1
Loose.............	65	59.1	49.1		56	62.9
Baking............	96	87.3	75.7		75	84.3
Piece.............	78	70.9	62.2		65	73.0
Receive...........	67	60.9	51.7		38	42.7
Laughter..........	98	89.1	71.4		87	97.8
Distance..........	82	74.5	67.2		69	77.5
Choose............	82	74.5	46.3		69	77.5
Strange...........	94	85.4	74.2		78	87.6
Picture...........	101	91.8	87.5		85	95.5
Because...........	90	81.8	83.9		85	95.5
Thought...........	94	85.4	72.4		82	92.1
Purpose...........	85	77.3	47.3		60	67.4
Learn.............	101	91.8	84.9		86	96.6
Lose..............	63	57.3	53.1		59	66.3
Almanac...........	57	51.8	21.5		60	67.4
Neighbor..........	91	82.7	66.6		73	82.0
Writing...........	81	73.6	74.0		70	78.7
Language..........	86	78.2	62.8		80	89.9
Careful...........	80	72.7	58.6		79	88.8
Enough............	97	88.2	68.0		82	92.1
Necessary.........	66	60.0	21.5		49	55.1
Waiting...........	82	74.5	66.8		74	83.1
Disappoint........	39	35.5	27.4		55	61.8
Often.............	102	92.7	57.5		85	95.5
Covered...........	94	85.4	62.6		79	88.8
Mixture...........	77	70.0	62.6		70	78.7
Getting...........	88	80.0	74.4		84	94.4
Better............	108	98.2	91.8		88	98.9
Feather...........	94	85.4	84.1		83	93.3
Light.............	93	84.5	90.5		83	93.3
Deceive...........	38	34.4	46.3		30	33.7
Driving...........	97	88.2	77.1		86	96.6
Surface...........	59	53.6	79.1		72	80.9
Rough.............	82	74.5	69.8		79	88.8
Smooth............	69	62.7	51.3		74	61.9
Hopping...........	97	88.2	58.1		80	89.9
Certainly.........	68	61.8	36.0		48	53.9

RICE SENTENCE TEST IN SPELLING USED BY BUCKINGHAM

GRADE		6B			6A	
NUMBER IN GRADE		85			74	
		CORRECT			CORRECT	
	BLOOMINGTON		BUCKINGHAM 6TH GRADE		BLOOMINGTON	
	No.	PER CENT	PER CENT		No.	PER CENT
Running...........	75	87.1	76.8		69	93.2
Slipped...........	54	63.5	42.7		55	74.3
Listened..........	71	83.5	53.5		71	95.9
Queer.............	60	70.6	77.3		62	83.8

TABLE CXIV (*Continued*)

RICE SENTENCE TEST IN SPELLING USED BY BUCKINGHAM

GRADE	6B			6A	
NUMBER IN GRADE	85			74	
	CORRECT			CORRECT	
	BLOOMINGTON		BUCKINGHAM 6TH GRADE	BLOOMINGTON	
	No.	PER CENT	PER CENT	No.	PER CENT
Speech............	60	70.6	72.0	55	74.3
Believe............	77	90.6	64.4	63	85.1
Weather...........	84	98.8	82.8	74	100.0
Changeable.......	48	56.5	46.7	47	63.5
Whistling..........	62	72.4	49.0	64	86.5
Frightened........	65	76.5	55.6	66	89.2
Always............	78	91.8	78.5	69	93.2
Changing..........	67	78.8	74.5	68	91.9
Chain.............	75	87.1	75.3	67	90.5
Loose.............	52	61.2	45.2	56	75.7
Baking............	77	83.5	83.6	72	97.3
Piece.............	64	75.3	69.9	62	83.8
Receive...........	61	71.8	59.8	54	73.0
Laughter..........	78	91.8	75.5	69	93.2
Distance...........	78	91.8	75.8	72	97.3
Choose............	68	80.0	56.8	58	78.4
Strange...........	80	94.1	86.9	71	95.9
Picture............	83	97.6	94.4	73	98.6
Because...........					
Thought...........					
Purpose...........	76	89.4	66.9	67	90.5
Learn.............	83	97.6	93.2	73	98.6
Lose.............	63	74.1	56.8	52	70.3
Almanac..........	64	75.3	38.6	59	79.7
Neighbor..........	79	92.9	65.2	73	98.6
Writing............					
Language..........					
Careful............	75	87.1	68.9	69	93.2
Enough............	83	97.6	80.3	71	95.9
Necessary..........	60	70.6	42.7	45	60.8
Waiting...........	77	90.6	82.3	71	95.9
Disappoint........	53	62.4	34.6	54	73.0
Often.............	82	96.5	75.8	72	97.3
Covered...........	81	95.3	77.5	72	97.3
Mixture...........	80	94.1	83.3	66	89.2
Getting...........	81	95.3	87.4	72	97.3
Better............	83	97.6	94.9	74	100.0
Feather...........					
Light.............					
Deceive...........	50	58.8	53.5	36	48.6
Driving...........	80	94.1	88.1	72	97.3
Surface...........					
Rough............					
Smooth...........					
Hopping..........	73	85.9	68.4	71	95.9
Certainly..........	68	80.0	57.1	66	89.2
Grateful..........	57	67.1	39.1	57	77.0
Elegant...........	48	56.5	53.5	44	59.5
Present...........	75	87.1	69.7	68	91.9
Patience..........	55	64.7	43.4	54	73.0
Succeed...........	75	87.1	53.0	66	89.2
Severe............	60	70.6	40.9	62	83.8

TABLE CXIV (*Continued*)

RICE SENTENCE TEST IN SPELLING USED BY BUCKINGHAM

GRADE	6B			6A	
NUMBER IN GRADE	85			74	
	CORRECT			CORRECT	
	BLOOMINGTON		BUCKINGHAM 6TH GRADE	BLOOMINGTON	
	No.	PER CENT	PER CENT	No.	PER CENT
Accident..........	62	72.9	45.5	61	82.4
Sometimes.........	80	94.1	52.5	73	98.6
Sensible..........	47	55.3	34.3	44	59.5
Business..........	51	60.0	46.0	51	68.9
Answer...........	72	84.7	74.0	73	98.6
Sweeping.........	80	94.1	87.4	72	97.3
Properly..........	74	87.1	61.1	66	89.2
Improvement......	71	83.5	59.6	71	95.9
Fatiguing.........	19	22.4	12.6	28	37.8
Anxious..........	66	77.6	49.0	62	83.3
Appreciate........	43	50.6	31.8	41	55.4
Assure...........	56	65.9	58.1	69	93.2
Imagine..........	44	51.8	33.6	53	71.6
Peculiar..........	46	54.1	24.0	49	66.2
Character.........	47	55.3	40.2	56	75.7
Guarantee........	15	17.6	11.6	23	30.1
Approval.........	49	57.6	38.1	50	67.6
Intelligent........	22	25.9	37.1	30	40.5
Experience........	42	49.4	44.4	61	82.4
Delicious.........	51	60.0	31.2	54	73.0
Realize...........	52	61.2	53.5	49	66.2
Importance.......	67	78.8	47.5	61	82.4
Occasion..........	52	61.2	34.8	59	79.7
Exceptions........	54	63.5	48.2	52	70.3
Thoroughly.......	27	31.8	18.7	43	58.1
Conscientious.....	6	7.1	.3	10	13.5
Therefore.........	76	89.4	36.4	69	93.2
Ascending.........	34	40.0	37.6	34	45.9
Praise............	68	80.0	69.0	70	94.6
Wholesome........	52	61.2	56.3	53	71.6

RICE SENTENCE TEST IN SPELLING USED BY BUCKINGHAM

GRADE	7B			7A	
NUMBER IN GRADE	86			62	
	CORRECT			CORRECT	
	BLOOMINGTON		BUCKINGHAM 7TH GRADE	BLOOMINGTON	
	No.	PER CENT	PER CENT	No.	PER CENT
Running..........	81	94.2	85.0	61	98.4
Slipped...........	63	73.3	51.8	51	82.3
Listened..........	76	88.4	69.8	58	93.5
Queer............	73	84.9	79.0	53	85.4
Speech...........	60	69.8	77.1	37	59.7
Believe...........	72	83.7	62.1	54	87.1
Weather..........	83	96.5	88.0	58	93.5
Changeable.......	60	69.8	66.8	41	66.1
Whistling.........	70	81.4	68.7	55	88.7
Frightened........	78	90.7	71.4	54	87.1
Always...........	82	95.3	88.6	61	98.4
Changing.........	83	96.5	89.6	57	91.9

TABLE CXIV (*Continued*)

RICE SENTENCE TEST IN SPELLING USED BY BUCKINGHAM

GRADE	7B			7A	
NUMBER IN GRADE	86			62	
	CORRECT BLOOMINGTON		BUCKINGHAM 7TH GRADE	CORRECT BLOOMINGTON	
	No.	PER CENT	PER CENT	No.	PER CENT
Chain.............	77	89.5	88.0	60	96.8
Loose.............	65	75.6	63.2	54	87.1
Baking............	76	88.4	93.5	58	93.5
Piece.............	66	76.7	83.7	50	80.6
Receive...........	72	83.7	62.1	47	75.8
Laughter.........	80	93.0	88.8	59	95.1
Distance..........	84	97.7	88.0	58	93.5
Choose...........	68	79.1	83.1	56	90.3
Strange...........	78	90.7	93.5	62	100.0
Picture...........	83	96.5	97.5	60	96.8
Because...........					
Thought..........					
Purpose..........	83	96.5	74.7	61	98.4
Learn............	84	97.7	95.9	61	98.4
Lose.............	70	81.4	60.0	25	40.3
Almanac..........	61	70.9	58.6	54	87.1
Neighbor.........	79	91.9	85.0	58	93.5
Writing...........					
Language.........					
Careful...........	77	89.5	85.8	59	95.1
Enough...........	81	94.2	91.0	55	88.7
Necessary.........	65	75.6	37.6	51	82.3
Waiting..........	78	90.7	89.6	59	95.1
Disappoint........	59	68.6	32.4	53	85.4
Often.............	85	98.8	87.2	58	93.5
Covered...........	86	100.0	90.2	61	98.4
Mixture..........	83	96.5	91.0	56	90.3
Getting...........	82	95.3	94.6	59	95.1
Better............	86	100.0	98.6	62	100.0
Feather...........					
Light.............					
Deceive...........	60	69.8	54.8	37	59.6
Driving...........	84	97.7	65.7	58	93.5
Surface...........					
Rough............					
Smooth...........					
Hopping..........	83	96.5	81.2	62	100.0
Certainly.........	72	83.7	79.0	58	93.5
Grateful..........	50	58.1	58.6	44	70.9
Elegant...........	42	48.8	65.7	46	74.2
Present...........	83	96.5	79.0	47	75.8
Patience..........	58	67.4	63.0	55	88.7
Succeed...........	77	89.5	70.8	58	93.5
Severe............	66	76.7	61.3	56	90.3
Accident..........	66	76.7	68.9	53	85.4
Sometimes.........	83	96.5	67.3	62	100.0
Sensible..........	37	43.0	55.0	38	61.3
Business..........	45	52.3	53.7	52	83.9
Answer............	83	95.6	86.9	57	91.9
Sweeping..........	83	96.5	92.1	58	93.5
Properly..........	79	91.9	73.0	58	93.5
Improvement.......	80	93.0	69.5	56	90.3

TABLE CXIV (*Continued*)

RICE SENTENCE TEST IN SPELLING USED BY BUCKINGHAM

GRADE	7B			7A	
NUMBER IN GRADE	86			62	
	CORRECT			CORRECT	
	BLOOMINGTON		BUCKINGHAM 7TH GRADE	BLOOMINGTON	
	No.	PER CENT	PER CENT	No.	PER CENT
Fatiguing..........	19	22.1	25.3	31	50.0
Anxious...........	67	77.9	66.2	56	90.3
Appreciate.........	43	50.0	49.0	46	74.2
Assure............	60	69.8	68.9	51	82.3
Imagine...........	50	58.1	47.7	45	72.6
Peculiar...........	56	65.1	46.3	45	72.6
Character..........	57	66.3	47.1	52	83.9
Guarantee.........	13	15.1	19.9	20	32.3
Approval..........	68	79.1	56.9	50	80.6
Intelligent.........	30	34.9	43.6	41	66.1
Experience........	44	51.2	63.5	49	79.0
Delicious..........	59	68.6	61.6	53	85.4
Realize............	57	66.3	65.7	39	62.9
Importance........	75	87.2	73.3	59	95.1
Occasion..........	52	60.5	44.4	52	83.9
Exceptions........	80	93.0	57.2	53	85.4
Thoroughly........	46	53.5	31.1	42	67.7
Conscientious......	59	68.6	1.6	44	70.9
Therefore..........	74	86.0	62.4	59	95.1
Ascending..........	45	52.3	52.0	43	69.3
Praise.............	77	89.5	78.2	57	91.9
Wholesome.........	61	70.9	74.7	51	82.3

RICE SENTENCE TEST IN SPELLING USED BY BUCKINGHAM

GRADE	8B			8A	
NUMBER IN GRADE	61			29	
	CORRECT			CORRECT	
	BLOOMINGTON		BUCKINGHAM 8TH GRADE	BLOOMINGTON	
	No.	PER CENT	PER CENT	No.	PER CENT
Running...........	61	100.0	93.4	28	96.5
Slipped............	54	88.5	70.9	24	82.8
Listened..........	57	93.4	86.9	28	96.5
Queer.............	58	95.1	87.3	26	89.7
Speech............	49	80.3	80.7	22	75.9
Believe............	57	93.4	76.6	29	100.0
Weather...........	61	100.0	92.2	20	100.0
Changeable........	50	82.0	65.6	22	75.9
Whistling..........	56	91.8	74.2	28	96.5
Frightened.........	60	98.4	85.7	29	100.0
Always............	60	98.4	95.5	25	86.2
Changing..........	57	93.4	91.4	29	100.0
Chain.............	61	100.0	95.9	28	96.5
Loose.............	60	98.4	81.6	28	96.5
Baking............	58	95.1	97.5	26	89.7
Piece..............	54	88.5	90.6	21	72.4
Receive...........	52	85.2	80.7	28	96.5
Laughter..........	60	98.4	96.3	28	96.5
Distance...........	60	98.4	97.5	27	
Choose...........	59	96.7	85.7	29	100.0
Strange...........	61	100.0	92.6	29	100.0

TABLE CXIV (*Continued*)

<small>RICE SENTENCE TEST IN SPELLING USED BY BUCKINGHAM</small>

GRADE	8B			8A	
NUMBER IN GRADE	61			29	
	CORRECT			CORRECT	
	BLOOMINGTON		BUCKINGHAM 8TH GRADE	BLOOMINGTON	
	No.	PER CENT	PER CENT	No.	PER CENT
Picture............	61	100.0	98.8	29	100.0
Because............					
Thought...........					
Purpose...........	60	98.4	92.6	28	96.5
Learn.............	60	98.4	99.6	13	44.8
Lose..............	31	60.8	55.7	26	89.7
Almanac...........	54	88.5	72.1	28	96.5
Neighbor..........	59	96.7	93.4	28	96.5
Writing............					
Language..........					
Careful...........	60	98.4	88.1	28	96.5
Enough............	57	93.4	98.4	28	96.5
Necessary..........	58	95.1	61.5	29	100.0
Waiting...........	61	100.0	92.2	29	100.0
Disappoint.........	52	85.2	38.9	25	86.2
Often.............	61	100.0	92.2	29	100.0
Covered...........	61	100.0	97.1	29	100.0
Mixture...........	61	100.0	97.1	28	96.5
Getting...........	61	100.0	97.5	28	96.5
Better............	59	96.7	100.0	29	100.0
Feather...........					
Light..............					
Deceive...........	43	70.5	79.5	18	62.1
Driving...........	59	96.7	98.8	28	96.5
Surface...........					
Rough............					
Smooth...........					
Hopping..........	60	98.4	89.3	29	100.0
Certainly.........	58	95.1	91.0	28	96.5
Grateful..........	58	95.1	61.9	24	82.8
Elegant...........	60	98.4	69.3	24	82.8
Present...........	54	88.5	91.4	29	100.0
Patience..........	57	93.4	80.7	26	89.7
Succeed...........	57	93.4	80.7	24	82.8
Severe............	57	'93.4	70.9	28	96.5
Accident..........	54	88.5	85.2	26	89.7
Sometimes........	60	98.4	82.8	29	100.0
Sensible..........	59	96.7	65.2	22	75.9
Business..........	44	72.1	68.4	22	75.9
Answer...........	51	83.6	93.4	28	96.5
Sweeping.........	60	98.4	94.7	28	96.5
Properly..........	59	96.7	86.5	28	96.5
Improvement.......	61	100.0	86.5	27	93.1
Fatiguing.........	58	95.1	31.1	15	51.7
Anxious...........	28	45.9	84.0	28	96.5
Appreciate........	56	91.8	74.6	22	75.9
Assure............	53	86.9	86.1	27	93.1
Imagine..........	55	90.1	66.4	26	89.7
Peculiar..........	60	98.4	56.1	23	79.3
Character.........	47	77.0	78.7	26	89.7
Guarantee........	55	90.1	25.8	16	55.2
Approval.........	27	44.3	75.4	23	79.3

TABLE CXIV (*Continued*)

RICE SENTENCE TEST IN SPELLING USED BY BUCKINGHAM

GRADE		8B			8A	
NUMBER IN GRADE		61			29	
			CORRECT			CORRECT
	BLOOMINGTON		BUCKINGHAM 8TH GRADE		BLOOMINGTON	
	No.	PER CENT	PER CENT	No.	PER CENT	
Intelligent.........	56	91.8	50.4	17	58.6	
Experience.........	35	57.4	68.9	27	93.1	
Delicious..........	56	91.8	85.2	28	96.5	
Realize............	50	91.8	73.4	27	93.1	
Importance........	66	98.4	81.6	29	100.0	
Occasion..........	59	96.7	49.6	25	86.2	
Exceptions.........	47	77.0	76.2	25	86.2	
Thoroughly........	51	83.6	53.3	18	62.1	
Conscientious......	37	60.7	19.7	13	44.8	
Therefore..........	57	93.4	79.9	27	93.1	
Ascending..........	49	80.3	55.7	20	69.0	
Praise.............	59	96.7	95.9	29	100.0	
Wholesome.........	58	95.1	36.1	23	79.3	

7. COMPOSITION AND READING

The following is an outline supplied by Mr. Courtis covering tabulations of Courtis Standard Research Tests in English Composition and Rates of Reading in the Bloomington public schools, January 22, 1914.

NATURE OF TESTS

Tests Used — Courtis Standard Tests, Series C

"Children were shown the picture of child sitting on doorstep drinking from a bowl of milk. First part of story about picture was dictated to them; they were then asked to complete the story. Work interrupted at end of five minutes. These papers are called 'Original Stories' in this report.

"Children were then given the printed second and third parts of the story to read. The second part they were asked to read at their normal rate, the third part carefully for reproduction. The number of words read in one minute was determined for scores. These scores called 'Normal Reading' and 'Careful Reading,' respectively.

EXAMINATION AND SCORING

"All classes from 4th to 8th grades inclusive in four school buildings in Bloomington, Indiana. Tests given by superintendent of schools in three buildings, by principal of building in one building, and scored by a single paid assistant under Mr. Courtis' direction.

Details of Scoring

"Method of scoring that used by Rice, Bliss, and others. The details are given in the following pages from the folder of instruction: pp. 11–12–13, Folder C, Parts I and II. Method unsatisfactory for three reasons:

"(1) Difficulty of keeping standards of judgment uniform.

"(2) Variability of standards from scorer to scorer.

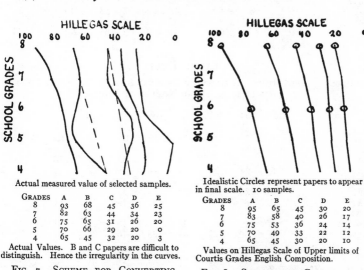

Actual measured value of selected samples.

GRADES	A	B	C	D	E
8	93	68	45	36	25
7	82	63	44	34	23
6	75	65	31	26	20
5	70	66	29	20	0
4	65	45	32	20	3

Actual Values. B and C papers are difficult to distinguish. Hence the irregularity in the curves.

FIG. 7. SCHEME FOR CONVERTING COURTIS ENGLISH GRADES INTO HILLEGAS SCALE.

Idealistic Circles represent papers to appear in final scale. 10 samples.

GRADES	A	B	C	D	E
8	95	65	45	30	20
7	83	58	40	26	17
6	75	53	36	24	14
5	70	49	33	22	12
4	65	45	30	20	10

Values on Hillegas Scale of Upper limits of Courtis Grades English Composition.

FIG. 8. SCHEME FOR CONVERTING COURTIS ENGLISH GRADES INTO HILLEGAS SCALE.

"(3) Lack of progress shown by the results. A median score of 3.2 in the 4B class does not mean at all the same as 3.2 in the 8A class owing to change in the meaning of a 3 ("C") paper from the 4th to the 8th grade.

"(1) First difficulty avoided as far as possible by checking work, by rescoring certain papers each day, also by setting up certain typical papers as standards and comparing each sample with the standards in all cases of doubt.

"(2) Very little can be done to eliminate the variability of standards from scorer to scorer until an adequate scale and method of measurement is devised. The comparisons in this report are of value from one viewpoint only. The scores at least *show the estimate* of the scorer on the papers scored.

TABLE CXV

MEDIAN GRADE SCORES IN ENGLISH COMPOSITION, BLOOMINGTON

GRADE	SCORES COURTIS	VARIABILITY	EQUIVALENTS		SCORES HILLEGAS
4B................	3.2	44	3 = 30	(−10)	28
4A................	2.9	54	2 = 45	(−15)	35
5B................	3.1	44	3 = 33	(−11)	32
5A................	2.9	46	2 = 49	(−16)	35
6B................	2.5	54	2 = 53	(−17)	45
6A................	2.5	55	2 = 53	(−17)	45
7B................	2.6	38	2 = 58	(−18)	47
7A................	2.4	45	2 = 58	(−18)	51
8B................	2.3	52	2 = 65	(−20)	59
8A................	2.6	41	2 = 65	(−20)	53

TABLE CXVI

ENGLISH COMPOSITION. QUALITY OF ORIGINAL STORY. PER CENT EACH QUALITY IS OF TOTAL NUMBER OF SCORES

	A		B		C		D		E	
	GEN.[1]	B[2]	GEN.	B	GEN.	B	GEN.	B	GEN.	B
4B..........		17		27		32		19		5
A..........	4	36	27	22	32	30	35	12	2	0
5B..........		19		28		33		18		2
A..........	5	24	22	28	44	38	22	8	7	2
6B..........		36		29		25		9		1
A..........	12	35	32	29	37	19	17	14	2	3
7B..........		19		41		18		3		2
A..........	14	30	25	48	33	16	22	5	6	1
8B..........		38		38		20		2		2
A..........	8	22	25	48	37	22	22	8	8	0

" (3) The median scores of the various grades in English composition (Table CXVI) show slight progress from 4th to 8th grade, but to reveal the absolute progress the attempt was made to convert the scoring by the method described above into absolute scores on the Hillegas Scale as follows. For each class, a single typical 'A,' 'B,' 'C,' etc., paper was selected. From all the 'A' papers of a grade, again the most typical paper was selected. The final twenty-five papers thus form a scale illustrating the judgments upon which the scoring given in this report was based. These were then scored by the Hillegas Scale. The results are given graphically and in figures in Fig. 7. Note the A values; they show a regular progress from 4th to 8th grade. Note the B papers. The 8th grade 'B' is almost directly over the 4th grade 'A.' Practically the same thing is true of each of the other papers and suggests that the stand-

[1] Gen. = General.   [2] B. = Bloomington.

ard for the various grades change at such a rate that the 4th grade qualities A, B, C, etc., are equivalent to the qualities called B, C, D, etc., in the 8th grade; in other words, that which is called a 'good' paper for a fourth-grade child would be called 'fair' for an eighth-grade child. The B and C curves are less regular than the others, but this is known to be due to the effort to emphasize the distinction between he B and C papers in the progress of selection. Accordingly the results in Fig. 7 were generalized in Fig. 8. The curves of Fig. 8 could be verified by scoring a large number of typical papers and this will be done as ▾ opportunity offers.

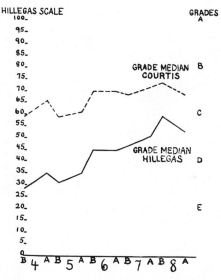

FIG. 9. DEVELOPMENT CURVE — ENGLISH COMPOSITION. BLOOMINGTON.

But for the present the values given in Fig. 8 will be used to convert the qualities by the Rice method into values on the Hillegas Scale. If a similar method were followed by different scorers it would be possible to equate their results.

"The median grade scores on both the Courtis and the Hillegas Scale are given in Table CXV and shown graphically in Fig. 9. This development curve for ability in English composition shows a fairly uniform progress, more rapid in later than in early grades. Either the 4A,

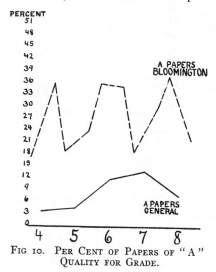

FIG 10. PER CENT OF PAPERS OF "A" QUALITY FOR GRADE.

6B, and 8B grades are rather better than the others, or the 4B, 5B,

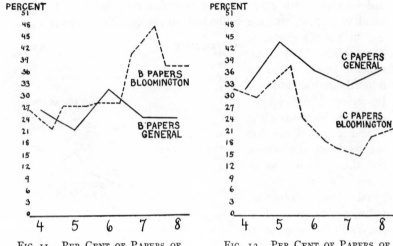

FIG. 11. PER CENT OF PAPERS OF "B" QUALITY FOR GRADE.

FIG. 12. PER CENT OF PAPERS OF "C" QUALITY FOR GRADE.

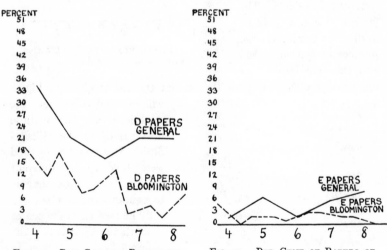

FIG. 13. PER CENT OF PAPERS OF "D" QUALITY FOR GRADE.

FIG. 14. PER CENT OF PAPERS OF "E" QUALITY FOR GRADE.

5A, 6A, 7B, 7A, 8A *worse.* The curve based on the Courtis values suggests that the median score of 2.5 'B' be adopted as a standard for the school system.

"From the viewpoint of efficiency, the per cents of various types of papers in each grade are the proper values to consider. For comparison such scores from other schools as are available are given.

They represent the scores of about 590 children from classes in some five different states. The facts of the table are shown graphically in Figs. 10 to 15. They show: (1) Either the results from the Bloomington schools are very good, (2) or the standards of the scorer were lower than that of scorers in the other schools.

"Probably both causes were at work, but the Bloomington sample papers compared with similar samples from other scales do not show the marked differences, while actual comparisons of many papers show the Bloomington scores high in other particulars also. The curves seem to show a larger number of A and B papers in the Bloomington schools with corresponding decrease in the C, D, and E papers.

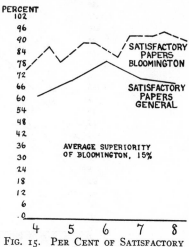

FIG. 15. PER CENT OF SATISFACTORY PAPERS "C" OR BETTER.

"Fig. 15 shows a comparison of results on the basis of total number of 'satisfactory' (A, B, and C) papers, a safer basis of comparison. The average superiority of the Bloomington schools by these results is about 15 per cent. That is, out of 100 children entering any grade in the Bloomington schools about 15 *more* will make a satisfactory grade or better in English composition than they would if they had attended the other schools from which returns have been received.

TABLE CXVII

RATE OF READING (NUMBER OF WORDS PER MINUTE)

	G M	TEST 4 B M	BLOOMINGTON VARIABILITY	G M	TEST 5 B M	BLOOMINGTON VARIABILITY
4B.........	118	168	57	70	113	37
A.........		187	30		125	31
5B.........	173	182	33	126	140	37
A.........		205	29		134	45
6B.........	214	231	28	142	180	26
A.........		258	27		208	27
7B.........	238	240	26	162	182	26
A.........		277	25		205	26
8B.........	262	270	20	212	187	28
A.........		244	24		180	21

G = General.　　　　B = Bloomington.　　　　M = Median.

RATES OF READING

"Table CXVII shows number of words read per minute in Bloomington and other schools. Fig. 16 shows same graphically.

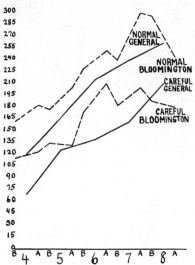

FIG. 16. RATES OF READING.
General is Medium Scores based upon 590 scores
from five states.

SUMMARY

Bloomington curves higher than general curves.
Rate for careful reading fairly constant from 6th grade on.
Same grade irregularities as noted before.
General values for normal reading probably safe standards.
A parallel curve at about 100 words less probably safe standard for careful reading.
Marked variation shown.
Light dotted line above traced from Fig. 15 to suggest correlation between classes that do well in English composition and in rates of reading.
Twenty-one out of 38 cases of marked agreement in scores.
Seven out of 38 cases of marked disagreement.
Suggestive of probable value of learning to read rapidly and understandingly as early in life as possible.
Need for standards.
Need for study of correlation in individual cases.

INDIVIDUAL VARIATION

"A study of the distribution of individual scores shows that in spite of the high class medians of Bloomington schools, the educational process itself is very inefficient. Range in 8th grade for rates of normal reading, for instance, from 140 words per minute to over 400 words per minute suggests the need for experimental use of definite standards derived from the median grade scores."

8. DRAWING

The drawing test was given and graded by Professor H. L. Childs, of Indiana University, and his class in school administration. The test was given in the grades March 16 and 17, 1914, and in the high school May 26, 1914. The test was given under the following directions:

1. *Materials:* White drawing paper, 6 x 9, drawing pencil, charcoal or crayon — black only.
2. *Preliminary data* on the back of the sheet: City, school, teacher, pupil, grade, age (years only), date.
3. Ask pupils to do the best they can and not to hurry.
4. *Subject:* Scene or picture with snow on the ground and boys or girls doing something as snow-balling, coasting, etc.
5. Be sure pupils understand just what they are to do and the time they are to have for doing it.
6. *Time:* Ten minutes, exclusive of all directions and recording of preliminary data.
7. Collect papers; tie papers of each grade in a package and label with subject, city, school, teacher and grade.
8. No assistance shall be given any pupil aside from interpreting the instructions and helping to fill in the data on the back of the sheet if necessary.
9. Distribute materials before giving the directions to the pupils.
10. Teachers should not know in advance the nature of the test to be given.

The scoring was done in accordance with the Thorndike drawing scale, published in the *Teachers College Record*, November, 1913. This scale, however, was supplemented in the following way before it was used:

THE SUPPLEMENTED THORNDIKE SCALE

The following samples of children's drawings were chosen from the Thorndike supplementary sheet numbered 101–117: Nos. 101, 102, 103, 104, 105, 106, 107, 108, 110, 111, 116, all of which represent snow scenes with action.

Seventeen judges, consisting of teachers, graduate students and seniors in Indiana University ranked these eleven drawings in order from poorest to best. The percentages of judgments favoring one sample over another were obtained from these rankings. Then, by use of Table 4, page 25, of *Teachers College Record*, November, 1913 (Professor Thorndike's table), these samples were given a relative placement. Samples 103 and 110 were dropped because judged to be approximately equal in value to 101 and 107 respectively.

The nine remaining samples were compared by ten of the judges mentioned above with various samples on the Thorndike scale and given a relative placement. By a combination of the two sets of

TABL[E]

DISTRIBUTION OF DRAWING ABILIT[Y]

NUMBER

SCORE	1B	1A	2B	2A	3B	3A	4B	4A	5B	5A	6B	6
0	1	....	....	....	....	....	....	....	....	....	....	..
1 to 1.99	1	....	1	....	....	1	....	....	....	....	....	..
2 to 2.99	2	....	4	....	....	1	....	....	....	....	....	..
3 to 3.99	13	16	18	5	....	3	....	....	1	....	....	
4 to 4.99	17	7	7	3	1	2	....	1	2	....	1	..
5 to 5.99	11	16	14	3	5	10	1	....	6	3	3	
6 to 6.99	27	34	18	23	14	18	15	6	15	13	6	
7 to 7.99	8	22	7	30	25	39	33	10	12	18	12	
8 to 8.99	6	19	12	33	39	40	23	57	23	48	42	
9 to 9.99	1	1	....	2	7	7	7	13	10	12	9	
10 to 10.99	....	....	....	1	3	3	....	5	8	9	17	
11 to 11.99	....	....	....	....	....	....	....	2	....	....	....	
12 to 12.99	....	....	....	....	....	....	....	1	....	....	....	
13 to 13.99	....	....	....	....	....	....	....	....	2	í	....	
14 to 14.99	....	....	....	....	....	....	....	....	....	....	....	
TOTAL	87	115	81	100	94	124	79	95	79	104	90	
MEDIAN	5.91	6.56	5.78	7.50	8.06	7.69	7.73	8.54	8.17	8.38	8.56	10.
P.E.	1.17	1.11	1.54	.86	.76	.85	.66	.18	1.13	.68	.63	1.

SUMMARY

1. A fairly steady progress, with one marked exception in grade 2B, is shown from [?]
that point there is a noticeable drop in the 7B grade with only a slight gain thereaft[er]
and eighth grades with the methods now used does not bring results comparable with t[he?]
from the beginning of the school term in the fall until the time of the test, though t[he]
years previous.

2. Median scores by grades range from 5.91 to 10.06, with an average for all grades [...]

3. The high school just about maintains the efficiency reached in the sixth, sever[th...]

relative placements values were assigned to the supplementary
samples on the scale, the original Thorndike values being in no case
changed.

VALUES ASSIGNED TO THE SUPPLEMENTARY SAMPLES

SAMPLE	VALUE ASSIGNED
116	5.5
107	7.2
106	8.0
111	9.3 (9.5 perhaps a better value)
108	11.0
104	13.0 (12.5 perhaps a better value)
101	14.0
105	15.3
102	17.5

Each paper was rated by two judges and the rank of any one grade
represents the combined judgment of not less than three judges and
generally of four or more.

CXVIII

1,690 Pupils, Bloomington Public Schools

7B	7A	8B	8A	Total	Per Cent of Pupils Receiving Each Score	9	10	11	12	Total	Per Cent of Pupils Receiving Each Score
....	....	....	....	1	.07	1	....	....	....	1	.35
....	....	....	....	3	.21	1	....	....	....	1	.35
....	....	....	....	7	.50	....	....	....	....	....	......
....	....	....	....	57	4.05	3	....	....	....	3	1.05
....	1	....	....	42	3.00	1	....	1	....	2	.7
....	....	....	....	73	5.20	5	3	2	....	10	3.51
3	2	....	1	198	14.09	6	8	3	....	17	5.96
7	2	5	7	243	17.30	18	14	11	....	43	15.09
39	24	23	17	462	32.88	20	32	27	4	83	29.12
13	31	9	6	141	10.03	19	18	20	....	57	20.00
7	34	8	13	139	9.89	11	12	15	2	40	14.00
1	1	1	5	15	1.07	5	4	6	1	16	5.61
1	3	....	....	8	.57	2	2	2	....	6	2.11
....	....	4	1	11	.78	3	2	1	....	6	2.11
....	....	3	....	‚5	.36	....	....	....	....	....	......
71	98	53	50	1405	100.00	95	95	88	7	285	100.00
8.67	9.66	8.96	9.00	8.17	......	8.65	8.72	9.00	8.75	8.80	......
.55	.72	1.01	1.12	1.04	......	1.25	.95	.97	1.09	1.04	......

Table CXVIII

1B grade to the 6A grade where the highest point of proficiency is reached. From There are two possible explanations. First, the effort given to drawing in the seventh effort. Second, the fact that no instruction in drawing was given in those grades pupils of those grades had had instruction in drawing the year before and for several

8.17.
and eighth grades.

Table CXVIII shows the number of pupils in each grade making scores of o, of 1 to 1.99 inclusive, of 2 to 2.99, etc. The percentage of all pupils in the grades and of all in the high school making any particular score is also given. These scores have not been compared with those of other schools because data from other schools were not available.

9. Reading

The Thorndike Visual Vocabulary Test and Understanding of Sentences Test were given in 1915 in a large number of Indiana towns. As soon as results are compiled comparisons can be made of Bloomington results with Indiana standard.

TABLE CXIX

Thorndike Visual Vocabulary Test, Bloomington, June, 1915

Grade	Sex	No.	No. of Errors per Line (large type), per Pupil (small)								
			4	5	6	7	8	9	10	10.5	11
	Boys...	58	26	51	132	201	225	266	213	270	160
			.44	.89	2.27	3.46	3.88	4.59	3.67	4.67	2.76
IVB.....	Girls...	46	20	46	72	133	169	198	158	213	131
			.43	1.00	1.56	2.90	3.67	4.30	3.43	4.63	2.85
	Both...	104	46	97	204	334	394	464	371	483	291
			.44	.93	1.96	3.21	3.79	4.46	3.57	4.64	2.80
	Boys...	68	45	57	105	199	243	277	247	312	173
			.66	.69	1.54	2.93	3.57	4.04	3.63	4.59	2.54
IVA....	Girls...	48	8	23	49	102	155	196	144	205	120
			.17	.48	1.02	2.13	3.23	4.09	2.37	4.27	2.50
	Both...	116	53	80	154	301	398	473	391	517	293
			.46	.68	1.33	2.60	3.43	4.08	3.37	4.46	2.53
	Boys...	35	30	38	50	104	135	169	134	190	113
			.88	1.08	1.43	2.97	3.83	4.83	3.83	5.43	3.23
VB.....	Girls...	38	8	20	36	72	108	143	109	168	98
			.21	.53	.94	1.89	2.84	3.76	2.87	4.42	2.55
	Both...	73	38	58	86	176	243	312	243	358	211
			.52	.79	1.19	2.37	3.33	4.27	3.33	4.90	2.90
	Boys...	64	22	30	66	127	217	229	181	277	160
			.34	.47	1.03	1.98	3.39	3.73	2.83	4.33	2.50
VA.....	Girls...	65	15	28	57	85	187	227	160	255	168
			.23	.43	.88	1.31	2.88	3.50	2.46	3.92	258
	Both...	129	37	58	123	212	404	456	341	532	328
			.28	.45	.95	1.64	3.13	3.53	2.64	4.12	2.54
	Boys...	50	13	15	51	80	151	146	144	216	75
			.26	.30	1.02	1.60	3.02	2.81	2.81	4.33	1.59
VIB....	Girls...	38	3	4	10	24	86	73	77	128	54
			.08	.10	.26	.63	2.26	1.92	2.03	3.37	1.42
	Both...	88	16	19	61	104	237	219	221	344	129
			.18	.22	.69	1.18	2.69	2.49	2.51	3.91	1.35
	Boys...	48	14	9	19	38	106	116	121	174	78
			.29	.19	.39	.79	2.21	2.42	2.52	3.63	1.63
VIA....	Girls...	53	0	8	6	32	93	118	107	181	97
			.00	.15	.11	.60	1.75	2.23	2.02	3.53	1.83
	Both...	101	14	17	25	70	199	234	228	355	175
			.14	.17	.25	.70	1.97	2.23	2.26	3.51	1.73
	Boys...	35	9	8	5	18	56	63	68	112	49
			.26	.23	.14	.51	1.60	1.30	1.94	3.20	1.43
VIIB...	Girls...	33	6	3	3	13	70	68	59	109	76
			.18	.09	.09	.39	2.12	2.06	1.79	3.30	2.30
	Both...	68	15	11	8	31	126	131	127	221	125
			.22	.16	.12	.46	1.85	1.93	1.87	3.25	1.84
	Boys...	25	7	2	3	15	45	61	55	83	34
			.28	.08	.14	.60	1.80	2.44	2.20	3.32	1.36

TABLE CXIX (*Continued*)

GRADE	SEX	No.	4	5	6	7	8	9	10	10-5	11
			No. of Errors per Line (large type), per Pupil (small)								
VIIA...	Girls...	54	5	2	8	12	76	103	88	166	88
			.09	.03	.14	.22	1.40	1.91	1.63	3.07	1.63
	Both...	79	12	4	11	27	121	164	143	249	122
			.15	.05	.14	.34	1.53	2.07	1.81	3.15	1.54
	Boys...	25	7	6	1	10	36	41	41	75	28
			.28	.24	.04	.40	1.44	1.64	1.64	3.00	1.12
VIIIB..	Girls...	45	5	1	3	9	56	51	55	105	58
			.11	.02	.07	.20	1.24	1.13	1.22	2.33	1.30
	Both...	70	12	7	4	19	92	92	96	180	86
			.17	.10	.06	.27	1.31	1.31	1.37	2.57	1.23
	Boys...	30	4	0	13	21	46	39	64	90	33
			.13	.00	.43	.70	1.53	1.30	2.13	3.00	1.10
VIIIA..	Girls...	36	2	0	6	13	48	43	61	93	57
			.05	.00	.17	.36	1.33	1.16	1.70	2.60	1.60
	Both...	66	6	0	19	33	94	82	125	183	90
			.09	.00	.29	.50	1.42	1.24	1.89	2.77	1.36

TABLE CXX

THORNDIKE UNDERSTANDING OF SENTENCES TEST, BLOOMINGTON, JUNE, 1915

GRADE	SEX	No.	TEST A	TEST B	TEST C	TEST D
			No. of Errors per Test (large type), Per Cent Errors (small)			
	Boys..............	59	9	56	101	182
			5.1	19.0	42.8	77.1
IVB.........	Girls.............	44	1	24	47	116
			75	10.9	26.7	65.9
	Both..............	103	10	80	148	298
			3.2	15.5	35.9	72.3
	Boys.............	72	6	54	95	199
			2.8	15.0	33.0	69.1
IVA.........	Girls.............	50	4	24	49	129
			2.6	9.6	24.5	64.5
	Both..............	122	10	78	144	328
			2.7	12.8	29.5	67.2
	Boys.............	46	9	27	51	124
			6.5	11.7	27.0	66.9
VB.........	Girls.............	39	1	21	38	106
			0.8	10.8	24.4	67.9
	Both..............	85	10	48	89	230
			3.9	11.3	26.2	67.3
	Boys.............	66	7	26	36	183
			3.5	7.9	13.6	69.3
VA.........	Girls.............	62	2	14	18	148
			1.1	4.5	7.2	59.7
	Both..............	128	9	40	54	331
			2.3	6.2	10.5	64.6
	Boys.............	50	4	23	36	126
			2.7	9.2	18.0	63.0

TABLE CXX (*Continued*)

GRADE	SEX	No.	No. of Errors per Test (large type), Per Cent Errors (small)			
			TEST A	TEST B	TEST C	TEST D
VIb	Girls	38	2	7	20	70
			1.7	3.7	13.3	46.0
	Both	88	6	30	56	196
			2.2	6.8	15.9	55.7
	Boys	48	4	11	26	93
			2.8	4.6	13.5	48.4
VIa	Girls	53	2	10	13	91
			1.2	3.8	6.1	42.9
	Both	101	6	21	39	184
			1.9	4.2	9.6	45.5
	Boys	55	1	9	17	66
			0.7	3.3	7.7	30.0
VIIb	Girls	29	0	9	24	62
			0.0	6.2	20.7	53.4
	Both	84	1	18	41	128
			0.4	4.3	12.2	38.1
	Boys	25	0	4	29	3
			0.0	3.2	29.0	38.0
VIIa	Girls	54	7	9	32	95
			4.3	3.3	14.8	43.9
	Both	79	7	13	61	133
			2.9	3.3	19.3	42.1
	Boys	25	1	8	23	38
			1.3	6.4	23.0	38.0
VIIIb	Girls	46	0	11	20	58
			0.0	4.8	10.9	31.5
	Both	71	1	19	43	96
			0.5	5.3	15.1	33.8
	Boys	31	1	7	28	50
			1.1	4.5	22.6	40.3
VIIIa	Girls	37	0	4	16	50
			0.0	2.1	10.8	33.8
	Both	68	1	11	44	100
			0.5	3.2	16.1	36.8

10. Country-Trained and City-Trained Pupils

A comparison of the performance of country-trained and city-trained pupils in the high school is given in the following pages. Those pupils who got their common school diploma from the city schools are counted as city-trained, and those who got their diploma from the country schools are counted as country-trained.

This study was made by Clifford Woody, at that time a graduate student in Indiana University, and extends over a period of six years beginning with the first semester of the school year 1907. It includes 418 pupils, 293 graduates of the Bloomington city schools and 125 from the Monroe County township schools. Entrance grades were obtained by taking the general average on the county examination for graduation for the country pupils and the general average for the last semester before entering high school for the city pupils. In computing entrance ages the actual age in years was taken; months and days were not considered.

TABLE CXXI
DISTRIBUTION OF CITY PUPILS ACCORDING TO RANK IN ALL SUBJECTS

RANK IN PER CENT		LIT.	COMP.	LATIN	GER.	MATH.	HIST.	BOT.	PHY. G.	PHYSICS
95–100....	Boys..........	5.42	1.19	16.00	1.60	10.54	8.60	1.69	8.62	6.67
	Girls.........	2.86	1.30	11.51	6.52	7.42	3.71	0.00	5.08	0.00
	Total........	3.84	1.26	13.54	5.06	8.63	5.33	.56	6.84	2.29
90–95.....	Boys..........	20.61	18.33	16.80	3.19	13.90	10.22	15.25	18.97	28.89
	Girls.........	28.90	26.22	25.66	20.22	15.69	18.57	13.75	15.25	3.49
	Total........	25.71	23.25	21.66	15.17	15.00	15.81	14.25	17.09	12.21
85–90.....	Boys..........	22.34	33.33	22.00	13.30	13.90	25.27	16.10	22.41	20.00
	Girls.........	30.26	45.10	24.01	25.17	22.82	24.14	24.17	18.64	8.14
	Total........	27.21	40.66	23.10	21.64	19.35	24.51	21.51	20.51	12.21
80–85.....	Boys..........	21.69	29.76	21.20	27.66	18.61	18.27	22.88	15.52	20.00
	Girls.........	21.84	20.75	18.75	22.25	16.98	20.95	31.67	22.03	24.42
	Total........	21.79	24.15	19.86	23.85	17.61	20.07	28.77	18.80	22.91
75–80.....	Boys..........	18.00	9.52	14.40	26.60	19.96	18.82	25.42	17.24	15.56
	Girls.........	10.85	3.75	11.84	16.18	19.69	22.55	22.08	22.03	50.00
	Total........	13.61	5.92	13.00	19.27	19.79	21.31	23.18	19.66	38.17
Failures...	Boys..........	11.93	7.86	9.60	27.66	23.09	18.82	18.64	17.24	8.89
	Girls.........	5.29	2.88	8.22	9.66	17.40	10.08	8.33	16.95	13.95
	Total........	7.85	4.76	8.84	15.01	19.62	12.97	11.73	17.09	12.21
Retards...	Boys..........	4.55	3.33	6.40	17.55	14.13	9.14	9.32	5.17	0.00
	Girls.........	1.49	1.30	4.93	6.52	10.84	4.51	4.58	10.17	4.65
	Total........	2.67	1.17	5.60	9.80	12.13	6.04	6.15	7.69	3.05

TABLE CXXII
DISTRIBUTION OF COUNTRY PUPILS ACCORDING TO RANK IN ALL SUBJECTS

RANK IN PER CENT		LIT.	COMP.	LATIN	GER.	MATH.	HIST.	BOT.	PHY. G.	PHYSICS
95–100....	Boys..........	2.20	.48	2.38	5.71	3.32	4.03	0.00	0.00	4.35
	Girls.........	4.75	2.33	23.44	10.55	11.48	3.38	2.30	2.94	3.45
	Total........	3.64	1.51	11.49	8.66	7.90	3.68	1.35	1.56	3.85
90–95.....	Boys..........	8.81	13.53	13.10	13.57	13.74	8.06	6.56	26.67	0.00
	Girls.........	18.98	22.18	20.31	23.39	16.30	14.19	10.34	20.59	13.79
	Total........	14.56	18.32	16.22	19.55	15.18	11.40	8.78	23.44	7.69
85–90.....	Boys..........	27.75	28.50	25.00	22.14	20.85	17.74	16.39	26.67	13.04
	Girls.........	24.75	31.91	14.06	25.69	21.11	21.62	21.83	20.59	31.03
	Total........	26.05	30.39	20.27	24.30	21.00	19.85	19.59	23.44	23.08
80–85.....	Boys..........	26.43	34.30	25.00	17.14	26.54	25.00	31.15	13.33	30.43
	Girls.........	20.68	26.07	12.50	16.51	17.78	22.30	25.29	17.65	34.48
	Total........	23.18	29.74	19.59	16.76	21.62	23.53	27.70	15.63	32.69
75–80.....	Boys..........	18.94	11.11	19.05	24.29	19.91	28.23	27.87	10.00	47.83
	Girls.........	17.29	7.00	10.94	13.30	17.41	24.32	26.44	20.59	13.79
	Total........	18.01	8.84	15.54	17.60	18.50	26.10	27.03	15.63	28.85
Failures...	Boys..........	15.86	12.08	15.48	17.14	15.64	16.94	18.03	23.33	4.35
	Girls.........	13.56	10.51	18.75	10.55	15.93	14.19	13.79	17.65	3.45
	Total........	14.56	11.21	16.89	13.13	15.80	15.44	15.54	20.31	3.85
Retards...	Boys..........	5.29	6.76	11.90	8.43	8.60	11.29	9.84	13.33	4.35
	Girls.........	5.76	5.06	9.38	5.51	9.63	8.78	5.15	11.76	0.00
	Total........	5.56	5.82	10.81	6.42	9.36	9.18	7.43	12.50	1.92

SUMMARY OF TABLES CXXI AND CXXII

(1) In rank 95–100: The city group has a higher per cent in the following subjects: literature, Latin, mathematics, history and physical geography. The country group in the following: composition, German, botany and physics. The country girl has a higher per cent than the city girl in this rank in all subjects except history and physical geography. The city boys excel the country boys in all subjects except German. In all cases except composition and German, the city boys have a higher per cent in the different subjects than the city girls. The country girls on the other hand have a higher per cent than the city girls in all subjects except history and physics.

(2) In rank 90–95: The city group has a higher per cent in composition, literature, Latin, history, botany and physics; while the country group has a higher per cent in German, mathematics and physical geography. The country girl has a higher per cent than the city girl in German, mathematics, physical geography and physics. The city boy on the other hand has a higher per cent than the country boy in everything except physical geography. The city girls in this rank have a higher per cent than the city boys in all subjects except physical geography and physics. The country girls excel the country boys in every subject except physical geography.

(3) In rank 85–90: The city group has a higher per cent in composition, literature, Latin, history and botany. The city girls have a higher per cent than the country girls in all subjects except German, physical geography and physics. The country boy has a higher per cent than the city boy in all subjects except composition, history and physics. The city girls have a higher per cent than the city boys in all subjects except history, physical geography and physics. The country girls have a higher per cent than the country boys in everything except literature, Latin and physical geography.

(4) In rank 80–85: The city group has a higher per cent in Latin, German, botany and physical geography. The city girls have a higher per cent than the country girls in literature, Latin, German, botany and physical geography. The city boys have a higher per cent than the country boys in German and physical geography. The city girls have a higher per cent than the city boys in literature, history, botany, physical geography and physics. The country boys have a higher per cent than the country girls in all subjects except physical geography and physics.

(5) In rank 75–80: The city group has a higher per cent in German, mathematics, physical geography and physics. The city girls have a higher per cent than the country girls in Latin, German, mathematics, physical geography and physics. The city boys have a higher per cent than the country, boys in German, mathematics and physical geography. The city girls have a higher per cent than the city boys in history, physical geography and physics. The country girls have a higher per cent than the country boys in only one subject, physical geography.

(6) Failures: The city group has a higher per cent of failures than the country group in German, mathematics and physics, while the country group has a higher per cent in all other subjects. The country girls have a higher per cent of failures than the city girls in all subjects except mathematics and physics. The city boys have a higher per cent of failures than the city girls in all subjects except physics. The country boys have a higher per cent of failures than the country girls in all subjects except Latin and mathematics.

(7) Retards: The city group has more retards in German, mathematics and physics and the country group in all other subjects. The city girls have more retardation in these subjects than the country girls. The city boys have more retardation than the country boys in German and mathematics only. There is more retardation among the city boys than among the city girls in all subjects except physical geography and physics. There is more retardation among the country boys than among the country girls in every subject except literature.

From this specific treatment of the per cents in the different ranks the following general conclusions can be drawn :

1. The city group in a majority of subjects have a higher per cent in the higher ranks and a lower per cent in the lower ranks.

2. In a majority of cases, the city group has a lower per cent of failures and retardation than the country group.

3. The country girls have a higher per cent in the higher ranks and a lower per cent in the failure and retardation ranks than the country boys.

4. There is more variation in the work of the city boys than of the city girls. The city boys have a higher per cent in the rank 95–100 and also a higher per cent in the failure class. This relation is not so apparent in the work of the country boys and country girls.

5. Everything considered, the city group has an advantage over the country group.

The following is a summary of Mr. Woody's conclusions in his comparison of city and country pupils by semesters:

First Semester. (1) During the first semester, the city group has a higher median grade in every subject except physical geography. (2) The country boys have a higher median grade than the city boys in algebra, botany, and physical geography. The city girls are superior in every subject. (3) This semester shows clearly a considerable advantage for the city group.

Second Semester. (1) In this semester the city group has a higher median grade in literature, composition, and Latin, while in German, botany, physical geography, and mathematics the country group is superior. (2) The country boys are superior to the city boys in German, algebra, and botany. The country girls are superior to the city girls in German, algebra, botany, and physical geography. (3) In a majority of these subjects for the semester, the country children have the advantage over the city, although in nearly every case the city pupils have less failures and retardation.

Third Semester. (1) In this semester the city group is superior in literature, composition, Latin, and history while the country group is superior in German and mathematics. (2) The country boys are superior to the city boys in literature, German, and mathematics. The country girls are superior to the city girls in Latin, German, and mathematics. (3) When the city and country groups are compared in the subjects for this semester, the advantage lies with the city group.

Fourth Semester. (1) In this semester, the city pupils are superior in literature, composition, Latin, and history, while the country group excels in German and mathematics. (2) The country boy is superior to the city boy in German and mathematics. The country girl is superior to the city girl in Latin, German, and mathematics. (3) In general there is a less amount of failures and of retardation as we proceed from semester to semester. In the country group the per cent is reduced much faster than in the city group. (4) Taking the groups as a whole, the advantage for this semester's work lies with the city group.

Fifth Semester. (1) The city group is superior to the country group in literature, composition, Latin, and history, while the country group excels in German and mathematics. (2) The country boy is superior to the city boy in literature, Latin, and mathematics. The country girl is superior to the city girl in Latin, German, and mathematics. (3) In general there is a less amount of failure and retardation among the country group than among the city group. (4) Taking the group as a whole, the advantage for this semester's work lies with the city group.

Sixth Semester. (1) The city group is superior to the country group in composition and Latin, while the country group is superior in literature, German, history, and mathematics. (2) The country boys are superior to the city boys in German and mathematics, while the grade in history is the same for both groups. The country girls are superior to the city girls in every subject. (3) Taking the groups as a whole, the advantage for this semester's work lies with the country group.

Seventh Semester. (1) The city group is superior in literature, composition, and history, while the country group is superior in Latin, German, and physics. (2) The country boys are superior to the city boys in German. The two groups receive the same grade in Latin and history. In the other subjects the city boys are superior. The country girls are superior to the city girls in literature, German, and physics. (3) In this semester, neither group has a clear advantage over the other.

Eighth Semester. (1) The city group is superior to the country group in literature, Latin, German, and history, while the country group is superior in composition and physics. (2) The city boys are superior to the country boys in everything but German. The city girls are superior to the country girls in Latin and history, while the country girls are superior in literature, composition, and physics.

The grade of both city and country girls is the same in German. (3) The groups, taken as a whole, show that the advantage here lies with the city group.

TABLE CXXIII

COMPARISON OF CITY AND COUNTRY PUPILS IN ALL SUBJECTS FOR ALL SEMESTERS

	CITY PUPILS						TOWNSHIP PUPILS					
	No. P'LS.	\multicolumn{3}{}{AVERAGE OF MEDIANS}		MEDIANS		No. P'LS.	AVERAGE OF MEDIANS			MEDIANS	
		B	G	T	B	G		B	G	T	B	G
Literature	1198	461	737	85.61	84.69	85.87	522	225	295	83.91	82.62	85.07
Composition	1114	416	677	87.04	85.94	87.50	464	207	257	85.52	83.36	86.51
Latin	554	250	304	86.86	86.78	87.02	148	84	64	85.31	82.99	87.81
German	633	188	445	84.90	79.30	86.28	358	140	218	86.90	83.75	88.31
Mathematics	1147	446	701	82.56	81.47	83.48	481	211	270	83.52	82.74	84.30
History	563	186	377	84.26	84.35	84.45	272	124	148	82.11	81.86	82.69
Botany	358	118	240	82.51	82.74	81.68	148	61	87	81.52	80.78	81.82
Phys. Geog.	117	58	59	83.41	84.44	81.81	64	30	34	84.37	81.04	84.06
Physics	131	45	86	80.34	86.19	78.67	52	23	29	83.01	79.98	85.16

	ENTRANCE GRADES						ENTRANCE GRADES					
Literature	1198	461	737	86.68	86.66	86.92	522	225	295	82.23	81.04	82.99
Composition	1114	416	677	86.93	86.84	86.93	464	207	257	82.31	80.99	83.15
Latin	554	250	304	87.89	87.57	88.01	148	84	64	81.90	80.26	82.90
German	633	188	445	85.83	85.26	86.09	358	140	218	82.27	81.07	82.57
Mathematics	1147	446	701	86.97	86.54	87.15	481	211	270	82.03	81.03	82.53
History	563	186	377	86.84	86.70	86.47	272	124	148	82.47	80.00	83.46
Botany	358	118	240	86.86	85.89	87.31	148	61	87	81.82	81.50	81.90
Phys. Geog.	117	58	59	87.22	87.02	87.40	64	30	34	80.74	84.06	80.31
Physics	131	45	86	86.91	87.50	86.47	52	23	29	82.04	79.25	83.22

Comparison of City and Country Pupils as to Scholarship: Table CXXIII makes a final comparison of the city and country groups in all subjects for all semesters and is based upon the averages of the median grades for the different subjects and different terms. By getting the sum of all median grades given for a subject and dividing by the number of semesters, we get the average median grade for that subject.

SUMMARY OF TABLE CXXIII

1. The city group has a higher average median grade in the following subjects: Literature, composition, Latin, history and botany; the country group, in the remaining subjects, i.e., German, mathematics, physical geography and physics.

2. The city boys have a higher median average than the country boys in all subjects except German and mathematics.

3. The city girls have a higher average than the country girls in literature, composition and history, while the country girls excel the city girls in Latin, German, mathematics, botany, physical geography and physics.

4. The city boys excel all groups in botany, physical geography and physics.

5. The city girls excel all groups in literature, composition and history. The country girls excel all others in Latin, German and mathematics. The country boy excels in no subject.

6. In the city group the highest grades are in composition and Latin, while for the country group the highest grades are in composition and German. The lowest grades in the city group are in botany and physics, while the country group made lowest grades in history and botany.

7. The city boys made the highest grades in Latin and physics; they make the lowest grades in mathematics and German. For the country boys the highest grades are in composition and German, and the lowest in physics and botany. For the city girls, the highest in literature and composition, the lowest in botany and physics; for the country girls, the highest in Latin and German, and the lowest in history and botany.

8. In the city group, the highest entrance grade is in Latin and the lowest in German; in the country group, the highest is in history and the lowest in physical geography.

9. The entrance grade for the girls in both groups is usually higher than for boys. It is significant that in most cases the girls make higher grades than the boys.

10. The correlation between the entrance grades and the actual grades made in high school is more marked in the city group than in the country group.

11. Taking everything into consideration, this table again shows the city pupils are superior in a majority of subjects to the country pupils.

Comparison of City and Country Pupils as to Entering Age, Attendance, and Previous Records

(1) *Comparison of Entering Age:* The table making this comparison shows the entering age for the country group was 14.89 years and for the city group, 14.43 years. It further shows that the entrance age for the city boys was 14.42 years, while for the country boys, 14.84 years; for the city girl 14.42 years, and for the country girl, 14.89 years. This shows that the country pupils are just about one-half year older than the city pupils; also that in each group the girls are a little older than the boys. The difference in age was much smaller than was expected, and since the difference in age is less than half a year, the factor of age will have no serious effect upon the problem.

(2) *Comparison of Attendance:* It was found that the average attendance for the city group was 83.80 days per semester, while that for the country group was 84.58 days per semester. The attendance of the city boys was 84.44 days per semester, while the average attendance for the country boys was 84.27 days; for the city girls, 83.39 days and for the country girls 84.58 days. Here, as in the case with the entering age, the difference is small and would have no vital effect on the general results of the study.

(3) *Comparison of Quality of Work Previously Done :* In the case of the country children, it has been continually asserted that only the very best students from the country attend the high school. On the other hand it is claimed that nearly all who graduate from the city system attend high school. This last statement is true for the Bloomington schools, where 90 per cent of the city graduates attend the Bloomington High School. In order to get some idea of the percentage

of the country graduates entering high school and to see whether only the best of them attended high school a study was made of those pupils who graduated from the Monroe County schools in 1912. This year, of course, would not answer for the whole study, but County Superintendent Jones says that it was a type year and hence should give trustworthy results.

In 1912, ninety pupils graduated from the Monroe County schools. Of this number, it was found that 79.89 per cent of them attended high school, although not all of them attended at Bloomington. The average grade of those who attended was 82.53 per cent and of those who did not attend, 80.78 per cent. The city girls who attended had a general average of 82.80 per cent and those who did not attend, 79.04 per cent. The boys who did not attend had a general average of 83.075 per cent and those who did attend, 80.21 per cent. These facts show that the group who attended high school had about 1 per cent higher general average than those who did not attend. This in itself is a small matter, when it is considered that about 80 per cent of the country graduates attend high school. These facts show that the country pupils considered represent the average ability of the country pupils and are not just the select few of them. The data and tables thus far given give us the following summary and conclusions:

General Summary

This study, taken as a whole, brings out the following significant facts:

1. The entrance grades for the city pupils are higher than for the country pupils.

2. The girls in both groups do better work than the boys.

3. The city group has a higher average median grade for all terms than the country group in literature, composition, Latin, history, and botany. The country group has a higher average median in German, mathematics, physical geography, and physics.

4. The city boys excel all others in science: i.e., botany, physical geography, and physics. The city girls excel all groups in literature, composition, and history. The country girls excel all others in foreign languages and mathematics.

5. The city pupils as a group are especially strong in English and Latin, while the country group is especially strong in German and mathematics. Both groups are weakest in botany.

6. In five out of eight of the semesters of the high school course, the city group has a higher median grade in a majority of subjects taught during the semester. The country pupils have a majority in two semesters and in the other semester each group excels in an equal number of subjects. This gives the city pupils a decided advantage.

7. Even though the city pupils have a higher median grade in a majority of subjects for a majority of terms, it cannot be denied that the country pupils are the "growers" in the high school and that they make more improvement over their first term's work than do the city pupils. The country pupils, as a rule, make their lowest grade in their first term and pull up semester by semester, while the city pupils do their best work in their first semester and then have a tendency to slump.

8. The country group has a higher per cent of failures and of retardation in literature, composition, Latin, history, botany, and physical geography. The city group has a higher per cent of failures and retardation in German, mathematics, and physics.

9. A significant fact is that a much higher per cent of both groups are in rank 95–100 in Latin than in any other subject.

10. There is a marked tendency on the part of country boys to slump during their senior year. This was shown in every subject except physics.

11. A study of the entrance grades shows that the less efficient from the country withdraw to a greater degree than those from the city. It is the less efficient city boys and the less efficient country girls who withdraw, while the less efficient city girls and country boys remain in school.

12. The work done by each group most nearly corresponds to their entrance grades during the early semesters of the high school course.

13. All facts considered, the city pupils have a rather marked advantage over the country children.

11. Withdrawals and Failures

Mr. J. H. Minnick made a study including all students entering the Bloomington High School during the four years beginning September, 1906. In all there were 150 boys and 243 girls represented. Tables CXXIV to CXXVII are taken from this study.[1]

---

[1] *The School Review*, Vol. XXIII, No. 2, pp. 73–84.

Table CXXIV shows the average grades made in the various high school subjects by those who for any reason were eliminated from school.

TABLE CXXIV
AVERAGE GRADES OF PUPILS ELIMINATED IN THE VARIOUS SUBJECTS

	MATHEMATICS	ENGLISH	LANGUAGE	HISTORY	SCIENCE
Boys	79.7	80.2	75.8	77.1	78.4
Girls	77.9	81.7	79.0	75.8	76.5

Table CXXV shows the per cent of eliminated students taking each subject who failed in that subject.

TABLE CXXV

	MATHEMATICS	ENGLISH	LANGUAGE	HISTORY	SCIENCE
Boys	32.6	19.3	28.4	32.3	24.4
Girls	31.9	18.0	21.6	31.3	30.9

Table CXXVI shows the per cent of eliminated students failing in only one subject.

TABLE CXXVI

	MATHEMATICS	ENGLISH	LANGUAGE	HISTORY	SCIENCE
Boys	6.0	0.0	6.3	6.3	1.8
Girls	7.1	1.0	3.7	1.8	2.4

Table CXXVII shows the per cent of eliminated students taking each subject who did not fail in that subject.

TABLE CXXVII

	MATHEMATICS	ENGLISH	LANGUAGE	HISTORY	SCIENCE
Boys	38.8	43.8	59.1	40.6	58.9
Girls	38.4	57.6	61.7	47.3	59.8

TABLE CXXVIII
ENROLLMENT, FAILURES, WITHDRAWALS, SECOND SEMESTER, 1913–14

SUBJECT	NUMBER ENROLLED IN SUBJECT DURING TERM			NUMBER DROPPED TO LEAVE CITY			TO QUIT SCHOOL			NUMBER REMAINING AT END TERM		
	B	G	TOTAL	B	G	TOTAL	B	G	TOTAL	B	G	TOTAL
English	141	173	314	3	2	5	15	11	26	117	173	290
Mathematics	125	153	278	5	4	9	14	5	19	107	142	249
Botany	18	22	40	1	0	1	4	0	4	13	32	45
History	72	109	181	2	3	5	7	3	10	64	102	166
Latin	66	101	167	2	3	5	4	3	7	60	94	154
Physics	23	35	58				0	2	2	23	33	56
German	99	120	219	2	0	2	12	11	23	82	108	190
Commercial	89	55	144	0	2	2	15	8	23	74	46	120
Physical Geography	9	21	30				1	1	2	8	20	28

TABLE CXXVIII (*Continued*)

SUBJECT	NUMBER REMAINING PUPILS FAILED			TOTAL FAILURES AND DROPPED TO QUIT SCHOOL			NUMBER REMAINING PUPILS CONDITIONED		
	B	G	TOTAL	B	G	TOTAL	B	G	TOTAL
English..............	15	5	20	30	16	46	5	4	9
Mathematics.........	15	11	26	30	11	41			
Botany..............	3	5	8	7	5	12	1	0	1
History.............	11	7	18	18	10	28	2	4	6
Latin...............	7	4	11	11	7	18	5	1	6
Physics.............	1	3	4	1	5	6	1	0	1
German.............	7	2	9	19	13	32	4	3	7
Commercial.........	6	3	9	21	11	32	6	3	9
Physical Geography...	1	0	1	2	1	3	0	1	1

TABLE CXXIX

SECOND SEMESTER, SCHOOL YEAR, 1913–14 PER CENT OF FAILURES BY SUBJECTS AND SEX OF THOSE REMAINING TO END OF SEMESTER

	ENGLISH	MATHEMATICS	BOTANY	HISTORY	LATIN	PHYSICS	GERMAN	COMMERCIAL	PHYSICAL GEOGRAPHY
9B —									
Boys..........	31.3	22.2	33.3		33.3		33.3	40.0	¹12.5
Girls..........	0.0	5.2	12.5		16.7		8.3	22.2	0.0
Total.........	12.5	10.7	18.2		23.8		16.7	31.6	3.5
9A —									
Boys..........	20.0	17.6	20.0		10.0		4.0	6.7	
Girls..........	7.4	2.2	16.7		7.1		0.0	0.0	
Total.........	11.9	8.8	17.6		8.3		1.8	4.8	
10B —									
Boys..........	10.5	18.2		57.1			15.8		
Girls..........	0.0	13.8		16.7			0.0		
Total.........	5.6	15.7		31.5			8.6		
10A —									
Boys..........	8.3	12.5		18.5					
Girls..........	3.1	11.8		11.5	12.5		5.3		
Total.........	5.4	12.1		15.1	6.7		3.2		
11B —									
Boys..........		5.3		50.0	12.5			7.6	
Girls..........		5.9		9.0	0.0			50.0	
Total.........		5.6		20.0	5.9			13.3	
11A —									
Boys..........	15.8	0.0			25.0		9.0		
Girls..........	5.7	14.3			0.0				
Total.........	9.3	9.5			10.0		5.3		
12B —									
Boys..........						²24.3			
Girls..........						9.1			
Total.........						7.1			
12A —									
Boys..........					11.1				
Girls..........					7.1	0.0			
Total.........					5.0	4.5			

¹ 9B and 9A combined in one class.   ² 12B and 12A combined.

TABLE CXXX

PER CENT OF FAILURES AND DROPPED TO QUIT SCHOOL TO THOSE ENROLLED SECOND SEMESTER 1913–14

	ENGLISH	MATHEMATICS	BOTANY	HISTORY	LATIN	PHYSICS	GERMAN	COMMERCIAL	PHYSICAL GEOGRAPHY
9B —									
Boys	42.8	63.2	57.1		36.4		63.4	62.5	22.2
Girls	17.4	5.3	12.5		14.3		21.5	27.3	4.8
Total	31.4	34.2	33.3		24.0		40.0	48.1	10.0
9A —									
Boys	40.9	24.3	27.3		10.0		22.6	30.0	
Girls	10.7	8.2	28.6		7.1		11.8	40.0	
Total	24.0	15.1	28.0		8.3		17.0	33.3	
10B —									
Boys	14.3	17.4		72.8	18.2		19.0	12.5	
Girls	14.3	6.3		20.0	4.4		11.1	0.0	
Total	14.3	10.9		42.3	8.8		15.4	6.3	
10A —									
Boys	8.0	5.9		21.4	0.0				
Girls	3.1	5.9		14.8	12.5		10.0	28.6	
Total	5.0	5.9		18.2	6.7		6.1	14.3	
11B —									
Boys		18.2		50.0	12.5			20.0	
Girls		4.8		9.1				6.7	
Total		11.6		23.5	5.9			27.8	
11A —									
Boys	20.0			8.3	40.0		7.7		
Girls	12.5	13.3			25.0		10.0		
Total	15.0	9.1		2.3	30.8		8.7		
12B —									
Boys						4.3			20.0
Girls				10.0		14.3	10.0		
Total				5.3		10.3		7.1	11.1
12A —									
Boys					11.1				
Girls				7.1	0.0				
Total				5.0	4.5				

12. CORRELATION OF RANK IN ENGLISH, MATHEMATICS, LANGUAGE, AND HISTORY [1]

The method used to determine the degree of correlation was to determine a numerical relation for the grades made by the eighty-six pupils, while in the four subjects considered.

If a pupil should make "E" grades in English, mathematics, grammar and history, the four subjects considered, then the degree of correlation of standing in these subjects would be 100 per cent. If he should receive four different grades, the degree of correlation would be zero. These are the two extremes. Between them exists a great number of possible combinations of grades which would have

[1] Part of the study made by Charley Bruner. See page 89 for more complete statement of method of this study.

almost as many different values of correlation as there are cases of variation in grade. The value of the various combinations was determined by the number of points the ranks were separated from each other. If a pupil had three "e's" and an "s" or a "g" that condition lacked only one point of having a perfect correlation. If a pupil had three "e's" and one "f" or two "e's," one "s" and one "g," he lacked two points. If he had three "e's" and one "p," or two "e's," one "s" and one "f," or two "e's" and one "g" and one "f," he lacked three points. If he had three "e's" and one "n.p.," or two "e's" and two "f's" or two "e's," one "s" and one "p," or two "e's," one "g," and one "p," he lacked four points. If he had two "e's," one "s" and one "n.p.," or two "e's," one "g" and one "n.p.," or two "e's," one "f" and one "p," he lacked five points. If he had two "e's" and two "p's," or two "e's" and one "n.p.," he lacked six points. If he had two "e's," one "p" and one "n.p.," he lacked seven points. If he had two "e's" and two "n.p.'s" he lacked eight points.

Similar relations exist if we take any of the ranks as the basis for correlation. All conditions in which there were four different ranks were classed together. All possible conditions were then arranged in order of their value. The table thus formed consisted of eleven possible conditions from a perfect to a zero correlation as follows:

1. Four grades of equal rank.
2. Three grades of equal rank and one grade in adjoining rank.
3. Three grades of equal rank and one grade two points away.
   Two grades of equal rank and two grades one point away.
4. Three grades of equal rank and one grade three points away.
   Two grades of equal rank and one grade two points away, and one grade one point away.
5. Three grades of equal rank and one grade four points away.
   Two grades of equal rank and two grades two points away.
   Two grades of equal rank and one grade two points away, and one grade three points away.
6. Three grades of equal rank and one grade five points away.
   Two grades of equal rank and one grade one point away, and one grade four points away.
   Two grades of equal rank and one grade two points away, and one grade four points away.
7. Two grades of equal rank and two grades three points away.
   Two grades of equal rank and one grade five points away, and one grade one point away.
   Two grades of equal rank and one grade two points away, and one grade four points away.
8. Two grades of equal rank and one grade three points away, and one grade four points away.
   Two grades of equal rank and one grade two points away, and one grade five points away.
9. Two grades of equal rank and two grades four points away.
   Two grades of equal rank and one grade three points away, and one grade five points away.
10. Two grades of equal rank and two grades five points away.
11. All different.

Values were assigned to the various conditions as follows: Condition one valued at 10 units, 100 per cent; condition two valued at 9 units, 90 per cent; condition three valued at 8 units, 80 per cent; condition four valued at 7 units, 70 per cent; condition five valued at 6 units, 60 per cent; condition six valued at 5 units, 50 per cent; condition seven valued at 4 units, 40 per cent; condition eight valued at 3 units, 30 per cent; condition nine valued at 2 units, 20 per cent; condition ten valued at 1 unit, 10 per cent; and condition eleven valued at zero.

On the basis of this comparison correlations were worked out for both the common school and the high school.

1. *Correlation in the Common School.* Twenty-five pupils had grades in condition one, twenty-nine in condition two, twenty-one in condition three, and two in condition four, making a total of 759 units out of a possible 860. The per cent of correlation, therefore, was 87.7 per cent. This means that if a pupil makes good in one subject, he has seven chances to eight to make good in the other subjects in common school.

English tended to raise the total average for any given pupil above the average for the other three subjects. There were fourteen cases and in only two cases did English tend to pull it down. Mathematics tended to pull the total average down in thirty-three cases and up in only four. Language caused the total average to be higher than the average for the remaining three subjects in ten cases, and lower in only five cases. History caused seven cases to be higher and seventeen cases to be lower. This makes it appear that the most difficult subject in the common school course is mathematics, the next is history, the next language, and the easiest English. Of the twenty-five cases in which there was a correlation of 100 per cent, fourteen pupils belonged to the "G" rank, six pupils to the "F" rank, and five pupils to the "E" rank. Of the twenty-nine cases in which there was a correlation of 90 per cent, there were seventeen pupils whose predominating grade was "G." This shows that the pupil in rank "G" or the average pupil is most evenly balanced in all the subjects. Sex difference is not noticed.

2. *Correlation in the High School Subjects.* There were only eighty-five cases correlated in high school. Pupil number 68 having no history grade was therefore eliminated.

Of these eighty-five pupils, four had grades in condition one, twenty-six in condition two, twenty-six in condition three, twenty-three in condition four, five in condition five and one in condition eleven, making a total value of 673 out of a possible 850. The per cent of correlation for the high school, therefore, was 79.2 per cent. The girls on the whole made better grades than the boys, but the four cases in which there was perfect correlation belonged to the boys, who, therefore, had a slightly higher per cent of correlation than the girls. Of the cases of perfect correlation among the boys, no two cases fell in the same rank. One had "S," one had "E," one had "G," and one had "F."

The following table shows the number of cases for each subject in which it tended to raise or lower the total average above or below the average of the remaining subjects:

TABLE CXXXI

SUBJECT	NUMBERS OF CASES IN WHICH THE AVERAGE WAS RAISED	NUMBER OF CASES IN WHICH THE AVERAGE WAS LOWERED
English..........................	26	7
Mathematics.....................	2	33
Language........................	20	11
History..........................	13	14

This shows again that mathematics was the most difficult subject and English the easiest. Language is slightly easier than history.

The following are important extracts from the general summary and conclusions reached by Mr. Bruner:

The change from common school to high school does not give rise to an abnormal decrease in retention of grades received. One finds in the common school and high school a decrease in retention towards the end of the course, but the decrease in retention from the common school to the high school is not much out of keeping with the retentions before and after.

The correlation for the four subjects is greater in the common school than in the high school. In the common school it is 87.7 per cent and in the high school it is 79.2 per cent. In other words, a pupil in the common school has seven chances out of eight to receive the same grades in all four subjects, while in high school his chances are four out of five.

Those pupils maintain the highest per cent of correlation whose grades fall in most cases in rank "G." This is true for both the common school and the high school.

13. DISTRIBUTION OF GRADES

It is not enough to know that a certain percentage of the pupils in a school system passed and a certain other percentage failed. In order to have an intelligent conception of the work that is being done by pupils it is necessary to know the percentage of the grades

falling in the various ranks as good, excellent, etc. The percentage
of pupils receiving the highest marks should approximate the percentage receiving the lowest marks. It is just as much of a failure
for a pupil capable of making "excellent" to make "good" as for a
pupil capable of making just a passing grade to make a failing grade.
The immediate penalty may be a little greater in the latter case
because the work has to be repeated, but even in the first case
there is an immeasurable penalty in the form of habits that hold
one's work on a level lower than native ability would justify.
Pupils are marked in the Bloomington schools by letters S, E, G,
F, P, N.P. S = 96–100 per cent; E = 91–95 per cent; G = 86–90
per cent; F = 81–85 per cent; P = 75–80 per cent; N.P. = below
75 per cent and below a passing grade. Table CXXXII shows for the
second semester, 1911–12, by grades, subjects, and sex the percentage
of grades falling within each group. Tables CXXXIII and CXXXIV
show some of the same things for the first semester 1914–15 and for
the second semester 1912–13. Failures are based upon number enrolled at end of semester. Conditions are counted as failures.

TABLE CXXXII

DISTRIBUTION OF GRADES, SECOND SEMESTER 1911–12, BY YEARS, SUBJECTS,
SEX

			96–100 Per Cent	91–95 Per Cent	86–90 Per Cent	81–85 Per Cent	75–80 Per Cent	Below Passing
Whole school system all pupils, all subjects..			5.4	15.1	29.3	26.5	18.5	5.2
"	"	" " boys " " ..	4.5	12.9	27.5	28.2	21	5.9
"	"	" " girls " " ..	6.2	17.1	30.8	25.1	16.2	4.7
Grades	1–4	all pupils, all subjects......	7.	17.6	36.2	26.4	10.4	2.4
"	"	" boys " "	6.	16.2	34.6	28.9	11.7	2.6
"	"	" girls " "	8.1	19.2	37.9	23.7	8.7	2.3
Grades	5–8	all pupils, all subjects......	4.5	13.	25.4	27.4	23.7	6.1
"	"	" boys " "	3.2	9.7	22.5	27.9	29.3	7.3
"	"	" girls " "	5.5	15.4	27.3	27	19.6	5.1
Grades	9–12	all pupils, all subjects......	2.7	14.3	18.6	23.4	28.1	12.9
"	"	" boys " "	2.4	10.7	14.7	25.6	31.	15.6
"	"	" girls " "	2.9	16.9	21.5	21.8	25.9	11.
Grades	1–8	all pupils, all subjects......	5.7	15.2	30.6	26.9	17.3	4.3
"	"	" boys " "	4.7	13.2	29.	28.5	19.9	4.8
"	"	" girls " "	7.	18.	32.	26.	14.9	3.9
Grade	1B	all pupils, all subjects......	5.1	16.	29.	26.5	12.	11.7
"	"	" boys " "	3.5	14.7	31.7	27.3	12.6	9.7
"	"	" girls " "	8.7	19.1	21.7	23.5	10.4	16.5
Grade	1A	all pupils, all subjects......	7.4	21.2	39.	23.4	6.4	2.5
"	"	" boys " "	5.8	20.9	37.	27.	7.	2.4
"	"	" girls " "	9.2	21.6	41.3	19.7	5.5	2.5

TABLE CXXXII (*Continued*)

			96–100 PER CENT	91–95 PER CENT	86–90 PER CENT	81–85 PER CENT	75–80 PER CENT	BELOW PASSING
Grade	2B	all pupils, all subjects......	7.	20.	42.7	21.1	6.1	3.3
"	"	" boys " "	4.8	20.2	38.7	25.8	8.1	2.4
"	"	" girls " "	10.1	19.1	48.5	14.6	3.4	4.4
Grade	2A	all pupils, all subjects......	9.	17.8	34.3	29.4	7.8	1.7
"	"	" boys " "	6.3	16.2	31.3	35.2	9.5	1.4
"	"	" girls " "	11.4	19.2	37.1	24.1	6.2	2.
Grade	3B	all pupils, all subjects......	10.5	14.	38.5	22.6	12.7	1.7
"	"	" boys " "	8.8	11.3	37.6	26.3	13.8	2.3
"	"	" girls " "	12.3	16.9	39.5	18.7	11.4	1.2
Grade	3A	all pupils, all subjects......	7.2	21.5	39.1	23.8	7.6	.9
"	"	" boys " "	7.8	18.5	37.3	27.1	8.4	.8
"	"	" girls " "	6.3	25.4	41.1	19.4	6.5	1.
Grade	4B	all pupils, all subjects......	7.	19.	36.2	27.6	9.1	1.1
"	"	" boys " "	5.2	19.2	33.2	27.9	12.8	1.7
"	"	" girls " "	8.3	18.8	38.6	27.4	6.3	.7
Grade	4A	all pupils, all subjects...,..	3.1	12.6	32.2	32.5	18.	1.8
"	"	" boys " "	3.9	10.6	30.9	33.5	19.2	1.8
"	"	" girls " "	2.4	14.3	33.3	31.4	16.9	1.7
Grade	5B	all pupils, all subjects......	6.2	17.2	26.6	24.4	22.3	3.3
"	"	" boys " "	4.7	13.7	22.4	26.1	29.7	3.3
"	"	" girls " "	6.9	18.9	28.6	23.6	18.7	3.2
Grade	5A	all pupils, all subjects......	3.4	14.6	32.	27.3	16.7	5.9
"	"	" boys " "	2.3	13.	29.9	27.6	20.1	7.1
"	"	" girls " "	3.8	15.7	33.5	27.1	14.4	5.1
Grade	6B	all pupils, all subjects......	2.1	9.8	26.6	31.9	23.5	6.
"	"	" boys " "	.9	4.9	27.5	32.1	26.9	7.8
"	"	" girls " "	3.	13.8	26.	31.9	20.8	4.4
Grade	6A	all pupils, all subjects......	1.8	7.9	19.4	29.2	33.	8.6
"	"	" boys " "	1.6	6.5	18.3	26.6	35.9	11.1
"	"	" girls " "	2.1	9.1	20.4	31.5	30.3	6.5
Grade	7B	all pupils, all subjects......	6.3	17.8	25.	26.5	19.5	4.9
"	"	" boys " "	3.2	12.9	20.7	29.5	27.2	6.9
"	"	" girls " "	8.3	21.9	27.8	24.6	14.5	3.6
Grade	7A	all pupils, all subjects......	6.5	12.4	25.3	26.2	23.5	6.
"	"	" boys " "	7.2	10.1	20.7	26.4	31.4	4.2
"	"	" girls " "	5.9	14.7	30.	26.	15.7	7.7
Grade	8B	all pupils, all subjects......	1.4	8.6	18.5	26.8	33.1	11.5
"	"	" boys " "	0.	3.8	15.4	28.5	38.5	13.8
"	"	" girls " "	2.5	12.7	21.	25.5	28.6	9.6
Grade	8A	all pupils, all subjects......	8.5	14.1	23.5	26.4	21.9	5.6
"	"	" boys " "	3.3	13.8	20.4	27.6	26.5	8.3
"	"	" girls " "	12.3	14.3	25.8	25.4	18.4	3.7
Grade	9B	all pupils, all subjects......	2.7	13.3	19.1	20.2	26.6	18.1
"	"	" boys " "	2.9	5.7	16.2	22.9	30.5	21.5
"	"	" girls " "	2.4	22.9	22.9	16.9	21.7	13.3

TABLE CXXXII (*Continued*)

		96–100 Per Cent	91–95 Per Cent	86–90 Per Cent	81–85 Per Cent	75–80 Per Cent	Below Passing
Grade	9A	all pupils, all subjects......	2.3	19.4	20.6	23.2	21.9	12.6
"	"	" boys " "	0.	16.2	16.2	21.7	25.6	20.1
"	"	" girls " "	3.9	21.5	23.8	24.3	19.3	7.1
Grade	10B	all pupils, all subjects......	.9	9.3	10.2	27.8	35.2	16.7
"	"	" boys " "	0.	7.	4.6	27.9	39.5	20.9
"	"	" girls " "	1.5	10.8	13.8	27.7	32.3	13.8
Grade	10A	all pupils, all subjects.....	1.7	12.6	25.3	20.7	27.	12.7
"	"	" boys " "	0.	6.8	24.7	24.7	30.1	13.7
"	"	" girls " "	3.	16.8	25.7	17.8	24.8	11.9
Grade	11B	all pupils, all subjects......	2.8	5.6	17.7	26.2	28.	19.6
"	"	" boys " "	6.8	6.8	11.4	31.8	31.8	11.4
"	"	" girls " "	0.	4.8	22.2	22.2	25.4	25.4
Grade	11A	all pupils, all subjects......	5.6	12.3	16.1	32.1	27.8	6.2
"	"	" boys " "	9.5	11.1	12.7	33.3	27.	6.3
"	"	" girls " "	3.	13.1	18.1	31.3	28.3	6.1
Grade	12B	all pupils, all subjects......	2.3	21.3	16.9	19.1	28.1	12.3
"	"	" boys " "	4.4	21.7	8.7	30.4	26.1	8.7
"	"	" girls " "	1.5	21.2	19.7	15.1	28.8	13.6
Grade	12A	all pupils, all subjects......	4.3	19.1	16.	14.9	42.6	3.1
"	"	" boys " "	0.	19.4	8.4	19.4	50.	2.7
"	"	" girls " "	6.9	18.9	20.7	12.1	38.	3.4
Grades	1–8	all pupils, reading..........	8.3	18.6	31.4	22.9	13.8	5.2
"	"	" boys "	6.6	15.4	29.5	27.2	15.3	6.
"	"	" girls "	9.9	21.5	32.9	18.9	12.5	4.4
Grades	3B–8A	all pupils, arithmetic.......	5.4	13.4	25.	21.2	23.1	11.9
"	"	" boys "	6.7	14.	27.	21.2	19.6	12.1
"	"	" girls "	4.9	12.9	21.3	23.1	26.	11.7
Grades	2B–8A	all pupils, { language and grammar }	3.1	13.6	30.5	27.7	17.4	7.6
"	"	" boys "	1.5	9.6	29.1	30.	19.3	10.5
"	"	" girls "	4.5	17.	31.7	25.8	15.8	5.2
Grades	4B–8A	all pupils, history..........	1.9	9.3	22.5	26.1	29.7	10.5
"	"	" boys "	3.	8.5	23.9	26.	29.4	9.1
"	"	" girls "	1.	8.5	21.4	26.1	30.	11.6
Grades	4B–7A	all pupils, geography.......	3.1	13.4	36.6	23.1	19.1	4.7
"	"	" boys "	3.1	16.1	39.1	21.8	16.1	3.8
"	"	" girls "	3.1	11.4	34.8	23.9	21.4	5.4
Grades	3B–8A	all pupils, spelling..........	23.5	29.6	24.3	13.7	6.8	2.1
"	"	" boys "	19.6	27.2	21.5	18.5	9.5	3.7
"	"	" girls "	26.9	31.6	26.7	9.5	4.5	.8
Grades	1B–2A	all pupils, phonics..........	18.1	22.5	31.2	16.4	4.8	7.
"	"	" boys "	12.5	21.9	33.5	19.2	6.3	6.7
"	"	" girls "	24.7	23.2	28.4	13.2	3.2	7.4

TABLE CXXXII (*Continued*)

			96–100 Per Cent	91–95 Per Cent	86–90 Per Cent	81–85 Per Cent	75–80 Per Cent	Below Passing
Grades	4B–7A	all pupils, physiology	1.1	15.	32.4	32.8	17.7	.9
"	"	" boys "	1.2	13.1	33.8	33.5	16.9	1.5
"	"	" girls "	1.1	16.4	31.3	32.3	18.2	.6
Grades	1B–8A	all pupils, drawing	.6	6.9	32.8	40.9	18.	.7
"	"	" boys "	.5	6.1	28.3	41.4	22.7	1.
"	"	" girls "	.7	7.7	37.2	40.5	13.6	.3
Grades	1B–8A	all pupils, writing	2.5	17.5	37.8	26.5	14.2	1.6
"	"	" boys "	1.9	15.8	33.4	27.6	19.1	2.1
"	"	" girls "	2.7	19.2	42.1	25.5	9.4	1.1
Grades	1B–8A	all pupils, music	2.4	13.2	32.8	27.8	23.2	.5
"	"	" boys "	1.3	7.4	28.1	28.7	33.8	.7
"	"	" girls "	3.5	18.8	37.2	27.	13.2	.4
Grades	7B–8A	all pupils, industrial	3.6	6.6	24.9	55.3	9.1	.5
"	"	" boys "	0.	0.	14.6	64.6	19.5	1.1
"	"	" girls "	6.1	11.3	32.2	48.7	1.7	0.
Grades	9B–12	all pupils, English	.6	16.9	20.8	25.8	27.8	8.
"	"	" boys "	1.5	12.5	14.7	31.6	29.4	10.3
"	"	" girls "	0.	20.3	25.4	21.5	26.5	6.2
Grades	9B–12A	all pupils, Latin	6.	17.2	22.5	21.1	23.4	9.8
"	"	" boys "	6.6	6.6	25.	20.	31.7	10.
"	"	" girls "	5.5	26.	20.5	21.9	16.4	9.7
Grades	9B–12A	all pupils, German	5.6	14.8	17.9	22.2	30.9	8.6
"	"	" boys "	1.6	12.9	16.1	22.6	35.5	11.3
"	"	" girls "	8.	16.	19.	22.	28.	7.
Grades	9B–11A	all pupils, mathematics	4.1	14.6	18.5	23.	21.9	17.8
"	"	" boys "	4.1	13.9	9.8	26.2	23.	23.
"	"	" girls "	4.2	15.2	24.8	20.6	21.2	14.
Grades	10B–12A	all pupils, history	.8	14.4	17.4	25.8	31.	10.6
"	"	" boys "	0.	8.7	19.6	30.4	28.3	13.1
"	"	" girls "	1.2	17.4	16.3	23.2	32.6	9.3
Grades	9B–9A	all pupils, physical geography	3.7	16.7	27.8	14.8	25.9	11.1
"	"	" boys "	3.6	14.3	25.	14.3	28.5	14.3
"	"	" girls "	3.8	19.2	30.7	15.4	23.1	7.7
Grades	9B–9A	all pupils, botany	0.	5.	8.3	30.	33.3	23.3
"	"	" boys "	0.	0.	0.	23.8	42.8	33.3
"	"	" girls "	0.	7.7	12.8	33.3	28.2	18.
Grades	12B–12A	all pupils, physics	0.	4.2	8.3	18.7	58.3	10.4
"	"	" boys "	0.	12.5	0.	31.3	56.2	0.
"	"	" girls "	0.	0.	12.5	12.5	59.4	15.6
Grades	9B–12A	all pupils, commercial	0.	2.	9.8	15.7	33.3	39.2
"	"	" boys "	0.	2.7	10.8	13.5	43.2	29.7
"	"	" girls "	0.	0.	7.1	21.4	7.1	64.3
Grades	12B	all pupils, French	0.	23.1	30.8	38.5	7.6	0.
"	"	" boys "	0.	0.	25.	50.	25.	0.
"	"	" girls "	0.	33.3	33.3	33.3	0.	0.

TABLE CXXXII (*Continued*)

			96–100 Per Cent	91–95 Per Cent	86–90 Per Cent	81–85 Per Cent	75–80 Per Cent	Below Passing
3B — Arithmetic —	All pupils		10.2	18.4	33.7	15.3	15.3	7.1
" "	"	boys	11.5	13.5	36.5	13.5	15.4	9.6
" "	"	girls	8.7	24.	30.4	17.4	15.2	4.3
3A — Arithmetic —	All pupils		10.3	21.4	34.1	17.5	11.9	4.8
" "	"	boys	13.9	20.8	33.3	16.7	11.1	4.2
" "	"	girls	5.6	22.2	35.2	18.5	13.	5.6
4B — Arithmetic —	All pupils		11.1	14.8	34.6	19.7	11.1	8.6
" "	"	boys	8.3	16.6	27.8	24.9	11.1	11.1
" "	"	girls	13.3	13.3	39.9	15.6	11.1	6.7
4A — Arithmetic —	All pupils		5.9	9.4	34.1	22.4	20.	8.2
" "	"	boys	7.7	7.7	35.9	15.4	25.6	7.7
" "	"	girls	4.3	10.9	32.6	28.3	15.2	8.6
5B — Arithmetic —	All pupils		4.3	16.3	29.3	22.8	19.6	7.6
" "	"	boys	0.	20.	33.3	23.3	16.7	6.7
" "	"	girls	6.5	14.5	27.4	22.6	21.	8.1
5A — Arithmetic —	All pupils		1.3	7.9	26.3	26.3	21.1	17.1
" "	"	boys	3.2	9.7	32.	25.8	16.1	12.9
" "	"	girls	0.	6.7	22.2	26.7	24.4	20.1
6B — Arithmetic —	All pupils		0.	7.9	17.1	26.3	31.6	17.1
" "	"	boys	0.	5.9	20.6	29.4	23.5	20.6
" "	"	girls	0.	9.5	14.3	23.8	38.1	14.3
6A — Arithmetic —	All pupils		1.3	7.6	12.7	24.1	34.2	20.3
" "	"	boys	0.	13.5	10.8	21.6	29.7	24.3
" "	"	girls	2.4	2.4	14.3	26.2	38.1	16.6
7B — Arithmetic —	All pupils		1.9	17.3	13.1	23.	23.	21.6
" "	"	boys	0.	10.	25.	25.	15.	25.
" "	"	girls	3.1	21.9	6.3	21.9	28.1	18.8
7A — Arithmetic —	All pupils		3.9	7.9	13.2	21.1	35.5	18.4
" "	"	boys	5.4	10.8	18.9	16.2	35.1	13.5
" "	"	girls	2.6	5.2	7.8	25.5	35.9	23.1
8B — Arithmetic —	All pupils		0.	5.	10.	12.5	55.	17.5
" "	"	boys	0.	0.	11.8	23.5	41.2	23.5
" "	"	girls	0.	8.7	8.7	4.3	65.2	13.
8A — Arithmetic —	All pupils		6.8	18.6	18.6	23.7	25.4	6.8
" "	"	boys	4.2	29.2	16.7	37.5	8.3	4.2
" "	"	girls	8.4	11.4	20.	14.3	37.1	8.4
4B — History —	All pupils		1.4	18.6	34.3	41.4	4.3	0.
" "	"	boys	3.4	31.	27.6	31.	6.9	0.
" "	"	girls	0.	9.8	39.	48.8	2.4	0.
4A — History —	All pupils		1.2	8.3	33.3	29.8	27.4	0.
" "	"	boys	2.6	7.9	39.5	26.3	23.7	0.
" "	"	girls	0.	8.7	28.3	32.6	30.4	0.
5B — History —	All pupils		3.3	15.2	20.7	23.9	33.7	3.3
" "	"	boys	6.7	16.7	20.	23.3	30.	3.3
" "	"	girls	1.6	14.5	21.	24.2	35.5	3.2

TABLE CXXXII (*Continued*)

		96–100 PER CENT	91–95 PER CENT	86–90 PER CENT	81–85 PER CENT	75–80 PER CENT	BELOW PASS- ING
5A — History —	All pupils..............	2.6	21.1	36.7	21.1	11.8	6.6
" "	" boys	3.2	19.3	35.5	25.8	9.7	6.5
" "	" girls	2.2	22.2	37.8	17.8	13.3	6.7
6B — History —	All pupils..............	0.	3.9	26.	28.5	26.	15.5
" "	" boys	0.	0.	35.3	23.5	32.4	8.8
" "	" girls	0.	6.9	18.6	32.6	21.	21.
6A — History —	All pupils..............	2.5	5.1	12.7	13.9	40.5	25.3
" "	" boys	5.4	2.7	16.2	13.5	32.4	29.7
" "	" girls	0.	7.1	9.5	14.3	47.6	21.4
7B — History —	All pupils..............	3.9	3.9	11.8	23.5	43.1	13.7
" "	" boys	5.	0.	20.	10.	45.	20.
" "	" girls	3.2	6.5	6.5	32.3	41.9	9.7
7A — History —	All pupils..............	1.3	1.3	8.	26.7	44.	18.7
" "	" boys	0.	0.	13.5	27.	48.6	10.8
" "	" girls	2.6	2.6	2.6	26.3	39.5	26.3
8B — History —	All pupils..............	0.	0.	10.3	28.2	41.	20.5
" "	" boys	0.	0.	0.	50.	50.	0.
" "	" girls	0.	0.	17.4	13.	34.8	34.8
8A — History —	All pupils..............	1.7	8.5	22.	25.4	33.9	8.5
" "	" boys	4.2	4.2	16.7	41.7	25.	8.3
" "	" girls	0.	11.4	25.7	14.3	40.	8.6
1B — Reading —	All pupils..............	9.2	20.4	18.4	23.5	9.2	19.4
" "	" boys	7.5	17.9	23.9	23.9	9.	17.9
" "	" girls	13.	26.	6.5	22.5	9.7	22.6
1A — Reading —	All pupils..............	12.4	28.8	30.1	18.3	4.6	5.9
" "	" boys	7.7	32.1	32.1	18.	3.8	6.4
" "	" girls	17.3	25.3	28.	18.7	5.3	5.3
2B — Reading —	All pupils..............	7.7	25.	40.4	17.3	1.9	7.7
" "	" boys	6.9	27.6	27.6	27.6	3.5	6.9
" "	" girls	8.7	21.7	56.5	4.3	0.	8.7
2A — Reading —	All pupils..............	13.2	23.7	25.4	28.1	7.9	1.8
" "	" boys	9.1	18.2	25.5	36.5	9.1	1.8
" "	" girls	17.	28.8	25.4	20.3	6.8	1.7
3B — Reading —	All pupils..............	14.2	12.1	41.4	18.2	12.1	2.
" "	" boys	9.8	7.8	45.1	19.6	15.7	2.
" "	" girls	18.7	16.7	37.5	16.7	8.4	4.2
3A — Reading —	All pupils..............	14.4	18.4	37.6	20.	8.	1.6
" "	" boys	14.1	12.7	35.2	24.	12.8	1.4
" "	" girls	14.8	26.	40.8	14.8	1.9	1.9
4B — Reading —	All pupils..............	13.8	18.8	32.5	27.5	7.5	0.
" "	" boys	8.6	17.2	31.4	34.4	8.6	0.
" "	" girls	17.8	20.	33.3	22.2	6.7	0.
4A — Reading —	All pupils..............	4.7	15.3	42.4	22.4	14.1	1.2
" "	" boys	2.6	10.2	43.6	28.2	12.8	2.6
" "	" girls	6.5	19.6	41.3	17.4	15.2	0.

TABLE CXXXII (*Continued*)

		96–100 PER CENT	91–95 PER CENT	86–90 PER CENT	81–85 PER CENT	75–80 PER CENT	BELOW PASSING
5B — Reading —	All pupils	19.	30.8	30.8	13.2	12.1	2.2
" "	" boys	13.3	16.7	26.7	20.	20.	3.3
" "	" girls	9.8	37.7	32.8	9.8	8.2	1.6
5A — Reading —	All pupils	3.9	21.1	35.5	30.3	9.2	0.
" "	" boys	6.5	12.9	22.6	38.7	19.4	0.
" "	" girls	2.2	26.7	44.4	24.4	2.2	0.
6B — Reading —	All pupils	4.1	21.6	16.2	31.1	19.	8.1
" "	" boys	0.	15.6	12.5	37.5	15.6	18.8
" "	" girls	7.1	26.2	19.	26.2	19.	2.4
6A — Reading —	All pupils	0.	7.6	20.2	26.6	36.7	8.9
" "	" boys	0.	5.4	21.6	30.	35.1	8.1
" "	" girls	0.	9.5	19.1	23.8	38.2	9.5
7B — Reading —	All pupils	1.9	21.2	38.5	26.9	11.5	0.
" "	" boys	0.	14.3	38.1	33.3	14.3	0.
" "	" girls	3.2	26.	38.7	22.6	9.7	0.
7A — Reading —	All pupils	0.	2.7	42.7	26.7	21.3	6.7
" "	" boys	0.	5.4	40.5	35.1	18.9	0.
" "	" girls	0.	0.	44.7	18.4	23.7	13.2
8B — Reading —	All pupils	0.	0.	25.6	17.9	43.6	12.8
" "	" boys	0.	0.	11.8	17.6	58.8	11.8
" "	" girls	0.	0.	36.4	18.2	31.8	13.6
8A — Reading —	All pupils	1.7	8.5	20.3	23.7	35.6	10.2
" "	" boys	0.	8.3	8.3	25.	37.5	20.8
" "	" girls	2.9	8.6	28.6	22.9	34.3	2.9
2B — Language —	All pupils	0.	0.	35.3	47.1	17.7	0.
" "	" boys	0.	0.	30.	60.	10.	0.
" "	" girls	0.	0.	42.9	28.6	28.6	0.
2A — Language —	All pupils	1.3	13.2	42.2	31.6	10.5	1.3
" "	" boys	0.	8.1	40.5	37.8	13.5	0.
" "	" girls	2.6	17.9	43.6	25.6	7.7	2.6
3B — Language —	All pupils	5.2	10.4	37.5	28.1	16.7	2.1
" "	" boys	2.1	6.1	42.9	32.7	14.3	2.
" "	" girls	8.5	14.9	31.9	23.4	19.1	2.1
3A — Language —	All pupils	3.3	20.7	41.3	27.3	7.4	0.
" "	" boys	1.5	19.3	37.3	32.8	9.	0.
" "	" girls	5.6	22.2	46.3	20.4	5.6	0.
4B — Language —	All pupils	6.2	27.2	34.6	20.	11.1	1.2
" "	" boys	5.6	16.7	36.1	19.4	19.4	2.8
" "	" girls	6.7	35.6	33.3	20.	4.4	0.
4A — Language —	All pupils	1.2	10.6	28.2	40.	16.5	3.5
" "	" boys	2.6	10.5	18.4	47.4	18.4	2.6
" "	" girls	0.	10.6	36.2	34.	14.9	4.3
5B — Language —	All pupils	4.3	17.4	21.7	28.3	22.8	5.4
" "	" boys	3.3	10.	20.	33.3	26.6	6.7
" "	" girls	4.8	21.	22.6	25.8	21.	4.8

TABLE CXXXII (*Continued*)

			96-100 Per Cent	91-95 Per Cent	86-90 Per Cent	81-85 Per Cent	75-80 Per Cent	Below Passing
5A — Language —	All pupils		1.3	10.5	38.2	30.3	14.5	5.3
" "	"	boys	0.	6.5	41.9	19.4	22.6	9.7
"	"	" girls	2.2	13.3	35.5	37.8	8.9	2.2
6B — Language —	All pupils		1.3	14.5	31.6	21.	19.7	12.
" "	"	boys	0.	8.8	32.4	14.7	23.5	20.6
"	"	" girls	2.4	19.	31.	26.2	16.7	4.8
6A — Language —	All pupils		1.3	8.9	21.5	29.1	22.8	16.5
" "	"	boys	0.	8.1	24.3	29.7	18.9	18.9
"	"	" girls	2.4	9.5	19.	27.6	26.2	14.3
7B —Language —	All pupils		5.8	9.6	34.6	23.1	15.4	11.5
" "	"	boys	0.	0.	25.	25.	35.	15.
"	"	" girls	9.4	15.6	40.6	21.9	3.1	9.4
7A — Language —	All pupils		1.3	9.3	17.3	29.3	29.3	13.3
" "	"	boys	0.	13.5	13.5	37.8	21.6	13.5
"	"	" girls	2.6	5.3	21.1	21.1	36.8	13.2
8B — Grammar —	All pupils		0.	5.	2.5	27.5	25.	40.
" "	"	boys	0.	0.	0.	11.8	17.6	70.6
"	"	" girls	0.	8.7	4.3	39.1	30.4	17.4
8A — Grammar —	All pupils		8.5	13.6	25.4	15.2	23.7	13.6
" "	"	boys	4.2	0.	12.5	16.6	37.5	29.2
"	"	" girls	11.4	22.9	34.3	14.3	14.3	2.9
4B — Geography —	All pupils		1.3	15.2	40.5	31.6	11.4	0.
" "	"	boys	0.	20.6	41.2	29.4	8.8	0.
"	"	" girls	2.2	11.1	40.	33.3	13.3	0.
4A — Geography —	All pupils		3.6	13.1	36.9	25.	20.3	1.2
" "	"	boys	5.3	15.8	39.5	26.3	13.2	0.
"	"	" girls	2.2	10.7	34.8	23.9	26.1	2.2
5B — Geography —	All pupils		7.6	13.	22.8	18.5	29.3	8.7
" "	"	boys	10.	6.7	23.3	23.3	30.	6.7
"	"	" girls	6.5	16.1	22.6	16.1	29.	10.
5A — Geography —	All pupils		1.3	11.8	32.9	23.7	17.	13.1
" "	"	boys	0.	19.4	41.9	16.1	13.	9.7
"	"	" girls	2.2	6.7	26.7	28.9	20.	15.
6B — Geography —	All pupils		2.7	12.	38.7	28.	17.3	1.3
" "	"	boys	3.	9.1	48.5	27.3	12.1.	0.
"	"	" girls	2.4	14.3	31.	28.6	21.4	2.3
6A — Geography —	All pupils		1.3	16.5	34.2	15.1	27.8	5.1
" "	"	boys	2.7	18.9	35.1	8.1	27.	8.1
"	"	" girls	0.	14.3	33.3	21.4	28.6	2.4
7B — Geography —	All pupils		3.8	13.5	51.9	21.2	7.7	1.9
" "	"	boys	0.	19.	42.9	28.6	4.8	4.8
"	"	" girls	6.5	9.7	58.1	16.1	9.7	0.
7A — Geography —	All pupils		2.7	12.	42.7	21.4	16.	5.8
" "	"	boys	2.7	18.9	40.5	18.9	16.2	2.7
"	"	" girls	2.6	5.3	44.7	23.7	15.8	7.9

Table CXXXII shows that when all of the grades of all of the pupils of the whole school system are considered there is a normal distribution of grades. A little over 5 per cent are in the highest group, a little over 5 per cent are in the lowest group, the next two groups adjacent to the highest and the lowest contain 15.1 per cent and 18.5 per cent respectively, while the two central groups contain 29.3 per cent and 26.5 per cent. The above showing would seem to indicate that the grading was satisfactory. A further analysis, however, shows the markings in grades one to four inclusive running a little high; whereas the markings in grades five to eight inclusive pull towards the low end, and grades nine to twelve inclusive show a marked piling up at the low end of the curve.

A further analysis on the basis of separate years shows the 1B grade with about twice as many failures as superiors. In the 1A grade the tendency is in the other direction. The same thing is true in grades 2B, 2A, 3B, 3A, 4B. In the 4A and 5B this tendency is not so noticeable, while in the 5A grade the markings begin to bunch more toward the failing end of the distribution. This tendency gradually grows in grades 6B and 6A. A more nearly regular distribution occurs in grades 7B and 7A. In the 8B grade there is a marked tendency toward the low end, but in the 8A grade there is a running back to an approximately normal distribution.

In the 9B grade, however, a marked drop in markings occurs. This condition is somewhat improved in grade 9A but falls again in 10B, maintains about the same position in 10A, and gets even worse in 11B. In 11A the condition is considerably improved, only to drop again in the 12B grade. In the 12A grade there is a considerable improvement.

An analysis on the basis of subjects shows a very satisfactory distribution in reading in grades 1 to 8 inclusive. In arithmetic in grades 3B to 8A inclusive there is a noticeable leaning toward the lower markings. In language and grammar, the conditions in grades 2B to 8A inclusive are fair; in history, grades 4B to 8A inclusive, much less satisfactory. In geography, grades 4B to 7A inclusive, there is a return to approximately normal conditions. Spelling in grades 3B to 8A inclusive leans strongly toward the high end of the curve, which condition is wholly in accord with the results from the Buckingham tests. Something of the same conditions prevail in phonics, grades 1B to 2A inclusive. In physiology, grades 4B to 7A inclusive, there is a high piling up in the middle of the curve. A similar condition is found in drawing, grades 1B to 8A inclusive;

writing, grades 1B to 8A inclusive; music, grades 1B to 8A inclusive; industrial work, grades 7B to 8A inclusive.

In high school English, grades 9B to 12A inclusive, the curve of distribution of grades leans noticeably toward the low end. In Latin, grades 9B to 12A inclusive, the curve straightens up fairly well. In German, grades 9B to 12A inclusive, it is still more nearly normal. In mathematics, grades 9B to 11A, another slump occurs toward the low end, followed closely in the subject of history, grades 10B to 12A inclusive. In physical geography, grades 9B–9A, a slight recovery occurs. But in botany, grades 9B–9A, there is a landslide towards low grades. · The botany record is about equalled in physics, grades 12B to 12A inclusive, and is surpassed in an undesirable direction by the commercial department, grades 9B to 12A inclusive.

An analysis on the basis of years and subjects shows conditions more definitely. Only some of the striking results along this line are here mentioned. From the 3B grade through the 4B grade there is a leaning of the curve toward the high end in mathematics. From the 4A grade on there is rather a steady reversal of the form of the curve up to the 8A grade, where the distribution of markings is fairly normal. In history the worst conditions are in grades 6B, 6A, 7B, 7A, 8B. Some improvement occurs in grade 8A.

In reading there is a rather heavy piling up in the failure group in grade 1B. From grade 1A on, however, through grade 5A, there is a leaning toward high markings. From the 6B grade on there is a general tendency toward the lower marking, with some relief, however, in grade 7B.

Language begins to get difficult in the 4A grade, grows in difficulty rather steadily until the 8B grade, where there is a marked piling up of failing grades. In the 8A grade, however, the recovery is almost complete.

The distribution of grades in geography is fairly normal.

TABLE CXXXIII

DISTRIBUTION OF MARKINGS FOR THE SECOND SEMESTER, 1912–13

	96–100 PER CENT	91–95 PER CENT	86–90 PER CENT	81–85 PER CENT	75–80 PER CENT	BELOW PASSING
Arithmetic						
Grade 3B all white pupils......	7.1	17.2	31.3	16.2	19.2	9.1
" 3A " " "	12.5	17.5	40.	17.5	12.5	0.
" 4B " " "	2.9	22.3	31.1	28.2	7.8	7.8
" 4A " " "	5.5	14.5	34.5	26.4	13.6	5.5
" 5B " " "	....	....	....	....	....	....
" 5A " " "	4.	17.	20.	31.	14.	14.

TABLE CXXXIII (*Continued*)

	96–100 Per Cent	91–95 Per Cent	86–90 Per Cent	81–85 Per Cent	75–80 Per Cent	Below Passing
Arithmetic (*Continued*)						
Grade 6B all white pupils......	6.8	10.2	20.4	21.6	20.4	20.4
" 6A " " "	9.1	5.7	30.7	28.4	17.	9.1
" 7B " " "	0.	12.5	4.2	20.8	38.9	23.6
" 7A " " "	1.8	3.5	7.	12.3	47.4	28.
" 8B " " "	2.	6.	6.	18.	44.	24.
" 8A " " "	0.	4.3	15.	21.3	49.	10.6
Total Arithmetic.............	5.1	13.1	25.2	22.9	21.6	12.
History						
Grade 4B all white pupils......	3.	11.9	34.3	29.9	16.4	4.5
" 4A " " "	7.3	10.	35.5	28.2	18.2	.9
" 5B " " "	6.3	30.2	16.7	26.	18.7	2.1
" 5A " " "	9.9	18.8	32.7	16.8	11.9	9.9
" 6B " " "	3.4	18.1	27.3	6.8	20.5	23.9
" 6A " " "	2.3	9.3	27.9	16.3	32.5	11.5
" 7B " " "	0.	1.4	16.7	19.4	41.6	20.8
" 7A " " "	0.	1.8	15.8	31.6	38.6	12.3
" 8B " " "	0.	8.	12.	16.	36.	28.
" 8A " " "	0.	2.2	17.4	32.6	34.8	13.
Total History...............	4.1	12.7	25.1	21.7	25.	11.5
Reading						
Grade 1B all white pupils......	5.4	13.1	33.7	21.7	10.9	15.2
" 1A " " "	14.3	12.3	34.4	28.6	4.5	5.8
" 2B " " "	15.5	21.1	39.4	19.7	1.4	2.9
" 2A " " "	11.2	26.8	33.6	21.6	6.	.8
" 3B " " "	10.6	18.8	38.8	27.	4.7	0.
" 3A " " "	9.2	23.3	33.3	25.	7.5	1.7
" 4B " " "	12.6	15.5	33.9	27.2	7.8	2.9
" 4A " " "	8.2	20.	35.5	27.3	9.1	0.
" 5B " " "	3.8	23.1	38.5	25.6	7.7	1.3
" 5A " " "	2.6	17.1	43.4	23.7	11.8	1.3
" 6B " " "	7.	12.8	36.	23.2	11.6	9.3
" 6A " " "	3.6	16.8	33.6	19.3	21.6	4.8
" 7B " " "	0.	22.2	36.1	20.8	16.7	4.2
" 7A " " "	0.	1.7	15.5	32.8	36.2	13.8
" 8B " " "	1.9	7.5	17.	22.6	28.3	22.6
" 8A " " "	2.1	0.	19.1	31.9	34.	12.8
Total Reading.............	7.8	17.	33.7	24.8	11.5	5.2
Grammar and Language						
Grade 4B all white pupils......	1.	17.3	38.5	29.8	9.6	3.8
" 4A " " "	8.2	12.7	35.5	23.6	17.3	2.7
" 5B " " "	8.2	22.4	24.5	22.4	16.3	6.1
" 5A " " "	7.1	25.5	32.6	21.4	9.2	4.1
" 6B " " "	10.2	17.	22.7	23.8	18.2	8.
" 6A " " "	6.	15.6	37.3	18.1	13.3	9.6
" 7B " " "	1.4	15.2	25.	9.7	23.6	25.
" 7A " " "	1.7	5.1	17.	18.6	15.3	42.4
" 8B " " "	2.	19.6	11.8	15.7	29.4	21.6
" 8A " " "	2.2	4.4	15.6	31.1	17.8	28.9
Total Grammar and Language.	5.3	16.5	28.1	21.8	16.1	12.3

TABLE CXXXIII (*Continued*)

	96–100 PER CENT	91–95 PER CENT	86–90 PER CENT	81–85 PER CENT	75–80 PER CENT	BELOW PASSING
Geography						
Grade 4B all white pupils	1.6	12.5	40.6	25.	15.6	4.7
" 4A " " "	8.	23.	31.	23.	9.7	5.3
" 5B " " "	6.2	12.4	42.2	15.5	17.5	6.2
" 5A " " "	11.7	18.4	33.	15.5	16.5	4.9
" 6B " " "	6.8	17.	23.9	21.6	21.6	9.1
" 6A " " "	4.9	15.9	31.7	22.	20.7	4.9
" 7B " " "	0.	16.6	27.7	43.1	9.7	2.8
" 7A " " "	3.4	3.4	32.8	32.8	24.1	3.4
Total Geography	5.9	15.8	32.8	23.6	16.5	5.3
Spelling						
Grade 2B all white pupils	29.6	25.4	32.4	9.9	2.8	0.
" 2A " " "	25.4	23.1	32.8	11.2	6.7	.7
" 3B " " "	26.5	22.9	21.7	19.3	7.2	2.4
" 3A " " "	25.8	28.3	27.5	11.7	6.7	0.
" 4B " " "	24.3	27.2	31.1	11.6	4.9	.8
" 4A " " "	14.7	37.6	33.	9.2	4.6	.9
" 5B " " "	20.2	38.4	28.8	3.8	6.7	1.9
" 5A " " "	16.7	36.3	19.6	14.7	8.8	3.9
" 6B " " "	20.5	25.	29.5	13.6	8.	3.4
" 6A " " "	25.3	31.3	24.1	16.9	2.4	0.
" 7B " " "	75.	12.5	1.4	11.1	0.	0.
" 7A " " "	82.8	10.3	5.2	1.7	0.	0.
" 8B " " "	64.6	25.	10.4	0.	0.	0.
" 8A " " "	70.4	20.5	9.1	0.	0.	0.
Total Spelling	32.	27.2	24.2	10.4	5.	1.1

TABLE CXXXIV

DISTRIBUTION OF SCHOLARSHIP MARKS GIVEN IN VARIOUS SUBJECTS AND GRADES, FIRST SEMESTER, 1914–15

BY PER CENTS

Part I. — Distribution by Subjects and Grades

SUBJECT AND GRADE	SUPERIOR, 96–100	EXCELLENT, 91–95	GOOD, 86–90	FAIR, 81–85	PASSING, 75–80	NOT PASSING, BELOW 75
Reading						
1B	10.8	16.7	24.3	24.3	11.7	12.2
1A	2.2	21.7	26.1	32.7	9.8	7.6
2B	5.7	23.6	35.7	22.8	7.9	4.3
2A	11.4	27.6	36.2	15.2	6.7	2.9
3B	3.9	24.5	31.6	16.8	19.4	3.9
3A	8.	31.	34.	19.	7.	1.
4B	10.9	21.2	29.9	24.1	10.9	2.9
4A	4.	18.2	32.3	21.2	20.2	4.
5B	2.4	22.4	33.6	28.8	12.	.8
5A	10.3	15.5	42.3	21.6	10.3	0.
6B	.9	15.3	29.7	27.	24.3	2.7
6A	1.3	11.3	15.	30.	30.	12.5
7B	3.5	17.6	18.8	16.5	34.1	9.4
7A	1.4	10.9	19.2	16 4	39.7	12.3
8B	0.	12.5	25.	29.2	18.1	15.3
8A	0.	6.7	20.	21.	43.3	8.3

TABLE CXXXIV (*Continued*)

SUBJECT AND GRADE	SUPERIOR, 96-100	EX-CELLENT, 91-95	GOOD, 86-90	FAIR, 81-85	PASSING, 75-80	NOT PASSING, BELOW 75
Geography						
4B................	2.5	13.8	46.3	31.3	6.3	0.
4A................	15.2	20.2	34.3	12.1	9.1	9.1
5B................	3.2	11.1	32.5	23.8	23.8	5.6
5A................	4.2	9.5	41.1	32.6	10.5	2.1
6B................	0.	9.	24.3	20.7	34.2	11.7
6A................	0.	8.8	12.5	20.	46.2	12.5
7B................	0.	5.9	18.8	22.4	44.7	8.3
7A................	0.	9.7	23.6	25.	34.7	6.9
Arithmetic						
3B................	3.8	17.9	29.5	19.2	17.9	11.5
3A................	9.2	22.	29.4	22.9	12.8	3.7
4B................	0.	12.5	19.9	27.2	26.5	14.
4A................	10.1	18.1	31.3	13.1	18.1	9.1
5B................	2.5	12.3	26.2	22.1	32.	4.9
5A................	4.1	11.3	32.	22.7	19.6	10.3
6B................	.9	15.3	28.8	26.1	20.7	8.1
6A................	0.	7.5	22.5	28.8	26.2	15.
7B................	3.5	14.1	20.	15.3	25.9	21.2
7A................	1.4	17.	22.2	25.	34.7	9.7
8B................	0.	10.8	21.5	26.2	30.8	10.8
8A................	0.	4.9	6.6	31.1	50.8	6.6
Language and Grammar						
4B................	4.	14.2	37.	21.3	17.3	6.3
4A................	5.1	21.5	36.7	17.3	15.3	4.
5B................	3.2	16.1	30.	36.3	13.7	.8
5A................	3.1	14.4	35.1	30.9	12.4	4.1
6B................	.9	5.4	15.3	30.6	27.9	19.8
6A................	2.5	6.3	15.	18.8	40.	17.5
7B................	1.7	5.1	33.9	30.5	0.	28.8
7A................	5.6	13.9	11.1	22.2	18.1	29.2
8B................	0.	5.6	15.5	12.7	36.6	29.7
8A................	0.	3.3	23.3	23.3	30.	20.
History						
4B................	2.5	9.	36.	38.5	13.9	0.
4A................	8.1	21.6	41.9	10.8	13.5	4.1
5B................	3.1	11.8	32.3	41.7	10.2	.8
5A................	4.1	18.6	42.3	20.6	10.3	4.1
6B................	10.	8.2	22.5	15.3	28.8	15.3
6A................	5.	8.8	15.	22.5	27.5	21.2
7B................	0.	0.	7.7	33.	51.6	7.7
7A................	0.	4.2	15.3	15.3	52.8	12.5
8B................	0.	0.	18.3	26.8	35.2	19.7
8A................	0.	0.	15.	35.	41.7	8.3
Spelling						
3B................	8.4	33.7	32.5	9.	7.2	9.
3A................	18.	37.8	24.3	14.4	2.7	2.7
4B................	11.7	32.1	26.3	19.7	7.3	2.9
4A................	11.1	32.3	37.4	8.1	8.1	3.
5B................	7.9	29.8	35.1	21.1	4.4	1.8
5A................	13.4	22.7	29.9	21.6	10.3	2.1
6B................	39.	32.7	15.9	6.2	6.2	0.
6A................	43.8	23.8	18.8	7.5	2.5	3.8
7B................	58.8	21.2	9.4	2.4	7.1	1.2
7A................	44.4	27.8	16.7	7.	2.8	1.4
8B................	49.3	26.	11.	6.8	4.1	2.7
8A................	72.1	23.1	3.3	3.3	0.	0.

TABLE CXXXIV (*Continued*)

SUBJECT AND GRADE	SUPERIOR, 96–100	EX-CELLENT, 91–95	GOOD, 86–90	FAIR, 81–85	PASSING, 75–80	NOT PASSING, BELOW 75
Latin (High School)						
9B	25.8	22.6	16.1	25.8	6.4	3.2
9A	0.	15.4	23.1	30.8	15.4	15.4
10B	12.9	19.4	29.	12.9	6.5	19.4
10A	10.	15.	15.	25.	5.	30.
11B	6.3	12.5	37.5	18.8	18.8	6.3
11A	7.7	38.5	30.8	15.4	7.7	0.
12B	10.	50.	30.	10.	0.	0.
12A	28.6	42.9	14.3	14.3	0.	0.
German (High School)						
9B	0.	32.	14.	18.	22.	14.
9A	0.	6.3	18.7	25.	18.7	31.3
10B	0.	9.	24.4	17.8	31.1	17.8
10A	3.3	6.7	16.7	20.	26.7	26.7
11B	6.8	17.2	24.1	38.	10.3	3.4
11A	0.	18.2	36.4	18.2	18.2	9.
12B	0.	30.8	38.5	7.7	23.1	0.
12A	0.	16.7	16.7	16.7	33.3	16.7
English (High School)						
9B	0.	13.6	25.8	31.8	18.2	10.6
9A	2.9	17.1	20.	34.3	8.6	17.1
10B	1.9	11.3	35.8	13.2	20.8	17.
10A	0.	5.1	7.7	25.6	41.	20.5
11B	0.	10.9	13.	26.1	45.7	4.3
11A	0.	4.5	0.	22.7	45.5	27.2
12B	0.	11.3	30.2	22.7	30.2	5.7
12A	0.	9.	45.5	27.3	18.2	0.
History (High School)						
10B	0.	20.4	22.4	28.6	16.3	12.2
10A	....	....	....	....	....	....
11B	4.1	12.2	28.5	20.4	24.5	10.2
11A	0.	13.3	26.7	33.3	26.7	0.
12B	7.	9.3	53.5	16.3	9.3	4.7
12A	5.9	23.5	29.4	29.4	5.9	5.9
Mathematics (High School)						
9B	9.4	20.3	29.7	14.1	10.9	15.6
9A	8.	28.	28.	12.	4.	20.
10B	0.	15.3	22.	23.7	25.4	13.6
10A	5.	10.	17.5	20.	25.	22.5
11B	0.	8.7	21.7	23.9	32.6	13.
11A	11.1	7.4	11.1	33.3	29.7	7.4
Commercial (High School)						
9B	0.	29.4	17.6	29.4	11.8	11.8
9A	0.	7.7	15.4	23.1	53.8	0.
10B	4.3	39.1	13.	21.7	4.3	17.4
10A	0.	20.	0.	50.	30.	0.
11B	0.	16.1	29.	29.	19.4	6.5
11A	0.	9.	9.	27.3	36.4	18.2
12B	5.9	11.8	17.7	29.4	35.3	0.
12A	0.	16.7	66.7	16.7	0.	0.

TABLE CXXXIV (*Continued*)

SUBJECT AND GRADE	SUPERIOR, 96–100	EX-CELLENT, 91–95	GOOD, 86–90	FAIR, 81–85	PASSING, 75–80	NOT PASSING, BELOW 75
Physical Geography (*High School*)						
9A	17.7	23.5	47.1	5.9	0.	5.9
Physics (*High School*)						
12B	9.1	30.9	40.	16.4	3.6	0.
12A	0.	0.	100.	0.	0.	0.
Botany (*High School*)						
9B and 9A	0.	9.5	19.	33.3	19.	19.

Part 2. — *Distribution by Grades and by Subjects Combined*

This table gives the percentage of "Superior," "Excellent," "Good," etc., awarded in all subjects included in Part 1.

Elementary Schools by Grades						
1B	10.8	16.7	24.3	24.3	11.7	12.1
1A	2.2	21.7	26.1	32.6	9.8	7.6
2B	5.7	23.8	35.7	22.9	7.9	4.2
2A	11.4	27.6	36.2	15.2	6.7	2.8
3B	5.5	25.6	31.2	14.9	14.7	8.2
3A	11.9	30.3	29.1	18.7	7.5	2.5
4B	5.5	17.6	31.4	26.5	14.2	4.8
4A	8.6	21.5	35.4	14.6	14.6	5.4
5B	3.5	17.8	31.1	29.1	16.1	2.4
5A	6.4	15.1	36.4	24.6	12.	5.4
Department School by Grades						
6B	8.4	14.4	22.8	21.	23.7	9.6
6A	8.8	11.	16.5	21.3	28.7	13.7
7B	11.6	10.8	16.5	19.8	28.9	12.2
7A	8.8	12.2	18.1	18.5	30.5	12.
8B	10.2	10.	15.8	21.2	28.	14.7
8A	14.6	7.3	13.6	22.8	33.1	8.6
High School by Grades						
9B	5.7	22.	22.9	23.3	13.9	12.2
9A	5.1	15.3	23.7	22.9	16.1	17.
10B	2.3	16.7	25.8	20.2	19.4	15.6
10A	3.5	9.2	12.8	24.8	27.7	22.
11B	2.3	12.4	24.	25.8	27.6	7.8
11A	3.9	11.8	15.7	25.5	32.3	10.8
12B	5.2	20.3	37.5	18.2	16.1	2.6
12A	5.8	19.2	40.4	21.2	9.6	3.8

Part 3. — *Subject Averages, All Grades*

[1] *Department School*						
Reading	1.3	13.4	21.8	21.6	32.	9.9
Geography	0.	8.7	17.6	22.3	41.1	10.4
Arithmetic	1.1	10.7	20.1	25.5	30.3	12.3
History	3.2	4.1	14.1	23.3	40.5	14.8
Grammar	1.8	6.9	18.2	21.4	27.1	24.6
German	0.	0.	28.6	28.6	21.4	21.4
Latin	0.	8.3	33.3	25.	33.3	0.
Spelling	51.7	24.	13.1	5.4	4.3	1.5

[1] Department School includes grades 6, 7, and 8.

TABLE CXXXIV (*Continued*)

SUBJECT	SUPERIOR, 96–100	Ex-CELLENT, 91–95	GOOD, 86–90	FAIR, 81–85	PASSING, 75–80	NOT PASSING BELOW 75
High School						
English.............	.6	11.1	22.5	25.2	28.	12.6
Mathematics........	4.9	14.7	22.3	20.4	22.6	15.
Physical Geography..	16.7	22.2	44.4	5.6	0.	11.1
History.............	3.4	15.4	32.6	24.6	16.	8.
Latin..............	13.5	23.4	24.1	20.	7.8	11.3
German............	1.5	17.5	21.5	21.	23.	15.5
Commercial........	1.6	20.3	19.5	28.1	22.7	7.8
Physics............	8.3	28.3	45.	15.	3.3	0.
Botany.............	0.	10.5	21.1	36.8	21.1	10.5
Department School as a Whole...........	10.1	11.4	17.9	20.7	28.2	11.7
High School as a Whole..	4.	16.3	24.6	22.4	20.8	11.8

A comparison of Table CXXXIV with Table CXXXII shows the changes brought about in the three-year period:

1. For the high school as a whole some progress was made. The per cent of superior grades was raised from 2.7 to 4 and the per cent of failing grades was reduced from 12.9 to 11.8. The per cent of barely passing was reduced from 28.1 to 20.8.

2. In high-school English the condition in 1914–15 is not so good as in the earlier period. In mathematics it is better. In physical geography it is considerably better. In history there is a rather marked improvement. In Latin an improvement is also shown. In German there is a distinct loss. In commercial a remarkable gain. In physics a distinct improvement. In botany some improvement is shown.

3. In arithmetic improvement is shown in grades 4A, 5A, 6B, 7A, 8B, and a loss in grades 3B, 4B, 8A; while no marked gain or loss is noticeable in grades 3A, 5B, 6A, 7B.

4. In geography, gains in grades 4B, 4A, 5A, loss in grades 6B, 6A, 7B, 7A, and no marked gain or loss in grade 5B.

5. In reading, gains in grades 1B, 2B, 5A, 8B, loss in grades 1A, 3B, 3A, 4A, 5B, 7B, 7A, and no marked gain or loss in grades 2A, 4B, 6B, 6A, 8A.

6. In language and grammar, gains in 4A, 5B, 5A, 6A, 8B, loss in 4B, 6B, 7B, 7A, 8A.

7. In history, gains in grades 4B, 4A, 5B, 5A, 6B, 6A, 7A, loss in grade 7B, no marked gain or loss in grades 8B, 8A.

8. In all subjects combined there is a gain in grades 1B, 2A, 3A, 4A, 5A, 6B, 6A, 8B, 9B, 10B, 11B, 12B, 12A, a loss in grades 1A, 3B, 4B, 7A, 10A, 11A, and no marked gain or loss in grades 2B, 5B, 7B, 8A, 9A.

14. Retention in Rank of Eighty-six Pupils in the Bloomington Graded and High Schools[1]

The problem included all children who had graduated from the Bloomington high school from 1907–13 inclusive and had had all of their school work from the fourth grade through the high school in the Bloomington schools. The purpose of the study was threefold:

1. To discover the percentage of pupils retaining their standing from year to year.

2. To determine the percentage of pupils retaining their rank throughout the course, beginning with any year as a basis.

3. To ascertain to what degree the pupils who are good in one subject are good in all subjects and vice versa.

In this study the term "grade" means the actual per cent given on a basis of 100; rank is used to designate the different groups of grades. Rank "S" includes grades from 96–100, rank "E" 91–95, rank "G" 86–90, rank "F" 81–85, rank "P" 75–80, rank "N.P." all below 75.

TABLE CXXXV

Total Percentage of Retention in English

	5TH YR.	6TH YR.	7TH YR.	8TH YR.	9TH YR.	10TH YR.	11TH YR.	12TH YR.
Boys	60.	50.	33.3	36.8	45.5	47.6	47.6	36.8
Girls	64.7	50.	37.1	44.4	39.5	42.1	36.9	34.1
Total	61.7	50.	35.7	41.8	41.7	44.1	40.7	35.3
Boys	....	69.6	33.3	39.1	48.	54.2	48.	45.5
Girls	....	60.5	42.8	46.6	35.5	35.5	33.3	25.6
Total	....	63.6	39.4	44.1	40.	42.	39.1	32.8
Boys	....	....	42.9	57.5	51.7	65.5	48.3	46.2
Girls	....	....	42.	39.2	32.1	28.3	37.7	42.5
Total	....	....	42.3	45.5	39.	41.4	41.4	43.8
Boys	....	....	....	60.	35.7	46.4	32.1	36.
Girls	....	....	....	47.9	44.	36.	32.	45.4
Total	....	....	....	53.4	41.	39.8	32.	42.
Boys	....	....	....	....	44.	44.	44.	40.9
Girls	....	....	....	....	50.	45.8	35.4	33.3
Total	....	....	....	....	47.9	45.2	38.4	38.4
Boys	....	....	....	....	....	48.2	48.2	50.
Girls	....	....	....	....	....	45.1	37.2	37.8
Total	....	....	....	....	....	46.2	41.	42.
Boys	....	....	....	....	....	....	32.2	44.
Girls	....	....	....	....	....	....	46.	45.4
Total	....	....	....	....	....	....	41.	46.1
Boys	....	....	....	....	....	....	....	36.
Girls	....	....	....	....	....	....	....	36.4
Total	....	....	....	....	....	....	....	34.8

[1] A study made by Charley Bruner, a graduate student of Indiana University. See pages 89 and 219.

Table CXXXV summarizes the total percentage of retention throughout the nine years in the subject of English, beginning with any one year as a basis.

Summary of conclusions drawn from the above table and from other tables on English:

1. That the least retention occurs in the 7th year in the common school and in the 12th year in the high school. The latter has the lowest percentage of retention of any year.
2. The classification of pupils as to rank in the 6th year gives the most uniform retention throughout the remaining years.
3. In the lower school years the grades made by pupils fall almost exclusively in ranks E, G, and F. As we approach the 12th school year the grades made by the pupils are distributed more evenly throughout the ranks S to N.P.
4. More pupils are found in the G rank, for each year from the 4th to the 12th, than in any other.
5. There are no perceptible sex differences in the retention of rank.

Summary on retention and distribution of rank in mathematics:

1. The percentage of retention for mathematics is lower than that for English.
2. The retention in the 7th year is lower than in either the 6th or 8th year.
3. If each year is taken as a basis for comparison, the results show that the transition from common school to high school causes a decrease in retention.
4. There is a gradual shift in rank from the upper end of the scale to the lower end as the pupils pass from the 4th to the 12th year.
5. Sex differences are very slight.

Summarizing the facts on the distribution and retention of ranks in history, the following facts stand out most prominently:

1. The retention is lowest in the 6th and 12th years and highest in the 8th.
2. It made no difference what year was used as the basis, the retention in each case was about the same.
3. The retention and distribution for the boys was much the same as for the girls in all instances.
4. The high school gave rise to more "S" and "N.P." grades than did the common school.

Table CXXXVI, compiled at the beginning of the second semester 1913–14, shows a relatively large number of eighth-grade graduates entering the high school. The elimination that occurs appears before graduation from the grades or after entrance to high school. For the past eight years 89.3 per cent of the eighth-grade graduates have entered the high school. In the transition from grades to high school there is a loss of approximately 10 per cent, some years more and some less, the extremes for the 15 consecutive semesters being 2.8 per cent as the lowest loss and 19.6 per cent as the highest. Of all

TABLE CXXXVI

RECORD IN HIGH SCHOOL OF EIGHTH-GRADE GRADUATES FROM THE SCHOOLS FOR WHITE CHILDREN IN BLOOMINGTON THROUGH SEMESTER ENDING JANUARY, 1914, NOT INCLUDING PUPILS WHO DROPPED OUT A TERM OR MORE AT A TIME

Date of Graduation from Grades	No. in Class	No. Entered High School	Per Cent Entered High School	No. Withdrawn to Quit School	Per Cent Withdrawn	No. Still Remaining or Graduated	Per Cent Remaining or Graduated	Av. No. of Terms Withdrawals Remained in High School	Av. No. Credits of Withdrawals at Time of Withdrawal	No. Graduating in Regular Time	No. 1 Term Ahead	No. 2 Terms Ahead	No. 1 Term Behind	No. 2 or More Terms Behind	Av. No. of Credits per Undergraduate
Jan. '07	36	32	88.9	15	46.9	17	53.1	2.6	5.5	11	3	……	3	1	……
May '07	29	25	86.2	12	48.	13	52.	5.7	7.7	8	2	……	2	1	……
Jan. '08	34	31	91.2	17	54.8	14	45.1	3.7	4.3	9	……	1	2	2	……
May '08	39	34	87.2	25	73.5	9	26.5	4.	11.5	7	……	1	……	1	……
Jan. '09	31	28	90.3	14	50.	14	50.	3.7	14.8	8	1	……	3	2	……
May '09	46	42	91.3	10	23.8	32	76.2	5.	14.7	23	1	……	4	……	28.6
Jan. '10	25	20	80.	14	70.	6	30.	3.5	9.1	3	……	……	……	……	27.
May '10	17	16	94.1	6	37.5	10	62.5	2.5	8.9	……	……	……	……	……	27.7
Jan. '11	31	29	93.5	12	41.4	17	58.6	3.1	7.9	……	……	……	……	……	20.
May '11	62	58	93.5	19	32.8	39	67.2	2.2	7.2	……	……	……	……	,	18.7
Jan. '12	36	35	97.3	12	34.3	23	65.7	1.7	5.2	……	……	……	……	……	14.1
May '12	55	48	87.3	13	27.1	35	72.9	1.3	3.6	……	……	……	……	……	11.
Jan. '13	39	36	92.3	4	11.1	32	88.9	1.	4.	……	……	……	……	……	6.6
May '13	51	41	80.4	5	12.2	36	87.8	.3	0.	……	……	……	……	……	3.5
Jan. '14	30	26	86.7	.	……	……	……	……	……	……	……	……	……	……	……
Total	561	501	89.3	178	37.5	297	62.5	……	……	……	……	……	……	……	……

TABLE CXXXVII

ACHIEVEMENT OF BLOOMINGTON HIGH SCHOOL GRADUATES AS STUDENTS IN INDIANA UNIVERSITY

Showing for all undergraduates in Indiana University and for all undergraduates of Indiana University who were alumni of the Bloomington high school, the number and per cent of hours of work of the various qualities — A (100–95), B (94–85), C (84–75), D (74–65), E (Conditioned, Failed, and Incomplete) — for the school year 1910–11.

	WORK MARKED A		WORK MARKED B		WORK MARKED C		WORK MARKED D		WORK CONDITIONED, FAILED, OR INCOMPLETE	
	TOTAL NUMBER OF HOURS	PER CENT OF TOTAL NUMBER OF HOURS OF WORK TAKEN	TOTAL NUMBER OF HOURS	PER CENT OF TOTAL NUMBER OF HOURS OF WORK TAKEN	TOTAL NUMBER OF HOURS	PER CENT OF TOTAL NUMBER OF HOURS OF WORK TAKEN	TOTAL NUMBER OF HOURS	PER CENT OF TOTAL NUMBER OF HOURS OF WORK TAKEN	TOTAL NUMBER OF HOURS	PER CENT OF TOTAL NUMBER OF HOURS OF WORK TAKEN
Total Indiana University undergraduates for year 1910–11	....	21.7	....	35.8	....	24.3	....	9.8	....	8.3
Indiana University undergraduates who were alumni of Bloomington high school	619	23.	995	37.	701	26.	252	9.4	124	4.6

those who entered the high school from the Bloomington graded school during the 15 semesters 37.5 per cent have withdrawn and quit school, while 62.5 per cent still remain. Of those entering high school from January '07 to May '09 inclusive, who should normally have graduated by May '14, 55.5 per cent have withdrawn. The high school during those years held approximately only 45 per cent until graduation. For those same years the average number of credits held by withdrawals was 8.8 or slightly more than the equivalent of two years' work.

Table CXXXVII shows that Bloomington graduates compare favorably with graduates of other schools in quality of passing work done. The per cent of Bloomington graduates in the failing group is considerably less than that for the university as a whole.

TABLE CXXXVIII

THE FOLLOWING TABLE INDICATES THE SHOWING MADE BY BLOOMINGTON HIGH SCHOOL GRADUATES IN THE AWARD OF HONORS AT INDIANA UNIVERSITY

	TOTAL GRADUATES			GRADUATING WITH HIGH DISTINCTION		
SCHOOL YEAR ENDING	TOTAL INDIANA UNIVERSITY GRADUATES	TOTAL INDIANA UNIVERSITY GRADUATES ALSO BLOOMINGTON HIGH SCHOOL GRADUATES	PER CENT OF TOTAL NUMBER BLOOMINGTON HIGH SCHOOL GRADUATES	NUMBER INDIANA UNIVERSITY GRADUATING WITH HIGH DISTINCTION	NUMBER BLOOMINGTON HIGH SCHOOL GRADUATING WITH HIGH DISTINCTION	PER CENT OF HIGH DISTINCTION BLOOMINGTON HIGH SCHOOL GRADUATES SUPPLY
1909..........	205	18	8.8	3	0	0
1910..........	215	11	5.1	5	1	20
1911..........	202	17	8.4	5	1	20
1912..........	225	12	5.3	6	2	33.3
1913..........	265	20	7.5	12	1	8.3
Total.......	1112	78	7.1	31	5	16.1

	GRADUATING WITH DISTINCTION			BOTH HONORS		
SCHOOL YEAR ENDING	NUMBER INDIANA UNIVERSITY GRADUATING WITH DISTINCTION	NUMBER BLOOMINGTON HIGH SCHOOL GRADUATING WITH DISTINCTION	PER CENT OF DISTINCTION BLOOMINGTON HIGH SCHOOL GRADUATES SUPPLY	NUMBER INDIANA UNIVERSITY GRADUATES IN BOTH CLASSES OF DISTINCTION	NUMBER BLOOMINGTON HIGH SCHOOL GRADUATES IN BOTH CLASSES OF DISTINCTION	PER CENT OF BOTH CLASSES OF DISTINCTION SUPPLIED BY BLOOMINGTON HIGH SCHOOL GRADUATES
1909..........	9	1	11.1	12	1	8.3
1910..........	8	0	0.	13	1	7.7
1911..........	17	4	23.5	22	5	22.7
1912..........	16	5	31.3	22	7	31.8
1913..........	18	4	22.2	30	5	16.7
Total.......	68	14	20.6	99	19	19.2

TABLE CXXXXIX

GRADES, INDIANA UNIVERSITY FRESHMEN, FALL TERM, SCHOOL YEAR 1913–14, IN MATHEMATICS

Worked out by Prof. D. A. ROTHROCK, Indiana University

	Number Taking Test	Average Age	Examination			Mortality in Per Cent		Per Cent Receiving Grades			
			I	II	Final	Withdrawn	Failed	D¹	C	B	A
All students in University	250	19.	80.	67.	71.7	8.	14.	16.8	18.8	20.4	22.
Students from high schools belonging to the North Central Association	35	19.	81.4	70.2	76.	5.7	11.5	15.	16.	21.8	30.
Not in North Central Association	65	19	78.6	65.5	69.4	10.	15.	17.5	20.	20.	17.5
Six largest high schools in Indiana	10	18	77.6	72.8	78.	4.4	8.7	21.7	17.4	17.4	30.4
All other high school graduates	20	19.1	80.	66.6	71.	8.8	14.5	16.3	19.	20.4	21.
Bloomington High School graduates	8	18	81.	65.5	71.	10.5	0.0	10.5	26.5	31.5	21.

¹ For value of these grades see Table CXXXVII.

Table CXXXVIII shows that while Bloomington high school graduates furnish only 7.1 per cent of all the graduates from Indiana University during the first five years after the inauguration of the award of honor system, they furnish 19.2 per cent of all such graduates graduating with distinction or with high distinction.

In the fall of 1913 the mathematics department of Indiana University gave to the freshman students taking mathematics three examinations, one at the beginning of the term, one about the middle of the term, and a final one at the end of the term. The following table shows a comparison of the results by various groups of students.

Table CXXXIX shows that the Bloomington graduates are about average in achievement in freshman mathematics in the university. They start in a little above the average but take a "slump" before the term closes.

TABLE CXL

SIZE OF HIGH SCHOOL CLASSES

High school first month of fall term school year 1913–1914. Number of classes and number of pupils in each class.

Number in Class	Frequency	Total Pupils in Each Class Size	Number in Class	Frequency	Total Pupils in Each Class Size
4	1	4	20	2	40
9	2	18	21	10	210
10	2	20	22	4	88
11	1	11	23	1	23
12	5	60	24	6	144
13	1	13	25	2	50
14	5	70	26	2	52
15	6	90	27	3	81
16	3	48	28	2	56
17	6	102	29	1	29
18	2	36	30	3	90
19	3	57	31	1	31
		529			894

Number of classes, 74
Average number to a class, 19.2
Median size of class, 19
Extremes in sizes, 4 to 31
Middle 50%, 19 to 24

TABLE CXLI

SIZE OF HIGH SCHOOL CLASSES

High school first month, Second Semester, school year 1913–1914. Number of classes and number of pupils in each class. Eighty-one classes.

Number in Class	Frequency	Total Pupils in Each Class Size	Number in Class	Frequency	Total Pupils in Each Class Size
8	1	8	20	4	80
9	1	9	21	12	252
10	2	20	22	8	176
11			23	4	92
12	1	12	24	1	24
13	3	39	25	5	125
14	3	42	26	2	52
15	2	30	27	1	27
16	4	64	28	4	112
17	6	102	29	3	87
18	8	144	30	2	60
19	4	76			
	35	546		46	1087

Average number to a class, 20.2
Median size of class, 21
Extremes in sizes, 8 to 30
Middle 50 per cent, 17 to 23

SUMMARY OF CHAPTER VI

Assuming that the subject matter assigned to the various grades is the proper subject matter to be taught at that time, the test of a school system is its achievement in reducing retardation and failures and in increasing normal progress and acceleration and the percentage of pupils receiving the higher grades, without lowering the standard of work and without accompanying the achievement with an unwelcome by-product, such as an impaired nervous system or a distorted mental or moral habit.

Within the past few years the Bloomington schools have succeeded to some degree in reducing retardation and failures and in increasing normal progress and the per cent of pupils receiving the higher grades. This result has been accomplished while the standard of work has not been lowered, as is shown by the comparison of achievement in the Bloomington system with that of other school systems from time to time. Judged, too, from the results of the physical examinations of school children and from the absence of any increase of complaints of overworked children on the part of parents, the achievement reached in the mastery of subject matter has not been gained at any physical or moral sacrifice.

CHAPTER VII

TEACHERS

The teachers in the Bloomington schools are nominated by the superintendent and elected by the board of trustees. Qualifications for appointment in the high school are the equivalent of an A.B. degree from a college or university and successful experience in teaching. For the grades the requirements are two years' academic training in addition to high school and successful teaching experience.

The following table shows the qualifications of the teaching corps for the school year 1913–14. The data were collected at the beginning of the school year. Experience averages, therefore, do not take account of the experience during the year 1913–14. Academic work is given in hours. Forty-five hours represents full time work for a period of one college year of nine months.

TABLE CXLII

QUALIFICATIONS OF GRADE TEACHERS

Teacher	Attended Country School	Attended Graded Schools	Graduate of High School	Student Normal School	Undergraduate Student College or University	Postgraduate Student College or University	Number Hours Strictly Educational Subjects	Total Hours Credit Exclusive of High School	Business College or Other Institution	Number Years' Experience in Teaching	Years' Experience in Country Schools	Years' Experience in Graded Schools	Years' Experience in High School	Years' Experience in Other Schools	Years' Experience in Bloomington Schools	Years in Bloomington Work as at Present	Number of Different School Systems or Districts in which Taught	Age, October, 1913
1	.	x	x	Graduate	⅓ Yr.	.	45	150	.	11	1	10	.	.	5	5	5	33
2	x	x	x	"	.	.	35	165	.	12	3	9	.	.	7	7	3	32
3	x	x	1 1½ Yrs.	.	⅓ Yr.	.	45	165	.	5	.	.	.	.	1	1	3	24
4	x	.	x	Graduate	2 Yrs.	.	45	45	.	21	9	5	.	.	12	5	2	41
5	.	.	x	.	Graduate	.	50	150	1 Yr.	14	2	12	.	.	7	7	4	34
6	x	x	x	2 Yrs.	⅔ Yr.	1 Yr.	53	183	.	1	.	12	½	.	1½	1	1	23
7	.	x	x	.	Graduate	.	50	165	.	19	2½	1	.	.	11	7	5	46
8	.	x	x	.	"	⅓ Yr.	30	180	.	1½	.	16½	1½	.	.	.	1	25
9	x	.	x	.	.	.	24	196	.	½	.	.	½	.	½	.	1	23
10	x	.	x	⅓ Yr.	1½ Yrs.	3 Yrs.	30	198	.	7	6	.	1	1⅓	.	.	.	23
11	x	x	2 Yrs.	2.3 Yr.	Graduate	.	12½	93	.	4⅓	.	1	.	.	1	1	3	26
12	x	x	x	Graduate	1¼ Yrs.	.	32	250	.	11	4	4	⅓	.	4⅓	4	2	30
13	x	x	1 Yr.	"	.	.	60	90	.	7	5	7	.	.	7	7	1	30
14	.	x	"	"	.	.	35	90	.	15	.	2	.	.	15	14	1	26
15	.	x	x	.	.	.	10	180	.	15	.	15	.	.	15	.	.	37
16	x	x	x	.	.	.	50	145	.	12	1	11	.	.	6	6	4	33

TABLE CXLII (*Continued*)

Row																		
17	x	:	x	"	"	40	127½	...	3	2	1	:	:	:	:	.	2	23
18	x	x	.	Graduate	Graduate	35	180	...	3	1	2	:	:	:	2	2	2	24
19	x	.	x	Graduate	...	50	140	...	4	4	.	:	:	:	.	.	2	25
20	x	x	.	⅓ Yr.	1⅓ Yrs.	20	198	...	1	.	1	:	:	:	.	.	1	23
21	x	x	x	...	"	20	60	...	7	3	4	:	:	:	4	4	2	28
22	x	.	x	...	2 "	15	90	...	12	4	8	:	:	:	5	5	5	36
23	x	.	.	...	1⅔	15	90	...	11	4	7	:	:	:	6	4	5	32
24	x	x	x	⅓ Yr.	Graduate	15	90	...	8	1	7	:	:	:	7	7	2	30
25	x	.	.	"	"	38	195	...	9	2	7	:	:	:	7	7	2	30
26	x	x	.	Graduate	½-1½	45	140	...	5	3	2	:	:	:	2	2	4	27
27	x	x	x	⅓ Yr.	Graduate	20	200	...	12	.	12	:	:	:	12	12	1	34
28	2 Yrs.	x	x	Graduate	1⅓ Yrs.	70	170	1 Yr.	20	1	19	:	:	:	7	7	3	38
29	x	.	.	...	Graduate	30	181	...	3	2	1	:	:	:	1	1	3	27
30	x	x	x	Graduate	1⅓ Yrs.	40	140	...	11	5	6	:	:	:	1	1	5	33
31	x	x	.	...	2⅓	25	125	...	6	2	4	:	:	:	4	4	2	27
32	x	.	.	Graduate	...	20	96	...	6	4	2	:	:	:	2	2	3	28
33	x	x	.	1⅔ Yrs.	Graduate	45	100	...	16½	6	10	:	½	10	10	10	3	40
34	x	x	.	Graduate	1⅔ Yrs.	125	148	...	2½	.	2	:	½	2	2	2	3	28
35	x	x	.	"	1⅓	93	143	...	6	.	6	:	:	3	3	3	3	31
36	x	.	x	...	...	45	135	...	6	1	5	:	:	5	5	5	2	28
37	x	.	.	1⅓ Yrs.	⅔ Yr.	15	70	...	7	1	6	:	:	6	6	6	2	28

[1] Attended high school only 1½ years and did not graduate.

¹ TABLE CXLIII

QUALIFICATIONS OF HIGH SCHOOL TEACHERS

Teacher	Attended Country School	Attended Graded School	Graduate of High School	Student Normal School	Undergraduate Student College or University	Postgraduate Student College or University	Number Hours Strictly Educational Subjects	Total Hours Credit Exclusive of High School	Business College or Other Institution	Number Years' Experience in Teaching	Years' Experience in Country Schools	Years' Experience in Graded Schools	Years' Experience in High School	Years' Experience in Other Schools	Years' Experience in Bloomington Schools	Years in Approximately Same Work as at Present	Number of Different School Systems or Districts in Which Taught	Age, October 1913
English		x	x		Graduate	⅓	44	195		4			4		1	1	3	28
"		x	x		"	½	24	204		2½	1		1½		1	1	2	24
"		x	x		"	⅓	35	185		7	1	2	5			:	3	30
Head History Department	x	x	x	Graduate	"	2 Yrs.	90	350		16	1	4½	10½		4	4	7	39
History		x	x		"	⅙ Yr.	30	187½		1½			1½		4½	4½	2	23
Mathematics	x	x	x		"	1⅓ Yrs.	46	230		28	1		27		5	5	5	49
"		:	x		"	1 Yr.	31	243		17	1	8	8		7	7	4	41
"		x	x		"	⅔ "	45	215		11	5		6		1	:	5	37
Head of Botany Department	x		x	Graduate	"	⅔ "	62	332		7	2		5		:	:	4	29
Physics		x	x		"	:	32	170		5	2		3		1	1	4	26
German		x	x		"	½ Yr.	33	203		4		1	4		1	1	3	31
"	x	x	x		"	:	42	183		4	1	1	2		2	2	2	22
Latin		x	x		"	1 Yr.	17	182		6½	1½		4		2	2	3	29
"	x	x	x		"	:	30	231		2	1		2		:	:	1	24
Commercial	x	x	x	Graduate 3½ Yrs.	"		10	110		5		2	2		1	1	4	26

¹ Interpreted, Table CXLIII means that the first teacher listed teaches English, did not attend country school, did attend graded school, graduated from high school, did not attend normal school, graduated from a college or university, spent ⅓ year in post graduate work, took in university or normal school 44 hours of work that could be counted strictly professional, had in all 195 hours of credit exclusive of high school work, had 4 years of teaching experience, all of which was in high school and only one of which was in the Bloomington schools, and that one year was spent in approximately the same position now held (1913–14), and was 28 years old in October, 1913.

TABLE CXLIV

QUALIFICATIONS OF SUPERINTENDENT, PRINCIPALS, AND SUPERVISORS

	Age, October, 1913	Number Different School Systems or Districts in Which You Have Taught	Years in Bloomington Work as at Present	Years' Experience in Bloomington Schools	Years' Experience in Other Schools	Years' Experience in High School	Years' Experience in Graded Schools	Years Experience in Country Schools	Number Years' Experience in Teaching	Business College or Other Institution	Total Hours Credit Exclusive of High School	Number Hours Strictly Educational Subjects	Postgraduate Student College or University	Undergraduate Student College or University	Student Normal School	Graduate of High School	Attended Graded Schools	Attended Country School
Superintendent	38	5	4	4	.	6	.	.	15	......	380	125	......	Graduate 4 Yrs.	......	x	x	x
Principal High School	39	7	6	6	.	14	5	1	20	......	253	65	1½	"	......	x	x	x
Principal Central Building	38	5	12	15	.	.	17	3	20	......	190	35	2⁄3	"	......	2 Yrs.	x	.
Principal Mc-Calla Building	30	5	.	1	2	3	1	1	7	......	183	40	......	Graduate	......	x	.	x
Principal Fairview Building	51	3	17	21	.	.	24	.	24	......	180	45	......	"	......	x	x	.
Principal Colored School	40	6	4	4	.	.	12	2	14	3 Yrs.	90	15	......	2 Yrs.	⅓ Yr.	3 Yrs.	x	x
Supervisor Manual Training	29	4	2	2	2	2	2	1	7	......	183	25	......	Graduate	......	x	x	x

SUMMARY OF TABLE CXLII

Teachers in grades, 1913–14:

1. Total number, 37.
2. Average number of hours' credit in advance of high-school work, 142.3 or 3.2 years of college work.
3. Average number of credits in strictly professional subjects, 38.5 or 2.5 years of professional work.
4. Average number of years of experience in teaching, 8.2.
5. Average number of years' experience in Bloomington, 4.
6. Average number of years' experience in Bloomington in approximately the same position as at present, 3.8.
7. Average age, 29.9 years.
8. Extremes in ages, 23 to 46 years.
9. Middle 50 per cent in ages, 26 to 33 years.
10. Extremes in years of experience, ½ year to 21 years.
11. Middle 50 per cent in years of experience, 4 to 12 years.

SUMMARY OF TABLE CXLIII

Teachers in the high school 1913–14:

1. Total number: 15.
2. All university graduates with the exception of one who has had three and one-half years of university work.
3. Whole teaching corps averages .77 of a year of postgraduate work.
4. Average, .84 of a year's credit in strictly educational subjects.
5. Average, exclusive of year 1913–14, eight years of teaching experience.
6. Average 5.7 years' high-school teaching experience.
7. Average, 1.8 years' experience in Bloomington high school.
8. Average age is 30.5 years.
9. Extremes in ages: 22 to 49.
10. Middle 50 per cent of ages range from 26 to 31 years.

TABLE CXLV
SALARIES OF TEACHERS

	1909–10	1914–15	PER CENT OF INCREASE FROM 1909 TO 1914
Average salary of principals of buildings	$909.50	$1015.00	11.6
Average salary of high school teachers........	885.00	918.24	3.9
Average salary of grade teachers.............	576.13	622.65	8.1
Average salary of special supervisors.........	758.30	844.00	11.3

Since 1909 from 25 to 30 per cent of the teachers have been leaving the Bloomington schools each year. Of those that have left during this period 22.3 per cent left to continue their education, 16 per cent left to get married, 5.3 per cent left because of illness, 6.4 per cent left to enter another line of work, 7.4 per cent were dropped because of inefficiency, and 42.6 per cent left for better paying teaching positions.

CHAPTER VIII

SUPERVISION OF INSTRUCTION

According to the present arrangement, the superintendent is free to devote about half his time to the supervision of instruction, the other part of the time being taken up with general administrative problems. The principal of the high school has two-thirds of his time off for supervision, the office work being largely taken care of by a clerk who gives her whole time to it. The principal of the department sixth, seventh, and eighth grade school has half of her time off for supervision. She also has a clerk for full time for office work. Each of the other principals has from one-fourth to one-third time off for supervision. Two teachers give their whole time to supervising the instruction in special subjects, one in music and one in drawing.

The following table will give a detailed account of the supervisory work of the principals of the different types of school.

TABLE CXLVI

ANALYSIS OF WORK OF PRINCIPALS

	HIGH SCHOOL PRINCIPAL	DEPARTMENT PRINCIPAL	PRINCIPAL OF BUILDING WITH FIRST FIVE GRADES
Total hours per week devoted to school affairs	50	$46\frac{1}{2}$	40
Hours per week devoted to teaching and labors incidental thereto	10	15	22
Hours per week devoted to supervisory labors, any kind	35	20	8
Number of teachers supervised	17	15	8
Number hours per week to each teacher	2	1.33	1
Number of pupils in classes supervised	400	667	360
Number hours per week per pupil in classes supervised	.088	.03	.111
Salary per week	$55.00	$27.50	$22.25
Cost of service per hour	1.10	.591	.51
Weekly cost of supervision per teacher supervised	2.44	.79	.51
Weekly cost of supervision per pupil in classes supervised	.103	.0177	.0113
Hours per week to personal class-room supervision	2	9	4
Hours per teacher supervised	.118	.6	.5
Weekly cost of class-room supervision	$2.20	$5.319	$2.04
Cost per teacher supervised	.13	.355	.255

TABLE CXLVI (*Continued*)

	HIGH SCHOOL PRINCIPAL	DEPARTMENT PRINCIPAL	PRINCIPAL OF BUILDING WITH FIRST FIVE GRADES
Hours per week to office work of a purely clerical nature that could be delegated to clerks............................	None	4	2
Cost per hour of such clerical service.....		$ .591	$ .51
Weekly cost of such clerical service.......		2.364	1.02
Cost per pupil per week in classes supervised............................		.0035	.003
Cost per teacher supervised.............		.159	.113
Hours of clerical service per teacher supervised............................		.266	$\frac{1}{4}$
Hours per pupil in classes supervised.....		.006	1/180
Hours per week to office work of a professional sort that cannot be delegated to clerks, teachers' meetings, conferences with students, parents, school board, and others regarding school matters, etc....	19	5.5	2
Cost per hour........................	1.10	.591	.51
Weekly cost of these services............	$20.90	3.25	1.02
Cost per teacher supervised............	1.23	.217	.255
Cost per pupil in classes of teachers supervised............................	.052	.0048	.003
Hours of service per teacher supervised...	1.12	.366	$\frac{1}{4}$
Hours per pupil in classes supervised.....	.048	.0082	1/180

Principals observe work at their discretion and follow their own wishes in regard to the method of criticising work observed. Once a year, however, they make a written report on each teacher to be filed in the superintendent's office.

The report given below, from one of the principals, shows one use made of the form for reporting observation of recitations. A report was made near the beginning of the year, October 28th. A second report was made May 4th. The grading for both reports follows: P stands for poor, F for fair, G for good, and E for excellent.

PRINCIPAL'S REPORT ON OBSERVATION OF RECITATION

.......................PRINCIPAL   ....TEACHER VISITED

Arithmetic   SUBJECT OBSERVED   *11 : 00 A.M.*, TIME OF RECITATION

	October 28, 1913,	DATE
I. HYGIENIC CONDITIONS:	*October*	*May*
1. Ventilation................................	F	G
2. Use of available lighting.....................	P	E
3. Seating of those defective in hearing or eyesight.	E	E
4. Adjustment of seats to size of pupils..........	G	G
5. Posture of children........................		
a. At seats during study.................	G	
b. While reciting........................	G	F
6. Cleanliness of desks, floor, and room in general, as far as the janitor is concerned..........	F	F

	October	May
7. Cleanliness of desks, floor, and room in general, as far as the teacher and pupils are responsible	E	P
8. Decorations — pictures, plants, exhibitions of work, artistic drawing on blackboard, etc., general attempt to make room beautiful and homelike..............................	F	F
9. Neatness and orderliness of teacher's desk.....	-E	G
10. Neatness and orderliness of pupils' desks......	G	P
11. Quality and arrangement of teacher's blackboard writing...........................	F	F
12. Cleanliness of pupils, and attention of pupils to their general appearance..................	F	F

II. CLASS-ROOM ORGANIZATION:

	October	May
1. Promptness and orderliness of movement and response of pupils......................	F	G
2. Preparation and arrangement of tools of instruction................................	G	G
3. Economy of time in passing from one recitation to another, in having pupils leave room, pass materials, etc...........................	F	G
4. Relation of teacher and pupils toward extraordinary incidents...........................	E	
5. Lack of absence and tardiness...............	G	G
6. Situation in regard to leaving room during school hours...........................	E	F
7. Speaking out when not called on............	E	E
8. Public opinion of class.....................		
9. Degree to which strong desirable habits are manifested by class as individuals..........		F
10. Degree to which strong undesirable habits are manifested by class as individuals.........		

III. PUPILS' ATTITUDE:

	October	May
1. Evidence of genuine striving of pupils to conform to conventionalities of the school...........	E	G
2. Degree to which all pupils are busy all the time.	F	F
3. Consideration of feelings of others (Do pupils interfere consciously or unconsciously with recitation that pupil on the floor is making?).		G
4. Evidence of a stress by teacher upon both right ideas and right actions on part of pupils.....		G
5. Degree to which pupils enjoy their work — spontaneity instead of discouragement..........	F	F
6. Degree to which everyone listens when the teacher speaks.........................	G	F
7. Degree to which pupils respond freely and intelligently without having to be "pumped" for answers..............................		
8. Absence of cases of pupils working at other lessons or at something foreign to school work during recitations.......................	F	

IV. PERSONALITY OF TEACHER:

	October	May
1. Freshness and vigor brought to the work......	F	F
2. Self-control..............................		E
3. Tact....................................		
4. Sympathy...............................		
5. Adaptability.............................		
6. Quality of spoken English..................	G	G

		October	May
V. SCHOLARSHIP OF TEACHER:			
	1. Accuracy and confidence of teacher...........	G	F
	2. Degree to which teacher strikes out from text-book and supplements from other sources...		
	3. Preparation for the day and freedom from necessity of referring to text-book..............		
VI. ASSIGNMENTS:			
	1. Preparation for on part of teacher............	F	
	2. Preparation for on part of pupils.............	E	G
	3. Provide for individual differences.............		
	4. Raise real problems for pupils to meet........		
	5. Degree to which pupils feel problems are their own...................................		
	6. Help given to pupils for next day's work......		G
	7. Degree to which assignment helps to teach the pupils the real art of study................		
	8. Degree to which all members of class have definitely in mind assignment on which they are reciting.................................		
	9. Time given to it in relation to time given to recitation proper................................		
	10. Degree to which work outlined in assignment is attainable by class in preparation time available....................................		G
VII. QUESTIONS:			
	1. Concise and clear............................		
	2. Challenge attention of all members of class....		
	3. Did children have to think before answering...		
	4. Sequence of questions.......................		
	5. Questioning on part of pupils................		
	6. Distribution of among pupils.................		
	7. Advantage taken by teacher on every opportunity to ask good questions...............		
	8. Degree to which necessity of repeating questions and answers is avoided..............		
	9. Does teacher ask question or name pupil first..		Ask question
	10. Degree to which teacher avoids giving cues to right answers...........................	E	
	11. Large questions properly supported by more detailed ones............................		
VIII. SUBJECT MATTER:			
	1. Degree to which it is worth teaching..........	E	G
	2. Degree to which comprehended..............	E	G
	3. Degree to which fitted to grade.............		G
	4. Degree to which it interests pupils...........		
	5. Is it the proper amount for the period.........	Not enough	E
IX. RECITATION:			
	1. Degree to which pupils are interested.........	E	G
	2. Degree to which pupils contribute............	E	
	3. Degree to which pupils talk to each other rather than to the teacher......................		
	4. Divided logically............................		
	5. Degree to which teacher avoids "shooting over pupils' heads"............................		
	6. Degree to which teacher succeeds in keeping in the background........................	G	

	October	May
7. Real progress made by class during recitation..	F	F
8. Quantity of matter covered in relation to time given to recitation.......................	P	G
9. Success of teacher in refreshing attention and interest of pupils by pauses, sitting erect, rising, introducing unusual illustrations, in some manner breaking the monotony......	P	
10. Enthusiasm imparted to children through teacher.................................	P	P
11. Summary and driving home of instruction.....		
12. Degree to which pupils are helped successfully over individual difficulties................		
13. Articulation and enunciation.................		F
14. Degree to which teacher refuses to accept vague, indefinite, incoherent answers.............	G	
15. Degree to which teacher emphasized reflection and not merely memory work.............	G	

X. STUDY PERIOD:

1. Freedom from distractions..................	F	F
2. Industry of pupils........................	F	F

XI. ADDITIONAL POINTS OF STRENGTH AND OF WEAKNESS OBSERVED.

This teacher was not very promising to begin with and the results of the principal's efforts were not as encouraging as was hoped for but the supervision was undertaken in a systematic and thorough way and every available means was used to improve the work. The following is the report of the actual things that were done by the principal to improve the work of this teacher:

REPORT ON EFFORTS TO HELP *One* TEACHER IN .... SCHOOL

I. After several short visits at different times and in different kinds of work, I made this analysis of her weaknesses and of features of the work in which she needed help and direction.

1. Waste of time in changing from one class to another.
2. Failure to keep children in studying sections busy at profitable work.
3. Failure to analyze the real difficulties the children met in class work.
4. Lack of fire and spirit in all of the "so-called" drill work.
5. Poor arrangement of board work.
6. Permitting the children to acquire slovenly habits in written work.
7. Careless mistakes in checking up the children's work. She frequently gave 100 per cent on a paper that was not worth 100 per cent.

II. Efforts made to help *general* attitude.

1. Through general teachers' meetings we sometimes made one of these weaknesses a subject of discussion in a particular meeting. Teachers had a chance to express themselves freely on such phase of the work and valuable contributions were made by all. Through this discussion this particular teacher had a chance to benefit by the experience of others and she got the general feeling on this particular subject.
2. Through smaller group meetings, for instance a meeting of all arithmetic teachers. Here plans and devices were suggested by different teachers

which they had found to be good. Where I had observed some teacher using some such helpful device, I asked her to tell us all about it.

3. Through individual conference with this particular teacher after each visit made. By reference to my visiting book to which each teacher has access, we were able to talk about specific points observed, and the teacher had a chance not only to get my views, but I had a chance to get hers.

III. Efforts made to correct *particular* weaknesses:

1. Through visits to other teachers.

    a. To Miss —— (Fourth Month).

    Miss —— excels in ability to pass quickly from class to class and to get the children settled down to work with very little time cost. I went with this teacher into Miss ——'s room, having told her before that this was the thing I wanted her to observe.

    b. To Miss —— (Fourth Month).

    Miss —— excels in neatness and arrangement of board work and in quality of black-board writing.

    c. To Miss —— (Fourth Month).

    Miss —— excels in drawing work, in neat appearance of her room and in good drill work in arithmetic.

In each visit the teacher knew beforehand the specific thing which she was to observe, and in a conference with me after each visit we brought out prominently the contrast between the work observed and her own work.

2. Through suggestions of the principal.

    a. In my visiting book December 1st, 8th, and 16th, February 5th and 10th, and April 2d.

    b. In individual conferences.

    c. By taking a class in arithmetic one period to show the economy of finding out who in the class needed help and how to give it to them, and at the same time keep the rest of the class profitably employed.

    d. By discovering a few cases wherein the children had been permitted to form wrong habits without the teacher's knowing wherein the trouble was, I tried to make her see the importance of first being sure that each child knew the right method of procedure before giving *any* drill work.

    e. Called attention to lack of neatness in children's work.

    f. Encouraged children who were not doing their best work to come to me and show me their work whenever it was very good.

    g. Asked the other teachers with whom she was most closely associated to offer such suggestions as in their judgment could be offered tactfully. (In all cases where this was done, such suggestions were received in the spirit intended.)

    h. Two or three cases of complaint from patrons about carelessness in grading papers came to me. In each case I advised the patron to see this teacher and to call her attention to such mistakes, not in a critical or unfriendly way, but in the desire to help her.

This method of calling attention to such mistakes I felt to be more effective than my going to her and telling her that such complaint had come to me. (Am satisfied that it was the better method.)

i. We enlisted co-operation of the home in certain cases where children needed outside help and in other cases where children were troublesome in school. Teacher brought this about through notes or personal conferences with the parents.

j. By dropping into the room just for a minute or two, and commending anything at all that seemed good. These short stops I did not consider visits. (By a visit I mean observing during one or more full recitation periods. I have made this teacher fifteen such visits this year.)

The above report is an example of reports to superintendent that are highly efficient. Other reports by this same principal and others as well show that material improvement has been made in the teachers' work through such constructive criticisms. The principal, working according to a plan similar to the above, performs her main function as regards her free time during school hours; i.e., that of making poor teachers good ones; and good ones excellent ones. With such help if the poor cannot be made good there is a sound basis to work on in dropping them from the system.

Another example of a problem in supervision is furnished by the following study made by the principal of the high school; and first published by Indiana University during the spring of 1914 in "The Proceedings of a Conference on Educational Measurements."

AMOUNT OF TIME GIVEN TO PREPARATION AND RECITATION IN THE BLOOMINGTON HIGH SCHOOL

Mr. E. E. RAMSEY

This study was deemed advisable because of an occasional objection on the part of students, parents, and in some cases, teachers, regarding the amount of time that students were required to spend in preparation and class work. Under the poor housing conditions of the high school, it has for many years been the policy to allow students to leave at both morning and afternoon sessions at the close of their recitation work. Preliminary to this investigation, it was found by inspecting the programs that about 10 per cent of the students were required to put in but five forty-five minute periods per day, and more than 50 per cent were not required to put in more than six periods per day. This suggested that it was highly probable that there was an excessive amount of home work in many cases because of the low average amount of time in school. The problem was thus reduced to one of determining the total time of preparation, and an adjustment between school preparation and home preparation if the results of the study warranted it.

The method employed was that of the questionnaire, one of which was submitted to each student in the high school, and another to the teaching force. The former list was submitted to all students at the same time and was required to be answered at once. The list submitted to the teachers covered a week's work.

The following are the essentials in the student's list relating to individual subjects:

Name............................ *Date*..............................

Answer ALL of the following questions as accurately as you can. Answer all time questions in minutes or in hours.

English. ——— (Here fill in the grade of English you are carrying.)
1. How long does it take you to prepare a literature lesson?
2. How long does it take you to prepare a rhetoric lesson?
3. How long does it take you to prepare a theme assignment?
4. When do you make your preparation for English?
5. Rank English as hardest, second hardest, third hardest, or easiest.

Mathematics. ——— (Here give grade of mathematics you are carrying.)
1. How long does it take you to prepare your mathematics lesson?
2. When do you make your mathematics preparation?
3. Rank mathematics as in the English.

Similar lists were submitted in language, history, science, and commercial work.
1. What are you doing during period 1?
2. What do you do during period 2?
3. What do you do during period 3?
4. What do you do during period 4?
5. What do you do during period 5?
6. What do you do during period 6?
7. What do you do during period 7?
8. What do you do during period 8?
9. How many periods per day are you in recitation, laboratory and type-writing practice?
10. How many periods per day are you in a regular assembly? The regular assemblies are 1, 2, 3, 5, and 6.
11. How far do you come to school?
12. What subject requires most time to prepare?
13. Why?
14. How many subjects are you carrying?

The following is the list of questions and directions given to the teachers, except that the complete list covered a full week's work:

Teacher's List for the week of December 9–13, inclusive

Answer the following points as carefully and as fairly as you can. I would much prefer that the entire list be answered before there is any communication among you on the points called for, or on the purpose of the questionnaire. Please remember that you are answering these questions from the student's standpoint rather than from your own. Assign your work throughout the week in a regular way. Answer all the time questions in minutes.

Report of (Subject)..*for December 9th*

Teacher............................

Text for which these questions are answered.

1. Number of pages regular text work assigned.
2. Time it should take to prepare this assignment.
3. Number of pages library work assigned.
4. Time it should take to prepare this assignment.
5. Number of pages of permanent notes, maps, etc., assigned.
6. Time allowed for these.
7. Amount of theme work or written report work.
8. Time allowed for this work.
9. Time any other assigned line of work may take.
10. Total time for this recitation.
11. Has this been an average week for all these lines of work?

To the above list was appended a supplementary list of general questions. They are as follows:

The English, history, and mathematics teacher should make an estimate of time spent by students belonging to the various organizations in their respective departments, as to the amount of time per semester that must be spent by students belonging to each organization in actual attendance on meetings and in preparation for assigned duty.

Number of students belonging to ——— club ———.

English and history teacher should make an estimate of the amount of time necessary for the preparation of outside reading per semester.

Do you make longer or more difficult assignments than you have made in other high schools with which you have been connected?

If so, estimate the increased time or difficulty in percentage.

Do you believe that the standard of work in the high school is beyond the reach of an average student ——— or that it is too onerous? ———

Do you believe that better work would be gotten by holding students in assembly for periods four and seven?

All answers submitted by students bore evidence of a desire to answer fairly as was shown by the lack of wide ranges in the estimates, and by the fact that the few wide ranges could be readily explained by a knowledge of the pupils who answered in this way. But one list from the students was rejected.

The result of the tabulation of preparation time as given by students and teachers is shown in the following table:

TABLE CXLVII

TIME SPENT IN RECITATION AND IN PREPARATION ON PART OF PUPILS IN BLOOMINGTON HIGH SCHOOL, TEACHERS' ESTIMATES AND PUPILS' STATEMENTS

SUBJECT	AVERAGE TIME RE- PORTED BY TEACHER	AVERAGE TIME RE- PORTED BY PUPIL	STUDENT'S ESTIMATE LESS TEACHER'S ESTIMATE	TEACHER'S ESTIMATE LESS STU- DENT'S ESTI- MATE	TEACHER'S ESTIMATE VARIES FROM AVERAGE OF STUDENT'S ESTI- MATE FOR DEPARTMENT
English 1 — Literature....	40	54	14	..	−15
" 2 — "	35	49	14	..	−20
" 3 — "	43	47	4	..	−12
" 4 — "	50	54	4	..	....
" 5 — "	60	69	9	..	+5
" 6 — "	50	54	4	..	−5
" 7 — "	60	63	3	..	+5
" 8 — "	45	51	6	..	−10
Average.................	42	55	..	..	....
Sum equals.............	..	..	..	..	−52
English 1 — Rhetoric......	33	51	18	..	−18
" 2 — "	55	49	0	6	+4
" 3 — "	45	44	..	1	−6
" 4 — "	60	44	..	16	+9
" 5 — "	60	56	..	4	+9
" 6 — "	65	49	..	16	+14
" 7 — "	60	49	..	11	+9
" 8 — "	45	67	..	22	−6
Average.................	53	51	..	..	....
Sum equals.............	..	..	..	..	+15
English 1 — Composition..	55	80	25	..	−37
" 2 — " ..	55	55	10	..	−37
" 3 — " ..	58	69	11	..	−34
" 4 — " ..	60	86	26	..	−32
" 5 — " ..	66	104	44	..	−32
" 6 — " ..	70	128	58	..	−22
" 7 — " ..	60	111	51	..	−32
" 8 — " ..	75	89	14	..	−17
Average.................	62	92	..	..	....
Sum equals.............	..	..	..	..	−243
Latin 1..................	55	66	5	..	−24
" 2..................	67	66	..	15	−12
" 3..................	75	100	25	..	−4
" 4..................	70	82	12	..	−9
" 5..................	75	84	9	..	−4
" 6..................	75	79	4	..	−4
" 7..................	70	88	18	..	−9
" 8..................	75	87	12	..	−4
Average..................	70	79	..	..	....
Sum equals.............	..	͞.	..	..	−70

TABLE CXLVII (*Continued*)

German 1	44	52	7	..	−15
" 2	49	53	4	..	−10
" 3	48	53	5	..	−11
" 4	55	54	..	1	−4
" 5	57	62	5	..	−2
" 6	48	66	18	..	+11
" 7	58	65	7	..	−1
" 8	67	66	..	1	+8
Average	53	59	..	..	....
Sum equals	..	..	..	..	−24
Mathematics 1	76	49	..	27	+14
" 2	68	79	11	..	+6
" 3	47	49	2	..	−15
" 4	56	67	11	..	−6
" 5	93	58	..	35	+29
" 6	65	67	7	..	−2
Average	67	62	..	..	....
Sum equals	..	..	..	..	+26
History 1	61	52	..	9	−7
" 2	77	81	4	..	+9
" 3	62	53	..	9	−6
" 4	81	78	..	3	+13
" 5	65	66	1	..	−3
" 6	87	76	..	11	....
Average	72	68	..	..	....
Sum equals	..	..	..	..	+6
Physical Geography 1	55	42	..	13	+11
" " 2	47	45	..	2	+3
Average	51	44	..-	..	....
Sum equals	..	..	..	..	+14
Botany 1	52	45	..	7	−2
" 2	60	63	3	..	+6
Average	56	54	..	..	....
Sum equals	..	..	..	..	+4
Physics 7	65	70	5	..	−6
" 8	76	72	..	4	+5
Average	72	71	..	..	....
Sum equals	..	..	..	..	−1
Commercial 2	59	61	2	..	−12
" 3	57	111	54	..	−14
" 4	41	73	32	..	−30
" 5	41	81	40	..	−30
" 6	46	68	22	..	−28
" 7	45	57	12	..	−26
" 8	50	47	..	3	−21
Average	48	71	..	..	....
Sum equals	..	..	..	..	−158

Table CXLVII shows the estimates by teacher (col. 1), and by pupils (col. 2). Column 3 shows the difference between column 2 and column 1, thus showing that teachers have underestimated time of preparation. Column 4 shows the difference between column 1 and column 2, showing overestimation by teachers. Column 5 shows the difference between the average for a given department and the pupils' estimate, — the minus signs (−) indicating that teachers have underestimated, and the plus sign (+) showing overestimation.

Inspection of the summaries of each department as shown in column 5 reveals that (1) English composition shows the greatest underestimation, (2) commercial subjects, (3) Latin, (4) English classics, (5) German, (6) physics, (7) botany, (8) history, (9) physical geography, (10) rhetoric, and (11) mathematics following in the order named. It is a striking fact that mathematics has the heaviest overestimation.

The teachers' estimates show a rather wide range of variation between departments. The largest figures are in (1) history and (1) physics. Then follow (2) Latin, (3) mathematics, (4) English composition, (5) botany, (6) rhetoric and German, (7) physical geography, (8) commercial, and (9) English classics. Taking the highest estimates as a basis, the lowest subject, English classics,

TABLE CXLVIII

Time of Preparation of Subjects as Listed by Teachers and Pupils

Estimate of Time by	Class	English	Latin	German	Mathematics	History	Physical Geography	Botany	Physics	Commercial	Combined Time for Recitation	Laboratory	Total Time	Using Smaller Number as a Base the Other Estimate Varies by Per Cent
Teacher	9B	40	55	..	76	..	55	..	..	..	135	..	451	5
Student	9B	54	60	..	49	..	42	..	..	..	135	..	430	
Teacher	9B	40	55	..	76	..	..	..	..	55	180	..	406	0.5
Student	9B	54	60	..	49	..	..	..	..	61	180	..	404	
Teacher	9A	35	67	..	68	..	..	60	..	..	135	90	435	8
Student	9A	49	52	..	79	..	..	63	..	..	135	90	468	
Teacher	9A	35	..	49	68	..	..	..	..	59	180	..	391	7
Student	9A	49	..	53	79	..	..	..	..	61	180	..	422	
Teacher	10B	43	75	..	47	61	..	..	..	..	180	..	406	5
Student	10B	47	100	..	49	52	..	..	..	..	180	..	428	
Teacher	10B	43	..	49	47	..	..	..	..	57	180	..	376	17
Student	10B	47	..	53	49	..	..	..	..	111	180	..	440	
Teacher	10A	50	..	54	56	77	..	..	..	..	180	..	417	5
Student	10A	54	..	55	67	81	..	..	..	..	180	..	437	
Teacher	10A	50	70	..	56	..	..	..	..	41	180	..	397	14
Student	10A	54	82	..	67	..	..	..	..	73	180	..	452	
Teacher	11B	60	75	..	93	62	..	..	..	..	180	..	470	5
Student	11B	69	84	..	58	53	..	..	..	..	180	..	449	
Teacher	11B	60	..	57	93	..	..	..	..	41	180	45	476	4
Student	11B	69	..	62	58	..	..	..	..	81	180	45	495	
Teacher	11A	50	75	..	60	81	..	..	..	..	180	..	446	3
Student	11A	54	79	..	67	78	..	..	..	..	180	..	458	
Teacher	11A	50	..	48	60	..	..	..	..	46	180	45	429	12
Student	11A	54	..	66	67	..	..	..	..	68	180	45	480	
Teacher	12B	60	70	..	..	..	..	..	65	..	135	63	458	11
Student	12B	63	88	..	..	66	..	..	76	..	135	63	411	
Teacher	12B	60	..	58	..	..	..	..	65	45	135	108	471	10
Student	12B	63	75	65	..	..	..	..	76	57	135	108	517	
Teacher	12A	45	..	..	..	87	..	..	70	..	135	63	475	2
Student	12A	57	87	..	..	76	..	..	72	..	135	63	484	
Teacher	12A	45	..	67	..	..	..	..	70	50	135	108	475	2
Student	12A	51	..	66	..	..	..	..	72	47	135	108	479	

shows but 58 per cent as much time needed for the latter subject as for physics and history. The widest variation in the students' and the teachers' estimates exist in composition and commercial. Practically all other subjects are fairly uniform in these two items. Composition and commercial occupy the position mentioned largely because of the amount of writing in both lines and speed practice in the commercial work.

Table CXLVIII shows two possible programs for each class from both teachers' and students' figures. The striking fact is that, when summed, the two sets of results are very close together, thus leading to the important conclusion that individual departments needed adjustment rather than the course as a whole. The percentage column shows the degree of uniformity in the two results. Nine of the sixteen percentages of variation from the lowest estimate are practically negligible, while none is seriously large. Another important point brought out by this table — but a point which no attempt was made to determine — is the amount of time a high school student should actually spend in his preparation and recitation.

A rather peculiar relation between the number who failed in their "longest" subject is that there is no correlation between the length of subject and the failures. Hence the time of preparation reduces itself simply to a problem of the time element. Neither is the correlation between the most difficult subject and failures large at all.

It was noted above that teachers had overestimated in some subjects and underestimated in others. There is no correlation whatever between these estimates and the percentage of failure. Failures thus seem to resolve themselves into problems of the subject and not to the length or difficulty, or to the failure of either the teacher or student to estimate closely the time element.

On the question as to what subject requires the most time for preparation, the totals show that 62 per cent of physics students rank that subject so; 44 per cent of Latin students next; 29 per cent of English students next; then follow mathematics, 26 per cent; German, 19 per cent; history, 17 per cent; botany, 15 per cent; physical geography, 7 per cent; and commercial, 5 per cent. The reasons given for the amount of time required for preparation are of interest: Of the 362 students who report on this question, 173 of them speak of the difficulty of subject selected as being the cause; 68 believe that the length of assignments is the main factor; while 16 select length and difficulty combined as being the cause. No other reason assigned has any considerable number of votes. The number selecting length of assignments is indicative of the fact that was made previously, that assignments were not, on the average, too long.

All answers given in both lists have been tabulated, but the space allotted this paper precludes further discussion of these results. On the basis of the results obtained, recommendations were made to the following departments: (1) The rhetoric assignments were somewhat overestimated by the teachers while the composition work was seriously underestimated. It was recommended that there be an adjustment between these two lines of work. (2) The work in physics, while the two estimates of time agree closely, was deemed too heavy, and it was suggested that the work be made somewhat lighter. (3) The work in history was likewise rather heavy, and the same suggestion was made as for physics.

The following outlines indicate in a definite way the lines of work undertaken by supervisory and administrative officers of the schools and by the clerks in their offices. They also show the proportion of time devoted to each activity. It is immediately clear that principals of buildings should be more free from recitations in order to have more time for work of a supervisory character.

DIARY SHOWING THE DISTRIBUTION OF THE SUPERINTENDENT'S TIME FOR ONE MONTH (November 6 to December 6, 1913).

Thursday, November 6. Left on 4:10 P.M. train for Indianapolis to attend meeting of City and Town Superintendents' Association.

Friday, November 7. Attended Superintendents' meeting and came home Friday night.

Saturday, November 8. Met Dr. Strayer and with him went over organization of school system from the standpoint of the superintendent's office. At 10:00 A.M. held Teachers' Meeting with Dr. Strayer as speaker. In afternoon met three principals and five teachers for conferences.

Monday, November 10. Visited every teacher in system except two. Went in for from two to five minutes to get general view of all the work. In the afternoon answered four days' accumulation of mail. Had a conference with principal of high school on the plan for installing a clock system in the new High School Building, after which I went to the McCalla Building for a teachers' meeting from 3:45 to 5:15. Dr. Haggerty opened the discussion at the meeting.

Tuesday, November 11. Visited at McCalla Building:

First teacher — strong section in geography. Weak section in arithmetic.
Second teacher — two classes — 5B in arithmetic and 5A in reading.

Third teacher — 6ʙ grammar, 6ᴀ grammar, 6ʙ spelling, 6ᴀ spelling.

Talked with each teacher about strong and weak points observed.

From 11:45 to 12:15 discussed with principal the work I had seen and mentioned points I would like him to observe in the teaching of the three teachers observed.

In the afternoon, worked in office, planning for school survey, and gathering data for School Board meeting at 4:00 ᴘ.ᴍ. 4:00 to 5:30, meeting with School Board. 5:30 to 5:45, meeting with contractor for High School Building.

5:45 to 6:15, conference in connection with the problem of improving the teaching of composition.

7:00–8:00, met Dr. Haggerty for conference in connection with future McCalla teachers' meetings.

8:30–9:00, listened to a report of State Fire Protection Committee on advisable changes in school buildings to make them safer from fire.

Wednesday, November 12.

8:00–8:20, answered correspondence in office.

8:30 to recess, gave arithmetic test at Fairview to grades 3ᴀ–5ᴀ inclusive.

From recess to noon gave tests to Central at 3ᴀ–4ᴀ grades.

1:15–2:30, gave tests in arithmetic at Central to grades 5ʙ and 5ᴀ.

2:30–3:00, conference with Professor Black on experiment in reading to be made in Central Building.

3:00–3:15, conference with president of Public Library Board over possibility of an arrangement whereby School Board might aid in building the Library Building and in return have the privilege of putting the school administration offices in the Library Building.

3:15–4:15, prepared for meeting of principals.

4:15–5:30, meeting of principals.

Met book representative from 7–8:10 in conference on new series of primary readers.

9–9:30, read literary selections in search of suitable portions to use in reading experiment in 7th and 8th grades.

Thursday, November 13.

8:00–9:00, answered correspondence.

9:10–11:30, gave abstract arithmetic test in McCalla Building to grades 3ᴀ–6ʙ inclusive.

11:35–12:00, conferred with principal on defects shown in arithmetic test.

1:15–2:30, gave tests in abstract arithmetic at McCalla, 6ʙ and 6ᴀ grades.

2:15–2:30, conference with a representative of a book company.

2:45–3:35, gave arithmetic tests in Colored School, grades 4th, 5th, and 6th.

3:40–4:15, in office compared grades made on same test in same grades 2 and 4 years before.

4:15–5:10, conference with Mr. Mahurin, the architect for the High School Building.

7:00–9:30, meeting with School Board, architect, and contractor to discuss modification of plans of High School Building to bring total cost within the financial possibilities of the board.

Friday, November 14.

Morning spent in office.

From noon Friday to late Wednesday (including Tuesday night) visited schools in Gary, Ind., and Hammond, Ind., and attended State Charities Convention in Gary.

Wednesday, November 19.

8:00–9:15, in office.

9:15–10:30, observed the work of two teachers.

10:30–12:00, discussed with principal of Central Building some of the problems to be taken up for study this year.

1:00–2:00, in office.

2:15–3:45, observed the work of two teachers at Fairview.

3:45–4:15, meeting with Fairview teachers and Dr. Haggerty introducing the problem for careful study by Fairview teachers during the winter, "What should one know about an individual in order to give him the proper vocational guidance and how can the desired data be collected and profitably kept?"

Thursday, November 20.

Visited schools at McCalla all morning.

8:30–9:00, observed teaching in mechanical drawing.

9:00–10:10, observed one teacher, all three sections in reading.

10:10–10:25 (recess period), discussed with teacher points that I thought deserved emphasis.

10:25–11:15, observed work of a third teacher.

11:15–11:30, discussed work with this third teacher.

11:30–12:10, discussed with the principal of the building the work of teachers observed. Principal had visited one hour and a half with me.

1:00–2:00, in office, conference with truant officer advising with him in regard to granting requests for books and clothing that had been applied for.

2:00–3:00, at new High School Building discussing proposed changes with the contractor.

3:00–3:45, conference with high school principal in regard to proposed changes in the curriculum.

3:45–4:15, made final preparation for principals' meeting.

4:15–5:30, meeting of the principals.

5:30–5:40, met with committee presenting petition for use of school building for holding religious meetings.

Friday, November 21.

7:45–10:00, office work answering correspondence, directing some school visitors (teachers from Shoals, Ind.) to the various buildings where they could find the work they were looking for. Getting ready some estimates of future school expenses to be used in the School Board meeting.

10:00–12:00, meeting of the School Board to arrange final plans whereby the heating plant in the new High School Building could be financed.

1:00–2:00, received various callers on school business.

2:00–3:00, discussed with truant officer the advisability of bringing suit to compel attendance at school, and devising means whereby those who are unlawfully absent from school might be discovered with the least loss of time.

3:00–3:45, selected from a list of possible tests for measuring efficiency of pupils in regular schoolroom subjects the different ones that we shall want to try out in the Bloomington schools this year.

3:45–4:00, conference with Colored principal over some points of special application to Colored School that were not taken up in the principals' meeting yesterday.

4:00–5:00, kept office hours, and between calls worked on a form for financial tables to be used at the close of the year in the report to the School Board.

5:00–5:55, conference with music supervisor in regard to music in the grades.

Saturday, November 22.

8:00–9:00, conference with truant officer in regard to an especially difficult case to handle.

9:00–10:00, conference with committee on Night School preparatory to reopening the Night School.

10:00–10:45, conference with teacher regarding an especially delicate case in discipline that she was voluntarily asking my advice about.

10:45–11:00, signed letters.

Monday, November 24.

8:00–8:30, correspondence.

8:30–9:15, conference with applicant for position.

9:15–10:00, worked on a test in spelling to be given in all grades.

10:00–10:45, meeting with School Board.

10:45–11:15, continued work on spelling test.

11:15–11:35, conference with janitor of Central Building in regard to method of keeping track of supplies issued by him to janitors and principals of other buildings.

11:35–12:00, continued work on spelling test.

1:00–1:30, preparation for School Board meeting at 2:50.

1:30–2:45, conference with manual training teacher concerning a proposed change in some of the problems designed for 7th and 8th grade boys in the woodworking course.

2:50–3:50, School Board meeting.

4:00–5:30, meeting with McCalla teachers for discussion of the problem they are working on this year.

5:30–6:00, meeting with principal of McCalla Building on points brought out in the teachers' meeting.

Tuesday, November 25.

8:00–9:30, correspondence.

9:30–12:00, conferences with bidders and architect preparatory to meeting of School Board in the afternoon for the purpose of closing the contracts for heating and plumbing in the new High School Building.

1:00–5:15, School Board meeting in connection with financial arrangements for heating and plumbing for new High School.

Wednesday, November 26.

8:00–8:20, answered correspondence.

8:30–11:00, gave abstract arithmetic tests to 6B's and 6A's at Central, to the 6B's at Fairview, and to the 7th and 8th grades at the Colored School.

11:00–11:45, observed the 8th grade arithmetic and 7th grade grammar recitations at Colored School.

11:45–12:10, discussed with a teacher of above grades points that needed emphasis.

1:15–2:30, gave abstract arithmetic tests to 7th and 8th grades at Central.

2:40–3:30, conference with Professor Haggerty concerning the teachers' meetings at McCalla and Fairview, where special problems are being studied under the joint direction of Professor Haggerty and the superintendent of schools.

3:30–6:00, meeting with committee responsible for working out a questionnaire to be submitted next Monday afternoon at 4:00 o'clock to High School and Departmental teachers in connection with the proposed social, sanitary, industrial, and mercantile survey of the city.

Thursday, Thanksgiving Vacation, November 27.

Friday, November 28. Vacation.

8:00–12:00, worked on an abstract arithmetic test to be given in three weeks to see if weaknesses discovered in last test have been overcome.

1:30–5:15, worked on a table showing average ages of pupils in school fall term 1912.

Saturday, November 29.

8:00–12:00, conference with janitor of Central Building in regard to the purchase of some paint to be used on old blackboards. Conference with president of Public Library Board in regard to the possibility of providing school administration offices in the proposed new Library Building. Conference with manual training teacher in regard to new problems to be undertaken in the manual training classes. Conference with the county superintendent of schools looking toward a large representation of teachers from Monroe County at the State Teachers' Association at Indianapolis during the Christmas holidays. Worked during the remainder of the morning on age-grade tables for fall of 1912–13.

2:00–3:00, conference with treasurer of the School Board in connection with word received in regard to furnishing heat plant at High School.

3:00–4:30, inspected work on new High School Building.

Monday, December 1.

8:00–8:30, visited Central Building to arrange with principal and teachers for visits to observe work in primary grades and in history teaching in 6th, 7th, and 8th grades.

8:30–11:30, visited primary grades at McDoel and at Prospect.

11:40–12:00, outlined work for clerk in office.

1:00 to close of school in afternoon, visited primary grades at Fairview.

3:50–5:20, teachers' meeting at Fairview Building.

Tuesday, December 2.

9:00–12:00, visited all morning at McCalla Building: 1B's in all of their reading; 4B's in geography and language upon request of teacher in order to advise with her and the principal inregard to the desirability of giving three of the strong 4B's a trial in the 4A grade. Result — two of the three were put ahead.

1:15–2:00, visited another room of 1B's in McCalla.

2:00–2:25, visited music supervisor during the period she had the 5A's and 6B's together.

2:30–2:45, visited Colored School to suggest a change in the program on Thursday to accommodate me in my effort to see all of the history work of the system in grades, 6, 7, and 8, in the two days, Wednesday and Thursday.

2:50–5:00, in office answering correspondence and preparing for arithmetic meeting tomorrow afternoon.

Wednesday, December 3.

9:00–3:00, visited all day in Central School Building observing the history teaching in grades 6, 7, and 8.

4:00–5:15, held a meeting of all arithmetic teachers from third grade up to discuss the results of the test in fundamentals finished last week. Half of the period was given over to a report from the most successful teacher of the fundamentals in arithmetic telling how she gets her results.

Thursday, December 4.

8:00–8:30, conference with head of the history department in high school with whom visits were made yesterday observing history teaching in grades 6, 7, and 8.

8:30–9:00, observed 6B history at Fairview.

9:10–10:10, observed 6B and 6A history at McCalla.

10:10–11:30, further conference with head of history department in regard to teachers' meeting to be held at 4:00 o'clock.

11:30–12:00, in office answering correspondence.

1:15–2:20, observed 6B and 5A history at McCalla.

2:30–3:35, observed 6B, 7B, 8B history at Colored School.

4:00–5:15, teachers' meeting led by head of the history department in the High School; a criticism of work observed for past two days.

Friday, December 5.

8:00–8:25, answered correspondence in office.

8:30–11:15, visited with primary teacher at McDoel and primary teacher at Fairview (both new to their positions). At the Central Building observed the work of the teacher there in the primary grades.

11:15–11:50, conference with teachers over things observed.

1:00–2:00, conference with High School principal over proposed survey to be undertaken by High School and Departmental teachers.

2:00–3:30, observed teaching in the commercial department at the High School.

3:30–4:00, conference with commercial teachers over work observed and over the subject of teaching writing to the grade teachers.

4:00–5:00, meeting with grade teachers for the teaching of writing. Meeting conducted by commercial teacher.

5:00–5:30, conference with principal of Colored School over work observed yesterday in his history teaching in 6th, 7th, and 8th grades.

LIST OF DUTIES OF CLERK IN SUPERINTENDENT'S OFFICE AS OUTLINED BY THE CLERK AS A RESULT OF TABULATING HER OFFICE WORK FOR ONE MONTH

Notify members of School Board of meetings.

Attend Board meetings and write up minutes of meetings.

Make out warrants and mail for all bills allowed.

Make out warrants for pay roll each month and deliver to the different buildings.

Make out warrants for all bonds, coupons, and special estimates when presented for payment.

Post from warrant book to ledger, footing up both warrant book and ledger to balance.

Paste paid invoices in invoice book.

Keep itemized account of all orders sent out from office to local dealers.

Prepare teachers' contracts.

Make report to School Board each month.

Assist in making out pay roll at beginning of year, and calling into office licenses of teachers.

Make typewritten copy of pay roll, list of teachers, with addresses, etc.

Answer correspondence — mostly by dictation.

Order all materials used in the schools.

Fill out questionnaires and reports in regard to school system.

Prepare copies of teachers' application blanks, reports by classes, estimates on promotions, blanks for collecting data.

Summarize monthly reports from each building each month, and prepare yearly report at close of school.

Look after distribution of materials and supplementary readers.

Typewrite various reports sent in to the office.

Typewrite superintendent's addresses given at various teachers' meetings and superintendents' meetings.

Look after all record sheets and cards on file in superintendent's office.

Notify principals of all meetings called. Also all general announcements to be made to the teachers through the principals.

Typewrite points discussed in principals' meetings.

File correspondence, reports, etc.

Make typewritten copies of examination questions as made out by teachers for meetings. Typewrite revised lists. Typewrite all special examinations, tests, and directions for same.

Make copies of examination summaries.

Assist in working out special problems with the superintendent.

Prepare typewritten copies of courses of study.

Keep inventory of materials.

Prepare and send out claims for tuition of transfers to the various township trustees.

Make out yearly reports for county superintendent to be sent to the state and to the U. S. Commissioner of Education.

Answer telephone calls.

Fill in data on accumulation record cards in office from principals' cards.

Keep principals and school inspector in touch with each other in regard to school examinations.

Make out orders for truant officer for supplies for poor children.

Fill out work certificates.

Make secretary of Board's bill for supplies furnished poor children to be presented to county commissioners.

Make schedule of bonded indebtedness.

Make schedule of insurance.

WORK OF PRINCIPAL FOR ONE WEEK — HIGH SCHOOL
May 4–8, 1914

May 4:   Morning

Book sales
Excuses
Conferences with three teachers
Class — one period
Grading geography papers — one period
Assembly — one period
Work on problem of grades
Office work — one period — making stencils for questionnaire

                        Afternoon

Book sales
Excuses
Office work — three periods
Conference with teachers (5)
Conference with student (2)
Telephone calls
Teachers' meeting
Routine business
Presentation of results of study of class of 1905

May 5:   Morning

Book sales
Excuses
Conference with teachers (3)
Class — one period
Grading geography papers — one period
Assembly — one period
Office work — one period
Correspondence

Afternoon

Book sales
Excuses
Conference with observation students as to plan of work
Conference with teacher
Office work — two periods

May 6:   Morning

Excuses and book sales
Case of discipline
Class — one period
Grading papers — one period
Assembly and work on problem — one period
Correspondence and office work — one hour

Afternoon

Cases of discipline (4)
Observation with observation students for one period, conference at close of
period
Superintendent's office — one hour
Conference with candidate for a position
Office work
Conference with a committee of juniors

May 7:   Morning

Excuses and book sales
Conference with students (3)
Election of editor and manager of *Optimist*
Class work — two periods
Assembly, one period, combined with office work
Office work on problem

Afternoon

Excuses and book sales
Junior class meeting — one hour
Conference with teachers (5)
Change of program for P.M.
Conference with observation students
Conference with a candidate for a position
Conference at University, 3:00–5:00

May 8:   Morning

Book sales
Excuses
Conference with students (3)
Conference with teachers (3)
Class work — one period
Grading of papers — one period
Assembly, one period, and work on problem
Office work — correspondence — one hour

Afternoon
Excuses and book sales
Conference with students
Conferences with teachers (4)
Phone Dr. Foley concerning a candidate
Observation students — two periods — conference following
Office work — one period

WORK OF CLERK FOR ONE WEEK — HIGH SCHOOL PRINCIPAL'S OFFICE

December 1–5, 1913

December 1:

8:15–8:30, Library books

   8:33, Announcements
Telephone

   9:17, Library period
Attendance
Tabulation of same
Attendance record in books
Tardy records
Work on monthly report

10:00, Library
Monthly report
Telephone

10:45, Office
Sales
Stamping magazines
Report

11:30, Office
Report — tabulation

1:00–1:47, Office
Attendance
Tabulation
Work on records and cards

   2:33, Library
Records and cards

   3:17, Library
Records and cards

   4:00, Check out library books
Count paper for sale
Sales

December 2:

Library books
Notices to section rooms
Tardy excuses
Telephone

Library
  Attendance
  Tabulation
  Attendance in books
  Records and cards
Office
  Records
  Sales
Office
  Records
  Mimeograph
Office
  Stamping books
  Records
Office
  Attendance, tabulation
  Central office
Library
  Tabulation
Library
  Library books
  Sales

December 3:

Library books
  Sales
  Excuses
Library
  Attendance
  Tabulation
  Attendance recorded
  Copying mechanical drawing grades
Office
  Sales
  Stamp magazines
  Records
Office
  Records and cards
Office
  Tabulation
  Finished German examination
Office
  Announcements
  Attendance
  Tabulation
Library
  Tabulation
Library
  Tabulation
  Books and sales

December 4:

    Library books
      Notices to section rooms
    Library
      Attendance
      Tabulation
      Attendance and tardies recorded
      Tabulation
    Office
      Count paper
      Inventory of books on hand
    Office
      Mimeograph work
      Tabulation
      Attendance
      Stamp books
      Recorded Mathematics grades
    Library
      Tabulation
    Library
      List of omitted grades for the six weeks
    Library
      Books
      Letter; names of graduating class to college in Ohio

December 5:

    Books, sales
    Notices
    Library
      Attendance, tabulation of same
      Attendance and tardies
    Office
      Tabulation
    Office
      Páper and pens for sale
    Office
    Bank
    Tabulation
    Tabulation of attendance
    Office
      Attendance
      Cards
    Library
      Cards
    Library
      Cards
      Books
    Books in order

WORK OF PRINCIPAL OF CENTRAL BUILDING FOR ONE WEEK

December 1–5, 1913

Monday, December 1:
8:00– 8:40, Entered six children new to Bloomington
             O.K.'d excuses for absences
             Three children reported for tardiness
             Short conference with Superintendent
8:40– 9:10, Wrote business letters
             Planned building meeting
9:10–10:10, Teaching
10:10–10:25, Hall and playground
10:25–11:20, Visited third grade teacher
11:20–11:45, Visited geography teacher

12:55– 1:15, Entered one new pupil
             O.K.'d excuses
             Two telephone calls about absent pupils
             One mother called with child who had been absent
1:15– 2:00, Worked on monthly report
2:00– 2:30, Teaching
2:30– 2:45, Hall and playground
2:45– 3:15, Teaching
3:15– 3:45, Office work, making transfers, etc.
4:00– 5:00, Teachers' meeting

Tuesday, December 2:
8:00– 8:30, O.K.'d excuses for absences
             Placed one new pupil
8:30– 9:10, Conference with a parent
             Answered four telephone calls
             Prepared assignments for next day's classes
9:10–10:10, Teaching
10:10–10:25, Playground
10:25–10:50, Schedule for Mr. Smith and Mr. Williams for visiting history
             classes
10:50–11:50, Visiting classes

12:55– 1:15, O.K.'d excuses
             Answered telephone calls
1:15– 2:00, Visiting
2:00– 2:30, Teaching
2:30– 2:45, Playground
2:45– 3:15, Teaching
3:15– 3:45, Worked on distributing 6A and 7B into three classes with
             reference to buildings in which they got 6B training
3:45– 4:10, Miscellaneous business
4:10– 4:40, Conference with a second and a fourth grade teacher

Wednesday, December 3:

        Visited all day with Mr. Smith and, Mr. Williams in history classes except when teaching

4:00– 5:15, Attended an arithmetic round-table; Mr. Smith presiding

Thursday, December 4:

8:00– 8:30, O.K.'d excuses
            Sent children to Dr. Woolery
            Settled an unruly boy
            Talked with literature teacher about class of day before

8:30– 8:45, Writing letters

8:45– 9:10, Visiting fifth-grade teacher

9:10–10:10, Teaching

10:10–10:25, Playground

10:25–11:40, Visiting second-grade teacher

11:40–11:50, Showing office girl how to average spelling grades

1:15– 1:30, Conference with sewing teacher

1:30– 2:00, Made a round of department, two or three minutes in a room, to see how measles was affecting attendance

2:00– 3:15, Teaching

3:15– 3:45, Office work

4:00– 5:15, History round-table

Friday, December 5:

8:00– 8:30, Office work

8:30– 9:10, Visiting first-grade teacher

9:10–10:10, Teaching

10:25–11:30, Visiting second-grade teacher

12:55– 1:15, Office work

1:15– 2:00, Worked on comparative standing of pupils trained in 6B in the different buildings on the abstract arithmetic test given by Mr. Smith

2:00– 3:15, Teaching

3:15– 5:00, Worked on the returns for second six weeks in spelling

OFFICE GIRL'S WORK FOR ONE WEEK — CENTRAL

November 24–26, 1913

Monday, November 24:

Dusted
Recorded excused absences and tardies
Prepared writing material to be distributed to teachers
Answered telephone
Collected names of absent ones from each room
Kept record of books which the history pupils borrowed
Distributed writing material to teachers
Went to Miss McBride's room for arithmetic papers

Washed blackboard and copied her work
Reminded two teachers to bring in list asked for
Recorded excused absences
Answered telephone
Copied work for principal
Hunted for and found some music books for Miss Peterson — told her they
were in the office
Watched in the assembly room
Collected names of absent ones from each room
Watched children who had to remain after school while teachers attended a
meeting
Answered the telephone twice

Tuesday, November 25:

Went to Miss Ratcliff's room
Dusted office
Recorded absences and tardies
Made a transfer
Recorded absences for each room
Stopped at superintendent's office
Stopped at bank
Called Miss Kiff and Miss Ratcliff to the office
Kept record of books returned and borrowed by pupils
Recorded absences and tardies
Telephoned principal of McCalla Building and asked him to send sheets and
cards of transferred pupils to Central
Handed Miss Tudor a note
Sent Miss Graves and Miss Chambers their monthly reports
Watched in assembly room
Answered the telephone
Took a notice to all the teachers
Made a list of all pupils who did not know the alphabet in each room and
gave each teacher her list
Recorded names of afternoon absentees
Took messages to Miss Denny, Miss Ikerd, and Miss Hunter
Answered the telephone twice

Wednesday, November 26:

Handed each teacher her list of pupils who did not know the alphabet
Dusted
Gave each teacher her pay check
Made blanks for arithmetic test given by Mr. Smith — one for each section
Handed these to teachers
Gave Miss Denny and Miss Tudor sheets and cards for transferred pupils
Recorded excused absences
Kept record of books loaned to pupils
Stopped at bank
Recorded list of absent ones in each room
Answered telephone

Looked up standing of Lavender children — telephoned them to superintendent's office
Called third-floor teachers to office
Took two messages to Miss Denny
Took two messages to Miss Ikerd
Took a message to Miss Gourley
Took a message to Miss Osborne
Recorded excused absences
Answered the telephone
Returned records to teachers
Gave blank sheet and cards to Miss Ikerd for new pupil
Answered telephone
Took message to Miss Hunter's room
Watched in assembly room
Recorded names of absent pupils
Handed each teacher a blank for spelling test
Answered telephone
Called McCalla Building by phone
Took monthly enrollment
Made a total of all the monthly reports

WORK OF PRINCIPAL FOR ONE WEEK — McCALLA

Report of work of principal during hours not teaching:
Time — 8:00–9:50 A.M. 12:40–2:05 P.M.

Tuesday: Morning

Entered a child new to the system
Examined child on account of sickness and sent him to Dr. Woolery
Visited first-grade teacher for music, 25 minutes
Visited 3B teacher for music, 25 minutes
Visited 3A teacher for music, 20 minutes

Afternoon

Worked on children who were tardy, attempting to cut down tardiness
Visited rooms and impressed same on teachers

Wednesday: Morning

Continued work on tardiness
Worked with case of truancy
Visited one room for purpose of later making a grading

Afternoon

Settled business with art company
Visited one room to determine what should be done with two children

Thursday: Morning

Transferred child into building
Visited room with superintendent

Afternoon

Entered new pupil
Worked on tardiness
Visited room

Friday: Morning

Worked on a report for superintendent, 15 minutes
Case of sickness required 15 minutes
Case of tardiness worked with
Visited one room

Afternoon

Conducted music in each of four rooms for about 15 minutes

Monday: Morning

Conducted music in each of five rooms

Afternoon

Worked on music for five rooms as directed by Miss Peterson
Gave Miss Carmichael's room first of a series of examinations to determine
    cause of slowness of four pupils
(In the above report there is no mention of time spent with the truant officer
    or patrons, who came to discuss problems concerning children)

WORK OF PRINCIPAL FOR ONE WEEK — FAIRVIEW

About three-fourths of the time of the Fairview principal is taken up in regular
teaching.

November 17–21, 1913

November 17:

(Taught Eight Recitations)

Received two pupils who had been quarantined
Placed three new pupils
Telephoned to school office for janitor
Straightened out a street quarrel
Telephoned about transfers
Answered phone from office
Answered two calls from patrons
Sent record sheet and transfers to McCalla
Sent record sheets to office
Prepared for "building meeting"
Visited three rooms
Teachers' meeting

November 18:

(Taught Six Recitations)

Placed two new pupils
Phoned secretary of Board of Health
Telephoned to office about missing records
Answered call of patron

Truant report
Two telephone calls
Visited four rooms
Answered telephone
Received patron who came to see about a child

November 19:
(Taught Seven Recitations)
Settled street quarrel in which six pupils were involved
Fire drill
Talked in rooms that made mistakes in drill
Interviewed two tardy pupils
Repeated the drill
Answered call of truant officer
Called school doctor
Called patron about sick child
Looked up a fountain pen which had been lost
Interviewed a boy who had done wrong
Talked to girl who was failing in her work

November 20:
(Taught Seven Recitations)
Fire drill
Talked to three boys about coming too early
Answered phone call from Central
Called school office
Answered call from Dr. Woolery
Phone call for Miss Peterson
Sent child for Miss Peterson
Answered telephone twice
Visited two rooms
Attended principals' meeting

November 21:
(Taught Eight Recitations)
Phone call from school office
Phone call from patron
Delivered message to child from mother
Talked to six pupils about rest order
Phone call twice
Visited four rooms
Phone call
Arranged time for reading of book with different teachers

CHAPTER IX

SCHOOL BUILDINGS

LOCATION OF BUILDINGS

All school buildings are on well-drained sanitary lots. Two of them, the Central Building and the Departmental Grade Building, are too close to the railroad, and as a consequence the work of the school is noticeably interfered with. No nuisance of any kind interferes with the work in other buildings.

The following tables, showing distances pupils have to go to get to the buildings, give an idea of the degree to which the buildings are properly distributed over the city. These data were taken the second week after the Christmas holidays 1913–14.

TABLE CXLIX

HIGH SCHOOL (Pupils Attending from Within City Limits)

DISTANCE FROM BUILDING	9B	9A	10B	10A	11B	11A	12B	12A	TOTAL
Under 1 square [1]....	2	1	1	..	2	..	1	..	7
1 and under 2.....	2	4	3	1	3	1	1	..	15
2 " " 3.....	1	..	1	..	5	1	..	..	8
3 " " 4.....	4	2	3	1	2	..	..	2	14
4 " " 5.....	1	1	8	1	1	3	3	..	18
5 " " 6.....	3	4	..	1	6	1	2	..	17
6 " " 7.....	2	6	2	1	4	..	3	1	19
7 " " 8.....	2	4	5	1	3	3	2	..	20
8 " " 9.....	8	2	4	..	3	1	4	2	24
9 " " 10....	7	3	5	5	3	5	2	1	31
10 " " 11....	2	2	7	..	3	2	1	..	17
11 " " 12....	3	2	2	3	1	3	1	2	17
12 " " 13....	4	4	3	..	1	..	1	1	14
13 " " 14....	1	..	1	3	4	..	3	..	12
14 " " 15....	6	2	4	1	1	1	..	3	18
15 " " 16....	1	..	1	..	..	..	..	..	2
16 " " 17....	1	..	1	..	1	1	..	..	4
17 " " 18....	..	1	..	..	..	..	..	..	1
18 " " 19....	2	..	1	..	..	1	2	1	7
19 " " 20....	..	..	..	..	..	..	..	..	..
Total............	52	38	52	18	43	23	26	13	265

[1] Interpreted Table CXLIX means that 2 pupils in the 9B grade lived less than one square from the building, 1 pupil less than 1 square, etc.

TABLE CXLIX (*Continued*)

Central (Within City Limits)

Distance from Building	1B	1A	2B	2A	3B	3A	4B	4A	5B	5A	6B	6A	7B	7A	8B	8A	Total
Under 1 square	2	1	·	·	2	·	1	·	·	·	1	3	·	·	·	2	6
1 and under 2	3	2	1	3	6	·	5	5	2	4	3	3	2	2	·	·	36
2 " " 3	4	2	1	4	6	·	5	4	1	1	1	2	2	1	·	·	33
3 " " 4	7	3	3	3	4	·	3	1	2	2	5	1	4	2	2	·	40
4 " " 5	6	1	5	7	4	·	4	6	5	7	2	2	4	2	8	2	60
5 " " 6	7	·	3	4	1	·	6	1	5	2	1	4	8	8	3	1	62
6 " " 7	2	1	·	5	2	·	9	3	1	2	3	8	11	8	5	7	69
7 " " 8	2	1	·	2	3	·	2	2	4	3	2	3	2	6	6	4	44
8 " " 9	2	1	·	1	1	·	4	1	2	1	1	6	6	6	3	·	39
9 " " 10	·	·	4	1	·	·	2	2	1	3	2	9	10	8	4	3	43
10 " " 11	2	·	·	·	1	·	1	·	3	·	1	4	5	8	6	2	54
11 " " 12	·	·	·	·	·	·	1	·	·	·	·	4	7	3	4	2	20
12 " " 13	·	·	·	·	·	·	2	·	·	·	·	1	6	1	3	·	12
13 " " 14	·	·	·	·	·	·	·	·	·	·	·	2	3	3	1	3	10
14 " " 15	·	·	·	·	·	·	·	·	·	·	·	3	2	·	1	2	9
15 " " 16	·	·	·	·	·	·	·	·	·	·	·	·	1	2	1	·	6
16 " " 17	·	·	·	·	·	·	·	·	·	·	·	·	·	·	·	·	·
17 " " 18	·	·	·	·	·	·	·	·	·	·	·	·	1	2	2	·	4
18 " " 19	·	·	·	·	·	·	·	·	·	·	·	·	·	1	1	·	3
19 " " 20	·	·	·	·	·	·	·	·	·	·	·	·	2	·	·	·	·
20 " " 21	·	·	·	·	·	·	·	·	·	·	·	·	·	·	·	·	·
21 " " 22	·	·	·	·	·	·	·	·	·	·	·	·	·	·	1	·	2
22 " " 23	·	·	·	·	·	·	·	·	·	·	·	·	·	·	2	·	1
23 " " 24	·	·	·	·	·	·	·	·	·	·	·	·	1	·	2	·	2
26 " " 27	·	·	·	·	·	·	·	·	·	·	·	·	·	·	2	·	3
Total	37	14	17	30	30	..	45	27	26	28	22	55	77	63	55	28	354

TABLE CXLIX (Continued)

McCALLA (Within City Limits)

DISTANCE FROM BUILDING	1B	1A	2B	2A	3B	3A	4B	4A	5B	5A	6B	6A	TOTAL
Under 1 square	.	.	.	.	.	.	.	.	.	.	.	.	.
1 and under 2	1	2	3	2	3	2	2	.	1	1	.	.	17
2 " " 3	6	4	1	4	2	.	2	11	1	1	4	1	26
3 " " 4	8	3	5	4	2	2	2	5	3	2	6	3	51
4 " " 5	6	7	11	3	6	4	7	6	6	1	5	1	62
5 " " 6	8	4	6	6	5	5	9	2	1	8	4	2	64
6 " " 7	7	5	8	6	3	5	8	1	5	2	5	2	58
7 " " 8	11	4	4	5	8	1	6	5	4	6	6	1	57
8 " " 9	3	.	4	1	10	5	7	4	8	3	2	5	53
9 " " 10	4	3	6	2	6	3	6	2	4	5	4	2	49
10 " " 11	2	1	3	1	1	5	2	1	4	2	1	1	26
11 " " 12	3	1	1	1	2	3	.	2	2	.	2	2	17
12 " " 13	.	.	3	1	2	1	2	1	1	.	1	1	13
13 " " 14	.	1	2	1	1	3	.	2	4	.	.	2	18
14 " " 15	1	1	3	.	.	3	.	3	.	.	.	.	11
15 " " 16	1	1	1	.	1	.	2	.	.	.	1	.	2
16 " " 17	1	.	.	.	.	.	.	.	.	.	.	.	2
17 " " 18	.	.	.	.	.	.	.	.	.	.	.	.	.
18 " " 19	.	.	.	.	.	.	•	.	.	.	.	.	.
19 " " 20	.	.	.	.	.	.	.	.	.	.	.	.	.
	62	36	61	37	52	42	53	42	44	31	41	25	526

TABLE CXLIX (*Continued*)

FAIRVIEW (Within City Limits)

DISTANCE FROM BUILDING	1B	1A	2B	2A	3B	3A	4B	4A	5B	5A	6B	TOTAL
Under 1 square	:	:	:	:	:	1	3	:	:	:	:	4
1 and under 2	:	3	4	1	1	2	4	1	2	1	1	20
2 " 3	9	6	3	4	6	1	4	0	5	4	2	44
3 " 4	13	5	5	3	6	6	6	3	4	1	5	57
4 " 5	9	1	7	3	3	4	4	2	5	7	2	47
5 " 6	9	6	3	3	10	5	5	6	3	4	3	57
6 " 7	10	5	1	2	7	3	5	4	5	3	3	48
7 " 8	4	2	2	3	3	3	5	1	5	6	11	45
8 " 9	3	1	1	1	5	0	6	7	2	3	1	30
9 " 10	4	0	1	0	3	1	5	5	0	2	0	21
10 " 11	2	2	1	0	1	1	4	0	0	2	1	14
11 " 12	:	:	:	:	:	:	2	:	1	:	:	3
12 " 13	:	1	1	:	:	:	:	:	1	1	:	4
13 " 14	:	:	1	:	:	:	:	1	:	:	:	1
14 " 15	:	:	:	:	:	:	1	:	:	:	:	1
1 mile	:	:	1	:	:	:	:	:	1	:	:	3
1¼ miles	1	:	:	:	:	:	:	:	:	2	:	3
1½ "	1	:	:	:	:	:	:	:	1	:	1	3
Total	65	32	31	20	45	27	54	30	35	36	30	405

COLORED SCHOOL (Within City Limits)

DISTANCE FROM BUILDING	1B	2B	3B	4B	5B	6B	7B	8B	TOTAL
Under 1 square.....	..	..	..	..	..	..	..	..	..
1 and under 2.....	..	..	..	..	..	..	..	..	..
2 " " 3.....	..	..	..	..	..	..	..	..	..
3 " " 4....	1	3	1	1	..	..	1	1	8
4 " " 5....	1	2	1	1	2	1	2	..	10
5 " " 6....	2	2	3	2	..	1	..	..	10
6 " " 7.	..	..	1	..	..	..	..	..	1
7 " " 8....	..	..	..	..	..	1	..	..	1
8 " " 9.....	3	..	..	..	..	..	..	..	3
9 " " 10...	..	..	..	..	2	2	2	..	6
10 " " 11....	4	3	5	0	2	0	2	1	17
11 " " 12....	3	..	1	..	..	..	..	2	6
12 " " 13....	4	2	1	..	1	..	..	1	9
13 " " 14....	1	1	1	3	1	..	..	..	7
14 " " 15....	..	..	..	..	..	..	..	..	..
15 " " 16....	..	..	..	..	..	1	..	..	1
16 " " 17....	1	3	2	1	2	..	..	..	9
Total............	20	16	16	8	10	6	7	5	88

McDOEL BUILDING (Within City Limits)

DISTANCE FROM BUILDING	1B	2B	2A	3B	TOTAL
Under one square.........................	5	2	3	2	12
1 and under 2............................	1	..	..	1	2
2 " " 3............................	1	..	..	..	1
3 " " 4............................	1	1	..	..	2
4 " " 5............................	1	1	..	2	4
5 " " 6............................	2	..	1	1	4
6 " " 7............................	..	..	1	..	1
7 " " 8............................	..	..	..	..	..
8 " " 9............................	..	..	..	..	..
9 " " 10............................	..	..	..	..	..
10 " " 11............................	..	1	..	..	1
Total..................................	11	5	5	6	27

HIGH SCHOOL (Pupils Attending Outside City Limits)

DISTANCE FROM CITY	9B	9A	10B	10A	11B	11A	12B	12A	TOTAL
Under ½ mile.......	..	2	..	..	..	..	..	..	2
½ and under 1.....	..	..	..	1	..	..	..	..	1
1 " " 1½....	3	..	2	..	1	..	..	..	6
1½ " " 2.....	1	..	..	..	1	..	..	1	3
2 " " 2½....	5	2	2	1	1	0	1	1	13
2½ " " 3.....	..	1	3	..	1	..	..	..	5
3 " " 3½.....	2	..	..	..	3	1	3	2	11
3½ " " 4.....	2	..	..	..	1	..	1	1	5
4 " " 4½....	4	..	3	..	1	1	..	..	9
4½ " " 5.....	2	1	..	..	..	..	..	..	3
5 " " 5½....	4	1	..	..	..	..	..	..	5
5½ " " 6.....	..	..	..	..	..	..	..	..	..
6 " " 6½....	..	..	1	..	..	..	..	..	1
Seven.............	..	..	..	..	..	..	1	..	1
Total............	23	7	11	2	9	2	6	5	65

TABLE CL
CENTRAL BUILDING (Outside City)

DISTANCE FROM CITY	1B	1A	2B	2A	3B	3A	4B	4A	5B	5A	6B	6A	7B	7A	8B	8A	TOTAL
Under ½ mile																	
½ and under 1	4																4
1 " 1½		1	2					1	3	1		1	3	3	2	1	18
1½ " 2					3		1	1	1		1	2	2		1		12
2 " 2½									1	1						1	3
2½ " 3													1				1
3 " 3½															1		1
3½ " 4																	
4 " 4½																	
4½ " 5																	
Total	4	1	2	..	3	..	1	2	5	2	1	3	6	3	4	2	39

TABLE CLI

FACTS ABOUT EACH SCHOOL BUILDING. SPRING OF 1913

	OLD HIGH SCHOOL BUILDING—TO BE USED IN FUTURE FOR DEPARTMENTAL GRADE WORK	CENTRAL BUILDING	McDOEL BUILDING DATA ONLY APPROXIMATE	COLORED BUILDING	McCALLA BUILDING	FAIRVIEW BUILDING
Dimensions of lot	660 ft. by 660 ft.	317 ft. by 277 ft.	660 ft. by 400 ft.	132 ft. by 132 ft.	200 ft. by 320 ft.	134 ft. by 132 ft.
Outside dimensions of building	165 " 40 "	93 " 74 "	One wing, 45 ft. by 25 ft., the other 30 ft. by 23 ft.	40¾ " 26¼ "	54 " 90 "	70 ft. 4 in. by 91 ft. 6 in.
Material of which built	Brick	Brick	Main part brick; small wing wood	Brick	Brick	Brick
Height of building to the square	40 ft.	53 ft.	....	33 ft.	39 ft.	35 ft.
Width of entrance and exit space	....	Three, 5 ft. each	....	Two, 3 ft. One, 6 "	....	Front, 6 ft. 10 in. Back, 7 "
Width, and length of corridors	1st floor, one 69 ft. by 7 ft. Two, each 27 ft. by 12 ft. 4 in. 2d floor, one 22½ ft. by 6 ft. 10 in. Two each, 19 ft. by 12 ft. 3d floor, one 69 ft. by 7 ft. 7 in.	1st floor corridor, 27 ft. by 13 ft. 2d floor corridor, 27 by 13 ft.	....	....	One, 6 ft. by 42 ft. " 4 " 32 " " 6 " 18 " " 32 " 24 " " 52 " 24 "	1st floor, 29 ft. by 36 ft. 2d " 24 " 30 ft.
Height of ceiling	....	1st and 2d floors, 14 ft. 3d floor, 15 ft.	14 ft.	12 ft. 6 in.	....	12 ft.
No. steps to reach 1st floor	Three	Ten	Three	Two	Six	Nine
No. steps to each stairway	Two stairways, 22 steps each	Two stairways between floors, each with landing— 14 steps between landings	....	One, 20 steps	One, 6 steps Four, " 8 " Two, " 7 "	One, 9 steps " 14 " " 7 "

TABLE CLI (*Continued*)

Width of stairways...	1st floor to 2d floor, 3 ft. 11 in. / 2d floor to 3d floor 3 ft. 6½ in.	4 ft. 7 in.	....	3 ft.	Seven, 3 ft. 6 in. / One, " 9 " 10 "	One, 13 ft / " 7 " / " 4 "
Height of risers.......	7 in.	7 in.	....	8 in.	7 in.	....
Width of steps.......	1st to 2d floor, 11¾ in. / 2d to 3d floor, 12 in.	12 in.	....	12 in.	12 in.	12 in.
Length of stairways between landings....	....	....	....	No landings between floors	One, 6 ft. / Four, 12 " / Two, 8 " / 7 "	....
No. of drinking fountains.............	Eight	Sixteen	No fountains	....	Four	Eight
No. of wash basins...	Two	Four	....	....	Eight	....
No. of toilet seats for boys.	Six	Eight	Three	Three	Seven	Seven
No. of toilet seats for girls	Eight	Ten	Three	Four	Twelve	Nine
No. of urinals for boys..	One trough	One trough, 30 ft. long	....	One trough	Trough, 16 ft. long	Nine
Kind of toilet arrangement.......	Water flush system inside building	Water flush system within building	Water flush system within building	Dry closets outside of building	Water flush system within building	Dry Smead system
Nature of heating.....	Steam	Steam	Coal Stove	Stoves	Hot air	Hot air
Nature of ventilating..	Windows only	Windows and inadequate gravity system	Windows only	Windows	Forced air automatic regulation	Gravity system only fairly satisfactory

Considering all the buildings 41 per cent of the 1B's walk more than six squares or approximately one-half mile or more; so also 32 per cent of the 1A's; 42 per cent of the 2B's, 35 per cent of the 2A's, 60 per cent of the 3B's, 46 per cent of the 3A's, 42 per cent of the 4B's, 45 per cent of the 4A's, 54 per cent of the 5B's, and 47 per cent the 5A's.

As far as distance is concerned the lower grade children are accommodated most poorly in the McCalla and Fairview buildings. Conditions in these buildings indicate that the buildings next constructed should be in the southeast and in the southwest portions of the city. Available lots in those sections of the city should be obtained as soon as finances will permit in order to insure the possibility of a site that will accommodate the largest number of children with the minimum requirement of walking.

Children coming from outside the city are tuition children and do not have the same claim on the city that those within the city limits have.

Table CLI gives a summary of facts about each building under conditions existing at the close of the school year 1912–13.

All the buildings are substantially built and are in a good state of preservation. The Fairview and the McCalla Buildings are arranged for safe exit in case of fire through fire escapes reached from the second floor through Von Dupren latch doors. The old High School Building and the Central Building are equipped with fire escapes reached from each room of the building but reached through windows instead of doors. These buildings I should consider unsafe.

The heating systems of all buildings are adequate as far as amount of heat furnished is concerned. Only in the McCalla Building is there a thoroughly modern system of heat regulation and ventilation.

The playground facilities at Fairview are very inadequate. Steps should be taken immediately to relieve the cramped condition in the playground.

Toilet arrangements are adequate in the four large buildings considering the fact that at the High School Building and at Central the children are not all receiving their rest period at the same time of the day.

At the McDoel Building the toilets are necessarily outside the building, but the boys' and girls' toilets are separated by a good distance and are shut off from view by lattice work.

The toilets at the Colored Building are in very poor condition and the boys' and girls' closets join each other being separated by a pro-

TABLE CLII

HIGH SCHOOL BUILDING

1 ROOM	2 SIZE	3 SQ. FT. FLOOR AREA	4 CU. FT. CONTENT	5 SQ. FT. GLASS AREA	6 RATIO TO FLOOR AREA	7 RATIO OF WIDTH OF FLOOR TO HEIGHT OF WINDOW	8 POSITION OF WINDOW	9 NO. PUPILS ACCOMMODATED	10 FLOOR AREA PER PUPIL	11 CU. FT. PER PUPIL	12 LINEAR FEET	13 PER PUPIL
1	19×21×11	399	4389	68.25	.17	1.9	L	24	16.6	183.	25	1.0
2	18×21×11	378	4158	68.25	.18	1.9	L	24	15.7	173.	30	1.3
3	25×21×11	525	5775	81.25	.15	1.9	L	26	20.1	222.	40	1.6
4	32×21×11	672	7392	143	.21	1.9	L, B				28	
5	25×48×11	1200	13200	205.6	.17	2.3	L	24	50.	550.	30	1.3
8	25×48×11	1200	13200	205.6	.17	2.3	L	24	50.	550.	55	2.3
9	21×21×11	441	4851	59.5	.13	1.9	L					
10	21×25×11	525	5775	81.25	.15	1.9	L				27	.9
14	19×21×12	399	4788	87.9	.22	1.7	L	33	12.1	145.	30	1.1
15	18×21×12	378	4536	87.9	.23	1.7	B, L	28	13.5	162.	30	1.1
16	18×21×12	378	4536	87.9	.23	1.7	L	28	13.5	162.	40	3.1
18	21×35×12	735	8820	151.8	.20	1.7	L, B	13	56.5	678.	45	
19	48×26×12	1248	14976	234.4	.19	2.2	L	103	12.1	145.	40	2.4
21	35×26×12	910	10920	175.8	.19	2.2	L	75	12.1	145.	50	2.2
22	21×35×12	735	8820	151.8	.20	1.7	B	21	35.	420.	26	1.1
23	21×12×12	252	3024	50.6	.20	1.7	L	12	21.	252.	32	1.3
24	18×21×12	378	4536	75.9	.20	1.7	L	28	13.6	162.	30	1.3
25	18×21×12	378	4536	75.9	.20	1.7	L	23	16.5	197.2	37	
26	19×21×12	399	4788	87.9	.22	1.7	L	28	14.2	171.	12	
28	19×16×12	304	3648	47.4	.15			6	35.3		33	1.5
30	37×21×12	777	9324	158.2	.20	1.9	R, B	22	35.3	424.	15	.6
32	26×15×12	390	4680	94.8	.24		L	27	14.4	173.	32	1.1
33	24×21×12	504	6048	94.8	.19	1.9	L	30	16.8	201.6	70	
34	58×30×14	1740	24360	335.7	.19	SKYLIGHT	L	123	14.1	198.	78	
36	57×30×14	1710	23940	335.7	.20	"	L	149	11.5	161.		
37	39×21×12	819	9828	164	.20	1.9	W	32	25.6	307.	12	
38	22×21×12	462	5544	72.	.15	1.9	L	32	14.4	272.	36	.4
39	35×21×12	735	8820	164.	.22	1.9	L		21.7			

L = Light coming from left of pupils.   B = Light coming from rear.   R = Light coming from right-hand side.

TABLE CLII (*Continued*)

McCalla School Building

No.	Size	Sq. Ft. Floor Space	Cu. Ft. Content	Sq. Ft. Glass Area	Ratio to Floor Area	Ratio of Width to Height	Position of Window	No. Pupils	Floor Area Per Pupil	Space Per Pupil Cu. Ft.	Linear Feet	Feet Per Pupil
1	23×32×11	736	8096	131.3	.18		L, B	48	15.3	168	42	.8
3	32×24×13	768	9984	163.6	.21	1.8	L	42	18.3	238	35	9.8
4	32×24×13	768	9984	163.6	.21	1.8	L	48	16.	208	37	.8
5	32×24×13	768	9984	163.6	.21	1.8	L	46	16.7	217	48	1.0
6	32×24×13	768	9984	163.6	.21	1.8	L	48	16.7	208	50	1.0
7	32×24×13	768	9984	163.6	.21	1.8	L	46	16.7	217	52	1.1
8	32×24×13	768	9984	163.6	.21	1.8	L	48	16.7	208	37	.8
9	32×24×13	768	9984	163.6	.21	1.8	L	46	16.7	217	48	1.0
10	32×24×13	768	9984	163.6	.21	1.8	L	48	16.	208	37	.8
Average					.207				16.4			

Fairview School Building

No.	Size	Sq. Ft. Floor Space	Cu. Ft. Content	Sq. Ft. Glass Area	Ratio to Floor Area	Ratio of Width to Height	Position of Window	No. Pupils	Floor Area Per Pupil	Space Per Pupil Cu. Ft.	Linear Feet	Feet Per Pupil
1	25½×30×12 [1]	805	9660	113.8	.14		L, B	43	18.7	224.7	50	1.2
2	30×26×12	780	9360	97.5	.13		L, B	42	18.6	222.8	50	1.2
3	26½×27×12	716	8592	97.5	.11		L, B	42	17.	204.6	54	1.3
4	27×25½×12 [1]	689	8262	113.8	.13		L, B	41	16.8	201.5	48	1.2
5	30×26×12	780	9360	105.	.14		L, B	42	18.6	222.8	50	1.2
6	26½×27×12	716	8592	115.5	.13		L, B	35	17.	204.6	54	1.5
7	25½×30×12 [1]	805	7660	147.	.17		L, B	39	18.7	224.7	50	1.3
8	27×25½×12 [1]	689	8262	147.	.17		L, B	46	16.8	201.5	48	1.0

[1] + 40 sq. ft. additional in front part of building.

TABLE CLII (*Continued*)

DEPARTMENTAL SCHOOL BUILDING

1	2	3	4	5	6	7	8	9	10	11	12	13
	ROOMS				LIGHTING						BLACKBOARD	
No.	Size	Sq. Ft. Floor Space	Cu. Feet Content	Sq. Ft. Glass Area	Ratio to Floor Area	Ratio of Width of Floor to Height	Position of Window	No. Pupils	Floor Area Per Pupil	Cu. Ft. Per Pupil	Linear Feet	Feet Per Pupil
1	30×35¾×12½	1074	13425	110.7	.10	.....	L, B, R	56	19.2	239.	36	.7
2	33×21×12½	693	8662	69.9	.10	.....	L	40	17.3	217.	60	1.5
4	29½×20×12½	590	7375	78.7	.13	.....	R, B	28	21.1	263.	55	2.0
5	32½×21×12½	683	8537	69.9	.10	.....	L	44	15.5	194.	...	...
6	23×35¾×12½	823	10278	110.7	.13	.....	L, B, R	47	17.5	218.7	64	1.4
7	23×35¾×12½	823	10278	110.7	.13	.....	L, B, R	47	17.5	218.7	64	1.4
8	52×67	3484	.....	361.2	.10	.....	L, B, R, F	247	14.1	...	...	...
9	30×35¾×12½	1073	13413	125.5	.12	.....	L, B, R	50	21.5	268.	36	.7
10	30×35¾×10½	1073	11261	84.6	.08	.....	L, B, R	54	19.9	209.	36	.7
11	24×20×11½	480	5520	55.4	.12	.....	R, B	30	16.	184.	32	1.1
12	37×21×11½	777	8935	108.2	.14	.....	L, B	59	13.2	157.	57	1.
13	28×20×11½	560	6440	73.	.13	.....	L, B, R	31	18.1	208.	45	1.
14	23×35¾×11½	823	9456	84.9	.10	.....	L, B, R	50	16.4	189.	63	1.5
15	33×21×11½	693	7969	58.5	.08	.....	L, R	43	16.1	185.	34	1.3

TABLE CLII (*Continued*)

CENTRAL SCHOOL BUILDING

1 ROOM No.	2 SIZE	3 SQ. FT. FLOOR SPACE	4 CU. FT. CONTENT	5 SQ. FT. GLASS AREA	6 RATIO TO FLOOR AREA	7 LIGHTING RATIO OF WIDTH OF FLOOR TO HEIGHT	8 POSITION OF WINDOWS	9 NO. OF PUPILS	10 FLOOR SPACE PER PUPIL	11 SPACE PER PUPIL CU. FT.	12 BLACKBOARD LINEAR FEET	13 BLACKBOARD LINEAR FEET PER PUPIL
1	33×27×13¼	891.	12028	164.4	.18	....	B, L	51	17.5	236	54	1.1
2	34¼×29×13½	1000.	13500	164.4	.16	....	L, B	45	22.2	300	55	1.2
3	29×34½×13½	1000.	13500	164.4	.16	....	L, B	46	21.8	293	60	1.3
4	27×33×13½	891.	12028	164.4	.18	....	L, B	42	21.2	289	55	1.3
5	33×27½×14	907.5	12705	164.4	.18	....	L, B	47	21.1	295	60	1.4
6	27½×29×14	798	11165	164.4	.21	....	L, B	46	17.3	243	50	1.1
7	29×27½×14	798.	11165	164.4	.21	....	L, B	48	16.6	233	45	.9
8	26¾×33×14	882.8	12358	164.4	.20	....	L, B	47	18.8	263	60	1.3
11	27½×26¾×14	735.6	10298	164.4	.22	....	L, B	47	15.7	219	60	1.3
		COLORED SCHOOL BUILDING. E. 6TH STREET										
Downstairs	24⅔×24×12	593	7116	115.4	.19	....	L, R, B	49	12.1	145	51	1.
Upstairs	24⅔×24×12	593	7116	115.4	.19	....	L, R, B	49	12.1	145	57	1.2
Average					.19	....	......		12.1			

(The old Colored Building has been replaced, September, 1915, with a new modern building of six rooms.)

jecting wall. This condition would have been remedied last year except that plans are on foot to build a new building for the colored children of the city.

(Since the above facts were gathered two new buildings have been erected, one for high school purposes and one for colored school purposes. These last two buildings have been constructed according to the modern demands for school buildings.)

Table CLII sets forth certain facts about the physical school plant according to conditions at the close of the school year 1914–15.

TABLE CLIII
Drinking and Toilet Facilities

1 School	2 Boys in At-tend-ance	3 Girls in At-tend-ance	4 Drink-ing Foun-tains	5 Pupils per Foun-tain	6 Urin-als	7 Boys per Urinal	8 No. Boys' Toilet Seats	9 No. Boys' per Seat	10 Girls' Toilet Seats	11 Girls per Seat
High School.....	205	255	6	77	10	20.5	7	29.3	12	21.3
Departmental...	261	301	8	70	6	43.5	6	43.5	8	37.6
McCalla........	272	211	4	121	8	34.	7	38.9	10	21.1
Fairview........	181	189	12	31	9	20.1	7	25.9	9	21.
Central.........	243	196	14	31	8	30.4	7	34.7	10	19.6
Colored [1].......	48	50	Cistern	..	4	12.	3	16.	3	16.6
Totals........	1210	1202	44	..	45	..	37	..	52	..

Enrollment was taken on entrance, Fall, 1914.

Playground Facilities

1 School	2 Size Lot	3 Area Lot Sq. Ft.	4 Ground Area Building Sq. Ft.	5 Net Area Play-ground Sq. Ft.	6 No. Pupils	7 Area per Pupil Sq. Ft.
Fairview.................	134 × 132	17,688	6,351	11,237	370	30.4
Central.................	277 × 317	87,809	6,975	80,834	439	184.
McCalla.................	200 × 320	64,000	4,680	59,320	483	122.8
Departmental and High School.................	660 × 660	435,600	6,720	405,680	562	397.
	......	....	23,200	......	460	.....
Colored.................	132 × 132	17,424	1,050	16,374	98	165.
Average.................	......	....	....	......	...	237.

" Exclusive High School and Departmental, 120 sq. ft. High School and Departmental were taken together.

Summary of Tables CLII and CLIII

1. Location of Buildings. — The Central Building and the Department Building are located too close to the railroad.

2. Size of lots. — Except at the Fairview Building the playground is satisfactory in size.

[1] These data are for the old Colored School Building, now replaced by a modern six-room building.

3. Heating and Ventilation. — Heating plants are satisfactory except at the Fairview Building. Ventilation is poor at Fairview, Central, Department, McDoel, and good in other buildings.

4. Lighting. — The lighting is poor in the Department Building both as regards direction and amount. As far as direction of light is concerned the lighting is fair at Central and Fairview. As far as amount of light is concerned, the lighting is good at Central and poor to fair in Fairview. The McCalla, the New Colored, and the New High School Buildings are well lighted.

5. The toilet systems are poor in Fairview and McDoel Buildings, but from satisfactory to good in all other buildings.

6. Assuming, as most authorities do now assume, that 15 square feet of floor space per child accommodated in each room is satisfactory, approximately 15 per cent of the schoolrooms in Bloomington fall below the desired standard in floor space. A large percentage of this shortage is in the High School and the new Colored Building where for economical reasons the rooms were temporarily crowded beyond their expected capacity.

7. Assuming, as most authorities do, that 210 cubic feet of air space per pupil is satisfactory, approximately 21 per cent of the schoolrooms in Bloomington are too small. The same explanation as regards the New High School and Colored Buildings obtains in cubic feet per pupil as in square feet floor space per pupil.

8. Assuming that the window area should be at least 20 per cent of the floor area, then approximately 40 per cent of the rooms have too small a window area.

9. Assuming that the light in recitation rooms should come only from the left, approximately 44 per cent of the rooms are inadequately lighted in that respect.

10. Taking Dr. L. P. Ayres' standard of 65 square feet as a very good allowance for playground for each child, one building, the Fairview, is inadequately supplied with playground space.

11. Taking 35 boys to each urinal as a satisfactory standard, one building falls below standard in urinal facilities for boys.

12. Taking as a satisfactory standard 30 boys to each toilet seat, three buildings prove inadequate in toilet facilities for boys. With 18 girls to a toilet seat as standard, practically all buildings are inadequate.

13. Taking Dr. L. P. Ayres' standard of 70 children to a drinking fountain as being fairly satisfactory, one building is noticeably inadequate in drinking facilities.

GENERAL CONCLUSIONS AND RECOMMENDATIONS

1. The general plan of combining the efforts of the forces on the ground and outside guidance by experts in making the survey proved satisfactory except that too heavy a burden rested on the local people whose time was well occupied with other duties. The survey should continue, a little being added each year, but the School Board should furnish more clerical assistance in the future.

2. The partial success of this survey should awaken in the minds of university authorities and public school authorities, especially in communities where universities are located, the unlimited opportunities for mutual helpfulness in conducting surveys and in conducting experimental work in the schools. I should recommend a still closer co-operation on the part of the Bloomington public schools and Indiana University than even now exists.

3. The findings of this survey and of future additions to it should be made more public in the future than they have been in the past. A public so loyal to the schools in a financial way as Bloomington is has a right to expect published information from time to time. Such information might well be distributed through parent-teachers' associations if such organizations were in existence. There is a place for such organizations in Bloomington, and the opportunities along this line have been too long neglected.

4. The analysis of the education and the occupations of the wage-earning men and women of Bloomington suggests that something might possibly be done to help them more definitely to advance in their trades or to prepare them to enter trades or occupations that are fuller of promise to them than the ones they are now in. Especially would it seem an opportune time to open free evening schools and, in addition to the regular academic subjects, offer opportunities in commercial subjects, domestic art and domestic science, various lines of work in the stone industry, and especially cabinet making and carpentry, as a basis for advancement in the furniture factory and planing mills of the city.

5. Through the medical department of the schools information should be disseminated in regard to the dangers connected with

drinking Bloomington well water. The establishing of standards
for preserving health in the home along other lines, too, would be
a good investment for the community. The whole community has a
right to such information and the public schools should be a strong
supporter of the public health officers in getting such information to
the public.

6. Some further special effort, possibly along the line of modifying
the course of study for certain types of children, should be made
to bring about a further decrease in the percentage of retardation
and to decrease the percentage of elimination from school. Compared with other cities, Bloomington does not have a bad record
along these lines now, but there is certainly still much room for
improvement.

7. A study of the subjects and grades that take the greatest toll
in retardation and elimination will reveal the strategic points in
attacking this problem. Certainly the sixth and seventh grades and
especially the first year of high school should be studied carefully
with a view to carrying a larger percentage of the pupils through
these grades. The state law assists below these grades.

8. Tables XLVIII and XLIX show the necessity of carefully considering the basis upon which promotions are made in making
comparisons from time to time looking toward the reduction of
retardation.

9. The trouble to which the various school buildings have been
put of raising funds for decorations, improvement of grounds, equipment of buildings, etc., should soon cease and the school board
should assume this responsibility. Within two years at least the
board should be able to take care of all such reasonable demands.

10. There is need of further extension of the work in manual
training and domestic arts and science.

11. Kindergarten schools should be established. At least two un-
graded schools should also be established to take care of pupils who
do not fit well into the regular classes.

12. Work in physical education should now be offered in view of
the fact that a new gymnasium is available for use on the part of a
large percentage of the pupils.

13. The work in agriculture and school gardening should be extended. The large lot on which the Department Building and the
New High School Building are located and the large tract of land
in connection with the McDoel Building would furnish fine sites for
gardens.

14. As soon as funds will permit printed courses of study and an occasional printed copy of annual reports should be available. The course of study needs revision, though, especially in upper grade arithmetic, in English, and in physiology before it is printed.

15. The medical inspection force should be supplemented as soon as possible by a dental clinic and a school nurse.

16. Standardized tests reveal the fact that pupils in the Bloomington schools rank well when compared with pupils in other school systems. Nevertheless, many points of weakness are revealed by the tests. Special drill in the fundamentals of arithmetic brought rapid improvement up to a certain point after which accuracy began to be sacrificed for speed. Further experiment in these drills should be made before the exact amount and kind to be used can be determined. There was not the improvement we should have had in the working of reasoning problems. More emphasis should be placed in the future on concrete problems. The work in writing is still weak. The methods thus far adopted for its improvement have so far failed to bring expected results.

17. Mr. Woody's study reveals that on the whole city-trained pupils did better work in the Bloomington high school than did country-trained pupils; nevertheless, whereas the city-trained pupils maintained in the first year of the high school the same quality of work they did in the eighth grade and the country-trained pupils dropped noticeably, the city-trained pupils gradually went down in their work in succeeding terms of high school and the country-trained pupils gradually came up. This slump on the part of the city-trained pupils should be studied and, if possible, remedied.

18. Tables showing percentages of promotions indicate a gradual improvement in that a larger and larger percentage of pupils are promoted year after year. This fact alone is not significant, but coupled with the fact that accompanying this change there has been a gradual improvement in the achievement of pupils, as shown in the results of tests given and of success in higher institutions of learning, it becomes very significant. If these two results have been reached without damage, physical or moral, to teachers or pupils, a step toward efficiency has been reached. The medical inspection department of the schools has noticed an improvement rather than a loss as far as general health is concerned, and I think I can safely say from observation that the results on the part of pupils have been obtained without lowering the standard of conduct toward teachers and toward each other on the part of pupils.

19. The teachers in the Bloomington schools are exceptionally well trained for their work. They are so well trained and successful, in fact, that they are continually leaving the system for other better paying positions. From one-fourth to one-third of the teachers leave the system each year and the majority of them leave because of better salaries. While the city is not at present financially able to increase the salaries materially, I think that within two or three years at most substantial increases can and should be made. The number of pupils to a teacher should be materially reduced.

20. More clerical help should be allowed the grade principals and they should have more time free for supervision of instruction.

21. A new heating and ventilating system is badly needed at the Fairview Building. A satisfactory toilet system is also needed there.

22. Baths should be provided at all buildings such as are in the new High School Building and in the new Colored Building.

23. The playground should be added to at Fairview. A bond issue has been made partially for this purpose and I judge this matter will soon be taken care of.

24. The new High School Building could be economically joined with the Department Building for heating purposes, and a saving of several hundred dollars a year in coal and janitor service would follow.

25. Building sites should be purchased both in the southeast part of the city and in the southwest part. It will be some time before buildings are needed there, but before very long the available sites for schools in those vicinities will be built up with residences.

CRITICISMS OF BLOOMINGTON SCHOOL SURVEY

1. The survey as a whole was not outlined toward one definite end with the view in mind that anything not contributing to that end could be eliminated. Since the survey covered a rather long period of time suggestions grew, as it were. Moreover, certain types of study were made primarily not because they were the things most needed to be taken up, but because someone interested in one of those lines was available for the investigation. Such was especially the case in a large number of the studies made by university students.

2. Largely for the same reason, also, certain studies that were desired were omitted because of lack of time and facilities for working them up. The survey, therefore, lacks compactness and unity. At the same time, also, it lacks completeness.

3. There is too much undigested data included. Much of that could have been omitted. It was included with the idea that it was valuable material and might later be further interpreted for the Bloomington school system and certainly would be valuable as a basis of comparison later with other school systems.

4. Much data are included simply as basic data from which summaries are built. The summaries alone could have been included and much space would have been saved thereby. The full data were included primarily in order that conclusions might be checked by them and doubtful figures might be verified or corrected.

5. The brief discussion of the course of study has its greatest strength in showing the methods of improving the course. The discussion does not consider at all adequately the particular defects of the course.

VALUE OF A SURVEY SIMILAR TO THAT MADE OF BLOOMINGTON

1. It reveals the points of strength and the points of weakness in the system when comparison is made with other school systems.

2. It reveals the degree to which weaknesses have been eliminated and points of strength have been further developed from time to time.

3. With these points of weakness and strength revealed the points requiring greater effort are clearly set forth and a large part of what would otherwise be misguided effort is avoided and economy results.

4. Concentrated effort on the revealed strategic points leads to experimentation which almost invariably results in the discovery of a better and more efficient way of doing things.

5. A survey planned as was the Bloomington survey discovers and brings to the surface latent ability on the part of teachers, principals, and superintendent that was not suspected, and when this ability is once released it is not satisfied to become buried again. The result is that the system of schools continues to draw interest on this new capital.

6. A general survey is a source of stimulus to every one connected with the system, and this added stimulus alone means more concentrated, cheerful, and hopeful effort and consequently better results.

7. Effort to solve the difficulties of teaching connected with one subject somehow passes over unconsciously to others, so that progress in the subject in which conscious effort is put forth is accompanied

by progress in the other subjects.   Such a transfer was very evident in the Bloomington results.

8. Above everything else a survey of the Bloomington type results in riveting ultimately the surveyors' attention on individual pupils and their performances and away from the mass performance.   The result is that individual needs become more quickly evident and consequently more quickly ministered to.

9. Further, a survey of the Bloomington type faces a remedy to conditions as a general survey from the outside might not.   Teachers are from time to time measuring themselves with themselves, not simply with others, and they are frequently measuring themselves, not once only.   Frequency of measurement of the right sort drives teachers and pupils to a way out of weaknesses.

10. Finally this survey may be of some service in suggesting what can be done in a small school system by the local school authorities themselves in the way of self-examination.

DATE DE RETOUR

M-5   U